JAPAN BEFORE AND AFTER DEFEAT

IN WORLD WAR II

IN their current preoccupation with childhood socialization, sociologists have tended to neglect the evidence which indicates that socialization is not confined to youth but can occur throughout a person's lifetime. Miss Tsurumi here undertakes to remedy this imbalance by showing, both in theory and in fact, how individuals alter their ideological and affective postures in adulthood and even in old age in response to basic changes in society.

Taking as the focus of her discussion the society with which she is most intimately acquainted, Miss Tsurumi analyzes (in Part One) the structure and methods of the dominant agency of socialization in Japan before and during World War II— the Imperial army—and contrasts them (in Parts Two and Three) with the patterns of postwar socialization implemented by the International War Tribunal, informal study groups, urban and agrarian families, and student movement organizations. At the same time, she seeks to clarify the relationship between societal change and personality development and, to that end, explores the effects that major economic and social trends in Japan have had on the attitudes and roles of various segments of the population.

Personal documents, including letters, diaries, and autobiographical writings, are used extensively th[rough]out to reveal and define the affective postures of the group[s stud]ied. The data on student at[titudes] derive largely from a series of

SOCIAL CHANGE AND THE INDIVIDUAL

Social Change

and the Individual

JAPAN BEFORE AND AFTER

DEFEAT IN WORLD WAR II

BY KAZUKO TSURUMI

PRINCETON UNIVERSITY PRESS

PRINCETON, NEW JERSEY

1970

Chapter VII, "The Student Movement: Its Milieu,"
and Chapter VIII, "The Student Movement:
Group Portraits," originally appeared in the
Japan Quarterly, xv, No. 4 (Oct.-Dec. 1968),
430-455, and xvi, No. 1 (Jan.-March 1969), 25-44,
copyright 1968 and 1969 by the Asahi Shimbun
Publishing Company, Tokyo. They are reprinted here
with the permission of the editor.

TO MY FATHER

Yusuke Tsurumi

FOREWORD

KAZUKO TSURUMI has reunited what psychology and sociology have torn asunder—feeling and thinking, child and man, man and society. She is concerned as much with the socialization of feeling as with the socialization of thought, with the socialization of the adult as with the socialization of the child, with the humanization of society by man as with the socialization of man by society. It is a complex lattice, mirroring the varying degrees of freedom of men in society, but with conceptual parsimony. Thus the same affects are the focus of both parent-child and adult socialization. The same structure which is used to describe a personality is used to describe a society. The same structure which is used to describe the organization of affects is used to describe the organization of ideologies. The same structure which is used to describe a personality or a society at one point in time is used to describe a personality or a society across time.

Parsimony is not here purchased at the expense of theoretical power. Kazuko Tsurumi has seized upon that rarest of experiments—the experiment in nature—a society before and after a major transformation occasioned by a total military defeat. Such a radical change necessarily changes adult socialization. The earlier parent-child socialization now creates conflict for the adult who had been socialized for a different society. So severe a mismatch as that between adult socialization in Japan after World War II and the parent-child socialization of those who grew up before the war is of course a rarity, but an extraordinarily illuminating one. The customary continuity between early and later socialization exaggerates the significance of early socialization both in fact and in the minds of theorists who were influenced by this very usual state of affairs. It has tended to produce an overestimate of the stability and rigidity of both men and societies and an underestimate of their potential for change. This experiment in nature is also of interest as a methodological strategy. Psychologists have in general been much possessed by the promise of the experimental method. Indeed, they have been willing and even eager to pay whatever price seemed necessary for the power and rigor which is presumed to be the consequence of manipulating and independently varying components of situations which might otherwise covary in such a way as to confound understanding. Because we are not able, nor willing, to treat

human subjects as purely experimental animals, experimental
rigor has been purchased at the price of triviality. We have therefore assumed the trappings of experimental science as we surrendered its substance. In this work, by contrast, there is no
experimental control, but we can witness the impact of major
psychological forces upon men and societies who must come to
terms with them. Men deeply committed to an ideology are
faced with the demand for renunciation or the surrender of their
lives. A society socialized for Emperor worship and the glorification of death is confronted with the ideal of the pursuit of happiness and peace.

Finally, she has traced both the continuities and the discontinuities in the socialization of affects and ideologies in particular
individuals, which predispose them either to conform to their
societies or to become agents of social change.

SILVAN TOMKINS
Livingston College
Rutgers University
November 20, 1969

Acknowledgments

Chapters I through VIII of this book constituted the substantive part of a doctoral dissertation submitted to the Department of Sociology of Princeton University in 1966. The last three chapters have been added since then. I am indebted to many persons who have assisted me in this study. My deepest gratitude is due to Professor Marion J. Levy, Jr., my thesis supervisor. His book on *The Family Revolution in Modern China,* published in 1949, was the first to awaken my interest in a comparative sociological analysis of Chinese and Japanese social structures. I was fortunate in being able to work as his research assistant in Japan in 1960 when he was engaged in a study of the social structure of Tokugawa Japan. Later, as a graduate student, I learned sociological analysis and theory formation under his direction.

Through his seminars and writings Professor Wilbert E. Moore inspired me to formulate empirical problems in terms of a theory of adult socialization and social change. Professor Silvan S. Tomkins's highly stimulating works imparted to me his theory of affects and their relationship to ideologies. The theoretical underpinnings of this study have for the most part been forged from my understanding of the ideas of these three men.

For the empirical materials used in the chapters on the circle and on women, I owe much to Japanese friends in many walks of life with whom I have collaborated in various writing groups since 1952. For the data used in the chapters on the student movement, I am greatly indebted to Professor Lewis S. Feuer, through whose sponsorship I was granted an assistantship from the Center of Japanese Studies of the University of California for work with him in 1962 in research on student movements in Japan.

Numerous persons have helped me formulate my ideas. Foremost among them is Professor Margaret Prang of the Department of History of the University of British Columbia, where I taught in 1964 and 1965. Our frequent discussions of my work afforded me the opportunity to clarify my ideas, while her understanding and sense of humor did much to lessen the trials of thesis preparation in a language that is not my native tongue. More recently, she has read and commented upon most of the final draft of the manuscript.

Professor George DeVos advised me that, when one develops a

typology, it had better be illustrated to make its meaning plain. His admonition prompted me to expand Chapter I ("Six Types of Change in Personality") so that it would incorporate the empirical materials on thought conversion in the 1930's. At the University of British Columbia the Interdisciplinary Colloquium organized by Professor Ernest Landauer invited me to give a paper at one of its meetings. The comments and criticisms that followed my presentation of the substance of what is now Chapter I enabled me to reformulate ideas for later chapters. My brother Shunsuke Tsurumi, professor of communications at Dō-shisha University, pointed out the significance of the collected messages of the war criminals executed by the War Tribunal; it was at his suggestion that I wrote Chapter IV.

Many persons have aided me with English style. Professor Watson Thomson of the University of British Columbia examined the first five chapters of my manuscript. Mrs. Thomas Perry made some valuable stylistic suggestions for the early chapters, and Mr. and Mrs. Howard Van Zandt helped with the chapters on the family. Professor John F. Howes of the University of British Columbia gave freely of his time in assisting me with last-minute changes in my thesis.

I am indebted to many sources for financial aid. Princeton University provided generous grants which permitted me to study in an environment at once stimulating and tranquil for the two years 1962-1964. Princeton's Area Study Committee gave me a travel grant for the summer of 1964. The Research Fund of the University of British Columbia and the Social Science Research Council of Canada awarded me research grants in 1965.

My deep appreciation is due to Professors Ezra F. Vogel and Robert E. Ward, whose invaluable criticisms and suggestions enabled me to revise and condense my original manuscript into its present form. I also wish to express my sincere gratitude to Messrs. William McClung and Sanford Thatcher of the Princeton University Press—the former for the encouragement and thoughtful advice he gave me during the preparation of this work, the latter for his painstaking and rigorous editing of the manuscript.

Finally, I owe great thanks to my two typists, Mrs. C. W. Wrinch of Vancouver and Mrs. Yoshiyuki Tsurumi of Tokyo.

These acknowledgments are far from exhaustive; I owe to many persons whose names are not mentioned here my silent but no less heartfelt gratitude.

KAZUKO TSURUMI
Tokyo, Japan

Contents

List of Tables and Graphs

SOCIAL CHANGE AND THE INDIVIDUAL

Introduction

1. Major Themes

There are three main lines of inquiry pursued throughout this collection of essays. The first is an attempt to explore in substantive analysis the possibilities that socialization is not limited to childhood but takes place throughout an individual's life and that the individual can and does change his personality through socialization in adulthood and probably in old age also. Talcott Parsons defines socialization as "the acquisition of the requisite orientation for satisfactory functioning in a role."[1] It is the process an individual must go through in learning the language, values, norms, ways of feeling, thinking, and acting that are prevalent in a society or a subgroup of a society in order for him to become an integral member of it. I shall use the term in this sense but emphasize adult socialization rather than the childhood socialization with which Parsons and other contemporary theorists are primarily concerned. I feel it necessary to focus attention on adult socialization for the following reason. In many societies the basic value orientation of the society as a whole does not change, or changes only slightly, within the life span of an indi-

[1] Talcott Parsons, *The Social System*, Glencoe, Ill., The Free Press, 1951, p. 205. The term "socialization" was first used by Durkheim as follows: ". . . all education is a continuous effort to impose on the child ways of seeing, feeling, and acting which he could not have arrived at spontaneously. From the very first hours of his life, we compel him to eat, drink, and sleep at regular hours; we constrain him to cleanliness, calmness, and obedience; later we exert pressure upon him in order that he may learn proper consideration for others, respect for customs and conventions, the need for work, etc. If, in time, this constraint ceases to be felt, it is because it gradually gives rise to habits and to internal tendencies that render constraint unnecessary; but nevertheless it is not abolished, for it is still the source from which these habits were derived . . . the aim of education is, precisely, *the socialization of the human being*; the process of education, therefore, gives us in a nutshell the historical fashion in which the social being is constituted. This unremitting pressure to which the child is subjected is the very pressure of the social milieu which tends to fashion him in its own image, and of which parents and teachers are merely the representatives and intermediaries." (Author's italics.) Emile Durkheim, *The Rules of Sociological Method* (1895), tr. Sarah A. Solovay and John H. Mueller, Glencoe, Ill., The Free Press, 1938, p. 6.

For a detailed discussion of current preoccupation with childhood socialization and the emergent recognition of the importance of adult socialization, see Kazuko Tsurumi, "Personality and Society: A Critical Review of Current and Classical Views," *Bulletin of the Faculty of Letters*, Seikei University, No. 3 (Dec. 1967), pp. 6-25.

vidual member of that society. There are some societies, however, in which this fundamental value orientation of the overall group undergoes a drastic change within an individual's lifetime. In the former type of society, the individual is not expected to alter his primary scheme of values, once it is presumably established through childhood socialization. In the latter type of society, though, the individual is obliged to abandon his basic set of values after childhood in favor of a new value orientation. It is in the latter type of society especially that scholars are confronted with the problems of adult socialization and adult personality change. Japan after the Meiji Restoration of 1867 and after World War II happens to fall into the second category. I must confesss that my interest in changes in the values and attitudes of adults is rooted in the exigencies of the circumstances specifically of those two periods of Japan's history.

The second path of investigation involves the comparative study of two contrasting patterns of adult socialization. Japanese society from the outbreak of the Manchurian Incident in 1931 to defeat in World War II in 1945 was organized on the foundation of what we call the Emperor system (*Tennō-sei*). But the new Constitution of 1947 ideally abolished the Emperor system as formulated by the previous Constitution of 1889, bringing with it a radical alteration in the value orientation of the society as a whole. In Japan during the fifteen years of the war from 1931 to 1945, the underlying ethical presupposition was that the individual should die willingly for the sake of the Emperor, whenever such a sacrifice was demanded in times of national emergency, especially during a war. Great emphasis was placed on preparation for and performance in war and on the glorification of death in battle. In contrast, the new Constitution declared that each person has the right and duty to pursue peace and happiness. Thus the stress now is on peace and respect for human lives, including one's own. These two basic value orientations of Japanese society, during and after the war, provided divergent principles of adult socialization. The prototypical agency of adult socialization before and during the war was the army. It was the army that built up a most effective program of socialization for war and for death. The agency of adult socialization after the war consisted of voluntary and informal study groups or circles. They have attempted to reeducate adults in the values of peace and life.

These contrary types of socialization will be analyzed in terms of the affects emphasized in their implementation, the methods involved, and the structure of relationships formed between the socializing agent and the socialized individual. In this way we may arrive at some significant correlations among these factors in the two types of socialization.

The third concern of this study is to examine the relationship between societal change and personality change. What type of society is likely to produce what type of adult socialization, and what type of adult socialization in its turn is likely to bring about what types of personality change? The question, formulated in this general manner, cannot be answered on the basis of the scant materials we shall handle within the limits of this inquiry. It is possible, however, to trace some concrete processes of conversion that individuals undergo and to classify them into different patterns of personality development. Then we may ask what modifications in the structure of society and in the pattern of adult socialization can account for different types of personality development, if any significant differences are to be found. Our conclusion may amount to pure conjecture, but there is no reason why we should not make a modest attempt to find an answer.

2. Statement of the Problem:
Basic Tensions in Japanese Modernization

On the substantive level, our problem concerns the process of modernization in Japan. According to Feldman and Moore, "the pre-industrial diversity of currently industrialized societies continues in the form of strains and tensions that are ultimately grounded in a society's historical trajectory towards industrialism."[2] In the modernization of Japan, the traditional authority of the Emperor system as the dominant political institution, the preservation of the traditional family and village communities as social institutions, and the inculcation, as the ultimate norm of conduct, of the traditional value of the unity of loyalty to the Emperor and filial piety to one's own parents (since the Imperial Household was identified as the main family of all the families of the Japanese) were used to accomplish speedy industrialization. "Japanese spirit and Western technology" was the

[2] A. S. Feldman and Wilbert E. Moore, "Industrialization and Industrialism: Convergence and Differentiation," *Transactions of the Fifth World Congress of Sociology*, The International Sociological Association, Sept. 1962, II, 167.

catchword of early modernization. No one seriously asked whether the traditional values required change when modern technology was introduced from the West. This very use of traditional authority and values by a so-called "dynastic elite"[3] as the leverage for industrialization accelerated the rate of Japan's economic growth and also saved Japan from colonialism. At the same time, the reassertion of traditional values in the long run sacrificed the development of political democracy in the interests of rapid economic and military growth.[4] The resulting dependence on authority inhibited the expression of criticism within society, and lack of criticism meant that no one could prevent the outbreak of war. Thus the way was prepared for catastrophe.

Parsons classifies industrial societies as endogenous or exogenous.[5] Levy, following Parsons's distinction, classifies industrial societies as "indigenous developers" or "late comers." Indigenous developers "developed these structures [structures of industrialization] mainly on their own and relatively gradually over a long period of time."[6] The latecomers are those who imitate the models of industrialization erected by the indigenous developers. Japan shares with other latecomers, like China and the nations of Southeast Asia and Latin America, those tensions of industrialization peculiar to them.

In the first place, there is the tension resulting from the swift pace of economic growth. A literary critic, Mitsuo Nakamura, observes the speed of modernization in Japan and its impact on the Japanese literary style:

[3] Clark Kerr, John T. Dunlop, et al., in *Industrialism and Industrial Man* (New York, Oxford University Press, 1960), specify the type of "industrializing elite" as "dynastic elite, drawn from the landed or commercial aristocracy, or, less frequently, from military caste (as the samurai in Japan) or religious hierarchy, governmental bureaucracy, or tribal chieftains" (p. 52).

[4] Japanese critics deplore the lack of political democracy among the people so frequently that specific quotation is unnecessary. But such criticism is relatively rare among Western scholars studying the industrialization of Japan, who seem to be more interested and fascinated by "the rate of economic growth." Among the few I may cite Hagen's concluding remarks in his chapter on Japan: "A very important factor in the development of political democracy in the West was the fact that the common people demanded it. In Japan the corresponding demand has been weak and limited, though complex changes are going on at present. Up to the present the simple folk of Japan have remained far more traditional in personality than have the common people of the West." Everett F. Hagen, *On the Theory of Social Changes: How Economic Growth Begins*, Homewood, Ill., Dorsey, 1962, pp. 348-349.

[5] Talcott Parsons, "An Outline of the Social System," in *Theories of Society*, ed. Parsons et al., Glencoe, Ill., The Free Press, 1961, i, 77.

[6] Marion J. Levy, Jr., *Modernization and the Structure of Societies*, Princeton, Princeton University Press, 1966, i, 16.

'A generation' in Europe means the time span of thirty years during which men are born and reach maturity, and the group of offspring takes over their parents' role in various social activities. In Japan, the concept, generation, implies the time span of ten years instead of thirty years. Sometimes it is shortened to five or six years. This is not a new phenomenon after World War II. Literary trends in Japan since the Meiji Restoration may better be divided into ten- rather than thirty-year spans.

To say that ten years in Japan are comparable to thirty years in Western countries implies that the rate of change in Japan is three times as rapid as that of Western countries. The fact that the change is so rapid again implies that the change is superficial. Too rapid a change means no substantial change. Japanese writers have been obsessed with anything called 'new' and 'fresh,' and they have claimed that their styles were 'new,' while actually their styles of writing have not departed radically from their ancestors in Japan or from their forerunners in Europe.[7]

Although the indigenous developers took their time in evolving their own patterns, sequence, and optimum rate of industrialization, the latecomers cannot usually afford to proceed at a leisurely pace. Thus their industrialization is often accompanied by incongruities, superficialities, intense exploitation, ideological oscillation from one extreme to another, disorganization, and anomie.

Second, latecomers reap both the advantages and the disadvantages of borrowing. Latecomers borrow most of the advanced technological, political, economic, and ideological devices from indigenous developers and engraft them into their own preindustrial structures and ideologies. In addition to the pressure from the speed of industrialization, latecomers suffer more than indigenous developers from the lack of synchronization of the pace of change in the various subsystems of the society. As a result of the absence of synchronization, there arises in latecoming societies the problem of coping at the same time with the heightened tensions characteristic of the several phases of industrial development. In other words, latecoming societies must deal simultaneously with the tensions characteristic of preindustrial society and with those of the most highly industrialized society.

[7] Mitsuo Nakamura, "Meiji," in *Gendai Nihon Bungaku Zenshū* (*The Collected Works of Contemporary Japanese Authors*), Tokyo, Chikuma Shobō, 1959, Bekkan ɪ, 9-10.

According to various modern sociologists, the phenomenon of "mass society" is the plight of a highly industrialized social system. William Kornhauser distinguishes four types of society: communal, pluralist, totalitarian, and mass. A communal society is one in which "elites are inaccessible in that elite elements and standards are selected and fixed by traditional ascription. Non-elites are unavailable in that people are firmly bound by kinship and community." The prototype of this form of social organization is medieval European society. In a mass society "elites are accessible and non-elites are available in that there is a paucity of independent groups between the state and the family to protect either elites or non-elites from manipulations of mobilization by the other."[8] A highly advanced industrial system is a mass society. In Kornhauser's scheme, these two types of society are diametrically opposite, representing different epochs in Western history. But in a latecoming society, like Japan, these diametrically opposed types of organization coexist, with the result that serious tensions vex both the members of that society and observers of it.

The same coexistence of different phases of development can be discerned within individual personalities. David Riesman has defined three types of social character, corresponding to three stages of industrialization. The society of high population growth potential tends to develop among its people "the tradition-directed" type of personality. The society of "population explosion" encourages "the inner-directed personality." And the society of incipient population decline is likely to produce "the other-directed" type. In a society where primary industry predominates, the tradition-directed type prevails; in a society where secondary industry is the main mode of production, the inner-directed prosper; and, in a society where tertiary industry comes to its ascendancy, the other-directed flourish.[9] In a latecoming society, like Japan, both tradition-directed and other-directed types exist, not only among differing individuals but sometimes within the same personality.

Third, latecoming countries are poor. The differential allocation of scarce goods and services produces major tensions in any society. The scarcity of goods and capital accumulation, if

---

[8] William Kornhauser, *The Politics of Mass Society*, Glencoe, Ill., The Free Press, 1959, pp. 40, 41.

[9] David Riesman et al., *The Lonely Crowd*, New York, Doubleday, 1950, pp. 21-23.

not services, is even more acute among latecomers than among indigenous developers. Moreover, in a latecoming society where the preindustrial legacy of strict class distinction persists, as in Japan, inequalities in the distribution of income are likely to be greater than in indigenous developers, which are farther removed from their feudal inheritance. A latecoming society has a smaller national income coupled with greater disparities in its distribution than an indigenous developer. This difference is likely to produce greater tension within a latecoming society, where the ideology of equality and the rising expectation of higher standards of living become prevalent.

There is another important kind of inequality: inequality of income distribution between the indigenous developers and latecomers. According to a report of the United Nations Secretary-General to the Economic and Social Council, "the annual per capita income [in 1962] in the less developed areas averaged $136, while in the economically advanced countries of North America and Western Europe it averaged $2,845 and $1,033, respectively. . . . The gap of per capita income between rich and poor nations has continued to widen. . . ."[10] As long as there is a rising expectation of higher standards of living among the world's peoples and a relative decrease in the average income among the latecomers, we can predict increasing tensions not only within latecoming societies but also between latecomers and indigenous developers.[11]

Fourth, the tensions between latecomers and indigenous developers are not simply economic; they are also ideological. The latecomers have an extremely ambivalent attitude toward indigenous developers, whose models they have usually borrowed. Moore observes that latecomers are "trying at least to match 20th century America and in certain respects to excel their chosen models for imitation, chiefly in regard to welfare

[10] *The Globe and Mail*, July 10, 1965.

[11] "Surely the universal spread of the desire to be well off—to live at a high standard of living, to enjoy something more than minimum material existence (as these desires are reflected in the activities of the so-called underdeveloped countries, and as the legitimacy of these motives has come to be recognized by the better-to-do nations) has reminded us, if reminding was needed, that social stratification in the world society, however vague the lines of boundary of world organization may be, is a fundamental and far-reaching fact of life." Melvin Tumin, "Final Seminar in Social Stratification" (MS), Feb. 1963, p. 5. Moore also discusses the problem of "the stratification of the societies of the world" in his "Industrialization and Industrialism" (MS).

and what might be called the 'spiritual' quality of social life."[12] The attitude of imitation and emulation that latecomers take toward indigenous developers is expressed in a slogan like "overtake and surpass." This ambivalent attitude is exacerbated in Asian and African nations, which have been colonies of the Western indigenous developers.

In Japan during the war years, a group of literary critics, authors, philosophers, and scientists participated in a symposium entitled "Overcoming the Modern" (*Kindai no Chōkoku*).[13] The title of the symposium demonstrates the basic dilemma of the latecomer's attitude toward European models. Since "the modern" is identified in the course of the symposium as "Western civilization," "overcoming the modern" is tantamount to overcoming Western civilization. For some members of the symposium, this meant to overcome reason and rationalism, which are at the core of Western civilization, through adherence to the indigenous spirit of classical Japanese literature. The same attitude toward Western civilization led to the justification of Japan's war aims.[14] Other participants in the symposium interpreted the title "Overcoming the Modern" to mean overcoming Western imperialism. This interpretation, however, posed a dilemma. As far as China was concerned, Japan had been the imperialist aggressor par excellence.[15] How could Japan justifiably accuse the West while she perpetrated the very same evil? During the war years Japan played a double role in the world. In relation to the Western nations, she was a latecomer. But, for the Asian *later*comers, she played the role of an indigenous developer. The heritage of this double role is a part of the problem of contemporary nationalism in Japan.

Yoshimi Takeuchi wrote in 1948:

Japan, at the dawn of the modern period, possessed a marked inferiority complex toward Europe. . . . Since then Japan has tried to overtake Europe with ferocious speed.

[12] Moore, "Industrialization and Industrialism," p. 30.

[13] The symposium was printed first in a journal, *Bungakukai* (*The Literary World*), in 1942 and then published in book form in 1943. See Yoshimi Takeuchi, "Kindai no Chōkoku" ("Overcoming the Modern"), in *Kindai Nihon Shisōshi Kōza* (*Lectures on the Intellectual History of Modern Japan*), Tokyo, Chikuma Shobō, 1959, II, 227-281.

[14] This standpoint was represented by Yojūrō Yasuda of the Japan Romantic School.

[15] This standpoint was represented by Katsuichirō Kamei of the Japan Romantic School.

The Japanese believed that only by becoming like the Europeans would they be able to overcome their inferior position. They tried to escape from the position of slaves by becoming slave-owners themselves. . . . And today, the Japanese are so infiltrated with the ethos of slavery that even their political movements for emancipation are obsessed by a slave mentality.[16]

Takeuchi is the sharpest critic of the subservient attitude of the Japanese toward Western indigenous developers. In essence, his thesis is this. Japan's attitude of superordination vis-à-vis the "weaker" nations in Asia is an integral part of her attitude of subordination vis-à-vis the "stronger" nations of the West. Instead of depending upon outside force to "modernize" Japanese society, Japan should become an independent and self-reliant nation. In order to achieve actual national independence, each individual member of the society should become a locus of independent judgment. That state of independence, both in the nation and in the individual, can only be achieved by overcoming the slavish mentality. Thus, reinterpreted in the postwar context, "overcoming the modern" shifts from criticism directed primarily against the West to self-criticism of Japanese attitudes toward the capitalist indigenous developers. Takeuchi's criticism is also directed against the attitudes of the Japanese communists, who regard the first socialist country, Russia, as an indigenous developer. "Overcoming the modern" has now come to mean overcoming the slavish mentality of a latecomer toward the indigenous developers, both capitalist and socialist. Thus Takeuchi pinpoints the fundamental issue of adult socialization in a latecoming society: how can the members of a latecoming society expurgate certain parts of the personality structures inherent in their own preindustrial legacy? Can they find resources within their own tradition that will enable them to transform themselves without borrowing alien values and purposes from some outside model? Underlying Takeuchi's argument is the basic assumption that means and ends should conform to the same principle. If the goal is independence and freedom, the means of attaining that goal must be free and independent. In-

---

[16] Yoshimi Takeuchi, "Chūgoku no Kindai to Nihon no Kindai" ("Modernization, Chinese and Japanese"), *Takeuchi Yoshimi Hyōronshū: Nihon to Ajia (Selected Essays of Yoshimi Takeuchi: Japan and Asia)* Tokyo, Chikuma Shobō, 1966, III, 37-38.

dependence and freedom cannot be achieved through dependence upon outside forces or under outside compulsion.

Although the list is not exhaustive, these are the four most salient factors among the characteristic tensions of modern Japan as a latecoming industrial society.

3. Types of Tension Management in a Society

I subscribe to Moore's proposal to view a society "as a tension-management rather than a self-equilibrating system." He maintains that tensions "are intrinsic to social systems, not simply accidental accompaniments or the product of changes that impinge on the system from external sources. Once the tensions characteristic of all or of particular types of social systems are identified, they are predicted to be the probable sites of change."[17]

In classifying types of tension management in a society, I shall focus attention on tensions arising primarily from unequal access to power, prestige, and wealth. Added to this universal source of tensions are those particular tensions in a latecoming society which arise from the discrepancies between indigenous preindustrial patterns of relationships and values and exogenous industrial patterns. There is an isomorphism between the ways these two types of tension are handled. I shall characterize the types of tension management with reference to both kinds of tension.

These types apply both to a society at large and also to subsystems of a society.

A distinction is made between synchronic and diachronic patterns of tension management (see Table 1). A synchronic pattern refers to the pattern of management of tensions at one period

TABLE 1

Synchronic and Diachronic Types of
Tension Management in a Society

Synchronic	Diachronic
Monopolism	Monopolistic system
Compartmentalization	Many-layered system
Competition	Competitive system
Integration	Integrative system

[17] Wilbert E. Moore, *Social Change*, Englewood Cliffs, N.J., Prentice-Hall, 1963, pp. 91, 89.

—for example, during the Tokugawa period (1615-1867) or during the war years from 1931 to 1945. A diachronic pattern refers to the pattern of change over time from one period to another—for example, from the Tokugawa period to the Meiji period (1867-1911) or from the prewar (before 1931) to the postwar (after 1945) eras.

Monopolism – Monopolistic system. Monopolism is a pattern that encourages one group or one subgroup to dominate others in some sphere of action so that conflicts may be minimized. The encouragement the Meiji Government gave the *zaibatsu* (financial clique), the *gunbatsu* (military clique), and the *gakubatsu* (academic clique) to influence major policy decisions in their respective spheres is an example of monopolism. When monopolism persists over time, we call it a monopolistic system. The dominant monopolizing groups in different spheres tend to coordinate their forces where their interests coincide in order to constitute a regime, which makes the major political decisions for the society as a whole. Monopolism abets the ascendancy of either a preindustrial indigenous pattern of values and relationships or an industrial exogenous pattern.

Compartmentalization – Many-layered system. Compartmentalization is a technique of government used by the regime of a closed-class system, as in Tokugawa Japan. The population is divided into numerous groups of different occupations, status, ages, sexes, locations of residence, etc. Each group is assigned different norms of conduct, styles of life, and even different habits of speech and is kept isolated, being allowed only minimum contact with other groups. Thus the occasion for arousing the sense of relative deprivation is obviated, despite the fact that a high degree of differential allocation of power, prestige, and wealth exists.

When this pattern of tension management persists over time, we call it a many-layered system, wherein indigenous patterns of relationships and values of preindustrial periods remain as the substrata, on which accumulate superstrata of exogenous patterns common to advanced industrial societies. These different layers are kept separated so that mutual contact is minimized. Thus subsystems representing the most ancient to the most modern types of relationships and values coexist within a society with little mutual influence.

Competition – Competitive system. In contrast to monopolism and compartmentalization, competition as a pattern of tension management legitimizes and maximizes interaction among groups and among individuals. Whereas monopolism tends to minimize the opportunities of exposing the members of a society or a group to values and thoughts hostile to the dominant group or subgroup, competition promotes such opportunities. Thus groups holding various ideologies, both indigenous and exogenous, are encouraged to compete with one another for recognition. Competition breeds conflicts, both overt and ideological, to such an extent that the organization of a group or a subgroup may be disrupted. It is, nevertheless, a necessary condition for the development of the next pattern—integration.

Integration – Integrative system. Under integration the examination of the interests, values, and relationships of conflicting groups is urged for the purpose of sorting out the functional from the dysfunctional factors and establishing a new pattern of synthesis. It differs from compartmentalization and monopolism in that contrasting patterns are dissected into component elements and the original patterns, both indigenous and exogenous, preindustrial and industrial, undergo basic transformation. When this type of tension management persists over time, we call it an integrative system.

What the ruling elite considers functional is often dysfunctional for the large segment of population under its rule. Within a society, or within a subsystem of a society, more than one type of integration may emerge.

These four types of tension management are not mutually exclusive. Most societies can be characterized as one type with respect to a specific area and as another type in another area. In that sense they represent mixed types. In any particular society at any given time, however, some type of tension management predominates in the society at large, as well as in the subsystems of that society.

4. TYPES OF DATA

The materials used in this book are of two kinds. First, personal documents—letters, diaries, autobiographical sketches, and interviews, both published and unpublished—are extensively employed. In this respect, mine is a modest attempt to follow the classical example of Thomas and Znaniecki in their monumental work on *The Polish Peasant*.[18] Second, the last three chap-

[18] Thomas and Znaniecki emphasize the merit of using personal documents in sociological investigation: "We are safe in saying that personal

ters on the student movement constitute an analysis of the survey materials derived from intensive interviews of one hundred university students in Tokyo.

5. ANALYTICAL TOOLS: INDICES OF CHANGE

I should like to explain briefly the tools of analysis I use throughout this work.[19]

Classification of the Structure of Relationships

In order to gauge a change in the structure of relationships within a group, I shall employ those pattern variables originally developed by Parsons and reformulated by Levy.[20] The six categories and pattern variables, according to Levy's analysis, are set forth in Table 2.

TABLE 2

CLASSIFICATION OF THE STRUCTURE
OF RELATIONSHIPS WITHIN A GROUP

Aspects of Relationships	Pattern Variables
Cognitive aspect	Rational – Nonrational
Membership criteria	Universalistic – Particularistic
Substantive definition	Functionally specific – Functionally diffuse
Affective Aspect	Avoidant – Intimate
Goal orientation	Individualistic – Responsible
Stratification	Hierarchical – Nonhierarchical

Since these categories are not meant to be definitive, as Levy admits, I propose to make some terminological changes and

---

life-records as complete as possible, constitute the *perfect* type of sociological material, and that if social science has to use other materials at all, it is only because of the practical difficulty of obtaining at the moment a sufficient number of such records to cover the totality of sociological problems, and of the enormous amount of work demanded for an adequate analysis of all the personal materials necessary to characterize the life of a social group. If we are forced to use mass-phenomena as material, or any kind of happening taken without regard to the life-histories of the individuals who participate in them, it is a defect, not an advantage, of our present sociological method." W. I. Thomas and Florian Znaniecki, *The Polish Peasant in Europe and America*, New York, Dover, 1921, pp. 1832-33.

[19] For the full discussion of the tools of analysis, see Kazuko Tsurumi, "Adult Socialization and Social Change: Japan Before and After Defeat in World War II," Ann Arbor, Mich., University Microfilms, 1967, Ch. II.

[20] Parsons, *The Social System*, pp. 58-67; Levy, *The Structure of Society*, p. 281.

to add four more categories and sets of pattern variables as shown in Table 3.

TABLE 3

REVISED CLASSIFICATION OF THE STRUCTURE OF
RELATIONSHIPS WITHIN A GROUP

Aspects of Relationships	Pattern Variables	
	X	Y
Cognitive aspect	Rational – Nonrational	
Membership criteria	Universalistic – Particularistic	
Substantive definition	Functionally specific – Functionally diffuse	
Affective Aspect	Avoidant – Intimate	
Loci of decision-making	Independent – Dependent	
Goal orientation	Individualistic – Collectivistic	
Stratification	Hierarchical – Egalitarian	
Participation	Voluntaristic – Compulsory	
Communication	Open – Secret	
Exchange	Reciprocal – Exploitative	

If the structure of relationships among members of a group is found at time-point A to be predominantly on the X side in all ten aspects and is found at time-point B to be predominantly on the Y side in some of those aspects, then we say that the structure of relationships within that group has to a certain extent changed. The degree of change depends partly on the number of aspects with reference to which a shift is recognizable.

I shall here give definitions for only those terms which I use differently from the way in which Levy uses them and those which I have added to his list.

Rational – Nonrational. The definition of the term "rational" invites controversy. Weber and Pareto have given the term variant emphases. The central criterion of Weber's classification is the existence of an element of choice for the actor as regards means or ends of an act. In the "traditional action," neither ends nor means are chosen by the actor. The means-ends relationship is settled by precedents, and individuals are expected to follow the precedents set for them. In the *wertrational* action, the actor does not have a choice of ends, but he has a choice of means to achieve the ends. In the *zweckrational* action, the actor selects both means *and* ends from among various alternatives. Weber has not developed the concept of "affectual action" as clearly as he did that of "rational action." Tomkins finds, in contrast, that affect constitutes the basic motivational system of *any* action and cannot be separated from rational or traditional types of action. According to Weber's scheme, the nonrational action can be identified as the traditional action, and the pattern variable will consist of the polar terms of rational – traditional.

Pareto, on the other hand, introduces a distinction between subjective and objective aspects of an action. By a subjective aspect he means that aspect of an action which presents itself to the mind of the subject performing it. By an objective aspect he means that aspect of an action which is seen "from the standpoint of other persons who have a more extensive knowledge."[21] Levy, taking over Pareto's definition, defines rational action as "that action in which the objective and subjective ends of action are identical"[22] and in which both ends and means are empirical. If we push this definition in substantive analysis, some difficulties arise. There are many actions whose means-ends relationships have not yet been verified. In the present state of knowledge, especially in the social sciences, there will always arise in actual analysis the doubt whether any specific action should be categorized as rational or nonrational. Even Levy's "qualified scientific observers" may have conflicting opinions about the status of some specific means-ends relationships.

There is a third position in defining a rational action, represented by Karl Popper: "rationalism is an attitude of readiness to listen to critical arguments and to learn from experience. It is fundamentally an attitude of admitting that '*I may be wrong and you may be right, and by an effort, we may get nearer to the truth,*' "[23] Popper's delineation of the rational attitude presupposes what Charles Peirce calls "fallibilism."[24] Popper's definition of the term "rational" stresses the necessity of recognizing human fallibility in order to assist thought in more nearly approximating reality. Thus Popper saves us from the impasse of inability to classify any action until the hypothesis upon which it is based is proved. In the analysis which follows, I propose to use Levy's definition of a rational action with Popper's qualification.

[21] Wilfred Pareto, "On Logical and Non-Logical Action," in *Theories of Society*, II, 1061-62. See also Laurence J. Henderson, *Pareto's General Sociology: A Physiological Interpretation*, Cambridge, Harvard University Press, 1937, p. 98.

[22] Levy, *The Structure of Society*, p. 242.

[23] Karl Popper, *The Open Society and Its Enemies*, Princeton, Princeton University Press, 1950, p. 411.

[24] Charles Peirce, *Philosophical Writings of Peirce*, ed. Justus Buchler, New York, Dover 1955, p. 356.

Independent – Dependent. An independent relationship is one in which the actors make decisions aware that these are their own decisions, distinct from "the mind of the group," and are willing to take responsibility for the consequences. A dependent relationship is one in which the actors identify themselves with the mind of the group to such an extent that they cannot formulate their own decisions. As a result, it does not occur to them that they should personally take any responsibility for the consequences of the decisions made for them. The identification of themselves with the group is such that, even if some decisions are imposed upon them, they do not feel them to be coercive. Thus this category is distinct from the other pattern variable of voluntaristic – compulsory. It is also distinct from the individualistic – collectivistic category. In both individualistic and collectivistic relationships, the individual considers himself quite separate from others. In both, actors recognize that they are the loci of decision-making. What is problematic is whether they consider the consequences of their actions for themselves alone or for others as well. A dependent relationship is perhaps best defined in part by Cooley's description of primary groups.[25] It is important to set up this category specifically to analyze postwar changes in the structures of families and of village communities in Japan.

Individualistic – Collectivistic. An individualistic relationship is defined by Levy as one in which "each of the parties to the relationship may be expected to calculate how best to secure maximum advantage from the relationship for himself without regard to the goals sought by the other parties to the relationship." A collectivistic relationship is one in which "the emphasis is placed on one (or more) of the members safeguarding the relevant goals of the others if he is (or they are) to achieve his (or their) own goals at all."[26]

We may go beyond Levy to distinguish between a dependently collectivistic relationship and an independently collectivistic relationship. The former is a relationship in which each of the persons involved becomes oriented toward a collective goal without consciously going through his own distinctive decision-making process. An independently collectivistic relationship is one in which each of the persons involved identifies himself with a collective goal after conscious deliberation. The

[25] Charles H. Cooley, *Social Organization*, New York, Schocken Books, 1962, p. 23.
[26] Levy, *The Structure of Society*, pp. 272-273.

term "dependently individualistic" can be used only in reference to an intergroup relationship. In a dependently individualistic intergroup relationship, each of the groups involved has members whose ingroup relationships are dependent but who nevertheless, in an intergroup situation, act for the sole advantage of their respective groups. Similarly, the term "independently individualistic" can be used only to refer to an intergroup relationship in which the members of each group have independent relationships within their own groups and act in an intergroup situation for the sole advantage of their own groups.

Voluntaristic – Compulsory. A voluntaristic relationship is defined by Andrew Effrat as "one in which the actions involved are consciously conceived by the actor as being performed by him because he has . . . freely chosen so to do."[27] For the opposite of "voluntaristic," Effrat uses "nonvoluntaristic," to signify the absence of free choice on the part of the actor. I prefer, however, to use the term "compulsory." A compulsory relationship is one in which actions are performed out of compulsion exerted upon the actor by someone other than the actor himself.

Open – Secret. I define an open relationship as one in which no information or skills are intentionally withheld from any member of the groups involved. A secret relationship is one in which some information or skills are intentionally withheld from at least some members of the groups involved.[28]

Reciprocal – Exploitative. According to Gouldner, a reciprocal relationship is one in which "a mutually gratifying pattern of exchanging goods and services" is established. An exploitative relationship is one in which an unequal exchange of goods and services takes place. The equivalent return may not be in the same form as the benefits received.[29]

All these pattern variables are used, not as binary distinctions, but as means of pointing out a relative degree of preponderance of one characteristic over the other. Following Levy, I shall employ the modifier "predominantly" to indicate relatively high degrees of specific characteristics, as in "predominantly universalistic," "predominantly voluntaristic," etc.

[27] Andrew Effrat, "Another Analytic Aspect of Relationship Structures" (MS), p. 1.

[28] It is Simmel who makes secrecy an important category in social analysis. See *The Sociology of George Simmel*, ed. and tr. Kurt H. Wolf, Glencoe, Ill., The Free Press, 1950, pp. 345, 349.

[29] Alvin W. Gouldner, "The Norm of Reciprocity: A Preliminary Statement," *American Sociological Review*, xxv, April 1960, 164, 171.

For the purpose of the present work, these pattern variables are used for the general analysis of changes in society as a whole, the analysis of changes in subsystems of a society, the comparative analysis of different agencies of socialization in the same period, and the comparative analysis of analogous agencies of socialization in different periods.

Classification of the Content of Socialization: Affects

How do we gauge a change in the content of socialization? We do so by distinguishing the two aspects of the content of socialization, namely, affects and ideology. According to Tomkins, affect is the primary motivational system of all human actions. It is "the primary provider of blue prints for cognition, decision and action."[30]

Tomkins classifies the affects into positive and negative, distinguishing under these headings a total of eight affect sets. The positive affects are interest – excitement, enjoyment – joy, and surprise – startle; the negative affects are distress – anguish, fear – terror, shame – humiliation, contempt – disgust, and anger – rage.[31] These affects may be invested in any object, person, or activity. It is the way in which individuals invest their positive and negative affects in specific types of objects and activities with specific degrees of intensity, density, and duration that constitutes the basic character of socialization. Tomkins identifies his eight paired alternatives of affect socialization according to the dominant affects involved. He constructs these types primarily for the analysis of childhood socialization; I shall apply them in a modified form to adult socialization. (see Table 4).

TABLE 4
A PARADIGM FOR AFFECT SOCIALIZATION

Affects Involved	Positive Affect Types	Negative Affect Types
Excitement – Interest	P_1 Excitement is maximized. The excitement of one member of the socialization unit is transmitted to the others so as to maximize excitement.	N_1 Excitement is directed primarily toward the norm. The excitement of one member of the socialization unit is isolated from the other members of the unit so as to minimize excitement.

[30] Silvan S. Tomkins, *Affect, Imagery, Consciousness*, Vol. I: *The Positive Affects*, New York, Springer, 1962, p. 22.
[31] *Ibid.*, p. 337.

(*Table 4 Continued*)

Affects Involved	Positive Affect Types	Negative Affect Types
Enjoyment – Joy	P_2 Enjoyment is maximized. The enjoyment of one member of the unit is communicated to the others so as to maximize enjoyment.	N_2 Enjoyment is not maximized. The enjoyment of one member of the unit is isolated from the others lest enjoyment be maximized.
Surprise – Startle	P_3 Learning about new objects and discovering novelty are encouraged and are shared by members of the unit of socialization.	N_3 Learning about new objects and discovering novelty are discouraged and are not shared by members of the unit of socialization.
Distress – Anguish	P_4 Distress is minimized. When a member of the socialization unit is found to be in distress, maximum effort is exerted by other members to mitigate it.	N_4 Distress is maximized. When there is a chance for inflicting distress on socializees, the socializers tend to inflict maximum distress, in the interests of socialization.
Anger – Rage	P_5 Anger is minimized. Whenever a member of the socialization unit is angry, other members explore the sources of anger to seek means of reducing it.	N_5 Anger is maximized. Socializers use their anger as a means of socialization.
Fear – Terror	P_6 Fear is minimized. When a member of the unit is fearful and anxious, other members explore the sources of fear and anxiety to seek means of alleviating them.	N_6 Fear is maximized. Fear and anxiety are maximized by the socializers as means of socialization.
Shame – Humiliation	P_7 Shame is minimized. Whenever a member of the unit feels ashamed, other members of the unit explore the sources of shame to seek means of easing it.	N_7 Shame is maximized. Socializers make the most of any opportunity to inflict shame as a means of socialization.
Contempt – Disgust	P_8 Contempt is minimized. Anticontempt ideologies are specifically taught to minimize ingroup and outgroup contempt.	N_8 Contempt is maximized. Socializers not only use contempt as a means of socialization but also teach ideologies of contempt to cultivate ingroup and outgroup contempt.

The perfect positive type is classified as $P_1 \ldots P_8$; the perfect negative type is classified as $N_1 \ldots N_8$. All other combinations are called mixed types.

The second set of classifications of affects pertains to the level of density of affects (see Table 5), which is defined by Tomkins

TABLE 5

CLASSIFICATION OF AFFECT SOCIALIZATION

Vector	Density	
	High Densities	Low Densities
Positive Affect Socialization	Positive – High	Positive – Low casual habitual
Negative Affect Socialization	Negative – High	Negative – Low casual habitual

as follows: "we will now define ideo-affective density as the product of the intensity and duration of affect and the concurrent ideation about the object of the affect. Low ideo-affective density refers to those experiences which generate little or nor affect, and little or no ideation, or if the affect and ideation are intense, they do not last long. High density occurs whenever the individual has both intense feelings and ideation which continue at a high level over long periods of time."[32] Low density is further classified into two subcategories. One is "transient, casual"; the other is "recurrent, habitual."

In order to distinguish our two sets of classification of affects, positive and negative affects (see Table 4) are called "the vector," and high and low densities of affects are called "the density."

According to the types of affect socialization to which a person is exposed especially in childhood but also throughout his adult life, that person's affective postures are formulated and reformulated. The affective postures of an individual will be characterized here both by the predominance of either positive or negative affects and by the densities of affects.

Classification of the Content of Socialization: Ideology

I use the term "ideology" in the sense in which Tomkins uses it. According to him, an ideology is defined as "any organized

[32] Silvan S. Tomkins, "Ch. 7. Ideology and Affect in the Volume Ideology and Affect" (MS).

set of ideas about which human beings are at once most articulate, and most passionate, and about which they are least certain. . . . When the same ideas are firmly established and incorporated into the fabric of a science or tested and found wanting, they cease to constitute an ideology in the sense in which we are using the term."[33]

For the analysis of the ideological aspects of the content of socialization, I employ only four of the pattern variables already defined in reference to relationship structures. They are those which I consider most pertinent to the classification of values, ideas, and overt actions. I also add one set of alternatives to those already developed. The resultant five pattern variables are treated as indicators of the conflicting principles operating within both the agencies of socialization and individuals: Rational – nonrational; Universalistic – particularistic; Independent – dependent; Individualistic – collectivistic; Engaged – detached.

Engaged – Detached. If a person thinks that he should intervene in the course of events that occur outside of him to try to control and to transform his environment in the way he wants, such a person is "engaged" in his value, idea, or action. On the other hand, if a person thinks that he should not intervene in the course of events but instead should resign himself to the existing state of affairs, such a person is "detached" in his value, idea, or action.

Ideological postures are distinguished from an ideology itself. The latter refers to a system of ideas; the former refer to a person's style of approach to, and his pattern of interpretation of, a certain system of ideas. Thus the same ideology may be held by different persons or by the same person at different periods of his life with a variety of ideological postures. The ideological postures constitute cognitive aspects of one's personality and can be analyzed by the use of the same five sets of pattern variables that are used for the analysis of ideologies.

Classification of Methods of Socialization

Socialization would be impossible without communication, the process of sharing common meanings for the same symbols. The theorists of communication, such as Mead, Dewey, and

[33] Silvan S. Tomkins, "Affect and the Psychology of Knowledge," in *Affect, Cognition, and Personality,* ed. Tomkins and Carroll E. Izard, New York, Springer, 1965, p. 73.

Parsons, however, have hitherto emphasized only the positive end of communication to the neglect of a possible negative end, the discontinuity of communication, or *discommunication*.[34] I propose to consider communication in terms of degree and to construct two models of interpersonal (or intergroup) communication as polar types—communication and discommunication. Any actual process of communication falls at some point on the communication – discommunication continuum.

In the construction of a model of communication, we are well furnished with a philosophical and sociological groundwork. (1) The model of communication represents a process of interaction between two or more persons or groups. (2) In this process, a communicator A transmits a symbol to his communicatee B, and the symbol evokes the same meaning for B as that intended by A. This conveyance of meaning is possible because we presuppose that A and B belong to an organized group from which they have acquired conventions of speech (cognitive communication). (3) At first, A and B may not agree about the desirability of the action proposed by A. However, we assume that, if B tries to see things as A sees them and A tries to see things in the light of B's point of view, they will eventually arrive at a new conclusion on which both of them can agree (value consensus). (4) Then A and B cooperate in the activity on which they have agreed (overt cooperation). (5) By participating in the same activity, A and B come to identify each other in positive emotional communion and sympathy (affective communication). (6) Through this entire process of mutual exchange of ideas, values, emotions, and experiences, A and B not only act upon their environment to change it but are themselves changed.

This model of communication owes much to the theories of Mead[35] and Dewey[36] and also to Parsons's model of comple-

---

[34] The word "discommunication" was first used by the author in her essay "A Note on 'Twilight of a Crane,'" in Junji Kinoshita, *Twilight of a Crane*, tr. Kenji Kuraishi, Tokyo, Miraisha, 1952, pp. 43-47. See also Shunsuke Tsurumi, "Komunikeishion-ron" ("A Theory of Communication"), in *Dewey Kenkyū (Studies of John Dewey)*, ed. Kazuko Tsurumi, Tokyo, Shunjūsha, 1952. Kazuko Tsurumi, *Dewey Koraidosukōpu (Dewey Kaleidoscope)*, Tokyo, Miraisha, 1963, pp. 122-123.

[35] George H. Mead, *Mind, Self, and Society*, Chicago, University of Chicago Press, 1934.

[36] John Dewey, *Experience and Nature*, La Salle, Ill., Open Court, 1959, pp. 138-170.

mentarity.[37] It rests on two major presuppositions. First, it assumes a certain type of relationship between the communicator and the communicatee. They have to share, as a minimal requirement, the conventions of speech. In a society where different status groups have different conventions of speech and jargon, it would be very difficult, if not impossible, for the members of different groups to communicate cognitively. In Tokugawa Japan the official administrative language of the samurai consisted mainly of classical Chinese read in the Japanese manner (*kanbun*). In written language they mostly used Chinese ideographs, and their spoken language was a modified form of classical Chinese. On the other hand, the common people, who were officially stratified as peasants, craftsmen, or merchants, employed a vernacular with a grammar and vocabulary different from *kanbun* and wrote primarily with the Japanese alphabet (*kana*). This convention persists even though the closed-class system was abolished at the time of the Meiji Restoration of 1868. As late as 1962, when Marion Levy visited Japan to carry on his study of the structure of Tokugawa society, Kunio Yanagida warned Levy: "There are two kinds of Japanese. The first group speaks the square language [meaning Chinese ideographs], and the second group speaks the round language [meaning the Japanese alphabet]. The first group consists of intellectuals and this is the group visiting foreign scholars usually meet. However, unless you talk to the second group, the common people, you will not be able to understand the real Japanese life."[38] In the society described by Yanagida, the existence, in any strict sense, of common conventions of speech cannot be taken for granted.

Second, this model of perfect communication presupposes a relationship of equals holding independent opinions and judgments, who can talk back and forth without inhibition. It suffices only for a rational, egalitarian, independent, reciprocal, voluntary, and open relationship. In an irrational, hierarchical, dependent, exploitative, compulsory, and secret relationship, one party is superordinate to the other. The subordinate party may be afraid to "talk back" lest he antagonize his superior, lose favor, or even lose his life. In such circumstances the nec-

[37] Parsons, *The Social System*, p. 204. See also the Appendix of the present work.

[38] I am citing, from memory, from a conversation between Kunio Yanagida and Marion Levy at Yanagida's house in Tokyo in March 1962.

essary conditions for the free interchange of ideas, values, and emotions, which alone ensure perfect communication, may be completely lacking. That is why I propose to use, in my theory of socialization, another model—the model of discommunication.

(1) The model of discommunication represents a process of interaction between two or more persons or groups. (2) In this process, a symbol transmitted by communicator A does not evoke for communicatee B the same meaning as that intended by A. Instead, either the symbol evokes for B some meaning different from that intended by A or it evokes no meaning at all for B (cognitive discommunication). (3) Both A and B find, however seriously they have tried to communicate, that it is totally impossible for them to come to an agreement on the value judgments involved in the issues (value dissension). (4) In such circumstances, if A still wishes to have B accept his ideas and values and carry out his commands, A has to use force to make B succumb. Force may be either physical or verbal. Verbal force often takes the form of a threat: "If you don't obey me, something terrible will happen to you," etc. Socialization through discommunication is often characterized by physical punishments and verbal threats, which evoke negative affects in both socializer and socializee (affective discommunication). (5) Then one of two situations will arise. Either A and B fall into open conflict or they decide to discontinue their relationship and to have no further contact. If an open conflict develops between persons or groups of persons, it may lead to a drastic change in the relationship. If A and B decide to have no further contact, then the relationship ceases to exist. In reaching this decision, both A and B change themselves with respect to their ideas, values, emotions, and behavior.

Between the two polar models of communication and discommunication, there are various mixed types of imperfect communication.

PART ONE

ONE

Six Types of Change in Personality: Case Studies of Ideological Conversion in the 1930's

I REGARD personality as a system of tension management.[1] This view of personality corresponds to the conception of society as a tension-management system set forth in the Introduction (Section 3). A major source of tension in personality, according to Tomkins's theory, lies in the mismatches between an individual's ideo-affective posture and the ideologies available at a given period in a society. By an "ideo-affective posture" Tomkins means "a loosely organized set of feelings and ideas about feelings."[1a] Ideologies, he maintains, tend to polarize into opposing principles, such as idealism vs. realism in epistemology and humanistic vs. normative orientation in social theory. His first hypothesis states that those who hold positive ideo-affective postures are inclined toward idealistic (or humanistic) ideologies, whereas those who hold negative ideo-affective postures tend to sympathize with realistic (or normative) ideologies.[1b] His second hypothesis concerns the relationship between types of childhood socialization and commitment to certain ideologies. Those whose childhood socialization has been based on positive affects tend in their adulthood to commit themselves to humanistic ideologies, whereas those who have received a

[1] Personality is defined by Allport as "the dynamic organization within the individual of those psychological systems that determine his unique adjustments to his environment." Gordon W. Allport, *Personality: A Psychological Interpretation*, New York, Henry Holt, 1937, p. 48. Cattell defines it as *"that which permits a prediction of what a person will do in a given situation. . . . Personality is . . .* concerned with *all* the behavior of the individual, both overt and under the skin." Raymond Cattell, *Personality: A Systematic Theoretical and Factual Study*, New York, McGraw-Hill, 1950, pp. 2-3. In either case, as in other definitions given by various psychologists, the concept of personality refers to a persistent pattern, peculiar to an individual, of bio-social elements interacting within him. See Calvin S. Hall and Gardner Lindzey, *Theories of Personality*, New York, John Wiley and Sons, 1957.

[1a] Silvan S. Tomkins, "Ch. 7. Ideology and Affect in the Volume Ideology and Affect" (MS), p. 3.

[1b] Tomkins, "Affect and the Psychology of Knowledge," in *Affect, Cognition, and Personality*, ed. Tomkins and Carroll E. Izard, New York, Springer, 1965, p. 73.

childhood socialization based on negative affects tend to commit themselves to normatively oriented ideologies. If an ideo-affective posture and an ideology are matched, Tomkins calls the result an "ideo-affective resonance to ideology."[1c] The term "ideo-affective posture" will be used in the sense defined by Tomkins. I also use the expressions "affective posture" and "ideological posture." The former means an individual's tendency to invest a specific type of affect, positive or negative, in an object or an idea. The latter signifies an individual's cognitive style of approach to an ideology. (See the Introduction, Section 5.)

In any society there are some persistent patterns for the management of tensions. Similarly, in any personality structure there are characteristic tendencies through which strains are controlled. In analyzing the types of tension management peculiar to an individual, I am concerned specifically with those tensions which arise when an individual is exposed to differing or conflicting types of socialization (1) at one and the same period of his life and (2) at different periods of his life. The reaction to conflicting types of socialization at one point of time will be called "synchronic"; the reaction to conflicting types of socialization over time will be identified as "diachronic."

1. TYPES OF AFFECT DEVELOPMENT

Tomkins distinguishes four aspects of personality: affects, cognition, evaluation, and overt action.

> Discontinuities between perception, cognition, affect and action are the rule and not the exception. They are a source not only of stress and strain, but of development. . . . It is just because there is relative independence of perception, ideology, affect and action that human beings can be influenced to change.[2]

In the typology I develop, I shall make a distinction between only two aspects: affects and ideologies.[3] My intention is not

---

[1c] Tomkins, "Ch. 7, Ideology and Affect" (MS), p. 3.

[2] Silvan S. Tomkins, *Affect, Imagery, Consciousness*, Vol. II: *The Negative Affects*, New York, Springer, 1963, p. 303.

[3] Here I use the term "ideology" as Tomkins uses it in his "Affect and the Psychology of Knowledge" in *Affect, Cognition, and Personality*, p. 73: [An ideology is] any organized set of ideas about which human beings are at once most articulate, and most passionate, and about which they are least certain. When the same ideas are firmly established and incorporated into the fabric of a science or tested and found wanting, they cease to constitute an ideology in the sense in which we are using the term."

to ignore the interplay of the other aspects but to simplify the process of the construction of a typology.

For the types of affect development, I shall borrow Tomkins's models of the theory of affects. According to Tomkins, there are four basic models: "monopolism," "intrusion," "competition," and "integration." These are synchronic reaction types of affects.

When an individual is exposed to conflicting types of socialization of affects at two different stages of his life, the possible patterns of his management of tension can be categorized according to the following diachronic models of personality developed by Tomkins: "snowball," "iceberg," "coexistence" and "late bloomer."

Snowball. The magnitude of the affects involved is strong. There is great interdependence of affective experience, in which the present experience is continually reinterpreted in terms of the past. *Positive snowball*: The positive affects not only continue to dominate but increase their strength, even when exposed to negative affect socialization in later periods of the individual's life. *Negative snowball*: The negative affects not only continue to dominate but increase their strength, even when exposed to positive affect socialization in later periods of the individual's life.

Iceberg. The magnitude of affect involved is weak. There is "relative independence of minor and major elements in the personality."[4] *Positive iceberg*: The dominant adult personality consists of negative affects, but it is "vulnerable under specific, limited conditions to intrusion" from past experiences of positive affect socialization. *Negative iceberg*: The dominant adult personality consists of positive affects, but it is "vulnerable under specific, limited conditions to intrusions" from past experiences of negative affect socialization.

Coexistence. The magnitude of affects involved is strong. This type of tension management tends to interpret "new experience as independent of early experience."[5] Both positive and negative affects are coexisting and conflicting in an adult personality. The causes of such a conflict may stem either from a mixed type of affect socialization in childhood or in adulthood or from conflicts between childhood and adult socialization of affects.

[4] Tomkins, *Affect, Imagery, Consciousness*, II, 362, 302.
[5] *Ibid.*, pp. 362-363.

Late bloomer. The magnitude of affects is strong. The person employing this type of tension management tends to respond to "much of the novelty in his later experience without entirely surrendering his past experience, but continually reinterpreting the latter in the light of recent experience so that a higher integration is achieved."[6] "At some later period in development there is a confrontation of the warring affect theories out of which a harmonious integration is achieved by the late bloomer."[7]

2. Types of Ideological Development

As a parallel to the typology of affect development, I shall construct a typology of ideological development. Like the development of affects, the development of ideologies in a person may be divided into synchronic and diachronic reactions to ideological socialization.

Let us assume that a person is exposed to two conflicting ideologies at one point in his life. His reaction can be categorized in the following five possible ways:

Committed. The person is committed to one of the conflicting ideologies to the exclusion of the other.

Unsocialized (or desocialized). The unsocialized person accepts neither of the ideologies. The desocialized person has previously accepted an ideology but has abandoned it and has not accepted another in its place.

Compartmentalized. The person acts in accordance with one group ideology while he is with that group and in accordance with another while he is with that other. The characteristic of this type of tension management is the separation of the two opposing ideologies within the personality so effectively that the person may ignore the fact that they are incompatible.

Conflicting. In this type of reaction the individual is torn apart by the conflicting ideologies of the groups to which he belongs. The person in this conflict is neither totally committed to any group nor totally alienated from any. He is ambivalent toward both ideologies.

Integrated. The integrated person seizes some new way of synthesizing conflicting ideologies so that new values and new principles emerge.

Let us further assume that an individual is exposed to the op-

[6] *Ibid.*, p. 362.   [7] *Ibid.*, p. 303; see also pp. 83-85.

posing ideologies of different socializing agents at different stages of his life. The possible patterns of his management of tension can then be classified into the following six types of dia-chronic development:

Ever committed (related to committed). An ever committed person does not change the ideology he previously held. When confronted with conflicting ideologies, he is likely to harden his initial stand instead of making any compromise. This type of person can be found among both conservative and radical groups, and he is likely to be in a position of influence in the group. If his ideology is one of engagement, rather than detach-ment, he is a potential agent of deliberate social change or counterchange.

Reversely committed (related to committed). Confronted with an ideology diametrically opposed to the one he already holds, this type of person espouses the new ideology, replacing the one he previously held. He is "committed," but to different ideologies at different times. If this type of reaction repeats itself whenever the person is exposed to a new and overpow-ering ideology, he becomes a perpetual oscillator. On the other hand, if the change of his ideology occurs once and for all, the commitment to the new ideology may assume a form similar to that characteristic of the ever committed.

Perennial deviant (related to unsocialized). Confronted with conflicting ideologies, the person is incapable of commitment. The discrepancy between ideologies is so overpowering that the individual feels himself helpless to close the gap. When a person consistently reacts in this way whenever he is exposed to conflicting ideologies, he is committed to deviation. This type of person, whom I shall call a "perennial deviant," may become a sharp critic of the existing social structures, but he is incapa-ble of acting as an agent of social change, since he is not in a position of influence in any group.

Many-layered self (related to compartmentalized). The many-layered self compartmentalizes conflicting principles and ideologies over time, as well as at each point of time. If the principles of his childhood and adult socialization conflict, he compartmentalizes them. If his adult obligations to different groups conflict with one another, he compartmentalizes them. The structure of his personality is thus like a series of geologi-cal layers. Each layer is different and may conflict with others, but the structure of his personality is such that each layer is isolated so that logical inconsistencies in his principles, if any, do not enter into his consciousness. This may be a defense mechanism adopted in the face of an ideological mélange. This type of person is usually in and out of various groups whose values conflict. Ordinarily he establishes good relationships with several groups, although he has deep roots in none.

Conflicting self (related to conflicting). The marked difference between this type of personality and the many-layered self lies in the former's possession of a norm of consistency which helps him to recognize conflict in ideologies. This type of person suffers from the awareness of discrepancies and conflicts between the principles of his childhood and adult socialization and between the ideologies of contemporary groups to which he belongs. But the peculiarity of this type of person is his inability to accept or reject any of his existing ideologies totally. In more than one ideology he finds simultaneously elements which are both resonant and dissonant with his ideoaffective postures. His ambivalent attitudes toward existing ideologies make him oscillate from one group to another. He is potentially a member of the sixth category, the innovator, but for the present he cannot be an active agent of social change.

Innovator (related to integrated). This type of person usually experiences a long series of conflicts involving both affects and ideologies in childhood or adult socialization. His awareness of these conflicts prevents him from rashly committing himself to any one ready-made group ideology. He separates what he conceives to be desirable and promising in the ideologies to which he has been exposed from what he conceives to be undesirable and decaying, and out of that he tries to construct a new and workable synthesis. If his ideology is one of detachment, he does not attempt to influence others. If his ideology is one of engagement, on the other hand, he may try to persuade the members of any of the groups to which he belongs to act on his new image, and thus he may be able to transform the relationship structure of that group. To that extent he may become an innovator. The innovator of a large-scale social change, which constitutes macrodynamics, is a rare specimen. More common are the innovators of small-scale changes in the relationship structures of the groups to which they belong. Indeed, there are many innovators who undertake such innovations in everyday social life, which constitute the microdynamics of social change.

3. TYPES OF CHANGE IN PERSONALITY

Now we have four sets of types: the four types of synchronic affect reactions, the four types of affect development, the five types of synchronic reactions to ideologies, and the six types of ideological development. The types of synchronic affect reactions and the types of synchronic reactions to ideologies are related isomorphically; similarly, there is a structural congruence between the types of affect development and the types of ideological development (see Table 6).

TABLE 6
ISOMORPHIC PAIRS OF AFFECT AND
IDEOLOGICAL DEVELOPMENT IN PERSONALITY

Types of Synchronic Reaction		Types of Diachronic Reaction	
Affects	*Ideologies*	*Affects*	*Ideologies*
(1) Monopolistic Negative Positive	Committed	(1) Snowball Negative Positive	*Ever committed*
(2) Monopolistic Negative Positive	Unsocialized or Desocialized	(2) Snowball Negative Positive	*Reversely committed*
Intrusive Negative Positive		(3) Snowball Negative Positive	
Competitive		Iceberg Negative Positive	*Perennial deviant*
		Coexistence	
(3) Intrusive	Compartmentalized	(4) Iceberg Negative Positive	*Many-layered self*
(4) Competitive	Conflicting	(5) Coexistence	*Conflicting self*
(5) Integrative	Integrated	(6) Late bloomer	*Innovator*

In the substantive analysis which follows, only diachronic reaction types are used, and for that reason they are italicized.

4. RELATIVE PROPENSITIES FOR CHANGE OF IDEOLOGIES

Some individuals are more amenable to change than others when confronted with ideologies different from those they have previously held. One of the factors determining propensities for change in one's ideologies is the relationship between affective posture and ideological posture. Generally speaking, the ideological posture of an individual changes more rapidly than his affective posture. When a new ideology is inculcated in an adult, it is likely to be colored by the individual's preexisting affective posture, which in its turn may eventually undergo some metamorphosis under the impact of the new ideology. The interaction between ideological change and affect development within a person is thus a two-way operation. Owing to the relative slowness of change in affective postures, however, it will take time for the ideological and emotional aspects of the individual's personality to become congruent. For some adults, exposure to a new ideology totally alien to their previous affect socialization is so disruptive that they may not be able to achieve any harmony at all between their persistent affective postures and their newly acquired ideologies.

Of our six developmental types of personality, the ever committed and the innovator are the least vulnerable to the general ideological fluctuations of society. The assumption is that those who are more susceptible to the sway of ideological trends are less likely themselves to become the generators of deliberate social change. Thus both the ever committed and the innovator are more apt than the rest to become potential agents of deliberate social change.

Among the ever committed, those with lower levels of commitment are more liable to shift into one of the other four types (perennial deviant, reversely committed, many-layered self, or conflicting self) and are thus more vulnerable to general shifts in ideologies than those with higher levels of commitment.[8]

5. THE SIX TYPES OF CHANGE IN PERSONALITY ILLUSTRATED: CASE STUDIES OF IDEOLOGICAL CONVERSION IN THE 1930's

To illustrate the types of personality change, I shall present case studies of ideological conversion (tenkō) in the 1930's,

[8] For the concept of the level of commitment, see Silvan S. Tomkins, "The Psychology of Commitment," in *Affect, Cognition, and Personality*, pp. 149-158.

studies which reveal characteristic patterns of personality development in the intellectual history of modern Japan. Ideological conversion is defined by Shunsuke Tsurumi as "the change of one's thought under the coercion of power." By power is meant "the state power." The means of coercion include both direct and indirect violence. Arrest by the police, torture, court trial, imprisonment, and death belong to the former; job discrimination, praise or denunciation through mass communication media, and social pressure of various kinds belong to the latter. Between total coercion and total voluntariness (the absence of coercion) lies a range of intermediate conditions. Here, however, ideological conversion is defined as a change of thought, effected primarily with some degree of coercion exercised by the state.[9]

When the Japanese Communist Party was established in 1922 as a Japanese branch of the Comintern, it was an illegal organization. At the outset it was a united front coalition of all the left-wing leaders, including anarchists, Christian socialists, social democrats, syndicalists, and communists. Under police suppression it was dissolved in 1924. In 1926 the Communist Party reemerged as the organization of the communists, excluding social democrats and others, under the leadership of Kazuo Fukumoto (1894-   ). Fukumoto preached the importance of learning the theory of Marxism – Leninism to the neglect of observation and analysis of the actual situation of Japanese society. He advocated the separation of the orthodox Marxists from other socialists to keep the Communist Party "pure." He also stressed the necessity of maintaining it as "the vanguard party" of the proletariat, thus isolating the party from the working people at the grass roots. Although his leadership came to an end in 1927 when the Comintern criticized his approach, his central principles remained as an undercurrent in the communist movement in the prewar period. "Fukumotoism" stood for the fetishism of theory, overestimation of the elites, and the alienation of the party from the common people.[10]

[9] Shunsuke Tsurumi, "Kyōdō Kenkyū Tenkō ni Tsuite" ("On the Joint Study on Ideological Conversion"), in *Tenkō*, ed. Shisō no Kagku Kankyūkai, Tokyo, Heibonsha, 1959, ɪ, 5-6.
[10] For the history of the Japanese Communist Party, see Shōichi Ichikawa, *Nihon Kyōsantō Tōsōshōshi* (*A Short History of the Japanese Communist*

The Communist Party is unique in the history of Japan in the sense that it was first and foremost in publicly advocating the abolition of the Emperor system and in combating it consistently. To defeat the system required a struggle against traditional authority and nonrational values in the industrialization of Japan. It also involved a fight against the particularistic system of belief embodied in Emperor worship. Thus the Japanese communists were the most powerful organized group in the prewar period to espouse rationalism and universalism. In other countries where communist influence was strong—Russia, Germany, France, and China—universalism had been relatively diffused among the people either through Christianity or (for the Chinese) belief in the Way of Heaven before communism was introduced. In Japan universalistic religions such as Buddhism and Christianity did exist before communism, but their followers usually compromised their original beliefs to make them compatible with the particularistic structure of relationships in Japanese society and with the particularistic system of belief of ancestor worship.[11] Thus, from the 1920's to 1945, Japanese communists were in the unique position of having to fight almost single-handedly for universalism against a particularistic tribal system.[12] If industrialization means the change in the structure of relationships and in the patterns of action from

---

Party), Tokyo, Shōkōshoin, 1946. For an analysis of Fukumotoism, see Shunsuke Tsurumi, "Nihon no Yibutsuron—Nihon Kyōsantō no Shisō" ("Materialism of Japan—The Thought of the Japanese Communist Party"), in Osamu Kuno and Shunsuke Tsurumi, *Gendai Nihon no Shisō* (*Contemporary Japanese Thought*), Tokyo, Iwanami, 1956, pp. 29-70.

[11] "The people to whom a human nexus is important place great moral emphasis upon complete and willing dedication of the self to others in a specific human collective. This attitude, though it may be a basic moral requirement in all peoples, occupies a dominant position in Japanese social life. Self-dedication to a specific human nexus has been one of the most powerful factors in Japanese history. . . .

"Universal religions advocate the transcending of limited human relations. This fact of religion, however, is scarcely seen in Japanese religions. A feature common to various Japanese religions is their emphasis on group propriety. From ancient days the importance of an established, limited human nexus has been in the consciousness of the Japanese. As the psychological example parallel to it, we may cite the fact that the Japanese statement of judgment (or reasoning) is severely limited to the environment which includes the speaker and listener. Universal religions from abroad had to be transformed to suit such a tendency of thought." Hajime Nakamura, *Ways of Thinking of Eastern Peoples*, Honolulu, Hawaii, East-West Center, 1964, pp. 414-415.

[12] Shunsuke Tsurumi, "Nihon no Yuibutsuron," pp. 35-36.

nonrationalism to rationalism and from particularism to universalism, then the communist program was compatible with the process of industrialization. As long as the communists supported industrialization, it was functional, at least theoretically, from their standpoint. Their blunt advocacy of the abolition of the Emperor system, however, was actually dysfunctional for their purpose because it alienated them from the masses whose interests they claimed to promote.

In 1927, and again in 1932, the Comintern issued "theses" for Japan, which were adopted by the Japanese Communist Party as its program. Both theses defined the Emperor system, as established at the time of the Meiji Restoration, as absolutism, which, according to the Marxian theory of history, is the last stage of feudalism based "on the parasitic landlord class on the one hand and on the other the bourgeoisie rapidly increasing its wealth." The theses maintained that "the overthrow of this system is the major goal of the revolution in Japan."[13] They emphasized that the Japanese communists should first work for the abolition of the Emperor system in order to achieve the bourgeois revolution and only then precipitate the proletarian revolution. Thus they proposed revolution in two stages, the first being the transition from feudalism to capitalism and the second the change from capitalism to socialism. Kentarō Yamabe, one of the leaders of the Communist Party in postwar Japan, commented on the party's adoption of the Comintern theses in 1927 and in 1933:

> In 1928, when the people were looking forward to the first general election based upon universal manhood suffrage, with high hope for the operation of the constitutional monarchy, the communist party all of a sudden distributed leaflets demanding the abolition of the monarchy. No wonder their campaign was not received favorably by the people.
>
> The blame must be attached not to the thesis itself, but to the blunders of the Japanese communist party in its methods of propaganda and political activity.[14]

[13] Kentarō Yamabe et al., eds., *Kominterun Nihon ni kansuru Tēzē Shū*, (*Collection of the Comintern Theses on Japan*), Tokyo, Aoki Shoten, 1961, p. 81. "The 1927 Thesis" referred to the Emperor system by using a general term, like "monarchy"; it was in "the 1932 Thesis" that for the first time the Emperor system (*Tennō-sei*) was coined to refer specifically to the Japanese type of monarchy.

[14] *Ibid.*, p. 252.

Yamabe also admits that the Communist Party in the prewar period was isolated from the people. "On the whole the revolutionary movement of Japan did not tie itself to the democratic movements of the people. It was a minority movement of elites, and it relied heavily on the destructive criticisms of the status quo, but very seldom posited any practical proposals as alternatives."[15]

In spite of these shortcomings, the Japanese Communist Party worked vigorously in the general election of 1928, sending its candidates into the Farmer – Labor Party, which was a legal organization. The left-wing parties, including the Farmer – Labor Party and the Social Democratic Party, won 8 seats in the Parliament, compared with 435 together for Seiyūkai and Minseitō, the two major conservative parties.[16] In terms of ballots cast, the left-wing parties acquired nearly half a million votes out of a total of about twelve and a half million. The conservative government, which had followed a policy of intervention in China ever since 1915 when it presented the Twenty-One Demands to China, found it necessary to wipe out all opposition in order to further its interventionist policy.[17] On March 15, 1928, less than a month after the general election, more than one thousand communists and socialists were arrested; four hundred and fifty of them were prosecuted under the Peace and Order Preservation Law, which had been instituted in 1925 to suppress subversive activities. The law prohibited "the organization of and participation in groups aiming at the abolition of private property or the overthrow of the national polity [meaning the Emperor system]."[18] According to the law as established in 1925, the maximum punishment was imprisonment for ten years. In 1928 the law was revised to extend the maximum punishment to life imprisonment or death.[19] After the Manchurian Incident in 1931, the number of arrests increased yearly, reaching a peak in 1933. The range of people liable to arrest and prosecution was extended to include liberal scholars, as well as communists

---

[15] *Ibid.*, p. 256.

[16] Shigeki Tōyama et al., *Shōwashi* (*A History of the Shōwa Period*), Tokyo, Iwanami, 1959, pp. 43-44.

[17] For a partial translation of the Twenty-One Demands, see William T. de Bary et al., eds., *Sources of Japanese Tradition*, New York, Columbia University Press, 1958, ii, 209-210.

[18] Hiroshi Suekawa, ed., *Kihon Roppō* (*The Six Basic Laws*), Tokyo, Iwanami, 1962, p. 656.

[19] *Ibid.*

and socialists, as the years went by and Japan's war effort was intensified.[20]

Those arrested were often subjected to police torture, and some were tortured to death. They were given alternatives: if they announced that they had changed their ideas (*tenkō* – ideological conversion), they could expect better treatment from the police authorities, and their term of imprisonment might be shortened. But, if they refused to change their ideas (*hitenkō* – nonconversion), they were bound to face either imprisonment for an indefinite period[21] or death. The criterion of ideological conversion was determined by the police authorities and was subject to change from time to time. For instance, at an early stage, if a person agreed that he would not engage in political activities, although not specifically admitting that

[20] The numbers of persons arrested for having transgressed the Peace and Order Preservation Law are given in the following table:

TABLE 7

PERSONS ARRESTED AND PROSECUTED FOR
VIOLATION OF THE PEACE AND ORDER PRESERVATION LAW

Year	Arrested	Prosecuted
1931	1,187	309
1932	2,489	663
1933	4,288	1,282
1934	2,102	507
1935	654	112
1936	783	149
1937	661	205

SOURCE: Tōyama et al., *Shōwashi*, p. 96.

In 1938 nine professors of both national and private universities were arrested for violation of the Peace and Order Preservation Law. In 1939 Eijiro Kawai, professor of economics at Tokyo Imperial University, anti-Marxist scholar of the philosophies of John Stuart Mill and Thomas H. Green, was prosecuted on the charge of having broken the Publication Law.

In 1949 Sōkichi Tsuda, a liberal scholar whose field of expertise was the ancient history of Japan, was prosecuted on the ground that his work *Study of the Period of Gods* committed the crime of *lèse majesté*. His publisher, Shigeo Iwanami, was also prosecuted.

In 1942 Yukio Ozaki, the holder of the longest record of successive victories in parliamentary elections since 1890, who served as the minister of justice in the Ōkuma cabinet, was prosecuted on a charge of *lèse majesté*.

[21] In 1941 the Preventive Detention Law was passed, so that even those who had already served full prison terms might be detained for an indefinite period of time if the court decided that they were likely to commit any of the crimes defined by the Peace and Order Preservation Law. See Suekawa, ed., *Kihon Roppō*, p. 657.

his previous ideology was wrong, he was considered converted or at least "semi-converted." But, in order to be recognized as an ideological convert (*tenkō-sha*) at a later stage, a person not only had to admit that he had been wrong to uphold a left-wing ideology but also had to publicly support nationalism and Japan's war aims. Under this severe suppression of thought, an overwhelming majority of those arrested and prosecuted accepted ideological conversion, with varying degrees of change from their initial standpoints.[22] Of about five hundred authors who belonged to the left-wing literary leagues—NAPF (Nippon Proleta Artista Federation, 1928-1931) and KOPF (The Federation of Proletarian Cultural Organizations of Japan, 1931-1934)—more than 95 percent are said to have undergone ideological conversion.[23]

Such is the historical background of ideological conversion in the 1930's. Let us now examine six individual cases in terms of our six types of change in personality.

The Ever Committed: Takiji Kobayashi (1903-1933)

Takiji Kobayashi[24] was born in a village in Akita Prefecture in the northeastern part of Japan, the second son of a poor peasant. His family migrated from Akita to Hokkaido when he was four years old. He started writing poems and novels after finishing public school. Upon graduating from commercial school, he went to work as a bank clerk in Hokkaido. When he

[22] The numbers of ideological converts among those prosecuted, according to the figures published by the Ministry of Justice in March 1943, are shown in the following table:

TABLE 8

IDEOLOGICAL CONVERTS AMONG THE PROSECUTED

	Communists	Anarchists	Others	Ultra-nationalists	Total
Converts	1,246	26	78	27	1,377
Semiconverts	1,157	29	75	33	1,294
Nonconverts	37	1	1	0	39
Total	2,440	56	154	60	2,710

SOURCE: Shihōshō Hogoka, "Shisōhan Hogotaisha ni kansuru Sokōchōsa," *Shihō Hogoshiryō*, p. 190—cited in *Tenkō*, I, 23-24.

[23] Shūgo Honda, *Tenkō Bungaku Ron* (*Essays on Conversion Literature*), Tokyo, Miraisha, 1964, p. 180.

[24] For the life and work of Takiji Kobayashi, see *Kobayashi Takiji Shū*, *Gendai Nihon Bungaku Zenshū*, Tokyo, Chikuma Shobō, 1954, XXXVIII, 113-222, 397-403, 417-421, 425-427.

was twenty-three, he began to read Marx, Lenin, and Gorky and was deeply impressed by their writings. He became active in labor union activities in Hokkaido and, during the election of 1928, campaigned for a Farmer – Labor Party candidate. In March 1928, when the NAPF was organized, he joined the organization. This was the initial stage of his resonance with Marxism.

From this first stage to his early death, Kobayashi's life can be explained by what Tomkins calls the cycles of "the triads" of commitment, punishment and suffering, and increased commitment, resulting in increased risk-taking. Each subsequent cycle begins with a higher level of commitment than the level with which the previous cycle ends, so that the series of cycles forms a spiral rather than a merely repetitive pattern.[25]

The first cycle of commitment to Marxism in Kobayashi's life began with his writing of the novel *March 15, 1928*, in which he realistically described the terror and torture used by the police against the communists and socialists arrested on that eventful day. The work was subsequently suppressed, but this response merely intensified his commitment to the cause. In the following year he wrote his most celebrated novel, *The Cannery Boat*. There he depicted the sweat-shop labor of the four hundred workers on a crab cannery boat and told of the strike they attempted under the leadership of a student-worker, which was finally suppressed by the Japanese navy. The second cycle began with his labor union activities, his subsequent arrest and detention for two weeks, his discharge from the bank, and his decision to leave Hokkaido for Tokyo to take a more active part in political events. The third cycle started with his activities in the NAPF and his subsequent arrest and prosecution in 1930 under the Peace and Order Preservation Law. He was also arraigned on the charge of *lèse majesté* as the author of *The Cannery Boat*, which was adapted for the stage and performed while he was being detained. After he was released on probation in the following year, he officially became a member of the Communist Party. The fourth cycle began with his participation in underground work for the communist cultural organizations, which involved the highest degree of risk-taking and finally led to his arrest in January 1933. Several hours after his arrest, he was tortured to death in the police station. His death was a testimony to his unflinching commitment.

[25] Tomkins, "Psychology of Commitment," p. 158.

What was the affective posture that underlay this spiral process of ever intensified commitment? The type of affect development in Kobayashi's case was predominantly negative snowball, in which negative affects become dense as ideological commitment increases in intensity. In recalling how he produced his first novel, *March 15, 1928*, Kobayashi confessed: "In the latter half of the novel, I wrote with all the power within me, groaning at each word I put on paper. That was over the scene in the police station. . . . At that time, speaking the truth, I thought I was merely speaking for the fury that my comrades wished to express but could not express while they were bleeding from the torture inflicted upon them by the police."[26] A critic observes that this recollection of the author reveals "how intensely he had to fight against his own fear lest he himself might be punished by the police" for what he was writing then.[27] The identification with the victims of torture reinforced the author's anger against the police, but at the same time he was keenly aware of his fear that the same fate might befall him for his muckraking exposure of police torture. From the beginning his psyche harbored a conflict between the positive affect of sympathy for the oppressed and the negative affect of anger against, and fear of, the oppressors.

Kobayashi's last novel, *The One Who Lives for the Party*, which he wrote while engaged in underground political activities, reveals the later stage of his emotional struggle. This book tells the story of an underground worker who attempts to organize a strike in a factory as a protest against the discharge of six hundred temporary workers. Although it is written in fictional form, the description of the life and feelings of the narrator, "I," yields a clue to the author's own experiences as an underground political activist. Coming home to his small rooming house after a long day spent organizing the workers, the protagonist finds himself dead-tired.

> Recently, I can no longer sleep in a leisurely way lying on my back. I tend to lie on my face like a sick child. Perhaps my health has been ruined by my extreme fatigue. I am reminded of my father, when he was a peasant in Akita, who used to take

---

[26] Takiji Kobayashi, "Shojosaku no Koro o Omoo" ("A Reminiscence of the Days When I Wrote My First Novel"), 1931—quoted in Hideo Odagiri, "Kaisetsu" ("Commentary"), *Gendai Nihon Bungaku Zenshū*, xxxvii, 417-418.

[27] Odagiri, *ibid.*, p. 418.

naps lying on his face when he returned from the field, with his muddy straw sandals still on his feet. My father worked till he ruined his health. Because land rents for the tenant farms were too high to allow him to make both ends meet, he cultivated the waste land that was so full of pebbles that nobody cared to till it, so that he might supplement his insufficient family income. Because of his hard labor, my father was troubled by a bad heart. Whenever I cannot help lying on my face, I feel that I am growing to resemble my peasant father. My father tried to escape his misfortune by working to the extent of ruining his health, instead of demanding that his landlord lower the land rent. That was more than twenty years ago. But I am different from my father. I cut myself off from any contact with my mother, my sister and my brother, and in addition I have already sacrificed my life with Kasahara [his common-law wife]. On top of everything, my health is being ruined because of the kind of life I have been leading. All this means sacrifice of my own life as my father sacrificed his. However, there is a difference. In my father's case, he sacrificed himself in order to serve landlords and capitalists, but I am sacrificing myself in resistance to them. For me there is no vestige of life that can be called my own private life. . . . I shall be satisfied if I can approximate a mode of living in which my private life is completely integrated in a life dedicated to the class struggle.[28]

Here is an ascetic self-image of the communist, in which his negative affects against the oppressors are internalized to such an extent that they are now directed against himself. He denies enjoyment and excitement for himself. He denies himself the pleasure of the company of his common-law wife, whom he puts to work in a tea house to support him so that he may devote all his efforts to advancing the aims of the party. He rationalizes this exploitation of her by maintaining that, because he is sacrificing his life for the sake of the cause, she should sacrifice herself for him, since she is incapable of serving the cause directly. As he himself admits, his affective posture is very similar to his peasant father's, although the end for which he strives is precisely the opposite. Kobayashi, too, shared with his father the traditional posture of predominantly negative affects, with its emphasis on unquestioning loyalty to the

---

[28] Kobayashi, "Tōseikatsusha," *Kobayashi Takiji Shū*, pp. 216-217.

group to which one belongs, self-sacrifice for the sake of the group, and the mechanism of compensation for one's own distress by inflicting distress on others who are considered to be lower in one's hierarchy of values.

The personality of Kobayashi, the martyr symbol of "nonconvert" communists in the 1930's, exhibited a strange, tightly knit marriage between the ideally rational ideology of Marxism and the predominantly negative affective posture of traditionalism. It should be noted that, as suppression of thought and the use of police violence were intensified, and as the necessity of working underground increased, the communists became more and more isolated from the people. The relationship between Marxian ideology and the negative affective posture of the traditional type was therefore strengthened. Exploration of the development of this type of relationship may reveal that there exists a correlation between patterns of tension-management in personality and in society.

The Reversely Committed: Manabu Sano (1892-1953) and Sadachika Nabeyama (1901-   )

Sano and Nabeyama were from very different social backgrounds. Sano came from a family of ten generations of doctors, and he graduated from Tokyo Imperial University with a silver watch bestowed by the Emperor, the mark of the elite of all the young elites in Japan of that day.[29] At Tokyo Imperial University he was one of the founders of Shinjinkai (The Association of New Men), which eventually became the vanguard of the "V Narode" movement in Japan and a hotbed of socialist leadership. After graduating from the university, Sano became a lecturer at Waseda University.[30] In contrast, Nabeyama was born into the family of a petty official, and he had no regular schooling after the death of his father forced him to find factory work. Under the impact of the Russian Revolution, he became interested in the syndicalist labor movement; he was arrested and imprisoned for two months in 1920, an experience which, he claims, turned him to socialist labor movement ac-

[29] The prize of a silver watch, a gift from the Emperor, was bestowed only on the best students graduating from Tokyo Imperial University. This practice was discontinued in 1918.

[30] For biographical data on Manabu Sano, see Michitoshi Takabatake, "Ikkoku Shakaishugisha—Sano Manabu, Nabeyama Sadachika," *Tenkō*, I, 164-200.

tivities.[31] Both Sano and Nabeyama were appointed by the Comintern in 1927 to the Central Committee of the Japanese Communist Party along with three other members. They were both arrested in April 1929 and were sentenced to life imprisonment in 1932. It was after the verdict was delivered that they began to contemplate a change of ideology. The prison authorities allowed them to meet and exchange ideas and, finally, to draw up a joint statement. This statement (issued in June 1933, five months after the death of Takiji Kobayashi) was printed and circulated among the political prisoners by the Department of Justice. Within a month of their declaration, 30 percent (415) of the nonconvicted and 36 percent (133) of the convicted prisoners announced their decision to convert.[32] After the public announcement of their ideological change, their sentences were reduced in 1934 by a higher court from life imprisonment to fifteen years.[33]

The statement of conversion by Sano and Nabeyama comprised four major points.[34] The first and most important concerned the Emperor system. According to Sano and Nabeyama, the Japanese people had a deep-rooted respect and attachment for the Imperial Household. Thus to abolish the Emperor system, which had been one of the major goals of the Communist Party, would be to oppose the will of the people. The pattern of revolution in any country should reflect the different "social psychological factors" peculiar to "her own tradition and her racial origin." In Japan, they argued, a revolution should be carried out under the leadership of the Imperial Household, and it should be based on "one-nation socialism," rather than on international socialism.

The second point stressed the racial superiority of the Japanese. Sano and Nabeyama maintained that there were superior nations and inferior nations. Since Japan was a superior nation in Asia, she should annex weaker nations such as Korea, Formosa, and Manchuria in order to establish "the People's Government of Japan, Korea, Formosa and Manchuria." In essence, this idea adumbrated the concept of the "Great Asiatic

[31] The biographical data on Sadachika Nabeyama were taken from his *Watashi wa Kyōsantō o Suteta* (*I Have Left the Communist Party*), Tokyo, Daitō Shuppan, 1949.

[32] Takabatake, "Ikkoku Shakaishugisha," pp. 164-165.

[33] Nabeyama, *Watashi wa Kyōsantō o Suteta*, pp. 154-159; Takabatake, *ibid.*, p. 165.

[34] Takabatake, *ibid.*, pp. 166-167.

Co-prosperity Sphere" later advanced by the Total War Research Institute in 1942.[35]

The third point dealt with the justification of Japan's current war aims in Manchuria. Sano and Nabeyama came out in support of the war, characterizing it as a war of emancipation of the Asian people from Western imperialism. They urged that Japan ally herself with Soviet Russia and the Chinese soviet to form "The Proletarian Pan Asianism" in order to bring the war to a successful end.

The fourth point put forward a criticism of the Japanese Communist Party. The party was denounced for its subjugation to the Comintern. In place of the Communist Party, Sano and Nabeyama proposed a new political party that would carry out the program of "one-nation socialism" under the leadership of the Imperial Household.

Let us examine the process of ideological change in the personalities of Sano and Nabeyama. The first step was the sense of the defeat of their movement. Sano confessed:

> In Japan where we have a fine proletariat, the communist party which claims to be the only and the vanguard party of the proletariat is moving further and further away from most of the working class, in spite of the self-sacrificing activities of serious-minded youth. To say this may seem to be a public admission of our defeat. Yes. We are willing to admit our defeat in the aforementioned sense. . . . By recognizing our failures for what they are, we shall be able to make a fresh start.[36]

Nabeyama likewise acknowledged the party's ineffectiveness:

> In inverse ratio to the internal decadence of the party, their programs and slogans became more and more revolutionary. They directed a general strike on a nationwide scale which no one could even dream would be successful. They agitated for a strike and demonstration on the anniversary of the consumer's cooperatives. . . . They did not have the support of the people and consequently they could not put into practice even one hundredth of what they promised; they committed themselves to bold policies only in theory.[37]

[35] For a translation of the "Draft of Basic Plan for Establishment of Greater East Asia Co-Prosperity Sphere," see De Bary et al., eds., *Sources of Japanese Tradition*, II, 294-298.

[36] Quoted in Takabatake, "Ikkoku Shakaishugisha," pp. 173-174.

[37] Nabeyama, *Watashi wa Kyōsantō o Suteta*, pp. 148-149.

Sano and Nabeyama, by criticizing the Communist Party for its alienation from the people, expressed their desire "to re-examine" themselves and communism "by probing into the primary motives which first inclined them to socialism and the labor movement"[38] and their wish "to start all over again." What were these primary motives which drove them into revolutionary movements?

When Sano became a leader of the "V Narode" movement in 1917 and Nabeyama a leader of the labor movement in 1920, "the proletariat" or the "laborers" were sacred symbols for those attracted to the movements.[39] It has been pointed out by Lewis Feuer that both prerevolutionary Russian intellectuals and British Fabian socialists of aristocratic and bourgeois backgrounds were motivated by a "collective guilt consciousness" over their privileged origins.[40] This collective guilt consciousness sometimes produces in intellectual elites in socialist movements an inferiority complex in relation to the common people which in turn leads them to idealize the proletariat. Marx distinguished between the class unaware of its own self-interests and "the class aware of itself" and united in an organized political party to defend its interests against the opposing class.[41] When Sano and Nabeyama began to take the Communist Party to task for its alienation from the people and to voice their desire "to start all over again," their conception of the people began to deviate from the orthodox communist view. The distress they felt over the defeat of their movement was followed by a change in their conception of the people that modified the theory of class to fit the people as they were. Thus they became less committed to the previously held ideology, and at the same time they took an initial step toward accepting the counter-ideology, which was advocated by the police authorities. They thereby became less committed to the ideology they had previously held.

The second event that further altered their ideological stand was the news of the escalation of the Manchurian war. Nabeyama wrote:

[38] *Ibid.*, p. 150.
[39] Takabatake, "Ikkoku Shakaishugisha," p. 174.
[40] Lewis S. Feuer, *Psychoanalysis and Ethics*, Springfield, Ill., Charles C. Thomas, 1955, Part II, p. 3.
[41] Karl Marx, *The Poverty of Philosophy*, New York, International Publishers, pp. 145-146—quoted in Reinhard Bendix and Seymour M. Lipset, "Karl Marx's Theory of Social Classes," in *Class, Status and Power*, ed. Bendix and Lipset, Glencoe, Ill., The Free Press, 1953, p. 31.

Despite our desperate anti-war struggle, the war was spreading. The impetus of the war had increased so much that it could not possibly have been prevented either by individuals or by party effort. . . . If we had stuck to our party line, we would have been advocating the defeat of our own country. I came to detest the advocacy of such a defeat for my own country. Before the war began, I could justify myself in taking such a stand. However, after the war started, I could not possibly say that my country should be defeated. Not only could I not say it, I could not even think such a thing. . . .

If I gave up the advocacy of my country's defeat in the war, would this not automatically lead me to abandon communism? It may be so. Thus reasoning, I hesitated. . . . Is there not a way to oppose the war of aggression without having to advocate our country's defeat? . . .

If we attempt to direct our war toward that purpose [the emancipation of the Asians], we may end up without being defeated and without having committed aggression. . . . That is only a wish. *Or rather, it is a rationalization of wishful thinking. It is an extremely untenable position. However, I find this position more congenial to my feeling* than support of the defeat of my country. . . .[42]

It should be noted that the change of ideological posture from an antiwar stand to support of Japan's war aim was motivated, as Nabeyama himself admits, by "the feelings" of "hostility," or the negative affect toward communist ideology. It was not reasoning on the ideational level that prompted Nabeyama's ideological conversion but the sense of discord between his affective posture and his ideological posture, in which the former dominated the latter. The second cycle began, then, with the feeling of disgust both Sano and Nabeyama came to have for the antiwar ideology they had previously held, progressed further with their move toward the support of Japan's war aims, and culminated finally in their decision to make public the joint statement of their conversion.

The process of commitment, as we have already seen, follows a spiral path, signifying ever heightening degrees of commitment with the start of each new cycle. In contrast, the course of reversal of the previous commitment represents a counter-

[42] Nabeyama, *Watashi wa Kyōsantō o Suteta*, pp. 151-153 (italics in the original).

process, indicating a declining level of commitment to the previous ideology with the start of each new cycle. The salient feature of the reversely committed is that commitment to a new ideology takes hold in proportion to the intensity of deviation from the previous ideology.

After denouncing communist ideology, Sano manifested, in prison, a growing commitment to Emperor worship.

> There was some germ of the right thinking in my original idea [as expressed in the joint statement of ideological conversion]. . . . That right way of thinking arose from my awakening to a sense of the dignity of our national polity. . . . The essence of the Imperial System lies in the Emperor's position as the Head of the Main Family of the Japanese people and like the Imperial gods and goddesses, the Creator and Sustainer of heaven and earth. . . . What supreme bliss it is to be born a Japanese with the privilege of sacrificing oneself for the sake of the noblest and absolute being, the Emperor. . . . I am determined to annihilate everything personal in me and make myself one with the Emperor.[43]

The first step of Sano's and Nabeyama's ideological shift took them from the concept of the proletariat as the self-conscious class as Marx understood it to the acceptance of the proletariat as it actually was. This became a preliminary step toward further ideological changes. The process may be formulated as a syllogism. First, the failure of the Japanese Communist Party was its alienation from the majority of the people. In order to make amends for this failure, the two disillusioned activists argued, they should "start all over again" by trying to identify themselves with the majority of the people. Second, the majority of the people, they observed, adhered to Emperor worship and supported Japan's war aims. Therefore, they could switch from advocacy of the abolition of the Emperor system to support of it, from an antiwar stance to the endorsement of Japan's war aims, and at the same time still maintain their original position —"sincerity" and service to the mass of the people.[44]

[43] Manabu Sano, "Waga Gokuchū no Shisō Henreki" ("The History of My Thought in Prison"), in Shihōshō Keisei Kyoku (Bureau of Punishment Affairs of the Ministry of Justice), *Keisei Shiryō* (*Documents for the Administration of Criminals*), Vol. i, 1944—quoted in Takabatake, "Ikkoku Shakaishugisha," pp. 184-185.

[44] After the war Sano wrote: "With the increase of the freedom of discussion, people have become critical even on the matter of the Emperor

The experience of Sano and Nabeyama should be described as ideological *re*conversion, rather than conversion. No written statements on their positions before they committed themselves to communism are available, but we do know in a general way that both of them were brought up by parents who were not communists and that both went to elementary school (although Nabeyama did not finish) where filial piety and loyalty to the Emperor were the core of compulsory moral education. Their commitment to communism, then, can be taken as the first incident of conversion—conversion from the ideas and affects of familism and Emperor worship to the ideology that denied both familism and the Emperor system. Their shift from communism back to Emperor worship should therefore be called ideological reconversion. They did not simply revert to the ideological and affective postures of their childhood socialization; instead, they returned to the primary ideological stances of their childhood and adolescence with higher degrees of commitment.

Their ideological conversion from familism and Emperor worship to communism represents the shift from predominant nonrationalism to predominant rationalism, from predominant particularism to predominant universalism, from predominant dependent collectivism to predominant independent collectivism. Reconversion is a subcategory of the more general process of the reversal of one's commitment, in which a person replaces one ideology with another without necessarily returning exactly to the previous ideology. When the reversal of one's commitment takes the form of reconversion, we may establish a general hypothetical proposition, that the reconverted person tends to manifest a higher degree of commitment to the readopted ideology than he showed to the same ideology when he previously held it.

The Perennial Deviant: Osamu Dazai (1909-1948)

Osamu Dazai was a talented existentialist novelist.[45] He was

---

system. . . . My standpoint on the Emperor system is identical with that of the vast majority of the productive mass including industrial laborers, farmers, intellectual laborers, urban middle-class people, etc." Manabu Sano, *Tennō-sei to Shakaishugi* (*The Emperor System and Socialism*), 1946— quoted in Takabatake, *ibid.*, p. 189.

[45] According to Shunsuke Tsurumi, the "conversion literature" of Dazai, Yutaka Haniya, Tomoyoshi Murayama, and their fellow writers was "the first manifestation of existentialism in Japan." Shunsuke Tsurumi, "Nihon no Jitsuzonshugi" ("Existentialism in Japan"), in Kuno and Tsurumi, *Gendai*

born in 1909 in Aomori-ken, the northern part of mainland Japan, the sixth son in a landlord's large family of more than thirty persons, including servants. Although his family was wealthy and could afford to feed so many mouths, still Dazai was treated by his parents as one of the "surplus population," and he suffered from emotional deprivation.[46] The awareness of being "surplus" and of not being wanted by his parents set the leitmotif of his life—the sense of shame and guilt for the sheer fact of having been born. One of his autobiographical novels, *The Banner Bearer of the Twentieth Century*, opens with an apology: "I am sorry I was born." Another, *No Longer Human*, begins: "I have spent a shameful life."[47] Yōzō, the protagonist of this book, writes about his childhood:

> I was anxious lest my concept of happiness and that of everybody else in the world should be completely incompatible. That anxiety made me groaning and sleepless night after night to the point of driving me almost crazy. Am I really happy? From my early childhood people told me that I was very fortunate. But actually I always felt as though I were living in hell. Those who said that I was fortunate looked to me far happier than I was. . . . The more I thought, the more confused I became. More and more I suffered from fear and anxiety that I was alone and that I was completely different from others. I was almost incapable of carrying on a conversation with my neighbors. I did not know what to say or how to say it.
>
> Then it occurred to me that I might try to play a clown.

Nihon no Shisō, p. 164. For biographical data on Osamu Dazai, see Ken Hirano, "Kaisetsu" ("Commentary"), and "Dazai Osamu Nenpu," *Dazai Osamu Shū, Gendai Nihon Bungaku Zenshū*, Tokyo, Chikuma Shobō, 1954, XLIX, 416-418 and 426-430 respectively. See also Yasutaka Saegusa, *Dazai Osamu to Sono Shōgai* (*Dazai Osamu and His Life*), Tokyo, Shinbisha, 1965. According to Saegusa, Dazai was the sixth son; according to "Dazai Osamu Nenpu," he was the fourth son. The former counts the two elder brothers who died young, whereas the latter does not. Saegusa notes (pp. 41, 47) that it was because Dazai was born as the sixth son and was treated as "a surplus," receiving no love from his parents, that he felt shame and guilt for his birth.

[46] "Dazai Osamu Nenpu," *ibid.*, p. 426.

[47] Osamu Dazai, "Nijusseiki no Kishu," *Dazai Osamu Zenshū*, Tokyo, Chikuma Shobō, 1962, II, 57; *idem*, "Ningen Shikkaku," *Dazai Osamu Shū*, p. 339. The English version is entitled *No Longer Human*, tr. Donald Keene, Norfolk, Conn., New Directions, 1958. The translation used in this essay is my own.

I had been a very skilful clown ever since my early child-hood, because I could not even conceive of how my own fam-ily lived and suffered or what they were thinking, and could not bear to admit that I did not understand them. Thus, with-out my knowing when it happened, I became a child who never told the truth.[48]

The relationship of Yōzō's father with his sons was like that of most fathers in a large family of a landlord in a northern vil-lage, namely, predominantly nonrational, particularistic, inti-mate, and dependently collectivistic. Yōzō's relationship with his father and other members of his family, though, as far as the novel describes, was in the main rational and universalistic, since his daily behavior was based on the calculation of the effects of his conduct as expressed in his playing the role of a clown; and he referred to his parents, brothers, sisters, servants, friends, and strangers indiscriminately as "neighbors," "everybody else," or just "others." He distinguished only between "I" and the rest of mankind, rather than between the "we" of his own family and those outside the family. His conduct, moreover, was mostly avoidant, his sense of alienation from his family being so acute that he had to act *as if* he were intimately engaged in family activities, as he did when he tried to hide his lack of interest in such matters by pretending to want the toy lion brought to him from Tokyo by his father.[49] (He was also predominantly independent and individualistic. In declaring that his sense of shame was derived from the fear that he had often failed to act on his own judgment of alternatives,[50] he revealed his ex-treme sensitivity to the concept of the individual as the locus of decision-making.)

The description of Yōzō's childhood reveals that Dazai's early reaction to the norms of familism and the patterns of behavior founded upon them was revulsion and contempt. At the same time, however, he did not wish to displease the members of his family, so he began to act as if he were in sympathy with their values and norms. But it was exactly this continuous playacting that made him aware of the gap between what he actually felt and what he did to live up to the expectations of others. This was the source of the negative affect of shame.

Another source of Dazai's sense of guilt was his birth into a

[48] Dazai, "Ningen Shikkaku," p. 340.
[49] *Ibid.*, pp. 341-342.   [50] *Ibid.*, p. 341.

privileged family in the midst of the poverty prevalent in the northern villages. This sense of guilt and shame drew him to the Marxist student group after he entered Tokyo Imperial University in 1930 to study French literature. He writes in the novel: "I like them [the members of the communist cell]. They were congenial to my temperament. This sense of intimacy was not derived from ideological sympathy with Marx. I took a vague pleasure in the illegality of my position. . . . I felt at home."[51] Later he admits:

> There is an expression, "a person who lives in the shadows," which denotes the miserable man, the defeated man, the man of vice in a society. I feel that I have been a man living in the shadows ever since I was born. Whenever I meet a person labeled by others as a man who lives in shadows, I cannot help feeling kindly disposed to him.[52]

Yet, just as Yōzō could not feel at home with his family, so Dazai could not feel completely at one with the communist group either.

> . . . I received a lecture on Marxian economics from a very ugly-looking youth sitting at the head of the table. But all that was said seemed to me platitudinous. Although it must have been true, I protested within myself that there was something more than that in man, something more irrational and more terrible than the motives we usually call desire, vanity, passion, or carnal desire. I myself could not specify what, but there was something at the bottom of human society, something more monstrous than economics, which always disturbed me and terrified me. Although I accepted dialectical materialism as being as natural as water flowing downward, that alone could not relieve me of my fear of other human beings; it could not open my eyes to the green leaves of spring, so to speak, and give me the complete sense of joy and hope. However, I always attended their meetings which were called "R.S." (I may be mistaken.) It was like a comedy to see my "comrades," their faces stiffly serious, engrossed in the study of theories which seemed to me to be almost elementary arithmetic, such as one plus one equals two. So I tried to soften the atmosphere by acting like a clown, which was almost second nature to me by then. I suppose it helped to

[51] *Ibid.*, p. 352.   [52] *Ibid.*

break the icy coldness of the meeting, and I made myself extremely popular among them.[53]

Thus Dazai could no more commit himself to communism than he could to familism, even though he acted as if he were in complete sympathy with the group. Indeed, he acted out this role so well that he was forced into a leading position, which eventually precipitated his departure from the party.

> The P (the party was so called, as I recall, in our jargon, but I may be mistaken) constantly requested us to do this or that to such an extent that we had no time for rest or play. This situation became so demanding that my frail and sickening body could bear no more. Primarily I was attracted by the group's underground character and that was why I began to assist their activities. However, when the activities became so extremely demanding, just as a joke may unexpectedly produce a serious consequence, I could not help feeling secretly agitated. I wanted to tell the responsible people of the P that they should ask those under their direct control to do whatever they wished to be done, but not me, who was more or less an outsider. So I escaped. After my escape I felt badly, and decided to kill myself.[54]

In 1935 Dazai joined a nationalist literary circle called the Japan Romantic School (*Nihon Rōman Ha*). This group, under the leadership of Yojūrō Yasuda, stressed the primary importance of feelings, rather than reason, as the criterion of social and literary criticism. It further suggested that Westernization, which had been promoted since the Meiji Restoration under the name of modernization, should be overcome by a return to the indigenous tradition of the Japanese people. Although the leader claimed that the group was apolitical, it did in effect support Japan's war aims. According to Bunzō Hashikawa, Dazai's association with the group was "accidental," and he differed significantly both in ideological and affective postures from the group's leader.[55]

---

[53] *Ibid.*, pp. 352-353.   [54] *Ibid.*, pp. 353-354.

[55] See Bunzō Hashikawa, "Nihon Rōmanha to Dazai Osamu" ("The Japan Romantic School and Osamu Dazai"), *Nihon Rōmanha Hihan Josetsu* (*An Introduction to the Critique of the Japan Romantic School*), Tokyo, Miraisha, 1965, pp. 151-167. According to Hashikawa, Dazai's association with the group arose out of contingent circumstances rather than ideological commitment. Dazai and his friends began a literary journal called *The Blue Flower* in 1934, which was annexed to the organ of the Japan Romantic

His withdrawal from the Marxist organization and "escape" into an innocuous stance left Dazai with a sense of guilt and shame even deeper than that from which he had suffered before. Thus he wrote in 1936:

> In the moonless night I escaped alone. The rest of my comrades lost their lives, all of them. I am a son of a big landlord. The agony of a convert? How dare you say such a thing, you who have betrayed your comrades so cleverly? . . .
>
> If you are a defector, you should behave like one. I believe in dialectical materialism. . . . It has been my principle for ten years, and will still be ten years from now. However, I do not want laborers and farmers to overcome their hatred and revulsion toward us, not a bit. I do not want them to make an exception. Since I believe in their simple courage and I cherish it above all else, I cannot possibly bring myself to talk about the world view in which I believe. I would not permit myself to speak of tomorrow's dawn with my rotten lips.[56]

It was the sense of guilt and shame derived from his early childhood experience that made him sympathize with the Communist Party. But he could not identify himself completely with the communist group, any more than he could with his family. Thus, when overburdening duties were piled on him and police suppression came, so that he had to quit the group, he felt a greater sense of guilt and shame than ever.

The same pattern held for his attitude toward women. It was always out of a sense of guilt and shame that he was drawn to the unfortunate and lonely women, "women in the shadows." When he was twenty-two, he attempted suicide in company with a hostess from a bar; he survived, but his partner died. This was the first time he experienced an intensification of guilt in his relations with women. It was in the next year that he entered the communist group. Following his break with the party, he tried to kill himself but did not succeed. In 1937 he again made an abortive attempt at double suicide. After his marriage in 1939,

---

School in 1935. Hashikawa argues on this ground that Dazai came to join the latter "by accident" (p. 152). On the Japan Romantic School, see Hashikawa, pp. 7-100; Kenji Yamaryō, "Nihon Rōmanha," in *Tenkō*, I, 250-288; Yoshimi Takeuchi, *Kokumin Bungaku Ron* (*The Theory of National Literature*), Tokyo, Tokyo Daigaku Shuppankai, 1954, pp. 63-74.

[56] Osamu Dazai, "Kyokō no Haru" ("The Fictitious Spring"), *Dazai Osamu Zenshū*, I, 278.

he enjoyed a relatively stable period of life and work, until the end of the war. During the years of confusion that immediately followed defeat, he wrote his most widely read novels, including *The Setting Sun* (1947), *Villon's Wife* (1947), and *No Longer Human* (1948). In this period the intermittent drug addiction that had characterized his earlier life became a permanent habit. In June 1948 he was found dead with his mistress.[57]

We classify Dazai as a "perennial deviant" because he was never committed to the ready-made ideology of any group, either primary or secondary, but only to himself. The pattern of the development of his affects approximates the negative snowball. The negative affects of guilt and shame were intensified as the result of the decisions he made; the decisions in turn were motivated primarily by his sense of guilt and shame. He ended by annihilating himself.

The Many-layered Self: Tomoyoshi Murayama (1901-   )

Tomoyoshi Murayama was born in Tokyo. He matriculated at Tokyo Imperial University and later went to Germany to study fine arts. After returning to Japan, he became acquainted with proletarian authors and theatre movements and eventually served as one of their leaders. He was arrested in 1932, whereupon he underwent ideological conversion and was subsequently released after two years' imprisonment.[58] He withdrew from communist political activities and concentrated on writing a series of "conversion novels" for two years after his release.[59] *The White Night* is unique for its extremely vivid depiction of the psychological process of ideological conversion.

> While he was in the police station, hearing that Shikano and Kimura [the names of his comrades] never said a word when under interrogation, in contrast to his own conduct, he denounced himself by hitting his head against the wall of his cell. He could not but admit that their conduct was completely beyond the standard he could live up to. Sitting in

[57] It has been generally established that Dazai and his mistress committed double suicide. According to Saegusa, however, the police found evidence, which they did not make public, that the woman had practically strangled him to death before she dragged him into the river with herself. See Saegusa, *Dazai Osamu to Sono Shōgai*, p. 229.

[58] *Tenkō*, III, 497.

[59] Honda, *Tenkō Bungaku Ron*, p. 202.

the dark corner of his prison cell, visualizing the scene of torture by the police, he tried to torment his own body, and he ended up with the full recognition that he could not stand up to such conditions. Moreover, he learned that Shinzō Matsui, whom he had somewhat despised for his insensitivity and the irregularities of his political activities, acted in the same manner as Kimura. This was the final blow to the self-confidence he had cultivated in himself through long years of hard work. No excuse he might think of could possibly salvage his crumbling confidence in himself. . . .

He stayed in this frame of mind for almost two years in the prison. After his second summer there, absolutely shut away from fresh air, his mind was eroded by something undefined and invincible. He felt as though his flesh and blood, or rather something mysteriously a part of his own father and mother, and of their forebears from time immemorial, whose faces, names and lives had long since perished was eating away his existence, which was after all an infinitesimally small particle of their posterity. However hard he tried to cry out at them, to push them aside, and to drive them out, it was of no avail. In his struggle with his invisible foes, day in and night out, he groaned, struck his head with his fists, and scratched the wall with his nails.[60]

This is an acutely straightforward evocation of the nonrational ideo-affective posture of familism based on ancestor worship in a predominantly rational, Western-educated person. This case shows the sudden reappearance of the negative affects of distress, fear, terror, and humiliation in a personality whose affects theretofore had been mainly positive: enjoyment of his own work, interest in people, and respect for his own achievements. Thus it clearly represents the negative iceberg model.

The author, educated in both Japanese and German universities and converted to communism, considered himself a completely rational person committed to a universalistic, independently collectivistic, and engaged ideology. To his great consternation, however, when he was exposed to the socialization of police terror, the ideas inculcated in him in his childhood through his primary group socialization were activated. As

[60] Tomoyoshi Murayama, "Byakuya" ("The White Night"), *Murayama Tomoyoshi Shū, Gendai Nihon Bungaku Zenshū*, Tokyo, Chikuma Shobō, 1957, LXXVII, 345-347.

long as he was active in the communist movement, his personality was dominated by a rational, universalistic, independently collectivistic, and engaged ideological posture, and he was not aware of the persistence of the other, underlying self, which was irrational, particularistic, dependently collectivistic, and detached. Thus he possessed the ideological posture of the many-layered self without realizing it—until the prison situation made him conscious of this deeper layer of his personality.

This confrontation with the subterranean component of his ideo-affective posture and his recognition of its density and durability led Murayama to decide to abandon communism. He submitted a report to the police authorities to that effect and was released.

"We should no longer pamper ourselves, hide, and deceive ourselves," Murayama wrote. "We should completely reject all that. We should admit to ourselves all our own weaknesses. And thus we will face reality, and our literary work will be honestly rooted in our true selves. Otherwise, we will never be able to follow a straight and narrow path to victory."[61]

What distinguishes the many-layered self as represented by Murayama from the reversely committed as exemplified by Sano and Nabeyama is that the former tries to observe, analyze, and criticize thoroughly the subterranean self inculcated through primary socialization, to which the top layer, acquired through later socialization, has to succumb. Sano and Nabeyama pursued no such self-examination after their reconversion to their primary ideo-affective posture. On the contrary, their commitment to the primary ideology was intensified.

The Conflicting Self: Shigeharu Nakano (1902-   )

The literary works of Shigeharu Nakano, after he was released from prison upon admitting ideological conversion, begin where Murayama left off.[62] Nakano was the second son of an owner-cultivator farmer in Fukui Prefecture.[63] When he

[61] Murayama, "Sakkateki Saishuppatsu" ("To Start All Over Again as an Author")—quoted in Honda, Tenkō Bungaku Ron, pp. 207-208.

[62] Murayama, having written a series of "conversion novels," including The White Night, reverted to his original interest in the theatre and resumed the writing of plays, instead of novels. See Honda, ibid., pp. 202-203.

[63] For biographical data on Shigeharu Nakano, see "Nakano Shigeharu Nenpu," Nakano Shigeharu Shū, Gendai Nihon Bungaku Zenshū, Tokyo, Chikuma Shobo, 1954, xxxvii, 428-430.

was sixteen, his elder brother died, and he thus became the only son in the family. In 1924 he entered Tokyo Imperial University and studied German literature. In the following year he joined the Shinjinkai group and, in the year after that, the Proletarian Arts League. At the time of the general election in 1928, he campaigned for the Farmer – Labor Party and was arrested briefly. He was active in the proletarian literary movements, first in the NAPF and later in the KOPF. He was arrested in 1932 and was imprisoned for two years. In 1934 he confessed that he was a member of an illegal political organization and agreed that he would give up political activities; he was subsequently released. In his celebrated novel, *The Village House*, he described and analyzed the aftermath of his ideological conversion.

Benji, the character in the novel who personifies the author, returns to his father's house in his native village. His father, Magozō, had gone back to his farm in his old age, after working for some years as a petty civil servant in various small towns. Magozō owned and cultivated some six acres, which was a medium-sized farm according to Japanese standards, but too small for him to make ends meet. Although he had neither money nor prestige, he was a "man of integrity," respected and adored by his fellow villagers, as well as by his own family.[64] Not as highly educated as his son, the old man stood for the wisdom of the common man who had accumulated his knowledge and acquired his philosophy of life through his own hard work as a small farmer. Though an Emperor worshiper and a conservative, he had taken pride in his son's proletarian literary activities and had tried to understand his political views.[65] Magozō did not, however, approve of his son's ideological conversion. The father admonished his son:

> When we heard that you were converted, your mother and I were astonished. Do you mean that you had been engaged in political activities as a recreation? It looks now as though you had looked on them as mere games. . . . Whatever good literary deeds you may have done, have all been discounted now. . . . It is simply outrageous. . . . However clever you may be, you are good for nothing if you abandon your manliness. Even if you read and write well, unless you have integrity,

[64] Shigeharu Nakano, "Mura no Ie," *ibid.*, pp. 256-257.
[65] *Ibid.*, p. 264.

your achievements will be of no avail. Since we heard of your arrest, we have been expecting that you would return dead, and we managed to dispose of our domestic affairs on that assumption. We expected that you would die on the scaffold in Totsukagahara [the name of the place where political prisoners were executed during the Edo period]. . . .

I for one feel very strongly that you should give up your writing. . . . What use is there in writing to justify your shameful ideological conversion? . . . Whatever you may write would be of no use except to disgrace your past achievements. . . . You should become a farmer instead.[66]

According to the father's norm of conduct, his son's ideological conversion was a shameful act of disloyalty to the group to which he had once pledged his allegiance. Whatever the group was, and whatever the principle for which the group stood, it was the traditional samurai virtue of loyalty to stick to it even if doing so meant death. Self-sacrificing devotion to one's own group to the very end was the basic value for the father. The son, on the other hand, thought that to give up writing would be to lose the meaning of his existence. He felt he must continue to write, to explain how and why his organization had been defeated and why he himself had failed. Benji "thought he could explain his ideas logically. However, he thought it was utterly impossible to communicate his attitude to his father."[67]

The father in this novel represents the values and logic of the common people, especially the farmers, in the Japan of the prewar period, whereas the son represents those of the left-wing elites. The son's recognition of the impossibility of communicating his ideas to his father bespeaks the author's own realization of the existence of discommunication between the left-wing elites and the masses. Ryūmei Yoshimoto points out that, in this recognition of discommunication, the author of *The Village House* displayed a most significant self-criticism of the ideo-affective posture of the revolutionary movements in Japan. Their leaders failed to reach the subterranean currents of the common people's traditional affects and ideas.[68] Both Murayama and Nakano show that the gap between the top and the bottom layers of the personalities comprising the elites and the social hiatus between the elites and the masses

[66] *Ibid.*, pp. 267-268.
[67] *Ibid.*, p. 268.
[68] Ryūmei Yoshimoto, "Tenkōron," ("An Essay on Ideological Conversion"), *Gendai Hihyō*, Jan. 1959.

are two sides of the same problem. In the *White Night* the gap dividing the two layers within the author's personality remains unbridged. In *The Village House* the author reveals his ambivalent attitude toward his father as a representative of the masses and toward himself as a member of a left-wing elite. In reply to his father's admonition to change his occupation from writing to farming, the son resolutely stated: "I understand what you have said. However, I should like to continue to write." Thus the son did not accept his father's values, although, in the last passage, he realized how unjust he had been in his relation to his father. While he was in prison, he had asked his old father again and again to come from the distant village to Tokyo to testify in court on his behalf and to petition for his release. He remembered that each time he saw his father, he looked older and thinner.

> . . . Benji realized how cruelly he had treated this old father of his to serve his own interests and feed his egotism. Now he recognized how atrociously he drove his wife, his sisters and his parents to make them serve his selfish purposes. Quietly, a feeling of disgust with himself crept into him.[69]

Nakano's attitude toward his father exhibits a marked contrast to that of Sano and Nabeyama. The latter, in their ideological reconversions, yielded themselves to the values and ideas of the masses, whereas the former, even after his ideological conversion, did not compromise with them. The relationship of Nakano with his family also differed from the relationship of Takiji Kobayashi with his common-law wife. The latter justified his exploitation of his wife on the pretext that he was working for the people; the former recognized his own father and the rest of his family as an integral part of the people for whom he allegedly had been working, and he was therefore ashamed of himself for having exploited them for his own benefit. Kobayashi's commitment to communist ideology was motivated mainly by negative affects of hatred and fury against the weapons of exploitation, oppression, and terror used by the ruling class. In contrast, in Nakano, who was primarily a lyric poet,[70] the positive affects

---

[69] Nakano, "Mura no Ie," p. 268.

[70] Nakano began as a poet, and his earlier poem "A Farewell Before Dawn," published in 1926, established him as a proletarian poet. His autobiographical novel *A Farewell to Poetry* (1939) tells of his high school days when he was deeply immersed in reading and writing the Japanese traditional form of poetry—*tanka*. See Nakano, "Uta no Wakare," *Nakano Shigeharu Shū*, pp. 279-320.

of the enjoyment of the beautiful and his sympathy with those who suffer were just as strong as the negative affects of self-humiliation and hatred against what he considered ugly and unpleasant. Nakano's dual affective posture was the basis for the ambivalence in his ideological posture, which is the mark of the conflicting self.

The Innovator: Hajime Kawakami (1879-1946)

Hajime Kawakami is said to have had more influence than any other Marxist thinker on the young intellectuals of the 1920's and 1930's.[71] The crucial aspect of his personality was that he encompassed a variety of logically incompatible experiences and ideas and that he finally worked out a creative integration of them at a later stage of his life. In the development of affects, he belongs to the late-bloomer type, and, in the development of his personality as a whole, he represents the innovator.

Kawakami's life can be divided into five periods, each of which stands for a distinctive type of affect and ideology of socialization. In the first period he was brought up in traditional samurai familism; in the second period he was taught the spirit of *shishi* ("men of high purpose")[72] based upon Confucianism; in the third period he turned to Christianity and Buddhism; in the fourth period he switched from bourgeois economics to Marxism; and in the fifth period he arrived at an integration of his affects and ideas.

Early Childhood: Samurai Familism

Kawakami was born in a village in Yamaguchi Prefecture, a part of Chōshū during the Edo period, the eldest son of a former samurai family.[73] His father served as the village chief for most of his life. Before his birth, his mother was divorced from his father, who subsequently took another wife. Kawakami was taken to his father's house three months after his birth and was brought up by his paternal grandmother. When he was fourteen months old, his stepmother gave birth to a boy,

[71] Minpei Sugiura, "Kawakami Hajime Ron" ("On Hajime Kawakami"), *Shisō no Kagaku*, No. 44 (1965), p. 23.

[72] The term "men of high purpose" as a translation of *shishi* was first used by Marius Jansen in his *Sakamoto Ryōma and the Meiji Restoration*, Princeton, Princeton University Press, 1961.

[73] For biographical data on Hajime Kawakami, see his *Jijoden* (*Autobiography*), Tokyo, Sekai Hyōronsha, 1947, Vols. I-IV, and Etsuji Sumiya, *Kawakami Hajime*, Tokyo, Yoshikawa Kōbunkan, 1962.

and she began to maltreat Kawakami. He recalls that he was hung by one arm down a well, a brutal persecution that left him with a sprained shoulder. The stepmother was soon divorced, and, when he was three years old, his own mother was restored to her position as his father's wife.

Except for this short period of suffering, he was brought up amidst a profusion of love and affection lavished upon him by his parents and grandparents. No one in his family, at this stage at least, dared punish him. He was then a child who knew no fear.[74]

When he entered elementary school at the age of four years and five months, which was an unusually early time for a child to go to school, his father ordered a school janitor to carry him on his back to and from school every day. When his brother began to go to school, Kawakami, two years older, was still being borne on the janitor's back while the younger brother had to walk along beside them.[75] Kawakami was a spoilt child, as he himself admits.[76] This extreme favoritism was a manifestation of the survival of the norms of the traditional samurai family, where the eldest son, the heir of the family, was treated with the utmost affection and respect. Minpei Sugiura points out that it was this childhood experience of always being allowed to have his own way that developed in Kawakami the determination to make his will prevail whatever the circumstances. "During the Meiji period," Sugiura comments, "in a society heavy with the remnants of feudalism, the utilization of feudal customs in a direction traditionally not intended, was the only way to develop oneself to one's full possibilities."[77]

Within the family and the village community where the structures of relationships were predominantly nonrational, particularistic, hierarchical, exploitative, and dependently collectivistic, only those at the top in both family and village could afford the type of socialization which would encourage enjoyment, excitement, and novelty. Kawakami's childhood socialization, on the whole, was of that type. However, if we recall the short period in which he was punished by his stepmother for reasons he could not understand, his childhood socialization can be classified as a mixed type of two extremes—ex-

---

[74] Kawakami, *ibid.*, i, 16. [75] *Ibid.*, pp. 37-38.
[76] *Ibid.*, pp. 48-49.
[77] Sugiura, "Kawakami Hajime Ron," p. 25.

tremely positive and extremely negative affects, with the former predominating.

Early Adolescence: The Ethos of *Shishi*

Chōshū-*han* is well known as the birthplace of numerous *shishi*, including Shōin Yoshida (1830-1859), Aritomo Yamagata (1838-1922), and Hirobumi Itō (1841-1909), the leaders of the Meiji Restoration and the elder statesmen of the Meiji Government. Cultivation of the spirit of *shishi* was the goal of education for the samurai during the Tokugawa period. It was based primarily on the Confucian doctrine presented in the *Greater Learning*, which teaches:

> Their persons being cultivated, their families were regulated. Their families being regulated, their states were rightly governed. Their states being rightly governed, the whole kingdom [the world under the heaven—*tenka*] was tranquil and happy.[78]

The *shishi* are men dedicated to the welfare of society as a whole as if it were their own.[79]

Cultivation of this spirit of *shishi* was the aim of education at the high schools, supervised by the educational organization established by the former *daimyō* (feudal lord) of Chōshū-*han*.[80] Kawakami attended both junior and senior high schools of this type. The spirit of *shishi* inculcated in him at this stage of his life continued to motivate his later work.

In senior high school he majored in literature but, immediately before graduation, decided to go into law. He worked hard and passed the entrance examination of the Law School of Tokyo Imperial University in 1898.

> The desire to become a statesman had always been an undercurrent in my mind, and I had been constantly inspired by Master Shōin [Shōin Yoshida]. That latent desire was

[78] Legge's translation, Ch. 5—quoted in R. P. Dore, *Education in Tokugawa Japan*, Berkeley, University of California Press, 1965, p. 41.

[79] Shōin Yoshida defines *shishi* as men who "identify the fortune and misfortune of the state with their own." Sumiya, *Kawakami Hajime*, p. 22.

[80] The Bōchō Kyōiku Kai (Bōchō Educational Association) was established in 1884 by the former feudal lord Mōri with the recommendation of Kaoru Inoue, then the minister of foreign affairs and a native of Chōshū. See Kawakami, *Jijoden*, I, 55-56.

brought to life by a newspaper report of the emergence of the first cabinet in Japan based on political parties;[81] it came to dominate me. The news that party men such as Yukio Ozaki, Gitetsu Daitō, Masahisa Matsuda, who supposedly never had silk hats in their hands, suddenly had become cabinet ministers excited my youthful heart to hope that I too might be able to climb the ladder. Literature was not a challenging enough career for a man to pursue for his entire life. I would switch to the law school.[82]

Young Adulthood: Christianity and Buddhism

In his student days at Tokyo Imperial University, under the influence of Kanzō Uchimura (1861-1930)[83] and Naoe Kinoshita (1869-1937),[84] Kawakami became interested in Christianity and began to read the Bible. He was most deeply impressed by St. Matthew's version of the Sermon on the Mount: "whoever shall smite thee on thy right cheek, turn to him the other also; and if any man will sue thee at the law and take away thy coat, let him have thy cloak as well. . . ."[85] Referring to this passage in the Bible, he wrote:

This I felt was the imperative of absolute unselfishness. My conscience bowed to it categorically. Upon reflection now it seems strange, but at that time I cried out inwardly "that is right, that is right" without asking why it should be so. I thought that the absolutely unselfish attitude revealed in the passage ought to be the true ideal of human conduct. And I felt that at the bottom of my heart I should conduct my-

[81] In June 1898 Shigenobu Ōkuma (1838-1922), the chairman of the Kensei Hontō (Main Constitutional Political Party), became the prime minister and formed a cabinet to which Daitō, Ozaki, Matsuda, and other members of the Kenseitō (Constitutional Political Party) were appointed. This was the first cabinet based upon political parties in Japanese political history. See Shigeki Tōyama et al., *Kindai Nihon Seijishi Hikkei (A Compendium to the Political History of Modern Japan)*, Tokyo, Iwanami, 1961, pp. 31, 34, 138, 144.

[82] Kawakami, *Jijoden*, I, 91.

[83] Kanzō Uchimura is the most influential Christian thinker in modern Japan. For an excellent study of his life and work available in English, see John F. Howes, "Japan's Enigma: The Young Uchimura Kanzo," Ph.D. diss., Columbia University, 1965.

[84] Naoe Kinoshita was a Christian Socialist who organized the Social Democratic Party in 1901 and took an antiwar stand during the Russo-Japanese War.

[85] Matt. 5:39-40 (King James Version).

self *literally* according to that ideal. However, at the same time in my mind there was anxiety that I might destroy myself if I adhered to such an ideal. Thus for the first time a doubt was implanted in me about how I should regulate my life. This was the beginning of my ethical quest. I may call it the beginning of my mind's history.[86]

It should be noted that, impressed as he was by Christian teaching on the love of one's neighbors, Kawakami was keenly aware of the conflict between his own self-interest and the ideal of dedication to others. This awareness of conflict can be said to be grounded upon his early childhood socialization, which was characterized by a mixture of positive and negative affects. It was this awareness of conflicts between motives, and the tension produced by that awareness, that held him through his later life to his intense search for integration.

In 1901, when in his first year at the university, the Ashio Copper Mine pollution incident occurred. In 1877 the mine, which had originally been opened up by the Tokugawa Shogunate, was transferred to a private industrial capitalist. As the mine developed, copper pollution spread through river water over a vast area and threatened the livelihood of many peasants and fishermen. Shōzō Tanaka (1841-1913), who had been campaigning in Parliament since 1890 for legislative measures to solve the problem, made a direct appeal to the Emperor in 1901 in a final effort to assist the victims.[87] One evening when Kawakami attended one of the public meetings to enlist support for the victims, a bamboo basket was passed around for the receipt of contributions.

Listening to the speakers, I imagined a great number of people wandering around without clothes in the severe cold. Suddenly, I heard a clear voice saying to me: Give to him that asketh thee, and from him that would borrow of thee turn not thou away. I decided without hesitation that I should give all I had except for a few things I needed immediately. When I left the lecture hall, I handed to a woman in charge the cloak, the wrap, and the muffler I had on that night. After I went back to my lodgings, I put all my clothes in a trunk

[86] Kawakami, *Jijoden*, Vol. v—quoted in Sumiya, *Kawakami Hajime*, pp. 45-46.

[87] See Naoe Kinoshita, ed., *Tanaka Shōzō no Shōgai* (*The Life of Shōzō Tanaka*), Tokyo, Kokumin Tosho, 1928, pp. 95-325.

except for the kimono I had on and called a rickshaw man to deliver it to the office of the anti-copper pollution organization.[88]

Although he was drawn to practice the Christian gospel's teaching on the unselfish love of humanity, he cannot be said to have actually become a Christian convert. He did not, for instance, ever join a church.

In 1902 Kawakami graduated from the university and became a lecturer at the Agricultural School of Tokyo Imperial University, as well as a few other schools.[89] In the following year he began to write for the *Yomiuri Newspaper* a series of articles entitled "Essays on Socialism," which gained him a name in academic journalism. In 1905, when he was twenty-seven, he learned of a Buddhist priest, Shōshin Itō, who published a religious journal called *Muga no Ai (Selfless Love)* and had launched a religious group under that name. Kawakami rashly identified the title of the journal and the group with his own idea of unselfish dedication to something greater than oneself and quickly came to the conclusion that the group was practising what he had held simply as an ideal. He joined it, resigned from all his teaching positions, and discontinued writing his articles for the newspaper. Soon after he joined, he found to his disappointment that neither its leader nor its members were as devoted to the welfare of others as he had expected them to be.[90] In order to demonstrate to his fellow believers the example of a truly "selfless" man, Kawakami worked hard, "without rest and without sleep." One day, while he was writing an essay "on the essence of the universe," he suddenly felt his brain becoming "as transparent as crystal." He felt that his own "small ego was annihilated" and that his mind saw the "Mind [of the Universe]," "transcending the bifurcation of mind and matter."[91]

In his autobiography Kawakami describes this as "a strange religious experience" which gave him the lifelong motivation to work for the benefit of the group, which he considered to be

[88] Kawakami, *Jijoden*, Vol. v—quoted in Sumiya, *Kawakami Hajime*, pp. 48-49.

[89] He was appointed in the same year to the professorship at Peers' School and to the lectureship at Senshū School and Taiwan Kyōkai Professional School. See Sumiya, *ibid.*, pp. 321-322.

[90] Kawakami, *Jijoden*, i, 107-124.

[91] Kawakami, *Jijoden*, Vol. v—quoted in Sumiya, *Kawakami Hajime*, pp. 45-46.

greater than his own "small ego." Kawakami's biographers interpret this experience as the by-product of an epileptic seizure.[92] This explanation seems to be justified by his own description of the violent pain in the head and contraction of the muscles that followed "the moments of revelation." Whatever the origins of the experience, it is important to examine what Kawakami himself meant by its "religious" aspect.

The religious content of this experience, as Kawakami saw it, was an amalgamation of Confucianism, Christianity, and Buddhism. The Confucian ethos of *shishi* had implanted in him the belief that working for the welfare of the state and the peace and tranquility of "the kingdom under heaven" *(tenka)* was superior to working for one's own private interest. This ethos accorded well with Christian teaching about dedication of oneself to human brotherhood. This morality of unselfish dedication was in turn confirmed by the great religious experience of Kawakami's life which, according to his testimony, was comparable to the moments of revelation of Zen Buddhism.[93] The personal sense of humility and the attitude of devotion to something greater than oneself were elements these three religions which influenced Kawakami had in common. But the reference group to which one should pledge oneself, as he defined it, differed among the three doctrines: the state according to Confucianism; human brotherhood according to Christianity; and the "Mind of the Universe" according to Buddhism. At this stage he did not even consider the possibility of conflict among these three reference groups, especially between the first two. The most essential thing for him was to fortify himself with the attitude of dedication to a group higher in his hierarchy of values than his own person. He did not give much consideration to the character of the reference group itself.

This amalgamation of different religions to form an ethical norm may be taken to illustrate what Marion Levy classifies as the concept of "non-exclusive religion."[94]

[92] Sumiya, *ibid.*, pp. 98-99. Kawakami himself writes that his grandmother was epileptic and describes the scenes of her seizures. *Jijoden,* i, 38-40.

[93] Sumiya, *ibid.*, p. 92.

[94] "An *exclusivist religion* is one whose adherents believe that one may believe in one and only one religion at any given point in time without being considered a hypocrite. *Non-exclusivist religions* are those whose adherents have never raised the question or believe that one may believe in

Adulthood: From Bourgeois Economics to Marxism

From 1908 to 1928 Kawakami taught economics at Kyoto Imperial University. It was during this period that he gradually became transformed from a bourgeois economic theorist into a Marxian economist.

In his first ten years at Kyoto University, his lectures on economic theory were based on the work of Böhm-Bawerk (1851-1914), Frank W. Taussig (1859-1940), John B. Clark (1847-1938), Thomas N. Carver (1895-   ), Irving Fisher (1867-1947), and John B. Commons (1862-1945). Karl Marx was scarcely mentioned.[95] In studying these bourgeois economic theories, he was pursuing his own deep interest in the problem of the conflict between self-centered and collectivity-centered activities. In his most celebrated work, *The Tale of Poverty* (1917), the author explained why the majority of the Japanese people were poor and proposed three measures to overcome poverty: first, "the rectification of the hearts"[96] of the rich; second, the introduction of social legislation; and, third, the nationalization of industry.[97]

It was not until 1919 that Kawakami began to study Marx's *Capital* seriously, and it was not until 1923, when he finished his work on the history of the development of bourgeois economic theories (*The Historical Development of Capitalist Economics*) that he determined to make a thorough study of Marxism. Reflecting upon his own work in economics up to 1923, he wrote:

> For a long time I have been unable to arrive at the dialectical understanding of the conflict and unity of religious truth and scientific truth. For that reason, in my scientific pursuit of social phenomena, I have committed, unconsciously, the mistake of confusing religious truth with scientific truth, the world of mind with the world of matter, and of

an indefinite number of different religions without any insincerity being implied." Marion J. Levy, Jr., *Modernization and the Structure of Societies*, Princeton, Princeton University Press, 1966, I, 346.

[95] Kawakami, *Jijoden*, I, 178.

[96] According to the *Greater Learning*, one of the four books of Confucian teachings, "the rectification of one's heart" is one of the major aims of learning. See Legge's translation quoted in Dore, *Education in Tokugawa Japan*, p. 41.

[97] Kawakami, *Binbō Monogatari* (*The Tale of Poverty*), 1917—quoted in Sumiya, *Kawakami Hajime*, p. 157.

introducing metaphysical idealism into the world of science. Thus in my scientific inquiry, I have fallen into utter confusion. I said in 1924, after publishing *The Historical Development of Capitalist Economics*, that I had disproved "twenty-year-old thinking on the problem of the operation of self-interest." By that I meant that I was determined to dissociate myself from religion in my pursuit of scientific inquiry. I was then determined to abandon the religious attitude which had obsessed me. . . . Since I was then already forty-six years old, that determination was a metamorphosis of the attitude held for thirty rather than twenty years. It was a leap in which I risked my life. I was like a worm transforming itself into a butterfly, breaking its own cocoon.[98]

The Marxist scholars Tamizō Kushida (1885-1934) and Kazuo Fukumoto severely criticized Kawakami's economic theory. Kawakami took the criticism of the latter especially as a challenge to become a Marxist scholar.[99] Within the next four years his teaching showed the growing influence of Marx, until in the academic year 1927-1928 his lectures consisted entirely of a commentary on *Capital*. Thus, at the age of fifty, he was fully committed to Marxian theory. That year many of his students were among those arrested under the Peace and Order Preservation Law, and he was forced to resign from his professorship at the university because of his influence on their political activities.[100]

At this point, two features of Kawakami's commitment to Marxian ideology should be noted. First, Kawakami became fully committed to Marxian theory in 1928, the year in which extensive arrests and suppression of communists and socialists began. It was not so much external circumstances as the recognition of the theoretical weaknesses of his previously held ideologies that turned him toward Marxism. If one is committed to an ideology under the direct influence of external

[98] Kawakami, *Jijoden*, I, 205-206.
[99] *Ibid.*, pp. 190-196.
[100] The three reasons underlying the recommendation for him to resign from the professorship of Kyoto University were: (1) his short article for the advertisement of *Lectures on Marxism* contained some subversive sentences; (2) his campaign speeches for the Farmer-Labor Party exhibited some elements of subversion; (3) there were some subversive members among the students who belonged to the Social Science Study Group whose supervision the university had entrusted to him. Kawakami, *ibid.*, pp. 257-258.

circumstances, both personal and social, ideological conversion is likely to occur if and when those circumstances change. If, however, an individual commits himself to an ideology mainly because of the development of his theoretical thinking, we can predict that the change of external circumstances will not play the dominant role in converting his ideology.

Second, Kawakami became committed to Marxism only in the later stage of his adulthood, in his early fifties, after he had been exposed to many different types of ideology, whereas the other individuals we have already examined committed themselves to Marxism in their early twenties. Kawakami observed in 1928:

> I began my scholarly work with bourgeois economics and ended up with a theory diametrically opposed to what I started from, by approaching Marxism step by step in a long quest for the place where my mind would finally rest in peace. The achievement of this transformation occupied twenty years of my teaching career at Kyoto University. . . . Reflecting on my past, I can see that my complete transference to Marxian theory was realized only after despicably long years of hesitation and acceptance of eclectic attitudes. Since I have arrived at this point after long years of meditation and research, I feel strongly that I cannot bend my scholarly convictions even if I were to be burned to death for maintaining them.[101]

Old Age: The Mutual Accommodation of Ideology and Affects —Marxism and Religion

When he resigned from the university, Kawakami planned to confine himself to his study to concentrate on the translation of *Capital*. The assassination in February 1929 of Senji Yamamoto (1899-1929), however, had a tremendous impact on Kawakami. Yamamoto was a member of Parliament who had publicly opposed the addition of the death penalty to the Peace and Order Preservation Law against subversive activities. Now, less than a year after his resignation, Kawakami became convinced that participation in revolutionary ventures was a far greater contribution to humanity than scholarly work.[102]

[101] Kawakami, *Keizaigaku Taikō* (*The Fundamentals of Economics*), 1928 —quoted in Sumiya, *Kawakami Hajime*, pp. 184-185.
[102] Kawakami, *Jijoden*, I, 324-343.

He therefore abandoned his study to engage in political activities.[103]

In 1931 the Communist Party asked Kawakami to donate money to the cause; he gladly complied. In the following year, at the age of fifty-four, he joined the party. He was hiding out from the police when a messenger arrived to tell him that the Central Committee had approved his membership in the party. He accepted with deep emotional exaltation.

> Among the party members at that time, there were some inconsequential people. One might wonder why I was so pleased to become one of them. Let me explain why. When the Chinese Red Army moved from Jui Chin to Yennan marching on foot six thousand miles, Hsieh Rou Ts'ai, who was already fifty, managed to keep up with the younger people in crossing the greatest river and the highest mountains in China. Even this strong man Hsieh, when asked to become a member of the Communist Party, "wept with pleasure, over the thought that even an old man like myself could be of some use in the construction of a new world." I am not a strong man like Hsieh. Far from it. However, I wept like Hsieh, when I was given an opportunity to join the party when I was even older than Hsieh. I, the Marxist scholar until then, was able to transform myself into a full-fledged Marxist. It was not at all easy for me—then I still held the rank of *shō san mi kun san tō* [bestowed by the Emperor] —to reach that point.[104]

To celebrate his entrance into the Communist Party, Kawakami wrote a traditional *tanka* poem, which can be translated as follows:

> Having reached my destination at last,
> I look back and see
> So many rivers and mountains
> I have traversed.[105]

---

[103] Kawakami had already been engaged in the political campaign for Ikuo Ōyama, the chairman of the Farmer-Labor Party, in the general election of January 1928. This party was disbanded in April 1928. After resigning from the university, Kawakami reorganized the party to establish with Ōyama the new Farmer-Labor Party in 1929. Realizing, however, that the new party did not serve the cause of the Communist Party, then an illegal organization, Kawakami dissolved the new Farmer-Labor Party and parted company with Ōyama in 1930. See Kawakami, *ibid.*, pp. 360-435.

[104] *Ibid.*, II, 107.   [105] *Ibid.*, p. 106.

It was characteristic of Kawakami's personality development that he composed a poem in the traditional Japanese style at the critical moments of his life when he made a major commitment either to a new ideology or to a new group. He wrote a *haiku* poem when he joined the *Muga no Ai* religious group; he produced a *tanka* poem when he made the decision to switch from bourgeois economics to Marxian theory; and his commitment to the Communist Party was marked in the same way. This practice reveals at least two things. First, each stage of Kawakami's ideological commitment not only was founded on a deliberate process of rational thinking but was supported by intense affects, crystallized in the form of poetry. Second, his affects were persistently patterned after the traditional mode in which his poems were composed, quite independently of the indigenous or exogenous character of the ideology.

In August 1932 Kawakami was arrested at his hiding place. By the beginning of the following year, almost all the active members had been arrested, and the party had practically disappeared. In June 1933 Sano and Nabeyama announced their conversion (see above). Subsequently, the public prosecutor in charge of Kawakami's interrogation urged him to submit a statement of ideological conversion. Kawakami refused to renounce Marxism. He stated clearly that his scholarly conviction about the basic theory of Marxism would never be shaken. On the contrary, he declared that "as a scholar I will continue to adhere to Marxism as a theory." He did promise, however, that he would retire from political activity. Since a true communist, he argued, unites theory with political practice, his retreat from politics would mean the end of his career as an authentic communist. He made it perfectly plain that he had made his decision simply to save his life. He said he would bury himself in his own study "as a disabled soldier" for the rest of his days.[106]

Kawakami's statement fell far short of satisfying the authorities, who had expected him to denounce communism as an ideology. Rather than denounce communism, Kawakami had denounced himself for his inability to live up to its ideal pattern. He still hoped that he might be granted probation, though, since he had pledged that he would not engage in political activities. Instead, he was sentenced to five years' imprisonment

[106] *Ibid.*, pp. 440-445.

without probation. All through the period of his stay in prison, the prosecutors tried to get him to renounce Marxism. Kawakami held to his convictions until he was released after serving his full term.[107]

What sustained his faith in Marxism was the ethos of *shishi*, acquired during his adolescence.

> Even after I became a Marxist, I never forgot Japan or disliked the Japanese. On the contrary, because I desired the welfare of the Japanese as a whole and the prosperity of Japan as a nation, I subscribed all the more ardently to the reconstruction of this country in a soviet system. Even if a man hopes for the defeat of his own country in war, that does not necessarily deny the fact that he is a patriot. . . . The rulers of a capitalist country are capitalists. However, if the war situation begins to deteriorate, this ruling class could lose its political competence, become desperate and commit irresponsible acts which would lead them to lose popular confidence. Especially if the country loses the war, its system of rule would be completely disorganized and the rulers would lose popular support. . . . This provides the best opportunities for a successful revolution. That is why those *shishi*, who aspire to the revolutionary reform of the political system of the nation, sometimes ardently wish for their country's defeat in the war. Their attitude is derived from sincere feelings of patriotism in its true sense.[108]

It is clear from this passage that, although the ethos of *shishi* remained the firm basis of his motivation, the reference group to which it was oriented changed. In Kawakami's earlier work, *Economy and Life* (1911),[109] his *shishi* ethos was directed toward the state, identified with the Emperor. But, when he became a Marxist, the focus of this ethos shifted toward the revolutionary group whose aim was the overthrow of the Emperor system. The change was not, however, a one-way affair.

---

[107] His prison term was reduced by one-fourth through amnesty granted at the time of the Crown Prince's birth in 1934.

[108] Kawakami, *Jijoden*, ii, 67-68.

[109] In *Economy and Life* he writes: "In Japan the state and the Emperor are one and inseparable. Since the state is our god, the Emperor is the divine representative. In our country, therefore, patriotism is the supreme moral, and at the same time patriotism is synonymous with loyalty to the Emperor." Quoted in Sumiya, *Kawakami Hajime*, p. 134.

Because it was sustained in Kawakami by the traditional ethos of *shishi*, Marxian ideology also underwent change.

During his days in prison Kawakami's interest in religion returned, and he strove to integrate his Marxian ideology with his religious feelings. According to Marxism, religion is an opiate that prevents people from recognizing the reality of their existence and from arriving at class consciousness. Kawakami attempted to redefine the concept of religion to make it compatible with Marxism. He classified truth into two categories, the one scientific and the other religious, and identified Marxism with the former. Thus the relation between Marxism and religion was reduced to a relation between two kinds of truth. By scientific truth he meant knowledge about the external world which can be used for the manipulation of one's environment. By religious truth he meant "the consciousness of consciousness, the reflection of mind on mind."[110]

Scientific truth and religious truth are thus two great categories with different objects of recognition and orientation. Scientific truth is recognized primarily by the Occidentals, whereas religious truth is most deeply grasped by the Orientals (especially the Indians and the Chinese). . . . However, these two kinds of truth are not mutually exclusive. . . . On the contrary, . . . they represent a unity through which man's recognition of the two worlds of mind and matter is completed. (Herein lies an example of the dialectical concept of the unity of opposites.) We should recognize clearly the conflict of these two types of knowledge, and at the same time comprehend their unity.[111]

What, then, is the content of what Kawakami called religion?

More than thirty years have elapsed since I joined the *Muga no Ai* movement at the age of twenty-six. During all these years I have been aware of a grain of truth in religion, which is embodied in the faith of common men and women. . . . Actually, even in the days when young Marxists were busily engaged in anti-religious movements, I had hanging in my living room the framed calligraphy of Priest Shaku Sōen [a Zen priest] on which was written: Muga Ai [Selfless Love]. . . . However, after I became wholeheartedly involved in political movements in Tokyo, I abandoned the "Muga Ai" plaque

[110] Kawakami, *Jijoden*, iii, 462.   [111] *Ibid.*, p. 463.

and forgot about religion. The problem of integration between the worlds of matter and mind also remained unre-
solved for me. Then I was arrested and during almost five
years in prison I had the opportunity to read the books on
religion again in tranquility. Making full use of this opportunity, I have achieved the unity of the worlds of matter and
mind.[112]

For Kawakami, the *sine qua non* of scientific knowledge was
"the grasp of major empirical data as thoroughly as possible
on the subject under investigation."[113] A prison, obviously, does
not meet that essential condition of scientific inquiry. Thus he
admitted that he had not made any progress in his scientific
quest. The prison environment was, however, conducive to
religious meditation, and he claimed to have made significant
progress in this area. As we have already seen, Kawakami's
concept of religion was nonexclusive, free from adherence to
any particular religious organization or church. Basically, religion for him was the intense and durable positive affective
posture of dedication to a group higher, or more continuous,
than his own existence. Despite his insistence that Marxism
represented scientific truth, the manner in which Kawakami
upheld Marxian ideology through his days of imprisonment
gave it the status of religion according to his definition.

What I see is the world one hundred or two hundred years
from now. Even if the Japanese Communist Party becomes
defunct, and even if the Comintern becomes extinct, I would
never budge an inch in my scholarly conviction.[114]

Thus Kawakami achieved an accommodation between the exogenous ideology of Marxism and his basic religious motivation
by making Marxism partly a religion in which other religions
such as Christianity, Buddhism, and Confucianism were
merged. In this rare type of mutual accommodation, both Marxian ideology and the ethos of *shishi* underwent a metamorphosis.
On the one hand, Kawakami's concept of Marxism, unlike the
orthodox view, not only considered Marxism to be compatible
with religion but made religious feeling a necessary condition
of high motivation in a Marxist. On the other hand, the ethos

[112] *Ibid.*, p. 466.
[113] *Ibid.*, p. 456.
[114] Kawakami, *Gokuchū Zeigo* (*Leisurely Meditation in Prison*), 1947—
quoted in Sumiya, *Kawakami Hajime*, p. 267.

of *shishi*, originally bound to the state, was oriented instead toward the concept of the community of the people of the world, going beyond the boundaries of the nation-state. This accommodation between his ideology and affects was achieved according to the traditional concept of nonexclusive religion. Just as the samurai used the ethos of *shishi*, feudal in its origin, to overthrow the feudal structure at the time of the Meiji Restoration, Kawakami the innovator used tradition to overcome traditionalism in the process of integrating his ideology and affects.

TWO

The Army: The Emperor System in Microcosm

JAPAN was the first nation in the world to renounce war as a means of settling international disputes. Under Article Nine of the Constitution of 1947, Japan abjured all "land, sea, and air forces, as well as other war potential."[1] Theoretically, the Imperial army and navy were disbanded on the termination of the war in 1945.

Although, ideally, the Japanese army is dead, actually it is not. The evidence of its survival is threefold. First, even though the army has been abolished, most of the present male population over the age of forty were exposed to army socialization before or during the war years, and the effect of the army experience remains strong among them. These men have participated in the most influential of the prewar agencies of male socialization—the army based on a system of conscription, which existed from 1873 to 1945. Second, since this war was the first fought in modern times on Japanese soil and since it exacted an enormous toll of dead and injured among both military personnel and civilians, it had a profound effect on individuals and on society. During the war in China which started in 1937, 185,647 soldiers died and 325,806 were lost or wounded, even before Pearl Harbor. In the Pacific war which followed (1941-1945) deaths in the armed services amounted to 1,555,308, and 309,402 were wounded or missing; at the same time 299,485 civilians were killed, and 368,830 were reported injured or missing.[2]

---

[1] "Aspiring sincerely to an international peace based on justice and order, the Japanese people forever renounce war as a sovereign right of the nation and the threat or use of force as means of settling international disputes.

"In order to accomplish the aim of the preceding paragraph, land, sea, and air forces, as well as other war potential, will never be maintained. The right of belligerency of the state will not be recognized." "The Constitution of Japan," *Kihon Roppō* (*The Six Basic Laws*), ed. Hiroshi Suekawa, Tokyo, Iwanami, 1962, p. 71. See also Arthur E. Tiedemann, *Modern Japan*, Princeton, Van Nostrand, 1955, p. 159.

[2] Keizai Antei Honbu (Economic Stabilization Headquarters), *Taiheiyō Sensō ni yoru Wagakuni no Higai Sōgō Hōkokusho* (*A General Report on the Casualties in the Pacific War*)—cited in *Ningen Keisei no Shakaigaku* (*Sociology of the Formation of Man*), ed. Keiichi Sakuda, *Gendai Shakaigaku Kōza* (*Lectures on Contemporary Sociology*), Tokyo, Yūhikaku, 1964, v, 39.

Death is a traumatic experience for the individual who is bereaved, and the death of a generation is a traumatic experience for the surviving generations. The dead are still alive in the experience of the survivors. Since the end of the war, a great number of letters, diaries, messages, wills, and other records of those who died in the war have been published. Equally countless memoirs, records, and diaries about the dead have been and still are being written by the survivors. The voice of the dead has in this way become the common property of the surviving generations, even among those who suffered no personal loss.

Third, despite the Constitution's ban against the resurgence of the army, Japan now maintains a "self-defense corps" consisting of a "land self-defense force" of 171,500, a "sea self-defense force" of 34,963, and an "air self-defense force" of 39,553, all equipped with modern weapons.[3] Although the government maintains that the "self-defense corps" is *not* an army, it is actually a full-fledged armed force, the maintenance of which clearly violates Article Nine of the Constitution.[4]

Thus the historical and contemporary influence of military life has been so pervasive that a study of the army is essential for an understanding of changing patterns of personalities and social structure in postwar Japan.

THE CONSCRIPTION SYSTEM

Since the famous "sword hunt" of 1587 by Hideyoshi Toyotomi (1536-1598) and throughout the Tokugawa feudal period (1600-1767), the privilege of bearing arms was restricted to the samurai class, which constituted six or seven percent of the total population.[5] *Bushidō*, the Way of the Warrior, or—as *Hagakure*,[6] a classical work on the subject, defines it—"the determined will to die" was monopolized by the samurai class. In 1872, five years

[3] *Asahi Nenkan* (*Asahi Year Book*), Tokyo, Asahi Newspaper Publishing Co., 1965, pp. 308-309.

[4] Shunpei Ueyama, "Nihon Bōeiron" ("On National Defense"), *Daitōa Sensō no Imi* (*The Meaning of the Great Asiatic War*), Tokyo, Chūōkoron-sha, 1964, p. 65.

[5] Naotarō Sekiyama, *Kinsei Nihon no Jinkō Kōzō* (*The Population Structure of Recent Japan*), Tokyo, Nishikawa Kōbunkan, 1958, p. 312.

[6] *Hagakure*, a textbook of the samurai moral code compiled in the early eighteenth century by the Nabeshima fief administration, begins with the statement: *"Bushidō towa shinukoto to mitsuketari"* ("Bushidō, I have found, means that determined will to die"). Tsunetomo Yamamoto, *Hagakure*, ed. Tetsurō Watsuji et al., Tokyo, Iwanami Shoten, 1965, p. 23. For a further explanation of the concept of *Bushidō*, see Robert N. Bellah, *Tokugawa Religion*, Glencoe, Ill., The Free Press, 1957, pp. 90-106.

after the downfall of the Tokugawa Shogunate, the first conscription law was enacted; it was enforced one year later. Paradoxically, it was after the abolition of feudalism that the feudal samurai ethic of dying honorably for the sake of one's lord was transformed into a universal ethic for the entire population of Japan, through the requirement of honorable death for the sake of the Emperor.

It is important to note that equality is stressed in the Conscription Ordinance of 1872.[7] Two years earlier, in 1870, the feudal hierarchy of four classes—samurai, peasants, craftsmen, and merchants—with the Shogun at its summit was abolished and was replaced by a new system of stratification. The new hierarchy consisted of the Imperial Household (*kōzoku*), the peers (*kazoku* = former shoguns, lords, court nobles, and the small group of samurai who were responsible for the Meiji Restoration), the former samurai (*shizoku*), and commoners (*heimin* = peasants, craftsmen, merchants, and outcasts). The equality emphasized in the Ordinance referred to the abolition of the previous hierarchy but was not intended to eliminate the hierarchical arrangement of society. Nevertheless, the Conscription Ordinance did bring about a fundamental change in the criterion for membership in the army, a change from particularism to universalism. In theory, according to the law, it was the duty of every male subject to become a soldier at the age of twenty, a privilege previously restricted to members of the hereditary warrior class.

Actually, however, the Conscription Ordinance fell short of its target of universal conscription. From 1872 to 1873 peasant uprisings against conscription or the "blood tax," as it was commonly known, spread throughout the country.[8] Those who could afford to pay proxy money were exempted from conscription. In addition, the Ordinance made allowance for the exemption of individuals who were either the head of a family, the heir, the only son, or the only grandson of a family, or an adopted

---

[7] For an English translation of the Military Conscription Ordinance, see William T. de Bary et al., eds., *Sources of Japanese Tradition*, New York, Columbia University Press, 1958, II, 197.

[8] The Conscription Ordinance states: "The Occidentals call military obligation a 'blood tax,' for it is one's repayment in life-blood to one's country." It has been said that the term "blood tax" antagonized peasants and turned them against conscription. See Riken Ōkubo et al., eds., *Shiryō ni yoru Nihon no Ayumi: Kindaihen* (*A Documentary History of Japan: The Modern Period*), Tokyo, Yoshikawa Kōbunkan, 1951, pp. 52-54.

son. Many young men of the eligible age sought adoption or tried to establish a branch family to evade military duty.[9] Thus in 1889, according to the statistics of the Ministry of War, only 5.2 percent of the male population eligible for conscription were actually drafted; 60 percent managed to secure exemption for various reasons; and another 10 percent either disappeared or simply failed to report for the physical examination.[10]

All these facts confirm Norman's observation about the basic difference in motivation between the soldiers of the French *levée en masse*, on which the Japanese system was originally modeled, and the Japanese conscripts. In contrast to the French soldiers of the Revolution, for whom the revolutionary cause was identified with their own emancipation from feudal shackles, the Japanese—at least at the inception of the system of conscription—were unwilling draftees.[11]

Within the military bureaucracy, at the outset, there were two opposing groups advocating divergent plans for the future of the Japanese army. The first group, under the leadership of Akiyoshi Yamada (1844-1892), urged the adoption of a French-style army, whereas the second group, under the leadership of

[9] See Shunsuke Tsurumi et al., eds., *Nihon no Hyakunen* (*A Hundred Years of Japan*), Tokyo, Chikuma Shobō, 1953, ix, 168-174.

[10] TABLE 9

THE STATE OF CONSCRIPTION (1889)

	No.
Eligible male population at the age of 20	309,234
Those handed over from the previous year	50,664
Volunteers	459
Total	360,357
In service in the army and navy	18,782 (5.2%)
On reserve in the army and navy	74,561 (20.7%)
Conscription postponed	17,826 (5.0%)
Exempted (disease and other reasons)	211,256 (58.6%)
Disappeared and absent	35,940 (9.9%)
Others	1,992 (0.6%)
Total	360,357 (100.0%)

SOURCE: *The Third Annual Statistical Report of the Ministry of War*—quoted in Akira Fujiwara, *Gunjishi* (*Military History*), *Nihon Gendaishi Taikei* (*Contemporary Japanese History Series*), Tokyo, Tōyōkeizai, 1961, p. 56.

[11] See Herbert E. Norman, *Soldier and Peasant in Japan: The Origins of Conscription*, New York, Institute of Pacific Relations, 1943, p. 4.

Aritomo Yamagata (1838-1922),[12] supported the Prussian system. Yamada, influenced by French and Swiss liberal thought, emphasized the role of the army in raising the general level of education among the people. He favored a type of army socialization which would disseminate knowledge and encourage some independent thought among the soldiers.[13] Yamagata, in contrast, argued for an authoritarian type of army socialization based on regimentation and severe discipline. In the course of successive reorganizations of the military system between 1878 and 1889, Yamagata and his clique took the lead, and the group of officers subscribing to more liberal ideas was finally disbanded in 1889.

The "dynastic elites" within the military bureaucracy led by Yamagata were confronted with the problem of developing a body of *willing* fighters without endangering the newly created hierarchical structure in which Yamagata and his associates occupied the ruling position. Their problem was how to promote among unrevolutionary troops and in support of their own exploitative regime a zeal comparable to the spirit which infuses soldiers battling on behalf of a revolutionary regime. In the first and most significant reorganization, in 1878, the General Staff Office was separated from the Ministry of War. The Emperor was charged with the responsibility of being the supreme commander of the military forces, and the General Staff Office was placed under his direct control. Thus the supreme command was made independent of the Ministries of the Army and of the Navy. The military was therefore accountable neither to the government nor to the Diet, nor even to the people, but solely to the Emperor.[14] The armed forces became, in effect, the Emperor's army and navy. One consequence of this change was the eradication of discrimination against peasants in favor of the warrior class. Now all were equal as the children of the Emperor.

The second accomplishment of reorganization was the abolition of the rules of exemption, so that every male subject, at the age of twenty, would in practice take military training for three years. Those with education beyond the high school level were

[12] For Yamagata and his role in the modernization of the army, see Roger F. Hackett, "The Meiji Leaders and Modernization: The Case of Yamagata Aritomo," in *Changing Japanese Attitudes toward Modernization*, ed. Marius B. Jansen, Princeton, Princeton University Press, 1965, pp. 243-273.

[13] Fujiwara, *Gunjishi*, p. 69; Norman, *Soldier and Peasant in Japan*, p. 46n.

[14] Noboru Umetani, *Meiji Zenki Seijishi no Kenkyū* (A Study of the Political History of the Early Meiji Period), Tokyo, Miraisha, 1963, p. 129.

eligible for one year's training in a cadet corps. All graduates of institutions training elementary teachers were compelled to undergo a period of indoctrination in the army, although only for six months. The shorter training given to prospective teachers was designed to assist in the recruitment of teachers, while at the same time guaranteeing that the military influence would permeate the elementary school system.

The third feature of reorganization was the establishment of a division of labor between the newly formed gendarmes and the regular army. In the words of General Terauchi preaching to his military cadets, the armed forces were to be "His Majesty's claws and fangs."[15] Since its inception the army had been assigned a double role: suppression of internal disturbances and defense against external enemies. In order to solicit the cooperation of the people in the conscription policy, however, it would have been a mistake for the army to make too obvious the first purpose, the suppression of unrest. Thus the gendarmerie was instituted to specialize in counterrevolutionary activities, while the regular army was expected to concentrate on preparation for external warfare. The gendarmerie also served as a military police, exercising strict control over the conduct of ordinary soldiers.[16]

The fourth stage of reorganization directly concerned the socialization of soldiers. A series of textbooks for the ideological indoctrination of soldiers was completed during this period. The most important were the *Admonition to Soldiers* (*Gunjin Kunkai*), published in 1878; the *Imperial Precepts to Soldiers and Sailors* (*Gunjin Chokuyu*), issued in 1882; the *Infantry Drill Book* (*Hohei Sōten*), a book of military strategy brought out in 1891; and the *Rules of Domestic Affairs in the Army* (*Guntai Naimusho*), a book of regulations for the private lives of soldiers adopted in 1888. Most of the ideological socialization in the Japanese army consisted of verbatim memorization and recitation of these code books.

The *Admonition to Soldiers* states clearly that the ethos of the modern army must be founded on the traditional way of warriors.

> During the past feudal period, *bushi* [warriors] occupied a status superior to the three classes of commoners. Only *bushi* were expected to be loyal and courageous, to serve their

---

[15] Fujiwara, *Gunjishi*, p. 59.   [16] *Ibid.*, p. 63.

lords, to respect their honour, and in failure to admit their shame. The virtues of the *bushi* were widely known among commoners through proverbs and aphorisms. However, since the Meiji Restoration, any person, regardless of his class origin, is allowed to enter military service. This is a great privilege bestowed upon the three classes of commoners. Today's soldiers are undoubtedly *bushi*, even if their status is not hereditary. It is therefore beyond question that they should exhibit loyalty and courage as their prime virtues, according to the best tradition of the *bushi* of bygone days.[17]

The particularistic ethic of the samurai of feudal days was thus turned into the universalistic ethic of the entire male population. "The equality of the four classes," a catchword of modernization, actually amounted to the "samuraization" of the previously nonsamurai classes. This process took place typically in the army. A similar pattern prevailed in other spheres of life.

Kunio Yanagida observes that samuraization was the pattern of social change in the initial period of modernization in Japan not only among the ruling elites but also among the common people.

> The slogan of the equality of four classes had a tremendous impact. As soon as the rumor got around that "there is no more distinction between samurai and peasants," people rushed to imitate the life style of the samurai. This pattern is an interesting feature of Japanese society. Although the peasants formerly appeared to hate the samurai, in fact they must have been envious of them.[18]

In 1898 the General Supervisory Bureau of Army Education was instituted and placed under the direct control of the Emperor.[19] It was through this body that the extensive revision of military code books was completed after the Russo-Japanese War of 1904-1905.

The *Rules of Domestic Affairs in the Army* was revised in 1908, the *Infantry Drill Book* in 1909. A new set of regulations, *The Military Education Ordinance*, was promulgated in 1913. The technological development of weapons, especially the ad-

---

[17] Umetani, *Meiji Zenki Seijishi no Kenkyū*, pp. 170-171.

[18] Kunio Yanagida, *Kokyō Shichijūnen* (*Seventy Years of My Native Village*), Kobe, Nojigiku Bunko, 1959, p. 270.

[19] Shigeki Tōyama et al., *Kindai Nihon Seijishi Hikkei* (*A Compendium to the Political History of Modern Japan*), Tokyo, Iwanami, 1961, p. 89.

vent of machine guns at the beginning of the century, made it necessary for fighting to be conducted in open order, rather than in close order as before. In open-order combat each soldier is expected to fight on his own whenever he is separated from his commanding officer or when that officer has himself fallen in battle. Logically, this type of combat requires considerable initiative on the part of the individual soldier, but the military elites resisted this logic because it threatened the social order and the army's position in it. The military leaders attempted to solve this problem by an intensive inculcation of what they termed "aggressive spirit" among the soldiers. The revised *Infantry Drill Book* exhorted the soldiers to overcome "material forces" by means of "spiritual forces."[20] This emphasis on the spirit, which was an integral part of the traditional way of warriors, was increasingly stressed in proportion to the technological advances in armaments. The official *Reasons for the Revision of the Rules of Domestic Affairs in the Army* states:

> In future combat we shall not be able to surpass our enemy in military forces. Neither can we expect to excel the enemy in weapons and materials for arms. On any battlefield we should steel ourselves to winning glorious victory despite military forces and weapons inferior to the enemy's. Since we must be prepared for such a situation, it is self-evident that more spiritual education is necessary.[21]

"Spiritual education" was thus the poor man's substitute for superior weapons and material forces. The army's statement of its philosophy adumbrates with surprising precision the emergence of the suicidal tactics of the *Kamikaze* (Divine Wind) charge and of the *Kaiten* (Turning of the Heaven) by the Japanese human torpedoes, both of which were used toward the last stage of the Pacific war. These suicidal attackers were the end product of the socialization carried on in the army ever since the end of the Russo-Japanese War.

The military administrators also foresaw that difficulties might arise out of the extreme regimentation to which the soldiers were subjected. In order to avoid unrest, the revised *Rules of Domestic Affairs in the Army* established "familistic relationships" among soldiers and officers in the daily life of the army camps. "The army camp constitutes one great family," the manual

[20] Fujiwara, *Gunjishi*, p. 111.   [21] *Ibid.*, pp. 113-114.

affirmed, and "the superior officers treat their subordinates as if the latter are of the same flesh and blood."[22]

The pseudo-familistic relationship structure and the traditional ideology of samurai ethics were the two pillars of army socialization as it was instituted in the formative period of the Japanese army.

2. The Structure of Relationships in the Army

According to *The American Soldier,* the American army at the beginning of World War II was "a small organization of officers and men more or less isolated from the democratic society which rather grudgingly supported it, and possessing institutional characteristics which contrasted sharply with the civilian life around it."[23] The three points of contrast between American military and civilian life were:

1. Its authoritarian organization, demanding rigid obedience.
2. Its highly stratified social system, in which hierarchies of deference were formally and minutely established by official regulation, subject to penalties for infraction, on and off duty.
3. Its emphasis on traditional ways of doing things and its discouragement of initiative.[24]

In prewar Japan contrasts between civilian institutions and army organization also existed, but in different patterns. In Japan, just as in America, the members of the armed forces were separated from the civilians. The army was a society apart, with its own system of hierarchical relationships, its own ethics and norms of conduct, and its own conventions of language. Still, it was not as isolated as its American counterpart. The conscription system functioned as the connecting link between the army and civilian society. Theoretically, under the conscription system, all males over twenty years of age were either soldiers in active service or ex-soldiers. According to official army terminology, the army was *chūō* (the center) and the civilian society *chihō* (a province) or *shaba* (the secular world—from a Buddhist Sanskrit word, *sahā*). This terminological distinction had symbolic significance. The *Military Education Ordinance* asserts:

---

[22] *Ibid.,* p. 112.
[23] Samuel A. Stouffer et al., *The American Soldier: Adjustment during Army Life,* Princeton, Princeton University Press, 1949, p. 54.
[24] *Ibid.,* p. 55.

"The military are the essence of the Nation and occupy the principal position thereof."[25] In this way the army became a central agency of adult socialization for the Japanese male population. The army detached the conscripts from civilian society for the period of military training and then returned them to society with a new outlook, so that the army's socialization affected various organizations throughout the whole society. To understand army socialization, it must be remembered that the armed forces were under the direct supreme command of the Emperor. Theoretically, this arrangement gave the army a closer relationship to the Emperor than any civilian group in Japanese society. The analysis of the army organization is therefore basically an analysis of the characteristic patterns of the Emperor system as a whole, albeit in its most extreme form.

In discussing the army, we can distinguish the primary group situation from the overall structure of the army. The soldiers were grouped together into fighting units—platoons, companies, battalions, regiments, brigades, and divisions. These constitute the overall organization of the army. The soldiers were also grouped together as living units, "domestic affairs squads" (*naimu han*). The same structural principles apply to both types of group, but with varying emphasis: in the overall organization of the army loyalty to the Emperor was stressed, whereas in the primary group situation familistic relationship was emphasized. The overall structure of the relationships was predominantly universalistic in membership criteria, nonrational in its cognitive aspect, dependently collectivistic in goal orientation, hierarchical in stratification, exploitative in exchange, secret in communication, and compulsory in participation. In the primary group situation intimate and functionally diffuse relationships were stressed, in order to fortify the overall structure.

Universalism and Particularism

In contrast to the predominantly particularistic criterion of membership in the civilian society at large in prewar Japan, the universalistic criterion of recruitment and of promotion ideally held sway in the army. In civilian society the hierarchical order of *kōzoku, kazoku, shizoku,* and *heimin* was hereditary,[26]

[25] *Guntai Kyōiku Rei (The Military Education Ordinance)*—quoted in Masao Maruyama, *Thought and Behavior in Modern Japanese Politics,* ed. Ivan Morris, London, Oxford University Press, 1963, p. 14.

[26] In 1938, one year after the outbreak of the Sino-Japanese War, the compulsory filing of one's social status, as *kazoku, shizoku,* or *heimin,* in

whereas in the army the ranks from private to general were non-hereditary. Although the upper-class officer corps was composed of the graduates of the Military College, the Military Academy, and the Military Preparatory School, the conscripted men could become only noncommissioned officers by passing the qualifying examinations and completing the training for military cadets. Thus, in contrast to some European armed forces where officers were drawn mainly from the aristocracy, in the Japanese army opportunities to climb the military ladder were open equally to the sons of peasants and the sons of nobility. Social mobility within the army, according to Masao Maruyama, functioned as "an anesthetic" to alleviate the sense of dissatisfaction arising from the strict class distinctions which persisted in the civilian society after the Meiji Restoration.[27] Among conscripted men, who constituted the bulk of the rank-and-file soldiers and non-commissioned officers, universalism prevailed.

The upper-ranking officers, however, insisted on retaining their particularistic criterion of recruitment. From the time of the establishment of the military bureaucracy, the army was under the control of the Chōshū clique, formed by those who originally came from the Chōshū-*han*. The navy was under the control of the Satsuma clique, formed by those who originally came from the Satsuma-*han*. Most of the important positions in the Office of the Chief of Staff as well as in the Ministries of the Army and Navy were monopolized by cliques. They constituted the original stronghold of the *gunbatsu* (military clique). After World War I the cliques were organized on the basis of education rather than birthplace. The graduates of the Military College, the Military Academy, and the Military Preparatory School came to be the most influential among the military clique.[28]

Thus there was a dual structure in the membership criteria

---

curriculum vitae and in hotel registrations was dropped. After World War II the social distinctions *kazoku* and *shizoku* were abolished altogether. At the end of the war there were fourteen households among *kōzoku* (the Imperial Household), but they are now reduced to three households, not including the households of the Emperor and the Crown Prince.

[27] Maruyama's comment appears in the symposium on "The Place of the Army in the Japanese Thought," in Kōji Iizuka, *Nihon no Guntai* (*The Japanese Army*), Tokyo, Tōdai Kyōdō-kumiai Shuppanbu, 1950, p. 85.

[28] Fujiwara, *Gunjishi*, p. 65; "Gunbatstu," in *Nihon Rekishi Jiten* (*Encyclopaedia of Japanese History*), ed. Tarō Wakamori, Tokyo, Jitsugyō no Nihonsha, 1958, p. 158.

of recruitment in the armed forces: a universalistic criterion for conscripted men and a particularistic criterion for the upper ranks of the military bureaucracy.

Dependent Collectivism

Maruyama provides an illuminating analysis of the power structures of the Emperor system in general and of the Japanese army in particular:

> Now this sense of degree of proximity to the ultimate value or entity [the Emperor] was immensely important in Japan: in fact it was the spiritual motive force that drove, not only the various individual power complexes (the military, the *zaibatsu*, etc.), but the entire national structure. What determined the behavior of the bureaucrats and of the military was not primarily a sense of legality, but the consciousness of some force that was higher than they were, in other words, that was nearer the ultimate entity. Inasmuch as the formal quality of the national order was not recognized in Japan, it was inevitable that the concept of legality should be poorly developed. The law was not regarded as some general body of regulations that collectively circumscribed the ruler and the ruled, but simply as a concrete weapon of controls in the hierarchy of authority of which the Emperor was the head. . . .
>
> The standard of values, then, that determined a person's position in society and in the nation was based less on social function than on relative distance from the Emperor. . . .
>
> Thus the pride of the nobility lay in being "the bulwark of the Imperial House"; and the very lifeline of the army and navy was the independence of the prerogative of supreme command [see Section 1 of this chapter], "based on the fact that the armed forces are under the personal leadership of His Majesty the Emperor." What determined the everyday morality of Japan's rulers was neither an abstract consciousness of legality nor an internal sense of right and wrong, nor again any concept of serving the public; it was a feeling of being close to the concrete entity known as the Emperor, an entity that could be directly perceived by the senses.[29]

According to Maruyama's analysis, there was no room for the recognition of the individual as the locus of decision-making

[29] Maruyama, *Thought and Behavior in Modern Japanese Politics*, pp. 12-13.

within the structure of the Emperor system.[30] Even the Emperor himself was not considered to be the locus of individual judgment. Instead, he was an integral part of the group mind, the mind of the Imperial ancestors. Everyone in this hierarchy was held responsible to the one immediately above him until the chain of responsibility reached the summit, the Emperor, who was responsible only to his ancestral gods and goddesses. In this structure, no one had any opportunity to make a decision which he could consciously recognize as his own, and no one had to take responsibility for the consequences of any decision made or any act committed in the name of the collectivity. The lack of recognition of the individual as the locus of decision-making and the emphasis on collective goal orientations together constitute the type of relationship defined as dependently collectivistic. In Maruyama's terminology, it is the "system of irresponsibility."[31]

Nonrationality

The legitimacy of the Emperor's authority rested on the past, on his divine origin. The Emperor represented traditional authority in the Weberian sense. The Meiji Constitution of 1889 declared that "the Emperor is sacred and inviolable."[32] And, since the Emperor was divine, he was considered to be infallible. In the *Precepts to Soldiers and Sailors* it was made clear that the Emperor was the commander-in-chief of the armed forces and that "inferiors should regard the orders of their superiors as issuing directly from Us."[33] In other words, soldiers were expected to obey the orders of their superiors as if they were the orders of the Emperor himself. If the Emperor was by definition infallible and if the superiors' commands were identified as the Emperor's, then it logically followed that the superiors'

[30] *Ibid.*, pp. 19-20.

[31] *Ibid.*, p. 128. The discussion of the centrality of the Emperor with reference to the value system of prewar Japan is not limited to Maruyama's work. It has been developed by many Japanese scholars—rightist, leftist, and independent. For the view of a right-wing ideological leader, see Uzuhiko Ashizu, *Nihon no Kunshusei* (*The Japanese Monarchy*), Tokyo, Shinseiryokusha, 1966. For a Marxist historian's view, see Kiyoshi Inoue, *Tennō-sei* (*The Emperor System*), Tokyo, Tokyo Daigaku Shuppankai, 1953. For the most recent analysis by an independent political scientist, see Shōzō Fujita, *Tennō-sei Kokka no Shihaigenri* (*The Principle of Control of the Emperor-governed State*), Tokyo, Miraisha, 1966.

[32] A complete translation of the Meiji Constitution appears in Tiedemann, *Modern Japan*, pp. 114-123.

[33] *Ibid.*, pp. 109-110.

orders, whatever they were, were infallible too. Thus the infallibility of the Emperor was established in the Constitution and his independence from the government and the Diet in the control of the army were combined to justify absolute obedience to superiors in the military hierarchy.

The cognitive aspect of the relationship between superiors and subordinates in the army was accordingly nonrational, since it did not conform to what we have defined as "rational," namely, the recognition of human fallibility. The relationship based on the belief in the infallibility of the Emperor is closest to what Weber calls the *wertrational* relationship, in which the ends of action are supplied to the actor from an external source and he is expected to select only the means to achieve those ends.

Exploitation

Loyalty to the Emperor and filial piety to one's parents were justified by the Meiji elites on the basis of the feudal concept of *on* and the repayment of *on*. *On* is translated by Ruth Benedict as "indebtedness."[34] However, as Kawashima points out, Benedict confuses *on* with the consequence of receiving *on*. Indebtedness is the consequence of having received *on*.[35] *On* originally designated the fief or the benefices given by the lord to his vassal; the vassal was obliged to pay for the benefits received in the form of military service. Marc Bloch points out the difference between the type of lord-vassal relationship that prevailed in Europe and the kind that existed in Japan. In Europe this relationship was a "bilateral contract," in which the lord gave protection to his vassal while the latter provided military service to the former. The relationship was reciprocal in the sense that the violation of the contract by either party evoked retaliation or resistance from the other. In Japan, however, "vassalage was much more an act of submission than was European vassalage and much less a contract." In Japan the relationship was "unilateral," and the right of resistance by the vassal was lacking.[36]

[34] Ruth Benedict, *The Chrysanthemum and the Sword*, New York, Houghton Mifflin, 1946, pp. 98-113.

[35] Takeyoshi Kawashima, *Ideorogii toshite no Kazokuseido* (*The Family System as an Ideology*), Tokyo, Iwanami, 1959, pp. 103-104.

[36] Marc Bloch, *Feudal Society*, tr. L. A. Manyon, London, Routledge and Kegan Paul, 1961, p. 446.

The characteristic pattern of the unilateral operation of *on* is explained by Kawashima as follows:

> *On* is not a gift exchanged between equals, but it is a "benevolence" bestowed by a superior on an inferior as a *special favor*, for which the recipient must feel an indebtedness *unfathomably deep.* . . . Thus, since the quantity of *on* is immeasurable and infinite, the obligation to repay it is also infinite. Moreover, *on* has *already been given* by the benefactor, whereas the recipient is duty bound to go on repaying his *infinite debts forever*. The benefactor possesses only rights, whereas the recipient has nothing but obligations, which are limitless and must be acknowledged through *loyalty* to the benefactor.[37]

Both Bloch and Kawashima make it clear that the lord-retainer relationship in feudal Japan was based on the unequal exchange of benefits, namely, exploitation by the lord of his subordinates.

This feudal relationship of *on* was transferred from the context of the lord-retainer relationship to that of the Emperor-subject and the parent-child relationship in modern Japan. What, then, was the content of *on* bestowed by the Emperor and the parents? The *on* which parents conferred on children included sustenance and nurture, education, material benefits, and, loving care. But, above all else, the greatest *on* given to children by their parents was, according to the textbooks of compulsory moral education, the *on* of having given birth to them.[38] Similarly, the Emperor was the benevolent father of the whole nation; the individual owed his greatest *on* to the Emperor for the mere fact of his birth as a subject of the Emperor.

In this way the relationship structure, stemming from the ideology of loyalty and filial piety, was predominantly exploitative, a manifestation of the principle of exchange of unequal benefits. Within the army, as we have already seen, the superiors were proxies for the Emperor. In the army barracks the company commander was specifically designated as a surrogate father, a subofficer as a surrogate mother, and new conscripts as their children.[39] Thus, in both the overall structure of the army and in the primary group situation, the superior-subordinate relationships were exploitative.

[37] Kawashima, *Ideorogii toshite no Kazokuseido*, pp. 105-106.
[38] *Ibid.*, p. 93.
[39] Iizuka, *Nihon no Guntai*, p. 66.

Hierarchy

The military ranks of any army are hierarchically arranged. They constitute a vertical system of chain of command, directed from the top down. Where absolute obedience is required on the part of inferiors to their superiors, as it was in the Japanese army and navy, those in the relatively inferior positions tend to build up a sense of being suppressed. When this feeling of suppression mounts to a certain point, it tends to produce displacement of affects. In strict hierarchical systems, such as armed forces, the suppressed affect of a soldier tends to be projected onto his inferior, whose suppressed affect is in turn directed toward his inferior, and so on until the chain reaction reaches the very bottom. This type of hierarchical relationship is characterized by Maruyama as "the transfer of oppression."[40]

Maruyama argues that this phenomenon of transference was a unique characteristic of the Japanese military system as well as of the Japanese civilian society at large. And he interprets the atrocities committed by Japanese soldiers during World War II as functions of a system of relationships peculiar to Japan. The logical conclusion of Maruyama's argument would seem to be that atrocities were uniquely characteristic of the Japanese military. How, then, could we account for the atrocities committed by the soldiers of other countries?

As a general pattern of analysis, Maruyama's interpretation is useful, but he fails to see that this is a more or less universal feature of military hierarchies. Kōji Iizuka suggests a slightly different emphasis. He quotes from Leopold Infeld's autobiography the passages describing "infernal" experiences in the Austrian army during World War I. Infeld paints a situation analogous to that in the Japanese army: the officers were insulted and hazed by their superiors, just as the common soldiers were beaten and slighted by corporals. Iizuka also quotes from *The Naked and the Dead* by Norman Mailer the words of an American general who asserts that it is essential to put pressure on the soldiers so that they may effectively direct their hatred and fear against their enemies. In sum, Iizuka avers the exploitation of "the transference of oppression" is present to some degree in all military organizations.[41]

Further evidence of the practice of the American army is

---

[40] Maruyama, *Thought and Behavior in Modern Japanese Politics*, p. 18.
[41] Iizuka, *Nihon no Guntai*, pp. 151-158.

provided in Sanford M. Dornbusch's discussion of hazing in his study of the American military academy:

> The hazing system contributes directly to acceptance of the bureaucratic structure of the Coast Guard, for the system is always viewed by its participants as not involving the personal character of the swab or upper classman. One is not being hazed because the upper classman is a sadist, but because one is at the same time in a junior status. . . . The swab knows he will have his turn at hazing others.[42]

Allowing for the difference in degree of severity, we can see clearly that utilization of the "transference of oppression" in the military establishment was not peculiarly Japanese. But in the American military academy, as described by Dornbusch, hazing was allegedly exercised on an impersonal basis, whereas in the Japanese army it was legitimated not only by reference to the status hierarchy but also through a pseudo-familistic relationship which linked superior to subordinate. Iizuka also points out that Japanese soldiers were less able than their Western counterparts to escape from whatever sense of oppression they may have felt because most of the organizations to which they belonged outside the army, such as their families, village communities, schools, and places of work, were organized on the same principles.[43]

Secrecy

There were two different principles operative in the official lines of communication in the army. On the one hand, there was a steeply differential access to information, much of which was classified as "secret" and "top secret." The precept of Tokugawa administrators, "do not let them [the people] know, but make them rely on us," was jealously observed by the military as well as civilian government elites in modern Japan. All the war news was controlled by the General Staff Office during World War II, and news unfavorable to the Japanese military operation was kept from soldiers as well as from the general public.

On the other hand, the soldiers were not allowed to keep anything secret. Their conversations were overheard and reported, their diaries, memos, and any other writings scrutinized,

[42] Sanford M. Dornbusch, "The Military Academy as an Assimilating Institution," *Social Forces*, xxxiii, May 1955, 319.
[43] Iizuka, *Nihon no Guntai*, p. 158.

and their letters, both incoming and outgoing, strictly censored. In this way communication from superiors to subordinates was theoretically secret, whereas communication from subordinates to superiors was theoretically open. This unequal exchange of information constituted another exploitative relationship, this time in the sphere of communication.

The soldiers, moreover, were forbidden to disclose their whereabouts to their families or to make any unfavorable comments on the army or the war situation. A sergeant lecturing to new recruits told them not to write, for instance, "the march is hard," "we are tired of eating onions," or "it is very cold."[44]

In spite of these restraints, soldiers managed to establish informal channels of communication among themselves as well as with the outside world. Letters and diaries were brought back to their families by returning soldiers or mailed home unofficially by soldiers off duty, thus bypassing the military censorship. Some devices were used to trick the eagle-eyed military censors. A postcard written by a soldier in the early part of 1945 was addressed to "Ogasawara Ryūzō," in care of the soldier's father. His father, reading the characters used in the name of the nonexistent addressee, deciphered that his son had been sent to Iwō Island in the Ogasawara Archipelago and knew that he would never return.[45]

Compulsion, Intimacy, and Functional Diffuseness

The principle of prewar military education was to make "obedience to their superiors and strict adherence to their orders *the second nature*" of soldiers.[46] In other words, the aim of military socialization was the internalization of compulsion to such an extent that the socialized individuals would feel that they were acting on their own volition while in fact they acted under coercion. Thus relationships between superiors and subordinates in the army were predominantly compulsory.

The pseudo-familistic relationship established in the military camps was also used to internalize compulsion. In addition to

[44] Wadatsumi-kai, ed., *Senbotsu Gakusei no Isho ni Miru Jūgonensensō* (*The Fifteen Years' War Seen Through the Messages of the Students Who Died in the War*), Tokyo, Kōbunsha, 1963, pp. 67-68.

[45] Iwateken Nōson Bunka Kondan-kai (A Conference on Culture in Agrarian Villages of Iwate Prefecture), ed., *Senbotsu Nōmin Heishi no Tegami* (*Letters of the Peasant-Soldiers Who Died in the War*), Tokyo, Iwanami, 1961, p. 133.

[46] Iizuka, *Nihon no Guntai*, p. 25 (italics in the original).

his surrogate father, mother, and brothers, the new conscript was assigned to a senior private, his "fighting companion" (*sen yū*) or "big brother." The new recruit had to clean his fighting companion's gun, shine his boots, and generally perform whatever errands he was ordered to do—even to massage his back.[47] In short, the relationship was both intimate and functionally diffuse.

This intimacy and functional diffuseness were in turn used to justify violations of the individual soldier's privacy. The use of violence and torture by superiors on their subordinates was justified on the pretext that it was an expression of the parents' "benevolent feelings" (*on jō*) and would do the children good.[48]

One of the marks of bureaucracy, according to Weber, is the separation of public office from private role.[49] Because of the imposition of the official ideology of familism, however, the public relationships of superiors and subordinates in the Japanese military bureaucracy became entangled with private relationships. Thus a squad chief or a platoon, company, or battalion commander might appropriate the services of his subordinates and treat them as though they were his own patrimonial retainers (*kerai*). Actually, the highest-ranking officers, who were theoretically close to the Emperor, were at a disadvantage, since they were cut off from direct access to the services of the rank-and-file soldiers. The officers of the middle rank, such as company and platoon commanders, did not suffer from this disadvantage. As a result, they tyrannized their superiors. The phrase "rule by the lower of the higher" (*gekokujō*) is used to describe this phenomenon. It refers in particular to the period of extended civil war in Japan (1336-1568) when the lower and the middle ranks of the social hierarchy revolted against the upper ranks.[50] In modern times it has developed in the army on more than one occasion, most notably in the young officers' uprisings of 1936.

[47] Nihon Senbotsu Gakusei Shuki Henshū Iinkai (Committee for the Compilation of the Letters of the Student-Soldiers Who Died in the War), ed., *Kike Wadatsumi no Koe* (*Listen, the Voice of the Sea*), Tokyo, Tokyo Daigaku Shuppankai, 1952, p. 59.

[48] Iizuka, *Nihon no Guntai*, pp. 43-45.

[49] Max Weber, *The Theory of Social and Economic Organization*, tr. A. M. Henderson and Talcott Parsons, Glencoe, Ill., The Free Press, 1947, p. 331.

[50] Maruyama, *Thought and Behavior in Modern Japanese Politics*, p. 113.

THREE

Socialization for Death: Moral Education at School and in the Army

1. THE MANY-LAYERED SYSTEM IN EDUCATION

In order to build up a "wealthy nation and a strong army" within a short period of time, the Meiji Government introduced industry and technology from the West. At the same time, in order to compensate for its relative inferiority in material forces, it restored the feudal ideology of the way of the warrior and combined it with the primitive tribal religion of Emperor worship, which constituted the ethos of the Emperor's army. From the beginning there was a conflict within the principles of socialization: rationalism prevailed in the sphere of technology, traditionalism or nonrationalism in the sphere of morality. And these two spheres, of means and of ends, were compartmentalized in such a way that the intrusion of the principle of rationalism into the sphere of ends was strictly prohibited. One segment of the population was provided with the education of a relatively rational ideology, whereas the majority of the population was indoctrinated in a predominantly nonrational ideology.

The Emperor Cult:
A Nonrational Ideology of Compulsory Education

The central organ of the *gakubatsu* (academic clique) was the Ministry of Education established in 1871. It was through this central organ that the nonrational ideologies of militarism and nationalism were prescribed for elementary schools, while rationalism and liberalism were commended to professional schools and universities.[1] The ideology of the Emperor cult was inculcated in the entire population in their formative years through compulsory moral education (*shūshin*) based on the *Imperial Rescript on Education* (1890).[2]

[1] Michio Nagai, "Chishikijin no Seisan Rūto" ("The Route for the Production of Intellectuals"), *Kindai Nihon Shisōshi Kōza* (*Lectures on the Intellectual History of Japan*), Tokyo, Chikuma Shobō, 1959, ɪv, 205-206.

[2] For translations of the *Imperial Rescript on Education*, see William T. de Bary et al., *Sources of Japanese Tradition*, New York, Columbia University Press, 1958, ɪɪ, 139-140, and Arthur Tiedemann, *Modern Japan*, Princeton, Van Nostrand, 1955, pp. 113-114.

At least five different trends of thought were patched together to make up the ideology of the Emperor cult as formulated in the *Imperial Rescript on Education*. The first was militarism as represented by Aritomo Yamagata (1838-1922), the founder of the Japanese army, who was prime minister and minister of internal affairs at the time the *Rescript* was promulgated and was the one individual most responsible for it. The second was constitutionalism as conceived by Kowashi Inoue (1843-1895), then head of the Bureau of Legislative Affairs and later minister of education, who was one of the drafters of the *Rescript*. The third was the Confucian ethic of familism as expounded by Eifu Motoda (1818-1891), a Confucian scholar, official tutor to the Meiji Emperor, and one of the drafters of the *Rescript*. The fourth was the indigenous and persistent pattern of the family dating from the ancient period. And the fifth was the nineteenth-century European type of organismic theory of society as formulated by Tetsujirō Inoue (1855-1944), a scholar of Oriental philosophy and student for a time in Germany, who became the author of the official interpretation of the *Rescript*.

Militarism

The ideological continuity between the *Imperial Precepts to Soldiers and Sailors* (1882) and the *Imperial Rescript on Education* can be established by quoting Yamagata's own words:

> I remember it was in 1890 that from among the prefectural governors emerged demands for the unification of educational aims [of the people]. There were also similar demands among the cabinet members. . . . I wanted something similar to the *Imperial Precepts to Soldiers and Sailors* for use in the education of the general public.[3]

Both the *Precepts* and the *Rescript* were drafted and issued under the initiative of the same person, Aritomo Yamagata. In 1888 Yamagata warned that the danger of war in Asia between England and Russia had been increased by the completion of the Canadian Pacific Railway which "shortened the British route

[3] "A Record of the Interview of Aritomo Yamagata Concerning the Promulgation of the *Imperial Rescript on Education*," *Documents*, II, 453—quoted in Noboru Umetani, "Kyōiku Chokugo Seiritsu no Rekishiteki Haikei" ("The Historical Background of the Formation of the *Imperial Rescript on Education*"), in *Meiji Zenhanki no Nashonarizumu* (*Nationalism of the Earlier Part of the Meiji Period*), ed. Yoshio Sakata, Tokyo, Miraisha, 1958.

to the Orient," by the construction of the Siberian Railway which "accelerated the eastward movement of the Russian Army," and by the beginning of construction of the Panama Canal which would "connect the Atlantic and the Pacific Oceans." If and when a war broke out, he declared, "it is not likely that we could maintain neutrality. We shall be forced to take either one of the following alternatives. Should we decide then to side with Russia, we would be forced to fight against the British and the Chinese warships and armies. Should we choose to be on the side of Britain and China, we would have to fight against Russia."[4]

The issuing of the *Imperial Rescript on Education* was motivated, just as the promulgation of the *Imperial Precepts to Soldiers and Sailors* had been, by a desire to unite the population and prepare it for war. A chain of events linked these two edicts. After the inauguration of the conscription system in 1883, criticism was voiced by exponents of freedom and popular rights on the ground that it was simply unjust to conscript men while denying them the right to vote. In response to this criticism Yamagata, then home minister, established in the years 1888 to 1890 a system of local autonomous governments. The citizens were given the right to elect some local officials in village, town, district, and prefectural governments. This concession was intended as compensation for the strengthening of conscription.[5] Actually, however, the system of local governments functioned in such a way as to enhance the control of the central government over the countryside.[6]

In 1890 Yamagata summoned a conference of the heads of local governments. Some prefectural and district governors argued for uniform principles of education at elementary schools in their respective provinces. Yamagata quickly accepted these demands and embodied them in the *Imperial Rescript on Education*. In order to achieve this end, Yamagata first discharged Takeaki Enomoto (1836-1908), then minister of education, who was reluctant to introduce state-directed moral education, and replaced him with another man who would be under Yamagata's

[4] Noboru Umetani, "Yamagata Aritomo Gunbi Ikensho" ("Aritomo Yamagata's Memorandum on Armament"), *ibid.*, pp. 112-113.

[5] *Ibid.*, p. 109.

[6] Roger F. Hackett, "The Meiji Leaders and Modernization: The Case of Yamagata Aritomo," in *Changing Japanese Attitudes toward Modernization*, ed. Marius B. Jansen, Princeton, Princeton University Press, 1965, p. 264.

direct control.[7] This incident shows how the military clique influenced the policy of socialization in the early days of Japanese modernization.

The system of local government was established in 1888 and 1890, and the right to control education was delegated to the local authorities. In practice, however, the central government used this system to impose the ideology of militarism on the entire population as prescribed in the *Imperial Rescript on Education*. And this purpose was accomplished under the political leadership of the founding father of the military clique.

In the text of the *Imperial Rescript* the phrase "should any emergency arise, offer yourself courageously to the state" comes at the end of the enumeration of various virtues that both men and women in various positions in the human nexus should observe. The Emperor cult as expressed in the *Imperial Rescript* was an ideological device to produce subjects ready to die for the sake of the Emperor. This commendation of death for the state, a straightforward expression of militarism, set the goal of moral education for the entire nation. In order to effectively achieve this goal, other doctrines, both traditional and modern, endogenous and exogenous, were summoned to contribute to the formation of the ideology.

Constitutionalism

It was Kowashi Inoue, one of the drafters of the Meiji Constitution, who toned down Yamagata's manifest militarism in both the content and the form of the *Imperial Rescript on Education*. In a letter to Yamagata he wrote:

> According to today's constitutional polity, the monarch should not interfere with the freedom of the conscience of his subjects. . . . If an Imperial rescript is to be issued now to indicate the direction of education, it should not be promulgated as a political directive. Instead, it should be considered as the monarch's own proclamation to the public. It ought to be distinguished from a military ordinance for the army.[8]

According to the Meiji Constitution, the Emperor was sacred and infallible. He was beyond mundane political conflicts. If the *Rescript on Education* were issued as a political directive

[7] Umetani, "Kyōiku Chokugo Seiritsu no Rekishiteki Hakei," p. 106.
[8] Kowashi Inoue's letter to Aritomo Yamagata on June 20, 1890—quoted *ibid.*, p. 123.

on educational policy as Yamagata had originally intended, the Emperor might become involved in ideological conflicts and thus be made vulnerable to ideological controversy. From Inoue's standpoint, that eventuality would defeat the purpose of the Meiji Constitution. It was not, therefore, in defense of freedom of discussion but rather from fear of weakening the Emperor system that Inoue warned Yamagata against his rash promulgation of the *Rescript* as a political ordinance.[9]

Yamagata accepted Inoue's advice and issued the *Imperial Rescript* with the Imperial seal alone and without the signatures of the cabinet ministers. Usually, political orders were issued under the name of the Emperor with the cabinet ministers signing their names to indicate that it was not the Emperor but the ministers, the Emperor's assistants in the Imperial governance, who were responsible.

It was also at the suggestion of Inoue that the clause "always respect the Constitution and observe the laws" was written into the *Rescript* as one of the essential duties of the Emperor's subjects.

Thus, ideally, the *Rescript* was given a form compatible with constitutionalism and appeared to be an enumeration of virtues commended to the people. Actually, however, it was made to function as the most powerful apparatus of indoctrination in nonrationalism.

Familism

The Meiji leaders were keenly aware that the manipulation of affects is the key to socialization through indoctrination in patriotism. For this purpose they devised a way to channel the affects between parents and children in the family into the political relationship between the Emperor and his subjects in the state. Their method was to identify the state with the family and on that basis maintain that filial piety (*kō*) was identical with loyalty (*chū*) to the Emperor. The identification of the state with the family and of filial piety with loyalty was achieved by recourse to the two patterns of familism, the one indigenous and prevalent among the common people of Japan for centuries, the other Confucian and limited to the samurai class in the Tokugawa feudal period.

[9] Ryōen Minamota, "Kyōiku Chokugo no Kokkashugiteki Kaishaku" ("The Nationalistic Interpretation of the *Imperial Rescript on Education*"), in *Meiji Zenhanki no Nashonarizumu*, pp. 171-172.

According to Confucian ethics in its original formation, filial piety of the son toward his father was the primary human virtue, and loyalty to one's lord was subsidiary to that fundamental virtue. However, when Confucianism was adopted as the official doctrine of the Bakufu Government, the official Confucian scholars made loyalty rather than filial piety the essential samurai virtue. For the samurai, "filial piety to one's father and forefathers was allegedly achieved by giving loyal service to the lord who had bestowed upon them their fief which one inherited."[10] Thus Confucian ethics underwent a metamorphosis through adaptation as the official samurai ethics of Tokugawa Japan.

The predominant type of family in Japan since ancient times was "the stem family," in which "one of the sons marries and continues to live with the parents, while the other sons and daughters marry and go out of the family unit."[11] Marion Levy points out that "the stem family" was also the predominant type of family "in which the average Chinese lived during the 'traditional' period."[12] In the Chinese stem family, however, the members of the family were limited to the blood relatives through patrilineal lines. In contrast, in the Japanese stem family, persons related and unrelated by blood to the head of the family who came to live under the same roof were treated as integral members of the family. Thus servants as well as sons and daughters were treated as members of the family in the Japanese type of stem family, and they also were entitled to branch out.[13]

This fictitious family relationship in which servants were treated as though they were blood relatives originated, according to Yanagida, as "a labor organization without payment of wages." In this system "the servant is not paid for his labor directly in money or in goods, but he receives benefits from the master in the form of maintenance and protection of his daily life." Besides, the servant expects his master to establish him as the head of a branch family after a certain period of service, thus

[10] Takeshi Ishida, *Meiji Seiji Shisōshi* (*History of Political Thought in the Meiji Period*), Tokyo, Miraisha, 1954, p. 24.

[11] Marion J. Levy, Jr., *The Family Revolution in Modern China*, Cambridge, Harvard University Press, 1949, pp. 55-56.

[12] *Ibid.*, p. 55.

[13] Kizaemon Aruga, "Nihon no Ie" ("The Japanese Family"), in *Nihon Minzoku* (*The Japanese Race*), ed. Nihon Jinrui Gakkai (The Japanese Anthropological Association), Tokyo, Iwanami, 1959, p. 175.

making him independent.[14] This relationship allowed the agricultural employers to keep their labor force during the slack season and to put it to work during the busy season without paying
wages all the year round. For this reason Yanagida interprets
the origin of the fictitious family relationship as based primarily
on economic needs peculiar to the mode of agricultural production in the ancient period.[15]

Inheritance by the eldest son began in the Nara period (707-
781), and the eldest son stayed in the parents' family to continue the main family (honke), while cadets and servants left
the main family to establish branch families (bunke). The main
and branch families composed a union of families called dōzoku.

> The Japanese dōzoku does not necessarily consist of blood
> relatives. It is a group of families of the common patrilineal
> lineage, sharing the worship of the common family gods.
> Blood relatives may live far apart, but the dōzoku group is
> required to live in the same hamlet. The major function of
> the dōzoku is the worship of the family gods, and from that
> follow all types of cooperation in matters of daily life. Fami-
> lies belonging to the same lineage [dōzoku] lose their function
> as members of their dōzoku by not being able to cooperate in
> the daily routines of life. The requisites for membership in
> the dōzoku are firstly the sharing of the common ancestor,
> from which the lineage of the main and branch families
> evolved, and secondly living together in the same area. The
> dōzoku relationship persists, regardless of the death and birth
> of each member, as a social unit united by the worship of the

[14] Kunio Yanagida, "Nōson Kazokuseido to Kanshū" ("The Family System
and Custom in the Agrarian Village"), Yanagida Kunio Shū, Tokyo, Chikuma
Shobō, 1963, xv, 344.

[15] The fictitious parent-child (oya-ko) relationship has continued to
spread, as Yanagida points out, into various spheres of life and occupations
other than agriculture ever since the Middle Ages. Yanagida notes more
than thirty different types of oya still extant. For instance, those who assume
such various functions as midwife and wet-nurse, the man who presides at
the genpuku (coming of age) ceremony, the go-between in marriage, and
an employment agent may be called one's parents (oya). During the
Tokugawa period the master craftsman, the head of a merchant's family,
the head of a samurai family, and the head of a landlord's family in the
northeastern part of Japan were all called oyakata (parents) by their ap-
prentices or servants. In agricultural villages all over Japan, the eldest son
was usually called oyakata, since he supervised the labor of other members
of the family, Kunio Yanagida, "Oyakata Kokata" ("The Fictitious Parent
and Child"), ibid., pp. 370-390.

common ancestors. This relationship very seldom becomes extinct unless all the member families happen to die out or
migrate to some other areas. Thus *dōzoku* groups constitute the
major elements of Japanese hamlet life.[16]

In the *dōzoku* type of relationship, the main family is in a
superordinate position relative to the branch families. The hierarchy of unit families is emphasized in the *dōzoku* union. This
hierarchical relationship between the main and the branch families within a hamlet was usually identical with the superordinate-
subordinate relationship between the landlord and his tenants in
a hamlet.

The *dōzoku* system dates back to the clan system of the ancient
slave society (40 B.C. - A.D. 645).

> It existed since ancient days through the middle ages and
> persists up to the present. . . . It is generally accepted that
> the clan system collapsed after the Great Reform [645]. . . . The
> basic principle that gave rise to the clan system, however,
> underlies all the social relationships in Japan and persists
> under various metamorphoses. The *dōzoku* system is one among
> such persistent patterns.[17]

Although the right of inheritance by the eldest son began in
the ancient period, it was not until the Tokugawa feudal period
(1600-1867) that the right of primogeniture and the single inheritance by the eldest son of all the family property and privileges were firmly established. Even then they appeared specifically among the upper-class samurai families. It was also
during this period that the right of inheritance by the main
family came to carry the most weight.[18] In order to consolidate
the relationship between the Imperial family and all other Japanese families, the dynastic Meiji elites adopted the ancient
dōzoku in the form which prevailed among the upper-class samurai of the Tokugawa period. In the later official interpretations
of the Emperor cult, particularly in the 1930's, the indigenous
pattern of the *dōzoku* family relationship was especially emphasized. *The Fundamentals of Our National Polity*, issued by the
Ministry of Education in 1939, stated: "Our country is a great
family nation, and the Imperial Household is the Main Family

---

[16] Kizaemon Aruga, *Nihon Kazokuseido to Kosakuseido* (*The Japanese
Family System and Tenancy*), Tokyo, Kawade, 1943, p. 102.
[17] *Ibid.*, p. 114.   [18] Aruga, "Nihon no Ie," p. 184.

of the subjects, and the Emperor has been the center of national life from the past to the present. Thus the Emperor and his subjects are united into One."[19]

The Imperial Household allegedly had an "unbroken lineage for ten thousand years" and was directly descended from the Sun Goddess Amaterasu. By virtue of this divine origin, the Emperor presided as the paterfamilias of the main family of the Japanese people, who were ideally united in the common ancestor, the Sun Goddess.[20]

The combination of the Confucian ethics of familism and the indigenous pattern of familism in the formulation of the ideology of the Emperor cult is interpreted by Takeyoshi Kawashima as a joining of two class-based family types, and the samurai type of family oriented primarily to "norm-consciousness" and the common people's type of family oriented primarily to "emotive reactions."[21]

The Organismic Concept of the State

The influence of Herbert Spencer on the formulation of the ideology of the Emperor cult has been suggested in several anecdotes.[22] There is, however, no conclusive evidence to prove that Spencer was responsible for the Meiji leaders' adoption of the Emperor cult as the national religion, although it is true that Spencer's organismic theory of the state was used to justify the superordinate position of the Emperor. In the 1870's and 1880's there was increasing agitation, by the Freedom and Popular Rights Movement, for the establishment of a representative assembly elected by the people. The leaders of the movement, under the influence of the writings of Rousseau and Mill, advo-

[19] Monbushō (Ministry of Education), *Kokutai no Hongi* (*The Fundamentals of Our National Polity*), Tokyo, 1939, p. 13. A partial translation is provided in De Bary, *Sources of Japanese Tradition*, II, 278-288; a summary may be found in Tiedemann, *Modern Japan*, pp. 136-139.

[20] For the ideology of familism as the basis of the Emperor system, see Takeyoshi Kawashima, *Ideorogii toshiteno Kazokuseido* (*The Family System as an Ideology*), Tokyo, Iwanami, 1957, pp. 30-65.

[21] *Ibid.*, p. 44.

[22] On being asked by Arinori Mori in 1870, Spencer gave him his advice on the reconstruction of the educational system of modern Japan. Spencer, in his letter to Kentarō Kaneko (1853-1942), advised him to make full use of the patriarchal family system in the parliamentary organization in Japan. See Ishida, *Meiji Seiji Shisōshi*, p. 101. See also John Dewey, "Liberalism in Japan," *Characters and Events*, New York, Henry Holt, 1929, I, 165. This essay is an illuminating account of the role of the Emperor cult in ideological socialization in prewar Japan.

cated the theory of popular sovereignty on the ground that all human beings were born free and equal.[23] The Meiji Government ideologues were aware that, in order to counteract this theory and the demand for equality and freedom, they needed some theoretical weapons more effective than Confucianism and indigenous familism.

The government asked Tetsujirō Inoue to write an official commentary on the *Imperial Rescript on Education,* with the help of more than eighty prominent scholars. Among them Hiroyuki Katō (1836-1916), the chairman of the government's textbook committee, was the most important. In the interpretations of the relationship between the Emperor and his subjects that Inoue and Katō provided, we can trace clearly the organismic theory of the state.

Inoue maintained that there were two fundamental moral principles. The first was private, consisting of filial piety, respect for elders, loyalty to one's monarch, and trust in one's friends; the second was public, exemplified in cooperation and the love of one's country. The *Imperial Rescript,* according to Inoue's commentary, prescribed these two primary human virtues and held that they were united in an organismic theory of the state. The *Commentary on the Imperial Rescript* proffers the argument that, since the state is an organism and individual families are cells of the organism, "there should be one and only one principle [of unification], for if there were more than one principle the state would be divided."[24]

Katō, a convert from the theory of social contract to social Darwinism, justified the superordinate-subordinate relation between the Emperor and his subjects in terms of an organismic theory of the state. According to his logic, "the higher organism [such as the state] consists of the sole sovereign (the central organ of thinking) and its subsidiary organs." Within such a state "what is beneficial for the survival of the state is good and moral, and what is detrimental is evil and immoral." From such a criterion of moral judgment, he argued that "all the virtues

[23] See *Jiyū Minken Hen, Meiji Bunka Zenshū* (*The Collected Works of Meiji Culture*), Tokyo, Nihon Hyōronsha, 1927; Shōzō Satō, "Ningen Kaihō no Ugoki" ("A Movement for the Emancipation of Man"), in *Nihonjin no Shisō no Ayumi* (*The Development of the Thought of the Japanese*), ed. Saburō Ienaga, Tokyo, Rironsha, 1956, pp. 37-56; Ienaga et al., eds., *Jiyūminken Shisō* (*The Idea of Freedom and People's Rights*), Tokyo, Aoki Shoten, 1957.

[24] Ishida, *Meiji Seiji Shisōshi,* p. 184.

pertaining to the relationship between the sovereign and his subject can be considered as the means of achieving the end, loyalty to the sovereign. That principle is compatible with the characteristics of individual human beings as the cells composing an organism called the State."[25]

It was ironical that the philosophy of Spencer, the advocate of laissez faire and the principle of nonintervention by the state in personal conduct, was used by his Japanese protagonists to justify state control of education. What the Meiji leaders were promoting was more akin to Spencer's "military society," a stage in the evolution of society which he considered lower than "industrial society" based on voluntary cooperation.[26]

A year after the *Imperial Rescript on Education* was issued, the Ministry of Education issued a directive to the elementary schools declaring that moral education must be founded on it. Although textbooks had been approved by the government prior to 1903, thereafter all books used in the elementary schools were produced directly by the Ministry of Education, and the government thus had firm control over socialization in the schools.

In order to make effective the indoctrination of militarism based on the Emperor cult, the Ministry of Education had already in 1886 remodeled the training programs for elementary school teachers on the pattern of army socialization. Military drill was introduced into the regular curriculum at normal schools, and the students were required to live in dormitories which were designed like army barracks and which subjected the students to military discipline.[27] This policy was initiated in order to implant a military type of outlook in the future elementary school teachers and thereby make them even more effective agents of socialization than they would have been with only six months' service in the army.[28] The continuity between elementary school education and army socialization was complete.

[25] Hiroyuki Katō, *Shizen to Rinri* (*Nature and Ethics*), pp. 133-137— quoted *ibid.*, pp. 126-127; see also Kiyoko Takeda, *Tennō-sei Shisō to Kyōiku* (*The Idea of the Emperor System and Education*), Tokyo, Meiji Tosho, 1964, pp. 85-103.

[26] Herbert Spencer, *The Principles of Sociology*, New York, D. Appleton, 1896, Vol. ii, Part v.

[27] Tomitarō Karasawa, *Gakusei no Rekishi* (*History of Students*), Tokyo, Sōbunsha, 1955, pp. 66-70.

[28] Nagai, "Chishikijin no Seisan Rūto," pp. 208-209.

Rationalism Applied to Higher Education

Under the leadership of Arinori Mori (1847-1889), the first minister of education, divergent aims were established for elementary schools and institutions of higher learning. Elementary schools were set up primarily for the purposes of educating the masses and producing obedient and loyal subjects of the Emperor. In their curricula the nonrational ideology of the Emperor cult was emphasized. At the same time, the educational policy makers foresaw the urgent need of providing a rational type of education in professional schools and universities in order to produce industrial, technological, and administrative elites. The Tokyo Higher Commercial School (now Hitotsubashi University) and the Tokyo Higher Industrial School (now Tokyo Technological University) were founded in the 1880's as government professional schools. At the time of the institution of those schools, the chief of the Professional School Section at the Ministry of Education stated that "In our country, the industrial schools are founded not for the purpose of providing personnel to industries already established. On the contrary, we are attempting to provide graduates who are capable of creating industries."[29] Accordingly, in these professional schools the pragmatic attitude characteristic of science and technology was emphasized.

Under the Imperial University Ordinance of 1886, Tokyo Imperial University was established as the first government university encompassing departments of humanities, social and natural sciences, engineering, and agriculture.[30]

At the time of its inception, the board of councillors for the university was appointed by the Minister of Education. In 1892, however, the regulations were revised so that the board was elected by and from among the professors of the University.[31] Thus, unlike the public elementary schools, where the appointment of teachers was under the direct control of the Ministry of Education, the Imperial University came to enjoy more autonomy from government intervention. Rationalism in the pursuit of knowledge and liberalism in the government of the university administration stood in sharp contrast to the nonrationalism in

[29] *Ibid.*, p. 211.

[30] Nagai emphasizes the progressive role of Tokyo Imperial University, in contrast to European universities at this period, in including both humanities and engineering and technology in its curriculum. *Ibid.*, p. 209.

[31] *Ibid.*, pp. 210, 230.

ideological indoctrination and direct government control in school administration on the elementary level of education.

Yet even this rationalism and independence from government intervention was limited. A rational way of thinking was encouraged only insofar as it did not subject the Emperor system itself to critical scrutiny. According to the Imperial University Ordinance, "the Imperial University aims to teach arts and sciences and the pursuit of knowledge to its ultimate conclusion in order to meet the demands of the state."[32] Arinori Mori stated categorically that "the interests of the state had priority over those of learning."[33]

The application of rational thought to analysis of the Emperor system was a criminal offense punishable as *lèse majesté*. The whole history of the suppression of thought concerning the Emperor system shows a wide range of ideologies held by persons prosecuted under the charge of *lèse majesté*, from communism, anarchism, and socialism to Christianity, liberalism, and democratic constitutionalism.[34] These trials, together with the general

[32] *Ibid.* p. 210.

[33] *Ibid.*

[34] Here are some of the incidents that involved *lèse majesté*:

(i) In June 1910 hundreds of socialists were arrested, and twelve of them were sentenced to death for high treason. Shūsui Kōtoku (1871-1911), who was an intellectual leader among anarchists and socialists but had not himself been involved in the plot, was among those convicted and executed. This incident had a tremendous impact on contemporary intellectuals. See Shōbei Shioda, *Kōtoku Shūsui no Nikki to Shokan* (*The Diary and Letters of Shusui Kotoku*), Tokyo, Miraisha, 1954.

(ii) Kanzō Uchimura (1861-1930), one of the most influential Christian thinkers of the Meiji period, left his position at the First Higher Middle School in 1891 because he had allegedly failed to bow before the *Imperial Rescript on Education* at the ceremony which marked its receipt from the Emperor. Karasawa, *Gakusei no Rekishi*, p. 70. See also John F. Howes, "Japan's Enigma: The Young Uchimura Kanzo," Ph.D. diss., Columbia University, 1965.

(iii) Tatsukichi Minobe (1873-1948), professor of constitutional law at Tokyo Imperial University, developed a theory of the Emperor as the organ of the state. The military condemned his work in 1935 as blasphemy both against the Emperor and the national polity of Japan. His works were confiscated, and he was forced to resign from the House of Peers.

(iv) Yukio Ozaki (1859-1955), who was successively elected to the Parliament ever since the first election in 1890 until his death and who was identified as the most respected constitutional democrat, was prosecuted in 1942 on the charge of *lèse majesté*. The poem he cited in an election campaign speech was taken to be a criticism of the present Emperor, the grandson of the Emperor Meiji. The poem read: "House for rent, writes the third generation, in T'ang style calligraphy."

repressive measures carried out under the Peace and Order Preservation Law, especially in the 1930's,[35] had a tremendous psychological impact on graduates and students of colleges and universities. Fear of prosecution was so great that it established in the students a sharp sense of the limits beyond which they must not think rationally. The Emperor cult, with its apparatus of negative affect socialization through fear and terror, created a taboo out of any rational and scientific way of thinking on matters that might have even slight relevance to the Emperor and the Emperor system. Since all major government policies were proclaimed and executed in the name of the Emperor, criticism of government policy automatically became criticism of the Emperor. The Meiji Constitution specified that war must be declared in the name of the Emperor. Thus, by implication, to question war policy was tantamount to questioning the infallibility of the Emperor.

Under the Emperor system the recipients of higher education were expected to be relatively more rational persons than the recipients of elementary education. Owing to the existence of this negative affect apparatus, however, even recipients of higher education were only partially rational persons. They could afford to be rational as far as the techniques of pursuing ends were concerned but could not be rational where the ends and policies of the government came under consideration. Moreover, recipients of higher education attended the elementary schools in their formative years, and it is quite conceivable that the effects of the basically nonrational type of socialization provided there persisted as substrata of their personalities. Thus among the elites the type of development of personality tended to be what we have classified as the many-layered self or the conflicting self, whereas among the masses the recipients of the compulsory elementary education only tended to represent what we have classified as the ever committed.

After compulsory education for six years was instituted in 1907, elementary school attendance rose to 98 percent. In contrast, the recipients of higher education were a small minority. In 1935 only 1.6 percent of the population between the ages of

---

[35] The Peace and Order Preservation Law, instituted in 1925, prohibited all organizations and individual activities designated as intending to "change national polity and the system of private property." Under this law an enormous number of people, including communists, socialists, and liberals, were arrested and prosecuted. For a listing of the number of people who fell victim to this law between 1931 and 1937, see above, Ch. One, p. 41, n. 20.

fifteen and fifty-nine could boast of having received higher education, whereas 9.2 percent had had some secondary education, 82.1 percent had had only elementary schooling, and 7.1 percent had received no education.[36] These groups thus constituted four educational layers in the population.

For the male population of prewar Japan, conscription was a rite of passage marking the transition from adolescence to adulthood. Its significance for university graduates, though, was different from the meaning it held for elementary school graduates. University students had the privilege of postponing their military training until they graduated; hence, their three years in high school and four years in college served simply as the transition period between adolescence and adulthood. But, for those who had finished only compulsory elementary education, conscription played a more vital role. Thus for craftsmen, who normally did not pass beyond the elementary level, the physical examination required for admission to army training denoted the end of apprenticeship and the beginning of full-fledged craftsmanship.[37]

Subsequent sections of this chapter will illustrate from personal documents the differing function of army socialization in the lives of those with higher education compared with those without it.

In December 1943 the university students' privilege of postponing their military service until graduation was rescinded, and the students—except for those in medicine, science, and engineering—were mobilized and sent to the front, while keeping their status as university students. For this reason, in the discussion that follows, both university graduates and students who were drafted will be referred to as "student-soldiers." Those who were peasants before being drafted will be called "peasant-soldiers." The personal documents of the student-soldiers who came from various sections of the country will be compared with those of peasant-soldiers who came from the northeastern

[36] Monbushō Chōsa-kyoku (Research Bureau of the Ministry of Education) *Nihon no Seichō to Kyōiku* (*Japan's Growth and Education*), Tokyo, 1962, p. 59.

[37] See Kazuko Tsurumi, *Chichi to Haha no Rekishi* (*The History of Our Fathers and Mothers*), Tokyo, Chikuma Shobō, 1962, pp. 108-109. This book contains the life histories of some fishermen, peasants, craftsmen, and transportation workers which were collected by the author in 1961 through intensive interviews of forty persons in their forties and fifties.

part of Japan. None of these peasants had an education above the level of junior high school.

2. The Processes of Army Socialization

Emptying the Self: The Socialization of Negative Affects

"The army quarters is a space of 120 square yards enclosed by a palisade and code books. It is an abstract society built under strong compulsion. Within that society, human beings, being deprived of their humanity, become soldiers."[38] This definition appears in Hiroshi Noma's novel about the Japanese army in World War II entitled *Shinkū Chitai* (*Zone of Emptiness*). In an army barracks "even the air is expelled by force," leaving only emptiness. Army socialization, in Noma's probing analysis, is a process of dehumanization, or emptying of the self as the center of distinctively individual feeling, thinking, and acting.

As Erik Erikson points out, isolation is the *sine qua non* of indoctrination.[39] Thus isolation from the ordinary world and the destruction of privacy were the initial steps of army socialization. The new recruits were detached both physically and symbolically from civilian society. First they had to dress in a particular style, with close-cropped hair, khaki uniforms, field-service caps, gaiters, and boots. They were disciplined to speak in the manner befitting a soldier. When referring to "I," the soldier was to use *watakushi* in addressing his superiors and *ore* in speaking to his equals; all other ways of expressing "I" in ordinary language —such as *boku, watashi*, and *washi*—were to be eliminated. To refer to money, "one meter" should be used to mean one *yen*, and "one centimeter" one *sen*.[40] Not only were the vocabularies different from ordinary Japanese, but so also were the acceptable endings of the sentences. It was one of the sources of agony for new recruits to learn the new conventions of speech, since any

[38] Hiroshi Noma, *Shinkū Chitai*, Tokyo, Kawade Shobō, 1952. The English version is entitled *Zone of Emptiness*, tr. Bernard Frechtman, Cleveland, World, 1956. This quotation is translated by the author from *Gendai Bungaku Zenshū* (*Collected Works of Contemporary Literature*), Tokyo, Chikuma Shobō, 1958, lxxxii, 217.

[39] Erik H. Erikson, *Young Man Luther*, New York, W. W. Norton, 1958, p. 135.

[40] Kōji Iizuka, *Nihon no Guntai* (*The Japanese Army*), Tokyo, Tōdai Kyōdō-kumiai Shuppanbu, 1950, pp. 24-25. This work includes a series of symposia in which two former company commanders in the army related their World War II experiences. A vivid description of army language is found in Masaharu Fuji, *Teikoku Guntai ni okera Gakushū Jo* (*A Preface to Learning in the Imperial Army*), Tokyo, Miraisha, 1964, pp. 180-182.

mistake meant a punishment of several blows on the face.[41] The suppression of the ordinary conventions of speech and the substitution of the army jargon did, however, give the new recruits a compensatory sense of superiority over the civilian population.[42] The surrogate tongue fulfilled another function as well. Since recruits came from various provinces with different dialects and it was difficult for them to communicate with one another, the army language served as a substitute for standard Japanese.

The second step in army socialization was the destruction of privacy. The conscripts were placed under twenty-four hours' surveillance; they were under the strict control of the training officers during the day, and they were watched by their squad commanders during the night.

> For instance, when we tried to go to the toilet at midnight, we had to pass by a guard standing at the door. A new conscript had to report: "So and so is going to the bathroom." If his voice was too loud, he was admonished that he should not speak so loudly while his fighting companions were asleep. But if his voice was low, he was also chastised. Thus we had to live under circumstances which made us feel that we were always tied up with invisible hands.[43]

The third technique of army socialization was the use of violence. Every evening before bedtime there was a roll call, when each soldier's arms and belongings were checked. The field-service cap, overcoat, uniform, underwear, knapsack, boots, gun, and sword of each soldier were examined by his superiors to confirm that nothing was missing and everything had been properly attended to. If the belongings of any soldier were missing or dirty, his superior would shout at him: "How is it that you have time to eat but no time to clean your gun!" or "How could you dare find time to sleep while you have no time to do your laundry properly!"[44] The shouting was usually followed by a

---

[41] "A student in my squad said 'boku' [I] by mistake and was hit with a fist by his squad commander. Being hit, that tall man, to my surprise, sank and sat flat on the floor. It must have been very shocking to him." Wadatsumi-kai, ed., *Senbotsu Gakusei no Isho ni Miru Jūgonensensō (The Fifteen Years' War Seen Through the Messages of the Students Who Died in the War)*, Tokyo, Kōbunsha, 1963, p. 210. This book consists of the letters and diaries of forty-seven student-soldiers.

[42] Iizuka, *Nihon no Guntai*, p. 25.

[43] *Ibid.*, p. 105.   [44] *Ibid.*, p. 165.

shower of fist blows or kicks administered by the superior officer. New recruits called the evening roll call "the hour of terror."[45]

An ex-officer relates his experience of disciplining his new conscripts.

> [The purpose of discipline is] to give new conscripts shock treatments. When they first come into the army, they look sloppy and too relaxed. It is hard to explain exactly what is wrong with them. But we somehow feel that way about them. Whenever we find any impropriety in their attitudes, behavior, or speech, we chastise them while keeping them standing at attention. Usually soldiers do not understand what is wrong with them, while they are being punished. The ultimate purpose of shouting at them and hitting them is to make them feel miserable, and thus to hammer it into them that absolute obedience is imperative in the army and that neither criticism nor protest is allowed. When superiors chastise conscripts, the former may ask why the recruits committed this or that blunder. If the conscripts begin to give reasons for their deeds, they are hit for having tried to answer. If they keep silent, they are also hit. Either way there is no escape from being beaten. The best they can do is to reply "Yes, sir" to whatever is said to them.[46]

It is important to note that the disciplining of new conscripts was not based on any consistent system of abstract rules but only on the whim of their superiors. More often than not, when new recruits were hit or humiliated by their superiors, there were no reasons for the acts other than the need to drive home the necessity of unquestioning obedience. The relentless destruction of privacy and the extensive use of violence were methods of negative affect socialization; by these means anger and contempt were maximized in the socializing agents, while distress, fear, and humiliation were maximized in the persons socialized. Whenever new recruits attempted to think, write, say, or do anything of their own accord, they met with punishment through admonition or violence. After constant repetition of this treatment, the fear of encountering humiliation and violence became so ingrained within the personalities of the conscripts that they were inhibited from thinking, doing, or feeling anything of their own volition.

[45] *The Fifteen Years' War*, p. 74.
[46] Iizuka, *Nihon no Guntai*, p. 165.

One year's army life has drained the humanity out of everyone. Second-year privates treat us first-year privates as though we were their slaves or rather machines. They have no other job than hazing and torturing us. . . . Every night we are strapped with slippers. One of us was beaten with the sheath of a sword and was hospitalized with a wound that required four stitches. Even a corporal acts like a god toward us. . . . Were a second-year private to discover that I have written a letter like this in the toilet, I would probably be murdered.[47]

A student marine wrote two months after joining the Marine Corps:

The two things that made me suffer most after I entered the armed forces were the alternate attacks of physical and mental pain. Physical pain was the result of cold and extreme muscular fatigue, and the mental pain arose from being deprived of books. Hunger and a hankering for food occupied a great part of one's daily thought. . . .

Even when I read the news of heavy fighting, I feel differently from what I did when I was a civilian. When I was a civilian, I felt some determination to cope with a war situation growing ever more serious. But since I entered the Marine Corps, I have lost the freedom and composure necessary to have a will of my own, being enslaved physically and mentally from morning till night. . . .

When I began to feel some relief from the sense of oppression, toward the end of the second month as a sailor, I realized that my integrity in coping with problems had been gradually paralyzed. . . .

First I wished I could become spiritually nothing. I thought I had to put an end to the life and thought of a civilian.[48]

Eight months after he had entered the Marine Corps, the same marine noted in his diary:

The head sailor was giving "spiritual education" to the sailors in his charge, with an oak stick at his waist. . . . He told his men to step forward one by one, and then he began to

[47] Nihon Senbotsu Gakusei Shuki Henshū Iinkai (The Committee for the Compilation of the Letters of the Student-Soldiers Who Died in the War), ed., *Kike Wadatsumi no Koe (Listen, the Voice of the Sea)*, Tokyo, Tokyo Daigaku Shuppankai, 1952. This book consists of letters by seventy-nine student-soldiers who died in the war.
[48] *Ibid.*, pp. 177-178.

strike with his full strength at the hips of each man. . . . Each sailor stood with his back turned towards the head sailor, with his hands held up and legs open. I heard the dull sounds of bang, bang, hitting the pelvic bones of the sailors. I felt I was witnessing a disgusting scene; indeed it was more than merely disgusting.

On Sunday some weeks ago, I also saw the same head sailor hitting another sailor, because he had returned to the barracks only ten minutes before the deadline. . . . The sailor fell on the gravel, groaning. Another sailor tried to help him stand up, but . . . he fell on the ground again. I saw a streak of blood running down the back of his head onto the collar of his uniform.

Both the tyrant and the victim will eventually be my subordinates. What should I make of this fact? Anyway, it is useless to think. It is completely nonsensical to think seriously.[49]

There were various forms of punishment other than verbal reproach and hazing. Among them were the postponement of meals or the suspension of holidays. A more severe form of punishment was confinement to the barracks jail. The decision to inflict this penalty was mainly at the discretion of a subofficer and a company commander. Sometimes the unfavored "sons" of the subofficer and the company commander were sent to the front as punishment. Demotion was yet another penalty. The most serious punishment was court-martial and imprisonment in the army prison. The army prison was under the jurisdiction of the gendarmerie and was distinct from a barracks prison, which was under the control of regular army officers. Although they were usually justified, each of these forms of punishment was sometimes applied out of animosity, rivalry, and hatred. The accused had no way of protesting against such injustices.[50]

[49] *Ibid.*, p. 184.

[50] In his *Zone of Emptiness* Noma relates a story of a soldier who was demoted from superior private to first-class private because of a false charge against him. He was also imprisoned for two years. This soldier used to work in the accountant's office and knew that his superiors, noncommissioned officers, appropriated army money, food, and other goods for their private use. In order to cover up their illegal practices, the officers saw to it that the soldier was sent to prison, and that, when he got out, he was put on the list of soldiers to be sent to the front. In this novel, based on the author's own experiences, Noma tries to describe corruption within the army, personal animosities and hatreds arising from rivalry among officers for power and promotion.

Protest was a form of disobedience—a capital crime in the army.

Isolation from ordinary life, the relentless invasion of privacy, constant reproach and hazing, and imprisonment constituted the apparatus of negative affect socialization. Owing to the changes wrought in their personalities by this socialization, men ceased to act voluntarily and, instead, acted out of fear and terror. New conscripts were humiliated until they felt less worthy than their horses. Some squad leaders publicly announced that horses were more precious than men, since men could easily be recruited whereas horses could not be replaced overnight. Thus horses were treated with meticulous care. On the occasion of a horse inspection, the soldiers assigned to stop galloping horses suddenly were often kicked and injured by the horses, but they preferred to risk this danger rather than be reprimanded by their superiors.[51] It was not, then, only fear that motivated soldiers; it was also the hierarchy of fears and terrors that determined their conduct, and, in this hierarchy of fears, first place was assigned to fear of the consequences of disobeying one's superiors.

Indoctrination: Socialization for Death

Indoctrination in the army included the word-for-word citation of the basic code books. The qualifying examinations for cadets were drawn from these code books, and the new conscript memorized them during his first year of training.[52] A graduate of the Law School of Tokyo University wrote about his first examination in the army:

> On the second day after my entrance into the army, the first qualifying examination took place. The first question was "Deferentially write the part on loyalty in the *Imperial Precepts*." An examination on the *Imperial Precepts* is extremely hard. The *Imperial Precepts to Soldiers and Sailors* is a long piece, and it takes twenty minutes to recite it. The language [especially the Chinese characters used] is so difficult that we cannot read it accurately unless parallel readings are given in

[51] *Listen, the Voice of the Sea*, pp. 55-61; Iizuka, *Nihon no Guntai*, p. 113.

[52] Those who had finished higher education were allowed to take qualifying examinations at the beginning of their first year as new conscripts. Those who had received secondary education were allowed to take such examinations at the end of their six-months' basic training. See *The Fifteen Years' War*, pp. 135n, 141n.

the alphabet. In the examination, we are required to write exactly in the same manner as the original texts, using the archaic alphabet, wherever it is used in the texts. In the texts, sometimes *koto* [the fact that] is written in phonetics and sometimes in Chinese characters. The same applies to *mono* [those who]. We are expected to remember where *mono* is written in phonetics, and where *koto* is written in characters. . . .

The second question was "What is military discipline?" I thought about this problem on my own and wrote: "Military discipline is a system of norms, observance of which is essential for the maintenance of the various activities of the armed forces." This answer was rated as close to zero. The right answer was to write out the fourth article of the *Infantry Drill Book*: "Military discipline is the lifeline of the army. It is military discipline that makes the whole army, from generals to rank-and-file soldiers stationed in various places and assigned with various duties in the battlefield, consistently obedient and creates the unified policy necessary for concerted action. The destiny of the army hinges on the firmness or looseness of this military discipline." All the other examinations followed a similar pattern. In the army there is no room for what you think yourself. (We call our own thoughts "private code books.") We are expected to learn the military code books by heart, word for word. It is different from the kind of education we have received at the university, in which emphasis was placed on our own ideas. But considering the fact that the language in the military code books is the most exact and concise expression of certain ideas, it is only natural that word-for-word memorization is required of us.[53]

There was a continuity between military indoctrination and compulsory moral education at primary schools. The common denominator was the fetishism of words as words. In schools in the regular class in compulsory moral education, as well as on ceremonial occasions such as the Emperor's Birthday or the National Foundation Day (called *Kigensetsu,* the day when, according to tradition, the Japanese Empire was founded by the first Emperor Jinmu), the *Imperial Rescript on Education* was recited. Whenever any part of the *Imperial Rescript* was read aloud, the reader was expected first to raise the book of sacred teachings above his head and bow deferentially to it

[53] *Listen, the Voice of the Sea,* pp. 53-54.

before beginning his recitation. Not only was the Emperor sacred, but so were the words issued in his name. The fetishism of words was applied to the language of the military code books. As the passage quoted above shows, the language of these documents was difficult for a law school graduate to learn. It was even more so for those who had had only elementary schooling. Army indoctrination was a strictly one-way communication, in which only the socializer spoke and the socializee was expected to accept silently whatever was told him. It was an imperfect communication, since the socializee was not expected to understand precisely what these words meant but only to grasp vaguely what they were about. Their ambiguity created a halo of sanctity around the words of the Imperial dicta. The inexplicable was taken for profound thought, something to be held in awe and revered. Perfect communication, or at least an attempt at perfect communication through free discussion, was tabooed, since in discussion the veil of euphemisms might be torn aside to reveal the actual motivations of the designers of the ideology and the socializee might be encouraged to think about the possible consequences of following the precepts he was taught.[54] On the other hand, if the socializee failed completely to understand the meaning of the *Imperial Precepts* and other code books, then socialization through words was impossible.

Thus imperfect communication, instead of complete discommunication or perfect communication, was functional for the military elites as a method of indoctrinating soldiers in the ideology of death. The use of imperfect communication as a vehicle of army socialization was related to the functional diffuseness of its ideological content. Perfect cognitive communication defines and delineates precisely what one is expected to do. Imperfect communication, in contrast, expands the range of duties and obligations that can be demanded of the socializee almost without limits, at the discretion of the socializer.

Yanagida has pointed out that there is a sharp distinction between the formal or ceremonial (*hare*-clear) and the informal or everyday (*ke*-cloudy) languages in Japanese colloquial

---

[54] Peirce defined the meaning of a symbol as follows: "The entire intellectual purport of any symbol consists in the total of all general modes of rational conduct which, conditionally upon all the possible different circumstances and desires, would ensue upon the acceptance of the symbol." *Philosophical Writings of Peirce*, ed. Justus Buchler, New York, Dover, 1955, p. 290.

conventions. In learning ceremonial language, students were taught "to recite meticulously word for word, without paying any attention to misunderstandings of the meaning."[55] Yanagida regretted that in prewar schools only the stereotypes of ceremonial language, with its inhibition of invention and creativity, were inculcated, to the utter neglect of everyday language.[56] Following Levy, we have already distinguished between actual and ideal patterns of action. Ceremonial language is the linguistic form of expressing ideal patterns of thought and action, whereas everyday language is the linguistic form of expressing actual patterns of thought and action. This distinction leads to the hypothesis that, if we compare what a person expresses in ceremonial language with what the same person says in everyday language, we may be able to gauge the distance between his ideal and actual patterns of thought and action.

The *Imperial Precepts to Soldiers and Sailors*, the basic text of army socialization, was written in the most ceremonial of ceremonial languages. After first examining the ideological content of the *Precepts*, we shall analyze how this army socialization was accepted or rejected by the soldiers as shown in their diaries and letters. Unfortunately from the sociologist's point of view, the writers of these letters knew that their communications faced censorship, and probably some of the letters were for that reason written in more ceremonial language than they otherwise would have been.

The *Imperial Precepts* prescribed five primary virtues for soldiers: loyalty, propriety, valor, fidelity, and simplicity. Among these five virtues, loyalty ranked first:

> Soldiers and sailors, We are your Commander-in-Chief. Our relations with you will be most intimate when we rely upon you as Our limbs and you look up to Us as your head. . . .
>
> Remember that, as the protection of the state and the maintenance of its power depend upon the strength of its arms, the growth or decline of this strength must affect the nation's destiny for good or for evil; therefore, neither be led astray by current opinions nor meddle in politics, but with single heart fulfill your essential duty of loyalty, and bear in

---

[55] Yanagida, "Kokugo no Shōrai" ("The Future of the National Language"), *Yanagida Kunio Shū*, 1963, xix, 31.

[56] *Ibid.*, pp. 31-34.

mind that duty is weightier than a mountain, while death is lighter than a feather. Never by failing in moral principle fall into disgrace and bring dishonor upon your name.[57]

This glorification of death was an ideology that provided incentives for dying for the sake of the Emperor. Four main elements constituted this glorification of death: a taboo on the discussion of politics, an organismic concept of the state, familism, and the prestige to be gained by dying.

The phrase "neither be led astray by current opinions nor meddle in politics" has a historical significance. The *Imperial Precepts* was promulgated in the heyday of the Freedom and Popular Rights Movement. The leaders of the movement tried to win the soldiers over to the cause of popular rights. They defined the primary duty of soldiers as the defense of the people's rights against their oppressors. The movement's leaders declared:

> Soldiers should always be aware of public opinion. Who are the internal enemies? Since a country's policy should be guided by public opinion, those who threaten and interfere with public opinion are the internal enemies. . . . If the government interferes with public opinion, it should be denounced as an enemy. Soldiers must understand this.[58]

The popular rightists not only published these appeals to soldiers but organized public meetings for men eligible for conscription.[59] They also advocated vigorously the creation of a revolutionary army in the true spirit of the *levée en masse*. One of the immediate purposes of the *Imperial Precepts* was to isolate the soldiers from these agitators. In opposition to the ideology of engagement, the *Precepts* sternly prescribed an ideology of detachment. This counsel in favor of detachment from politics failed to prevent the military magnates from dictating the political course of the nation up until Japan's defeat in World War II. But it did succeed in establishing a taboo among the rank-and-file soldiers against the discussion of politics or war and, in effect, said: Shut your mouth and die quietly. This strong taboo against political discussion in the army accounts in part for the absence of criticism of the war policy by

[57] De Bary, *Sources of Japanese Tradition*, II, 198-200; Tiedemann, *Modern Japan*, pp. 107-112.
[58] Ienaga et al., eds., *Jiyūminken Shisō*, p. 104.
[59] *Ibid.*, pp. 105, 176-177.

soldiers and, indeed, by the entire male population who had received military training. They could not even think of any criticism.

Second, the official presentation in the *Precepts* of the relationship between the Emperor and the army as one organism of which the Emperor is the head and the soldiers are the limbs embodies the organismic concept of the state. Just as in the *Imperial Rescript on Education,* the organismic analogy was used in the *Precepts* to make identification of the soldiers with the father-image of the Emperor effective.

Third, loyalty to the Emperor was justified on the basis of traditional familism, as in the *Imperial Rescript on Education* examined earlier. Yet the Emperor-soldier relationship was, according to the *Precepts,* more "intimate" than the Emperor-civilian relationship. Soldiers were told that they were the Emperor's favorite sons. They were, then, even more deeply burdened with the Emperor's *on* than civilians and, consequently, were more heavily obliged to repay his *on* by demonstrating greater willingness to die for him than civilians.

There was another aspect of familism applied to the army. The treatment of new conscripts as "children" in the "family" of soldiers in the barracks was an important socializing device to make the ideology of death acceptable. Tomkins points out:

> Earlier affective response can be readily activated if another adult fails to treat us as an adult. So long as we are treated like adults, we act and feel like adults, but many adults can be made to feel like ashamed children by an overly authoritarian police officer who speaks to them as they might have been spoken to by their parents when they transgressed. It is always possible to activate earlier feelings by acting toward the adult as though one were his parent and he was the child.[60]

Even adults who in their civilian capacities were expected to act as independent and rational persons, such as university students or heads of families, had their childhood roles of dependence and obedience activated under the treatment accorded them as army recruits. The absence of privacy and the subjection to humiliation, terror, and anxiety also helped to evoke childhood roles of dependence and obedience. Since the new re-

---

[60] Tomkins, *Affect, Imagery, Consciousness,* Vol. II: *The Negative Affects,* New York, Springer, 1963.

cruits were treated as "children," they began to act like children
and became more submissive to the ideology of death than they
would have been if they had been allowed to sustain their adult
roles.

Fourth, soldiers were provided with positive incentives for
death, in the form of prestige. They were told that they would
become gods of the fatherland and would be worshiped in the
Yasukuni Shrine in Kudan, Tokyo. It is a folk belief that any
dead member of a family becomes a god and protects the surviving members of the family.[61] To be made a Yasukuni god is
a special honor bestowed only on national heroes. Whereas a
family god protects just his own family, a Yasukuni god protects
the entire fatherland. This mark of distinction ennobles not only
the individual soldier but his whole family, since his family
name is listed among the gods. According to the Confucian
doctrine as expressed in *Hsiao-Chin*, the achievement of fame
for one's family name is the ultimate stage of filial piety. Thus,
in the act of dying for the sake of the Emperor, the unity of
loyalty and filial piety was held to be fully realized. In contrast, to fail to die like a soldier and to allow oneself to be cap-
tured by the enemy was to disgrace not only oneself but one's
family and village community. This was the meaning of the
passage "Never . . . fall into disgrace and bring dishonor upon
your name."

How was this incentive to die according to the ideal pattern
understood by the soldiers in interpreting their own motivation? A student-soldier noted in his diary while at the front:

> Soldiers believe with extreme naiveté that they are heroes
> in the defense of their country. They are proud to be the
> saviors of their fatherland. That is an easy sentimentalism.
> But that is the anchorage of their emotion. It is a kind of
> soldiers' mental masturbation for which they are willing to
> waste their youthful energy. . . . This is sad. They do not
> possess enough reason to be critical of their own state of
> mind. Moreover, *should they deny this belief, they would
> have nothing left to sustain them in their hardships.*[62]

To accept the nonrational belief that they would become a national god was actually, then, a defense mechanism for many

[61] Yanagida, "Tamashii no Yukue" ("Where the Spirit Goes"), *Yanagida
Kunio Shū*, 1963, xv, 561.
[62] *The Fifteen Years' War*, p. 139.

soldiers. Without it they would have been unable to face the brutal fact that they were wasting their lives in a war over which they had no control.

In summary, prewar Japanese army socialization used imperfect communication as its method and was mainly negative in affect socialization. Its ideological content was predominantly nonrational, particularistic, dependently collective hierarchical, and detached.

3. The Soldiers' Attitudes toward Army Socialization

Comparison of the letters of peasant-soldiers with those of student-soldiers shows some marked differences in attitudes toward life and socialization in the army. The peasant-soldiers were less critical of the army and found more positive value in military experience than student-soldiers. The peasant-soldiers also accepted the army ideology of death more willingly than the student-soldiers.

Table 10 provides a classification of the themes of the letters written by peasant-soldiers in the collection *Letters of Peasant Soldiers Who Died in the War* and of those written by student-soldiers in the collection *Listen, the Voice of the Sea*. Because both of these collections consist of letters carefully screened by editors preparing books for commercial publication, the letters are no doubt relatively more thematic than others which might have been selected. At any rate, since the criteria of selection are more or less the same for both, the relative frequency of themes in the two collections can be taken to indicate differences in attitudes between the two types of soldier.

These differences in attitudes can be correlated first with the level of education. The student-soldiers had all had some higher education; a number had already graduated, but many were taken away from the universities to serve in the army. The peasant-soldiers had had elementary and junior high schooling. Differences in attitudes can further be correlated with agrarian and urban styles of life. Finally, they can be correlated with income level and the occupational status of the soldiers or their families. In the case of the peasant-soldiers, the size of their farms and their status—the distinction between owner-cultivators and tenants—are specified. In the case of the student-soldiers, their social origins are not mentioned. Context enables us to classify them roughly as of middle-class origin or above.

The first contrast between student-soldiers and peasant-

TABLE 10

THEMES OF LETTERS WRITTEN BY PEASANT-SOLDIERS
AND STUDENT-SOLDIERS

Themes	No. of Peasant-Soldiers	No. of Student-Soldiers
Complaints and criticisms about army life and training	3	18
Army life—better than civilian life	4	0
Army life—satisfactory	4	0
Doubts about the war and the legitimacy of authoritarian power	0	4
Doubts about Japan's victory	0	3
Anxiety about Japan's future	0	2
Reluctance to die	0	7
Ascription of a positive meaning to death	6	4
Resignation toward death	0	4
Concern about family and family maintenance	18	8
Love for a girl friend	0	3
Platoon commander's letter announcing the death of a soldier to his family	2	0
Regret at not having gone to high school	1	0
Agony of a wounded soldier	1	0
Poems (their own)	0	16
Greetings and other themes	11	8
Total	50	77

soldiers lies in their way of comparing army with civilian life. The theory of relative deprivation developed by Samuel Stouffer and others provides a useful method of analyzing this difference in attitudes between the student-soldiers and the peasant-soldiers, though it requires slight modification. In its original formulation the theory asserts "that people do not suffer in an 'absolute' way; they compare their lot with that of other people of their kind."[63] We propose to reformulate this proposition into the hypothesis that people do not suffer in an "absolute" way but compare their new experience with their own previous experiences.

In their letters and diaries, most of the student-soldiers expressed their agony over the absence of privacy in army life, whereas no peasants, as far as our sample shows, made such a complaint. The student-soldiers compared army life with their life at home where they usually had rooms of their own for

[63] Paul Lazarsfeld, "The American Soldier—An Expository Review," *Public Opinion Quarterly*, XIII, Fall 1949, 388.

study. Peasant-soldiers compared their life in the army barracks with their life in the farmhouse where they worked, ate, and slept with other members of the family in one big room with a dug-in fireplace in the center. Student-soldiers had much to lose by entering the army, including privacy, a style of life, and physical and material comforts. Peasant-soldiers had little to lose, since they had never been able to afford the kind of physical and material comforts or the privacy to which students were accustomed. For this reason the peasant-soldiers were more favorably disposed toward army life than student-soldiers.

The eldest son of a part owner-cultivator, part tenant farmer of 2.5 acres wrote of life in the army:

> Although there are very busy days in the army, life in general is easier here than at home. We get up at six in the morning. If I got up as late as that in our village, I would be very much ashamed of myself in front of my neighbors.
>
> You must be suffering from the shortage of rubber boots at home. Thanks to the army, I, Fujimi, am walking through the mud in a pair of fine rubber boots.[64]

Fishermen also found life easier in the army. One remarked:

> In 1938, I received a red paper [a conscription order], and was sent to Manchuria to do guard duty. As a civilian I was only a member of the crew on my boss's boat. The beating administered to a new army conscript was nothing compared to the hardships of a fisherman's life.[65]

A city streetcar conductor likewise commented that army life was less taxing:

> I was drafted in April 1944 and entered the army in Sakura, in Chiba Prefecture. Within a week of entering the army, I had put on weight noticeably. The army life was easier than the work on the streetcar.[66]

[64] Iwateken Nōson Bunka Kondan-kai (A Conference on Culture in the Agrarian Villages of Iwate Prefecture), ed., *Senbotsu Nōmin Heishi no Tegami* (*Letters of the Peasant-Soldiers Who Died in the War*), Tokyo, Iwanami, 1961. This collection includes the letters of fifty peasant-soldiers who came from Iwate Prefecture in northeastern Japan. None of these peasants received education higher than the level of junior high school.

[65] Kazuko Tsurumi, *Chichi to Haha no Rekishi*, p. 67.

[66] *Ibid.*, p. 89.

In the second place, army socialization was, for the peasant-soldiers, a functional substitute for professional education. It helped them get ahead in the world. For the student-soldiers, on the other hand, army socialization ran counter to their university and college education in both content and method. It was therefore dysfunctional for their professional careers.

A noncommissioned officer of twenty-six, the eldest son of an owner-cultivator of 2.6 acres, wrote from Manchuria:

> Today we again worked hard on English. We study everything—calligraphy, abacus, arithmetic, polygraphy, Japanese, ethics, and other subjects. It keeps me busy to compete with the others. I shall work hard to match your heavy labors in the fields.[67]

The son of a village shopkeeper, an apprentice in an auto repair shop, was sent to Manchuria and returned after the war to relate his experiences in the army:

> Usually people say that army life is hard to bear. But I think it did me good. In civilian life, we often failed to be punctual, and we were often morally loose. In the army we were beaten and we suffered from the discipline. But looking back I can see that the army made a man out of me. In the army I experienced the inside story of human life. Industry alone is not enough, neither is shrewdness. You should combine both in order to succeed in life. That is what I have learned from the army experience.[68]

After he came back from the war, this man married a woman who was introduced to him by his "fighting companion." With the help of his wife he worked hard to establish himself as an owner of an auto repair shop.

For the student-soldier, in contrast, army life was a deviation from their professional training, at least temporarily. One student-soldier complained:

> A new conscript has absolutely no time for reading and for being free. It was the greatest pain in the first year in the army not to be able to read books.[69]

---

[67] *Letters of the Peasant-Soldiers*, p. 123.
[68] Kazuko Tsurumi, *Chichi to Haha no Rekishi*, pp. 155-161
[69] *The Fifteen Years' War*, p. 152.

Another student-soldier in the Marine Corps confessed:

> For several minutes before the meal hour, while the soldiers on duty were busy arranging the table, and the clatter and clamor filled the dining hall, I sat on a hard bench and read and reread a leaflet describing mentholatum. Then I realized how hungry I had been for written words.[70]

A student at the Tokyo School of Physics wrote a year after he entered the army:

> The more I see of the evil and ugly side of military life the stronger becomes my passion for mathematics, which requires rigour and diligence. These were integral parts of my character before I entered the army. . . . Every night I long for a scholarly life such as Pascal's. I want to enter a life dedicated to mathematics and meditation.[71]

Most of the student-soldiers were agitated, especially in their first year in the army, by the loss of such student privileges as freedom and initiative in the pursuit of knowledge. They feared that army life would make them so stupid that they would be unable to resume their academic careers. Gradually another insight dawned upon them. For many of the students of middle-class origin and above, army life provided fresh contact with people of social origins other than their own. For the first time in their lives they lived with peasants, craftsmen, and industrial workers from all over the country. For the first time they realized what it was like to be poor, to be unable to go to school beyond the elementary level, and to be denied opportunities to advance beyond the economic and social position of their parents. Thus the army experience was dysfunctional for the student-soldiers as far as their professional careers were concerned, but it was functional in the sense that it expanded the range of their experience and their capacity to sympathize with others.

M. T., a graduate of Kokugakuin University who died as a lieutenant, wrote:

> My military life during this period of training as a cadet was extremely painful, and longer than the training taken by some others of my generation. But this I believe will become the best foundation for building up my self-confidence. . . .

[70] *Listen, the Voice of the Sea,* p. 179.   [71] *Ibid.,* p. 138.

I was put into an infantry platoon where the degrading and painful life provides an intelligent human being with a severe trial of his forbearance. Compared with the navy and air force, which are easier and more spectacular, the infantry platoon provides a very painful, long, and tedious training. Because I was placed in the infantry my war experience was certainly democratic. I was formerly too aristocratic to get my ideas across to the public. This experience will become the foundation of self-assurance in my future work. Up to now, the lack of experience made me hesitant to put forward my own arguments and convictions.

I was always troubled by an inferiority complex, and in order to hide it, I maintained my aloofness. My scholarly life was carried out in a highly intellectual atmosphere. I received no recognition, and I did not feel secure or at ease.[72]

For the student-soldiers, then, army life was functional even if the army socialization itself was not. Prewar Japanese society was highly stratified, and people of different social classes, occupations, and geographical sections were isolated from one another. One of the sharpest dividing lines separated those who had finished only elementary school education from those who had gone to universities. The army served as a mixer of men of different social origins. For some of the student-soldiers, the experience, in that sense, was comparable to the experience of the "V Narode" movement, albeit on a limited and compulsory basis.

The third point of contrast is to be found in the types of role conflict which the two groups had to face. The student-soldier was confronted with a conflict between his role as pursuer of knowledge and his role as a soldier; the peasant-soldier faced a conflict between his role as a family provider and his role as a soldier. All of the student-soldiers were under thirty years of age, and most of them were unmarried, whereas 26 percent of the peasant-soldiers were thirty or older and 41 percent were married. These differences in age distribution and marital status may appear, at first sight, as the essential factors in explaining the peasant-soldiers' greater concern about their families and their families' means of livelihood.[73] In fact, however, the ex-

[72] *The Fifteen Years' War*, pp. 160-161.
[73] The age distribution of student-soldiers and peasant-soldiers, as shown in *Listen, the Voice of the Sea* and *Letters of the Peasant-Soldiers*, is set

pression of concern for family maintenance by the peasant-soldiers cannot be correlated with age or marital status. Most of the peasant-soldiers worried that their mothers and their wives would overwork themselves because of the shortage of male labor at home. A nineteen-year-old lance corporal, the eldest son of a tenant farmer living on 0.5 acres of land, wrote:

> I have decided not to apply for admission to the school for noncommissioned officers. Remembering that I am the eldest son, I cannot go on leaving the hard work for my parents. Even for the sake of our country, I now feel that I cannot abandon my own family. Please do not worry; I am not going to the military school. I was wrong in thinking of going. Please forgive me. However long my military service may persist, I believe it will not exceed six years.[74]

For those who had finished only primary education, the great-est incentive as a soldier was to become a noncommissioned officer. To succeed, however, would make them liable to in-definite service whereas under normal circumstances a rank-

TABLE 11

AGE DISTRIBUTION OF PEASANT-SOLDIERS AND STUDENT-SOLDIERS

Age	No. of Student-Soldiers	No. of Peasant-Soldiers
18	1	0
19	1	2
20	3	0
21	5	2
22	12	2
23	11	2
24	7	11
25	3	3
26	4	5
27	3	4
28	3	0
29	3	2
30 or older	0	13
Not specified	21	4
Total	77	50

forth in Table 11. Among the student-soldiers, those whose ages are not specified cannot have been over 30, since they were drafted either while they were in school or immediately upon graduation.

[74] *Letters of the Peasant-Soldiers*, p. 161.

and-file soldier could expect his release after three years. Ideally, filial piety and loyalty to the Emperor were identical, but actually most of the peasant-soldiers, like the one quoted above, suffered from divided loyalties. Usually, loyalty to their families weighed more heavily on their consciences than duty to the state, until they found themselves in a situation where they had no choice. A sergeant of twenty-nine, the eldest son of an owner-cultivator with nine acres of land and forest, wrote from the fighting front to his family: "I am intending to study hard while I am in the army in order to take an examination for a job as supervisor of forestry in Saghalien, at a salary of about seventy yen a month. I am also thinking of becoming a policeman either in Korea, Hokkaidō, or Saghalien. . . ."[75] Later he informed his wife: "Now we are told that we shall be sent to a more dangerous zone than the one we are in now. We are preparing for the move. I do not know whether I shall return alive. Please be prepared to behave like a soldier's wife."[76]

Role conflict among the peasant-soldiers concerned objects of loyalty, rather than the principles of loyalty itself. As far as these letters show, no peasant-soldier raised any doubt about why he had to die for the Emperor, any more than he questioned why he had to work to support his parents, wife, and children. Both duties were simply taken for granted. The structure of relationships within the peasant family and in the army were more or less similar in that they were both predominantly non-rational, dependently collectivistic, intimate, functionally diffuse, hierarchical, and compulsory. There was also continuity between the ideological socialization of primary school and that of the army. Thus, at the moment when they had no choice but to die for the Emperor, they accepted their fate more easily than the student-soldiers.

A twenty-five-year-old noncommissioned officer in the para-troops, the fourth son of a farmer with three acres of land, told his parents:

> The time has come to do service to my country. My body is not mine alone. It does not make any difference where I blossom out [die] for my country. After I have parachuted into the enemy's sky, you will read about me in the newspaper. When I die in battle, I will shout *banzai, banzai*. . . . When you

[75] *Ibid.*, p. 93.   [76] *Ibid.*, p. 96.

hear that I have died in battle, I want you too to shout *banzai, banzai*. I beseech you to do so.

I will become a blossom in the enemy sky; thereafter I will become a god and continue my service for my country.[77]

All of those among the peasant-soldiers who expected to die in battle anticipated death in the stereotyped manner laid down in the army's indoctrination program.

The role conflict of the student-soldiers involved a disparity in principles. The ideological socialization provided in the university taught students to be rational, independently individualistic, and voluntaristic in pursuit of universalistic knowledge and values, whereas the ideology of the army required soldiers to be nonrational, dependently collectivistic, and compulsory in pursuit of particularistic values. A graduate of Tokyo Agricultural University wrote from China:

> A soldier in the Nakazawa platoon struck a Chinese civilian with a rock, and he fell on the ground with his broken skull bleeding. The soldier again kicked him and stoned him. It was an unbearable scene. The officers of the platoon were watching it callously. Apparently the incident took place on the orders of sublieutenant Takagi. What a cold-blooded fellow! Thinking of the innocent farmer, I accuse myself for not having helped him. I feel guilty.[78]

As a soldier he could not possibly have interfered with the execution of an order. Yet as a student, as a human being, he felt that he should have tried to stop the atrocity, even if doing so would have led to severe punishment or death. He questioned, though, whether he could so risk his own life. Here the army ethics of particularism conflicted with, and finally won out over, the universalistic ethics of a student.

Most of the student-soldiers wrote about their role conflicts, but not all of them succeeded in resolving them. M. T. at least tried to integrate his two roles.

> Since I developed a mission to reconstruct the army, I have been able to integrate my purposes as a soldier and as a student. . . . The making of an essentially scientific army!
>
> The modernization of the army! It is difficult enough to modernize the army, but it is even more difficult to "overcome

[77] *Ibid.*, p. 190.
[78] *Listen, the Voice of the Sea*, pp. 13-14.

the modern"[79] at the same time. In spite of the fact that the army is not modernized yet, individual soldiers have been educated entirely in the modern morality of individualism. . . . This makes the task of reconstruction difficult. . . .

It would give me supreme pleasure if I could make the army even a bit more scientific and a bit more modern, and at the same time help soldiers overcome the petty bourgeois ideology of modern individualism. . . .

My mistrust of hard-headed military education drives me to adopt a new and peculiar method of education. I am obsessed with the desire to practice my own theory of education. Will it succeed? Will intelligence win? Will the reliance on physical force be overcome? How different will the conscripts trained in the new method based on intellect be from those who were trained in the traditional way? The answer will determine my worth.[80]

This is the most active and creative attempt at the integration of the roles of a student and a soldier exhibited in the letters of the student-soldiers. This man's criticism is not directed against the war aims themselves, however, but against traditional military socialization, which was a means of achieving the war aims. A student-soldier who returned alive wrote immediately after the war:

At that time [during the war] we did not know that this was a war of aggression or a war of imperialism. Besides we did not dream of rejecting war in general as a crime. We believed that war is a universal inevitability. In the liberal education we had received, criticism was directed only against the ultranationalistic and militaristic trends of the day, and our hatred was focused only on the militarists and some of the rightists.[81]

Student-soldiers also accepted the war as inevitable. When the war situation became most critical, it was the student-soldiers who volunteered to be the pilots of *Kamikaze* planes and the operators of human torpedoes. Although army socialization was based on compulsion, they acted on the opposite principle, volunteering for certain death. Student-soldiers, in contrast to

[79] See Introduction, Section 2.
[80] *The Fifteen Years' War*, pp. 146-165.
[81] Takeshi Yasuda, *Sensō Taiken: Issen Kyūhyaku Shichijūnen e no Isho* (*My War Experience: A Will for 1970*), Tokyo, Miraisha, 1963, p. 19.

peasant-soldiers, were not bound by army stereotypes and tried to read their own meaning into their deaths. A sublieutenant in the navy, a former student at Tokyo University who died as a human torpedo, wrote:

> [The names of four women are listed.] These are my ideal women, at least temporarily. . . . I still have an unquenchable love for each one of them. My love for them symbolizes my love for my ideals. However, this love is all one way, for they do not know that I have loved them thus. Now on my way to attack an enemy warship, I remember my love for them and want to transform it into love for my fatherland. Is it a blasphemy? . . .
>
> We, the three corps of suicidal attackers, Rikukū, Kamikaze, and Kamishio, are the only soldiers in Japan who are able to do anything to turn the present desperate situation toward a favorable conclusion. . . .
>
> I have been silent for several days, and have arrived at a kind of resignation.
>
> Now I can announce clearly that I shall be next to none in fighting spirit in the service of my country.[82]

It was not out of negative affects of fear, anger, distress, or hatred but out of joyful love for his woman friends and for the protection of those whom he cherished that he was willing to die. It should be noted that he did not say directly that he was dying for the Emperor, as he had been taught. By this stage of the war the Japanese navy had lost most of its fighting capacity, and the soldiers believed this drastic action was the only way to meet the situation. Under the circumstances some took the view: "We were ready to die anyway, so to choose to die as a suicidal attacker was a genuine expression of our youthful pride to make our death most meaningful."[83] It was a rational calculation of means to achieve the given and absolute ends.

The student-soldiers tried to be rational as far as the methods of waging the war were concerned. But they were as blind and unquestioning as the peasant-soldiers about the war itself. This attitude of *wertrationalität* was a function not only of army socialization but also of the limited type of rationalism in prewar university socialization.

[82] *The Fifteen Years' War*, pp. 228-230.
[83] Shunpei Ueyama, *Dai Tōa Sensō no Imi* (*The Meaning of the Great Asiatic War*), Tokyo, Chūōkōronsha, 1964, pp. 2-3.

Yoshimi Takeuchi is one of the few scholars in postwar Japan who have made an objective assessment of the function of army socialization for the common people.

The army—the Japanese army of the past—was no doubt the root of much evil. We should be glad that it was dissolved, since the abolition of the army means the elimination of one of the major bottlenecks in the modernization of Japan. However, our rejoicing over the extinction of the army cannot be single-hearted. The reason is that we have not yet found a functional substitute for the army as an agent of adult socialization. The new educational system does not replace army education, which was a thoroughgoing compulsory education for adults in prewar days. Consequently, the new educational system is not fully supported by the public. An educational agency which meets the public demand for adult education is completely lacking today. Not only that, the need for the establishment of such an agency has not yet been fully recognized. Although it was based on compulsion, army education was suited to the actual needs of the public in Japan, since it provided free professional training, and it gave people moral training at a minimum level, although admittedly mistakes were made. If Japan were already a progressive civil society, it might be able to get along without any agency of adult education. But, if it had been such a society, an army of the prewar type could not have functioned as it did. It is a prejudice on the part of intellectuals to think that the mere extinction of the army means progress. The common people had reasons to look askance at the liberal education offered by the university.[84]

Takeuchi points out that university education was cut off from the needs of the common people, whereas army socialization met their demands better in spite of all of its shortcomings. He recognizes the necessity of creating new agencies of adult socialization which will cater to the interests of the masses and will be a functional equivalent for the prewar army.

[84] Yoshimi Takeuchi, "Guntai Kyōiku ni tsuite" ("On Army Education"), *Kokumin Bengaku Ron* (*Theory of National Literature*), Tokyo, Tokyo Daigaku Shuppankai, 1954, pp. 192-193.

FOUR

The War Tribunal: The Voice
of the Dead

ON THE FIFTEENTH of August 1945 Japan surrendered unconditionally to the Allied Powers, and on the second day of
September her representatives formally accepted the provisions
of the Potsdam Declaration. They included the following
clause: "We do not intend that the Japanese shall be enslaved
as a race or destroyed as a nation, but stern justice shall be
meted out to all war criminals including those who have visited
cruelties upon our prisoners."[1] In January 1946 the International
Military Tribunal for the Far East was established to implement
this clause. Representatives of eleven countries sat on the Tribunal: the United States, China, Great Britain, Soviet Russia, Aus-
tralia, Canada, France, the Netherlands, New Zealand, India,
and the Philippines.[2]

The Tribunal classified war crimes into three major categories: "Crimes against Peace, Conventional War Crimes, and
Crimes Against Humanity."[3] Individuals were grouped into
classes A, B, or C according to the type of crimes with which
they were charged. Class A war criminals were those charged
with the planning, preparation, initiation, and waging of an
aggressive war or a war in violation of international law or
treaties.[4] Those in class B were charged with ordering and direct-
ing atrocities, while class C comprised those charged with the
actual execution of atrocities.[5] All those accused of class A
crimes were tried by the Tokyo War Tribunal; the rest were
tried separately by the countries where they had been stationed

[1] International Military Tribunal for the Far East, *Judgment*, Nov. 1948,
Annex–1, p. 3.
[2] *Ibid.*, p. 1.
[3] *Ibid.*, p. 7.
[4] *Ibid.*, p. 32.
[5] Asahi Shinbun Hōtei Kishadan, *Tokyo Saiban* (*The Tokyo War Tribunal*), Tokyo, Tokyo Saiban Kankōkai, 1962, ɪ, 40.

during the war.[6] Out of some 4,000 arrested as war criminals, 1,068 were executed or died in prison from 1946 to 1951. Of this 1,068, only 14 were ranked as class A criminals.[7]

Of those who died as war criminals, 701 left personal documents in the forms of letters, diaries, essays, and poems. They were written on such diverse substances as writing paper, wrapping paper, toilet paper, handkerchiefs, a piece of sheet, and the margins of books. The whole collection was published under the title *Seiki no Isho* (*The Last Testament of the Century*).[8]

All the writers knew that their deaths were certain; there was nothing they could do to change their fate. These documents

[6] TABLE 12

WAR CRIMINALS CLASSIFIED BY COUNTRIES WHICH EXECUTED THEM

Country	No. Executed
Allied Powers	14
United States	167
China	175
Britain	254
Dutch East Indies	273
Philippines	17
French Indo-China	33
Australia	135
Total	1,068

SOURCE: *Seiki no Isho* (*The Last Testament of the Century*), ed. Sugamo Isho Hensankai, Tokyo, Shiragikukai, 1954, Appendix, pp. 2-5.

[7] TABLE 13

WAR CRIMINALS CLASSIFIED BY CAUSES OF DEATH

Cause of Death	Class A	Classes B and C	Total
Execution	7	901	908
Disease after convicted	5	60 ⎫	
before convicted	2	26 ⎬	93
Accident after convicted	0	12 ⎫	
before convicted	0	7 ⎬	19
Suicide after convicted	0	12 ⎫	
before convicted	0	23 ⎬	35
Cause not clear	0	13	13
Total	14	1,054	1,068

SOURCE: *Ibid.*, Appendix, p. 1.

[8] *Ibid.*, pp. 1-744.

can thus be taken to be fairly accurate and sincere revelations of the patterns of thinking, feeling, and action of these soldiers who were exposed to two principles of socialization diametrically opposed to each other, the one represented by the Japanese army and the other expressed by the War Tribunal.

In our analysis of these documents, we shall ask the following three related questions.

First, did the War Tribunal as an agent of resocialization of soldiers succeed in accomplishing its professed aim? According to the opening statement of Joseph B. Keenan, chief of counsel acting on behalf of the United States, the War Tribunal's goal was the prosecution of justice and the prevention of future calamities of war.[9] Since the War Tribunal was established ideally as the agent of socialization for peace, we can legitimately ask whether it succeeded in this purpose. The result intended by the War Tribunal in this respect was twofold. In the first place, it meant to make the soldiers themselves recognize their own "crimes against humanity." In the second place, the Tribunal was contrived to be an instrument of preventing the surviving generation of Japanese from committing similar crimes. We shall focus our attention mainly on the former aspect and leave discussion of the latter aspect to the concluding section of this chapter. The reason for emphasizing the former aspect is to be found in our contention that what the executed men thought and felt before they died has had a long-range effect on the attitudes of the succeeding generations of Japanese toward the matters of war and peace.

Second, what proved to be the effects of Japanese army socialization on these soldiers when they were confronted with the War Tribunal's contrasting principle of socialization? Did the soldiers change their affective and ideological postures as quickly and as drastically as the War Tribunal expected them to? To what extent and in what ways did the affective and ideological postures inculcated by the army socialization persist in their personality structure, if they persisted at all?

Third, what types of change in personality structure, if any, were observable among the soldiers executed by the War Tribunal?

9 Asahi Shinbun Hōtei Kishadan, *Tokyo Saiban*, p. 205.

1. Basic Data Concerning the Dead

The war criminals who were executed or otherwise died in prison were classified as shown in Table 14. More than 18 percent of the total were civilians.

TABLE 14

War Criminals Classified by Rank or Status

Status	Rank	No.
Military	Generals	59
	Field grade officers	118
	Officers below the rank of major	262
	Subofficers and chief warrant officers	89
	Noncommissioned officers	316
	Privates	28
Civilian	Civil officials, interpreters and civilian employees in the army and navy	196
Total		1,068

Source: *Seiki no Isho*, Appendix, p. 6.

Ages at the time of death, listed in Table 15, are known for only 672 of the war criminals. The majority of the dead were under thirty-five, and the youngest was twenty-two.[10]

TABLE 15

Ages of War Criminals at Time of Death

Age at Death	No.
25 and below	34
26-30	180
31-35	157
36-40	104
41-45	69
46-50	39
51-60	72
61-70	15
71 and above	2
Total	672

[10] *Seiki no Isho*, Appendix, p. 6.

The educational backgrounds of the 701 authors are summarized in Table 16, based upon *curricula vitae*. We may

TABLE 16

EDUCATIONAL BACKGROUND OF WAR CRIMINALS

Educational Background	No.
Graduate of military schools (including the military preparatory schools, the Military Academy, the War College, etc.)	92
University graduate or student	44
Professional and technical school and higher school graduate or student	86
Graduate of high school or youth school*	47
Educational background not specified	432
Total	701

* The youth schools, which combined professional and military training, were established in 1935.

assume that most of those whose educational backgrounds were not specified were graduates of primary schools. If so, about 60 percent of those who left messages had only had elementary schooling. According to the statistics for 1935, 82.1 percent of the entire Japanese population between the ages of fifteen and fifty-nine were graduates of elementary schools only.[11] In comparison to the prewar educational level of the general population, then, these authors had received comparatively advanced education.

Information on previous occupations, provided in Table 17, is available for less than half of the authors.

Although we have an adequate knowledge of the wartime status of these men as soldiers or civilians, the rank of the military personnel, the place of their deaths, and the ages at which they died, data concerning educational backgrounds and previous occupations are incomplete. Consequently, we cannot correlate attitudes toward death and ways of thinking with either education or prior occupation, as we have done in our analysis of letters from student-soldiers and peasant-soldiers in the foregoing chapter. In the present chapter our analysis must focus on whether soldiers and civilians sentenced to death by the

[11] Monbushō Chōsa-kyoku (Research Bureau of the Ministry of Education), *Nihon no Seichō to Kyōiku* (*Japan's Growth and Education*), Tokyo, 1963, p. 57.

TABLE 17

PREVIOUS OCCUPATIONS OF WAR CRIMINALS

Occupation	No.
Professional soldier (assuming the graduates of military schools to be such)	92
Farmer	90
Civil servant	34
White-collar worker	26
Commercial or industrial worker	15
Policeman or prison guard	15
Doctor: military doctor (5) civilian doctor (5)	10
Teacher	6
Fisherman	4
Transportation worker	3
Priest	2
Barber	2
Not specified	402
Total	701

War Tribunal changed the motivations and ideologies inculcated in them by socialization in the Japanese army.

2. THEMES OF THE MESSAGES

The form and content of the messages are not uniform. Some are long, whereas others are as short as one or two poems. Most are not autobiographical and do not relate changes in the authors' thought and feelings before and after imprisonment. All that we can learn from most of the documents is the state of mind of the author shortly before his death. Thus we cannot discuss change or constancy in ideology and affects individually over extended intervals of time. This drawback does not, however, prevent a general comparison between the final stages of the ideologies and affects of the war criminals as revealed in their messages with the ideologies and affects that we can assume had been implanted in them by the Japanese army. The content and method of army socialization and the relationship structure of the army as an agent of socialization have been discussed in the preceding chapters. In this chapter we shall seek to determine how many of those condemned to death changed their ideas and affects and what types of change were involved.

There are at least three basic themes running throughout the messages of the 701 war criminals: discussions whether or not they actually felt guilty of the charges on which they were convicted, search for the meaning of their own deaths, and accounts of their primary concerns on the verge of death. Within the discussions of guilt five different responses can be distinguished: guilty, guilty of failing in duty to the Emperor, not guilty but responsible, not guilty, and no mention of guilt. The attitudes of the war criminals toward death and their primary concerns on the verge of death can be broken down into the following fourteen categories.

(1) The author thinks that the trial was unjust and that his death will be avenged by retribution on the victor nations who were his judges. ("Antitrial")

(2) The author considers his death as an act of loyalty to the Emperor. ("For the Emperor")

(3) The author considers his death a sacrifice for his community. ("Sacrifice")

(4) The author believes that after death his spirit will return to his fatherland and protect it throughout eternity. ("Immortality I")

(5) The author believes that after death his spirit will return to his family and protect them. ("Immortality II")

(6) The author achieves tranquility of mind in the face of approaching death through resignation to his "destiny," religious faith, or the appreciation of everyday experiences. ("Tranquility")

(7) The author expresses concern and love for his family. ("Family")

(8) The author writes to his family only about his innocence of the charges on which he was convicted. ("Not guilty")

(9) The author expresses his despair in facing death. ("Despair")

(10) The author regrets having become a soldier and expresses his wish that his children will choose jobs in fields other than the military and the civil service. ("Regrets")

(11) The author criticizes the Japanese army and the Japanese people who shared the characteristic attitudes of the military. ("Antimilitary")

(12) The author writes only about the sense of guilt he feels for his conduct in the war. ("Guilty")

(13) The author expresses his conviction that war should be eliminated in the world of the future. ("Antiwar")

(14) The author does not mention any of the items used in the classification. ("Irrelevant")

These fourteen categories can be grouped into three major classes. The individuals who fall under descriptions (1) through (8) either expressly endorsed Japan's war aims or at least did not expressly reject or criticize them. We call those who voiced these types of views "ever committed." Their previous commitment to the military ideology of wartime Japan did not shift. Individuals in groups (9) to (13) either explicitly criticized Japan's war aims or at least expressed regret for having participated in the war. Since holders of these views deviated from the military ideology, they are classified as "not ever committed." Category (14) represents the nonclassifiable, so called because their messages are irrelevant to the subject of our discussion.

The ever committed are grouped in items (1) through (8). Within this class the categories are arranged to indicate the degree of commitment to the ideology previously inculcated. The lower the number of the category, the higher the degree of commitment to the war ideology of the Japanese army. This arrangement of categories in descending order does not constitute a perfect Guttman scale, but examination of individual cases reveals that a person who was critical of the trial administered by the War Tribunal quite often expressed his conviction that his death was an act of loyalty to the Emperor. Similarly, a person who considered his death a sacrifice to the state would often write about his belief in his immortal spirit and its protection of his fatherland. He might also mention his concern for his family. In contrast, persons classified under the category "tranquility" or "family" never referred to their immortality. Thus, with respect to the ever committed, the organization of categories from the highest to the lowest degree of commitment *approximates* the cumulative quality that is required of a Guttman scale. In this limited sense, we shall talk about the degrees of commitment.

On the other hand, categories relating to the not ever committed, such as the despair of death, changes in personal view toward the army, the sense of guilt, and antiwar conviction, do *not* demonstrate a cumulative quality. Most of the not ever committed showed that they had deviated from the military ideology in at least one respect, although in other respects they often shared the attitudes of the ever committed. Thus the not ever committed in our typology of personality change can be classified as either the reversely committed, the deviant, the many-layered self, the conflicting self, or the innovator. The classification depends on the data available to substantiate the relationship between the elements of agreement and disagreement with the military ideology which each individual held.

Tables 18, 19, and 20 show the distribution of persons who were ever committed to the military ideology compared with those who in some respect deviated from it and with the non-

TABLE 18

ATTITUDES OF CONVICTED WAR CRIMINALS
THE EVER COMMITTED

	(1) Anti-trial	(2) For the Emperor	(3) Sacrifice	(4) Immor-tality I	(5) Immor-tality II	(6) Tran-quility	(7) Family	(8) Not guilty	Total
Guilty	0	0	0	0	0	0	0	0	0
Guilty to Emperor	0	3	0	0	0	0	0	0	3
Not guilty but responsible	0	7	3	1	3	3	6	3	26
Not guilty	61	29	124	67	31	51	35	12	410
Guilt not mentioned	1	8	35	12	14	69	32	0	171
Total	62	47	162	80	48	123	73	15	610
%	9.0	6.8	23.1	11.4	6.8	17.8	10.4	2.1	87.4

TABLE 19

ATTITUDES OF CONVICTED WAR CRIMINALS
THE NOT EVER COMMITTED

	(9) Despair	(10) Regrets	(11) Antimilitary	(12) Guilty	(13) Antiwar	Total
Guilty	0	0	2	13	0	15
Guilty to Emperor	0	0	0	0	0	0
Not guilty but responsible	0	0	0	0	1	1
Not guilty	7	4	7	0	16	34
Guilt not mentioned	4	2	1	0	7	14
Total	11	6	10	13	24	64
%	1.5	0.8	1.4	1.8	3.4	8.9

classifiable. Of those condemned to death, 87.4 percent were ever committed, whereas only 8.2 percent were not ever committed.

TABLE 20
ATTITUDES OF CONVICTED WAR CRIMINALS
THE NONCLASSIFIABLE

	(14) *Irrelevant*
Guilty	0
Guilty to the Emperor	0
Not guilty but responsible	0
Not guilty	2
Guilt not mentioned	25
Total	27
%	3.7

3. ATTITUDES TOWARD GUILT

The war criminals' differing reactions on the question of guilt are summarized in Table 21. The table shows that the majority of the war criminals sentenced to capital punishment by the International War Tribunal believed that they were not guilty. This circumstance was the result of a high degree of discommunication between the judges and the judged concerning the concept of war guilt.

It has been observed by American social scientists like Ruth Benedict that in traditional Japanese culture there was a sharp distinction between the concepts "shame," which is based on

TABLE 21
ATTITUDES OF WAR CRIMINALS TOWARD GUILT

	No.	*%*
Guilty	15	2.1
Guilty to the Emperor	3	0.4
Not guilty but responsible	27	3.8
Not guilty	446	62.8
Guilt not mentioned	210	30.9
Total	701	100.0

"external sanction," and "guilt," which is based on "internal sanction." And Japan, Benedict argues, had a "shame-culture" in contrast to Western culture, which she classifies as a "guilt-culture."[12] George DeVos criticizes this dichotomy as an oversimplified division between guilt and shame. He bases his argument on an analysis of empirical data taken from his study of a postwar Japanese village. DeVos likewise finds fault with the distinction made between shame and guilt in the work of Piers and Singer. They identify shame as the motivation related to the ego ideal that "demands achievement of a positive goal" and guilt as the motivation related to the superego that "inhibits and condemns transgression."

> Although the ego ideal is involved in Japanese strivings toward success, day-by-day hard work and purposeful activities leading to long-range goals are directly related to guilt feelings toward parents. . . .
>
> Nullification of parental expectations is one way to "hurt" a parent. As defined in this paper, guilt in the Japanese is essentially related either to an impulse to hurt, which may be implied in a contemplated act, or to the realization of having injured a love object toward whom one feels some degree of unconscious hostility.
>
> . . . If a parent has instilled in a child an understanding of his capacity to hurt by failing to carry out an obligation expected of him as a member of a family, any such failure can make him feel extremely guilty.[13]

It is, we can see, too simple to explain away the lack of the admission of guilt among the war criminals in terms of the absence of a concept of guilt among the Japanese. It was rather the type of reference person or group whose expectations the Japanese soldiers tried to live up to that determined whether they judged themselves "guilty" or "not guilty." Most of those who pleaded "not guilty" admitted that they were "guilty" of preceding their parents in death and thereby causing them deep grief. A major who claimed that he was not guilty of the massacre of nonbelligerents in Nanking wrote to his mother: "I have

---

[12] Ruth Benedict, *The Chrysanthemum and the Sword*, Boston, Houghton Mifflin, 1946, pp. 222-223.

[13] George DeVos, "The Relation of Guilt toward Parents to Achievement and Arranged Marriage among the Japanese," *Psychiatry: Journal for the Study of Interpersonal Processes*, xxiii, No. 3 (Aug. 1, 1960), p. 290.

accumulated many acts of filial impiety, and moreover, now I am adding to your burden the duty of nurturing your two grandsons. That is the most impious act of all. I deeply regret that I have to do this to you. Please pardon my guilt."[14]

How did the concept of guilt held by the majority of the soldiers of Japan differ from that established by the International War Tribunal?

In order to accept the concept of war guilt, it was necessary to assent to the following four basic assumptions. First, all wars of aggression are denounced by the Kellogg-Briand Pact; the war that Japan waged was a war of aggression; therefore, it should be denounced, if one is to abide by international law. This reasoning involves a judgment about the character of Japan's war against China and later against the United States and her allies. Those who endorsed Japan's war aim would deny that it was a war of aggression, whereas those opposed to it would agree that it was so at least partially. Unless one recognizes it as a war of aggression, one cannot properly conclude that those who participated in the war were guilty. Thus the war criminals who overtly or tacitly supported Japan's war aim did not believe themselves guilty, except for those who felt guilty for failing in their duty to the Emperor. This is not to say that all those who were critical of Japan's war aim considered themselves guilty. In order to arrive at that conclusion, one would have to accept also the following three assumptions.

Second, the concept of war guilt assumes that on the battlefield the individual soldier acts in the conscious awareness that he, as an individual and not simply as a member of a collectivity such as the state or the army, functions as the locus of decision-making (independent individualism). Third, it presupposes the existence of a reference group higher in the value hierarchy than the state to which the individual soldier refers in making his value judgment (universalism). The very terminology of "crimes against humanity" points to a reference group called humanity existing above and beyond the nation-state. Fourth, it takes for granted that the individual soldier has the choice of obeying or not obeying the order of his military superior (voluntarism).

Japanese army socialization indoctrinated men in an ideology based on principles directly contrary to the ideals upheld by the

[14] *Seiki no Isho*, p. 41.

War Tribunal. Japan's war against China and against the United States and her allies was "a sacred war of emancipation of Asians from Western imperialism." Soldiers were discouraged from thinking of the individual as the locus of judgment and encouraged to act as an integral part of the collectivity (dependent collectivism). Loyalty to the Emperor and to the state represented by him was the supreme value (particularism). In the Japanese army, ideally, the possibility of disobeying a superior's order was denied, although actually disobedience did occur. All orders issued by superiors were identified with the supreme command of the Emperor himself, and soldiers were thereby obliged to pledge absolute obedience to them (compulsion). If the individual soldier refused to obey, he would certainly be tried for treason and condemned to death.[15] Karl Jaspers, in his discussion of the war guilt of the Germans, contends:

> I who cannot act otherwise than as an individual am morally responsible for all my deeds, including the execution of political and military orders. It is never simply true that "orders are orders." . . . so every deed remains subject to moral judgment.[16]

Jaspers, assuming that the individual is the locus of decision-making, asserts that, even when the individual is acting in accordance with his superior's order, it is actually possible for him to use his discretion either to aggravate or to mitigate the degree of inhumanity involved in the execution of the order. Thus we can argue that even in the most rigidly regimented army, such as the Japanese army was, there actually existed alternatives for individual soldiers to choose, either to execute orders with varying degrees of pain or to risk their own lives in an outright refusal.

The war criminals tried before the International Military Tribunal were exposed to conflicting ideologies and principles

[15] According to the statistics collected by Kunisaku Kikuchi from *Rikugun Nenpō* (*The Army Annals*) from 1920 to 1937, there were 4,702 cases (each case may involve more than one soldier) of soldiers who were court-martialed for using violence against their superior officers, disobeying their orders, organizing themselves for rebellions, rioting, escaping from the army, etc. During the same period 1,210 cases of suicide in the army were reported. See Kikuchi, "Tennōseika no Guntai ni okeru Itan" ("Heresy in the Army under the Emperor System"), *Misuzu*, Nov. 1964, pp. 2-13, 47.

[16] Karl Jaspers, *The Question of German Guilt*, tr. E. B. Ashton, New York, The Dial Press, 1947, pp. 31-32.

of socialization. The ideology in which they had previously
been indoctrinated was war oriented and was founded primarily on the principles of dependent collectivism, particularism, and compulsion. In contrast, the ideology which the International War Tribunal ideally stood for was peace oriented and
was based on the principles of independence, universalism, and
voluntarism. That the majority of the war criminals felt no guilt
demonstrates that their ideological orientation and principles
did not change because of their imprisonment or the pronounce-
ment of the death sentence.

A superior private in the navy gives an account of why he
pleaded not guilty:

> I was sentenced to death for carrying out my superior's
> order in suppressing the movements for independence in the
> island of Borneo where I was stationed as a member of the
> Special Police Force of the Navy. . . . As for this incident, I
> did not act out of my personal interests, but for the sake of
> the Empire, in conscientiously executing my duty in absolute
> obedience to the order of my superior. I swear by heaven,
> earth and the gods that I am not ashamed of myself. . . . I do
> not care what others may say, since I did my best to serve my
> country. I am sure that only gods know this.[17]

An army general states that within the armed forces of any
country obedience to the order of one's superior is a matter of
course, and he continues that, "if the content of the order is
wrong, responsibility rests with the authorities of the army and
navy and with the government, but not with the individual
recipient of the order."[18]

According to the logic of the above quotations, it is not the
recipients of orders who are responsible for the acts committed
in executing them but rather the authorities who issue them.
What, then, were the attitudes of the wartime leaders concerning
their responsibilities? Hideki Tōjō, the army general and wartime prime minister, wrote:

> As a man responsible for the waging of the war, I deeply
> regret that the war ended with our defeat. Personally I am
> not disturbed by my death penalty. However, my responsibility
> to my countrymen is so deep that I cannot fulfill it even with
> my death. However, I pleaded not guilty with reference to

[17] *Seiki no Isho*, p. 176.   [18] *Ibid.*, p. 313.

international crimes. I still insist on this point. I was forced
to surrender. . . . I deeply regret what I have done and apologize to the Emperor and to my countrymen. Ideally, the
Japanese army should have acted in accordance with the
benevolent will of his Majesty. But actually there were some
in the army who committed blunders. I regret that our Japanese army suffered from misunderstanding in the outside
world on account of those blunders.[19]

Tōjō, for one, was absolutely clear about the reference group
to which he was responsible. To the Emperor and his countrymen represented by him, Tōjō admitted his responsibility. But
he did not acknowledge responsibility toward any outgroup
members. His concept of responsibility, then, was particularistic
in its group reference. Moreover, he asserted that he was responsible for Japan's *defeat* in the war but not for having waged the
war itself. He still believed in the righteousness of Japan's war
aim.

So it is possible, as Tōjō's declaration makes clear, to deny
one's guilt while at the same time admitting responsibility. Most
of those who pleaded not guilty but recognized their responsibility fall into this pattern and are thus classified among the
ever committed, since they did not change their basic belief in
Japan's war aim.

Finally, a distinction has to be made between those who admitted that they were guilty and those who conceded merely
that they were guilty toward the Emperor. A subofficer in the
gendarmerie writes about the atrocities committed by him and
the soldiers under his command:

> We did not act according to our own will. We respected
> our order and acted out of our sense of duty and the sincere
> desire to do service to our country. . . . However, we should
> admit that this incident violated the true nature of the sacred
> war. Someone ought to atone for the sin in order to purify
> the stain. I only wish to beg His Majesty's pardon for having
> inflicted pain upon Him. I deserve to die ten thousand times
> for that crime.[20]

It is characteristic of those confessing guilt toward the Emperor
that they endorsed Japan's war aim and that their group reference was particularistic. It should also be noted that the three

[19] *Ibid.*, p. 683.   [20] *Ibid.*, p. 101.

who felt guilty toward the Emperor also believed that their deaths were a form of atonement for having failed the Emperor.

In contrast, those who confessed guilt fall into two groups. First, there are those who acknowledged their guilt without specifying what they did or against whom they did it. A sublieutenant in the navy writes:

> Upon reflection, I am terrified at the thought of the spiritual and internal sins I have committed up till now. I am tortured by my reflection on the law of retribution. I am ready to accept the just judgment of heaven and to atone for my sin with my death.[21]

Second, there are those who specified what they did or to whom they should apologize. A sergeant in the gendarmerie repented his crimes on his death bed in a hospital after being sentenced to twenty years of imprisonment:

> Reflecting in tranquility upon my past, I realize that I treated nonbelligerents cruelly. . . . The only thing I can do now is to pray for the repose of the souls of the victims of the incidents in which I was involved. Now that is the only way open to me to atone for my sins.[22]

In both instances these soldiers granted that they were, as individuals, responsible for what they did. In that sense they accepted the principles of independence of judgment and voluntarism. Both of them admitted their guilt toward the victims, members of a group outside of their own society. In that sense their group reference was universalistic. Yet none of those who admitted guilt referred specifically to their attitude toward Japan's war aim or toward any future war. Hence, even those who agreed that they were guilty of war crimes did not live up to the expectation of the War Tribunal, which assumed that, if these men recognized their guilt, they would change from a war-oriented ideology to a peace-oriented one. It should be added that six out of the fifteen who confessed guilt were civilians, who may not have received any formal military socialization.

The International War Tribunal as an agency of adult resocialization established in theory a new concept of war guilt, but actually it failed to get this concept across to the majority of the Japanese war criminals.

[21] *Ibid.*, p. 424.   [22] *Ibid.*, p. 166.

4. THE EVER COMMITTED

Criticism of the Trial ("Antitrial")

Out of the sixty-two who criticized the War Tribunal, thirteen persons specifically protested that the charges against them were false. All of them belonged to the war criminal classes B and C. Let us cite two of these claims of false charges. A sergeant major in the gendarmerie, sentenced to death in the Dutch East Indies in 1948, protested:

> I regret that I was mistakenly identified as the criminal. The actual criminal had already returned to Japan before the investigation of the murder case. . . . Those who were accomplices in the case were not called to the court. Moreover, we are under the order of our superiors in the gendarmes not to tell the truth about the incident.
>
> At the trial, I admitted straightforwardly what I had actually done. I had been prepared to accept the just punishment of erroneous acts I had actually committed. However, to be accused falsely as the criminal in a most atrocious murder case is something I cannot possibly accept. . . . My friend Kihara tried to expose the facts of the incident, and I was extremely grateful to him. However, his good intentions were suppressed by the order of our superior officers.[23]

A similar travesty of justice was reported by a civilian working for the army who was also executed in the Dutch East Indies:

> When Captain Numata and Sergeant Major Okamura of the gendarmes were dispatched to K Island for the investigation of espionage activities among the natives, they did not have their own interpreter. Thus I was temporarily assigned to them to serve as their interpreter. . . . I went with them with a company of infantrymen to four villages on the island. . . . Since both Numata and Okamura were newcomers on the Island, the natives did not know their names. However, since I had been stationed on the Island, my name was known among them. Besides, I was present all the time when both Numata and Okamura investigated the natives under arrest. After Japan's defeat, the natives gave my name, instead of Numata and Okamura, as being responsible for their maltreatment. . . .

[23] *Ibid.*, pp. 201-202.

At the trial, both Numata and Okamura declared that they knew nothing of the arrest and the maltreatment of the natives. The trial resulted in the death penalty for myself and Okamura while Numata received a sentence of only ten years' imprisonment. This is contrary to our common sense. Had we been tried under Japanese law, Numata, the commander and prosecutor, should certainly have received the heaviest punishment. . . .[24]

The quotations show that these two persons considered themselves victims of a double injustice. They felt that they had been betrayed by their former superiors in the Japanese army and at the same time had not been given fair treatment by the allied forces. Tsuneharu Tsukuba, who made a full examination of the records of the trials of all the war criminals, testifies that many of the war criminals of classes B and C did in fact suffer such twofold injustices. Their trials were accorded much less time and care than those of the class A criminals.[25]

Twenty-four of the sixty-two who criticized the War Tribunal specifically expressed their wish to be revenged on the country which sentenced them to death. Most of them defined the War Tribunal as an instrument of vengeance.

Were all the wartime activities of the allied forces justifiable in the light of international law? The use of atomic bombs that killed several hundred thousands of nonbelligerent women and children, the atrocious murder at Guadalcanal, the bombing of hospital ships—why are such acts by the allied forces not punished? . . . The law under which war crimes were punished is the arbitrary law of the victors. And the War Tribunal is the agent of vengeance exercised by the allied powers under the name of Law.[26]

This criticism points to the existence of discrepancies between the ideal pattern of principles expressed in the terms of reference of the International War Tribunal and the actual conduct of the victorious nations both in war and in the postwar trials. These discrepancies were major factors in promoting the belief among the war criminals that the trials were unjust and constituted acts of vengeance. If the allied forces took revenge upon them,

[24] *Ibid.*, p. 245.
[25] *Nihon no Hyakunen* (*A Hundred Years of Japan*), ed. Shunsuke Tsurumi et al., Tokyo, Chikuma Shobō, 1961, I, 67-69.
[26] *Seiki no Isho*, p. 484.

they reasoned, the allies in their turn should be punished. A lieutenant general in the army declared:

> After my physical death, my true spirit will soar in the sky and will never rest until it achieves its revenge for Japan's defeat. . . . The reconstruction of our Emperor's country will require the destruction of America and the conquest of China. As long as our country is under pressure either from America or from China, its rehabilitation will fall short of the realization of Greater Japan's world destiny. The reconstruction of our Empire in its true sense means victory in this war of revenge. I want you to reflect on this matter seriously and deeply. In this sense, even though I die, I want my spirit to be even more active than before. The more people agree with my intention, the more active my immortal spirit will become.[27]

In these appeals to posterity for the execution of vengeance, the traditional samurai mores of vendetta (*katakiuchi*) were frequently invoked.[28]

The divergence of the actual from the ideal in the actions of the Tribunal was pointed out not only by the war criminals themselves but by critics in the victor nations. Among Americans, Senator Robert Taft and Supreme Court Justice William O. Douglas were especially forthright and penetrating in their criticism.[29] Moreover, one of the judges of the Tokyo Tribunal, the representative of India, Radhabinod M. Pal, drew up a voluminous minority opinion in which he claimed that none of the defendants were guilty and recommended that they all be released immediately, since the spirit of vengeance that prevailed in the Tribunal was not conducive to thought. He maintained that the people should be left to themselves to search

[27] *Ibid.*, p. 51. This is a part of the general's own explanation of the poem he composed just before he was executed. It can be translated as follows: "In Kwantung, my transient body may fall, high in the sky will soar, the valiant spirit of mine."

[28] *Katakiuchi*, in which the close relatives or the retainers of the one who has been slain were under the obligation to kill the offender, was legally recognized during the Edo period. After the early eighteenth century, instances of *katakiuchi* increased among *chōnin* and peasants while they decreased among samurai. It was not until 1880 that this custom was entirely banned by the law. *Sekai Dai Hyakka Jiten* (*The Great World Encyclopaedia*), Tokyo, Heibonsha, 1959, v, 418.

[29] John F. Kennedy, *Profiles in Courage*, New York, Harper and Brothers, 1956, pp. 216, 218.

for their own way to overcome the ignorance and avarice that
had led them into the terror of war.[30]

Masajiro Takikawa, who served as a lawyer for some of the
defendants in the Tokyo Tribunal, commented on the discrimination he had encountered as a Japanese lawyer at the Tribunal:

> The drama of the Tokyo Tribunal was planned to present
> a façade showing that the prosecutors and lawyers acted on
> the basis of fair play. Therefore, the lawyers of the defeated
> nation should have been treated deferentially. In fact, we
> were treated as the equals of the American lawyers as long as
> we were on the stage, the court. But as soon as we were back
> stage, we were discriminated against. . . . The Japanese law-
> yers were allowed to use neither the main entrance [to the
> building where the trials took place], nor even the side entrance
> where the defendants entered. We had to use either the back
> entrance or the side entrance to the basement in order to go
> to our offices. . . . . The lawyers' offices were on the first and
> second floors. The American lawyers' offices were mostly on
> the second floor, whereas the Japanese lawyers' offices were
> on the first floor. . . . And these were typical features of the
> theatrical arrangement of the Tokyo Tribunal.[31]

Takikawa's observation points up the discrepancy between the
ideal principles of egalitarianism and universalism and the
actual hierarchical and particularistic character of the relationship between the lawyers of the allied nations and the Japanese
lawyers, and he sees this as a symbol of the whole structure of
the Tribunal.

Thus both the war criminals themselves and a variety of outside observers, both American and Japanese, were united in the
recognition that a gap separated the ideal and actual structures
of the Tribunal. Ideally, the Tribunal aimed at establishing the
principles of rationalism, universalism, independent individualism, and voluntarism. But, actually, the structure of the relationship between the socializers (the trial authorities) and the
socializees (the defendants) was nonrational insofar as it was
based on vengeance rather than justice, particularistic because
the concept of war crimes was applied only to the defeated
nations, and dependently collectivistic because of the failure of

---

[30] *Tokyo Saiban* contains the translation of Pal's statement on pp. 345-935.

[31] Masajirō Takikawa, *Tokyo Saiban o Sabaku (My Judgment of the Tokyo Tribunal)*, Tokyo, Tōwasha, 1952, pp. 11-13.

the judges to examine each case carefully to ascertain whether individual soldiers had acted blindly in conformity with the orders of superiors. In some instances those who had tried to save their enemies or prisoners of war contrary to orders were sentenced to death by the Tribunal for having used their own independent judgment. The actual relationship between the trial authorities and the defendants was predominantly compulsory, as any court situation demands. The affect socialization used in the trial and during imprisonment relied mainly on negative affects, in which distress, anger, fear, and shame were maximized. Some war criminals reported that they were even subjected to violence and torture by the local police during the term of their imprisonment.[32]

The actual structure of the relationship and the type of affect socialization employed by the War Tribunal were contributing factors in driving the sixty-two war criminals who had been classified as having "antitrial" attitudes into more intensified commitment to the Japanese military ideology. The Tribunal's attempt to resocialize produced the opposite effect.

Death for the Sake of the Emperor ("Emperor")

Types (2) through (7) of the ever committed exhibit the variety of meanings which those sentenced tried to see in their deaths. The choice to them was not between life and death but between a meaningless death, "a dog's death" (*inujini*), and a death becoming a man. Many of the accused wrote that "I do not want to die a dog's death" or "my death is not a dog's death." The desire to die a man's death involved two considerations. First, one's death should be meaningful; that is, one should die for some purpose. Second, it was best to die in "a good style" (*migotoni* or *rippani*). The first point pertains to the ethics of death, the second to the aesthetics of death. These two aspects are inseparable in the sense that, in order to die in a good style, one has to convince oneself that one's death is in some sense meaningful. Emphasis on one or the other, of course, may vary from person to person.

Forty-seven persons, according to our classification, openly avowed that they were dying for the sake of the Emperor (category 2). Since our classification assumes a cumulative quality, we can add to this number those who criticized the trial as unjust and reaffirmed the righteousness of Japan's war aims

[32] *Seiki no Isho*, pp. 178-179, 187-188, 232.

(category 1). Thus 15.8 percent out of 701 persons believed they were dying for the sake of the Emperor. Considering that this concept of death was central in army socialization, this percentage is extremely low.

Among those who were manifestly committed to the belief in death for the sake of the Emperor, two different types may be distinguished. The first type represents those who believed in Emperor worship and acted in conformity with it. The second type comprises those who actually lost faith in the Emperor after Japan's defeat but pretended in their messages that they still believed in the Emperor system and acted accordingly until the very last. One such person was a sergeant major in the gendarmerie who was critical of the military.

> The education for death which we received in the past does not work here. . . . M, a day before his execution, wistfully admitted that, although he did not really want to shout out *banzai* [ten thousand years' life or three cheers for the Emperor], he felt he should do so for the sake of his family, lest they suffer for his failure to live up to the ideal pattern of conduct expected from a soldier. He was quoted as saying, before he left for the execution field, that he would not give *banzai* for the Emperor.[33]

The writer claims that there were many who conformed in behavior to the ideology of Emperor worship even though they did not believe in it. This type of behavior is close to what Robert Merton calls "ritualism."[34] It is difficult to be certain how many of those who wrote and acted in keeping with the ideology of Emperor worship were actually "ritualist," rather than "conformist." It is quite conceivable, however, that at least some of those whom we classify as ever committed to the Emperor ideology were ritualist. As the sergeant major points out, some of them might have shouted *banzai* to the Emperor from fear of retributive social sanctions against their families. Keiichi Sakuda,

[33] *Ibid.*, p. 458.

[34] Robert Merton defines "ritualism" as a mode of individual adaptation in which the individual rejects prevailing values but "continues to abide almost compulsively by institutional norms." "Conformity" is defined as the acceptance of both cultural goals and institutionalized means. Robert Merton, *Social Theory and Social Structure*, Glencoe, Ill., The Free Press, 1951, pp. 140, 150. According to Irving Rosow's typology of socialization, "conformity in behavior [despite the rejection in values], out of expedience or of self-interest" is classified as "Chameleon." Irving Rosow, "Forms and Functions of Adult Socialization" (MS), Russell Sage Foundation, 1963, pp. 6-8.

who has made a sociological analysis of the messages of the war criminals, suggests another motivation for the ritualistic *banzais* of some war criminals. According to him, the utterance of three cheers for the Emperor was "a form of protest against" a Tribunal which they considered unjust.[35]

Death as a Sacrifice for One's Community ("Sacrifice")

According to Table 18, there are 162 persons in this category. Since our classification is a cumulative one, most of those who belong to "antitrial" and "Emperor" categories also described their death as a sacrifice. The point at which these three types diverge is their attitude toward the war. Those who emphasized their "antitrial" sentiment regarded the trial as a continuation of the war and, consequently, beseeched their posterity to carry on the war against their enemies for the sake of avenging their deaths. For those who viewed their deaths as expressions of loyalty to the Emperor, the situation was defined by the Emperor, and they were ready to accept whatever definition of the situation he gave. Since the Emperor accepted unconditional surrender to the allied powers, they too accepted Japan's defeat. Those who fall into this category urged their posterity to be loyal to the Emperor. This attitude implied that, if the Emperor were to declare war, their posterity would be bound to obey his order to fight again. In contrast, those who come under the category "sacrifice" accepted the Imperial edict of surrender but did not specifically encourage their posterity to obey the Emperor. Instead, they looked upon the situation after the defeat as requiring the people to work for the rehabilitation of their own community or nation. In army socialization the Emperor and Japanese society were identified, but an examination of the writings of these soldiers shows that, for them, the identification was not complete. Some emphasized the importance of the Emperor, while others emphasized the community of their countrymen, the Japanese. The former spoke of their loyalty to the Emperor as a person, while the latter felt more loyalty to the community of the Japanese people. Whether or not this split in reference was latent before the defeat and

[35] Keiichi Sakuda, "Shi to no Wakai—Senpan Keibotsusha no Ibun ni Arawareta Nihonjin no Sekinin no Ronri" ("Rapprochement with Death—The Logic of Responsibility of the Japanese as It Appeared in the Messages of the War Criminals Convicted to Death"), *Tenbō*, No. 72 (Dec. 1964), p. 64.

became manifest only afterward cannot be empirically verified. It is sufficient here to note that the difference between those classified under the category "Emperor" and those under the category "sacrifice" lies in the reference points of their loyalty.

Sakuda, in his analysis of the messages of the war criminals, groups them into four classes according to the attitudes they express toward death: "death as a sacrifice," "death as the achievement of solidarity with the dead," "death as atonement for one's sin," and "death as natural death."[36] Although our classification is different, this particular category, "death as a sacrifice," overlaps with his. "Death as a sacrifice" can be defined as an attitude which sees the meaning of one's death in sacrifice "for the sake of the future development of one's own group and its members."[37]

This is the attitude a first lieutenant in the navy expressed:

I deeply regret that I am going to be executed because of a false accusation. However, if Japan, after her acceptance of unconditional surrender, is to preserve her national polity, retain her territory, and save her people from annihilation, *reparation by blood* is necessary. Carrying this deep in my mind, I am willing to *sacrifice* myself as a part of that reparation. I want my parents, brothers, wife, and children to understand the thought and feelings with which I am going to die.[38]

A sublieutenant in the navy held a similar view:

Although I am not guilty, I am going to die with serenity, taking upon myself all the sins of others, as the commander responsible for my company and for the rebirth of the Japanese nation. I am happy to *sacrifice* myself to neutralize the evil feelings of the allied powers toward my country.[39]

A sergeant in the gendarmes explained:

Our country has lost the war. That is why those who are not guilty are put to death. I consider myself as a *human pillar* [*hitobashira*] for the reconstruction of our Emperor's domain.[40]

This image was echoed in the statement of a sergeant major in the army.

[36] *Ibid.*, pp. 55-69.   [37] *Ibid.*, p. 61.   [38] *Seiki no Isho*, p. 39.
[39] *Ibid.*, p. 406.   [40] *Ibid.*, p. 76.

I am a noncommissioned officer and as inconsequential as a bit of dust compared to generals and admirals. . . . Nevertheless, I happened to be chosen to play an important role as a war criminal. The responsibilities for this abominable war lie with our eighty million countrymen, especially with the military leaders and the politicians. However, I, the infinitesimally insignificant being, am forced into a position of high responsibility, namely, that of atoning for their sin. . . . My five-foot body is going to be a *corner stone* [*suteishi*] of peace. Without this *corner stone* there will be no peaceful Japan. I am happy to prepare the way for world peace.[41]

In these passages phrases like "blood reparation," "human sacrifice," and "human pillar," stand out. Sakuda relates "blood reparation" and "human sacrifice" to the ancient customs of clan society. Whenever a member of a clan A was injured by a member of another clan B, clan A would demand a human sacrifice as a reparation from the members of clan B. Any one of the members of clan B could be chosen as the human sacrifice—whether or not he was the offender. The war criminals' belief in death can be thus interpreted as the survival of ancient custom.[42]

The idea of death as a sacrifice for one's community involves, first, a strategy of action to achieve empirical ends (the rehabilitation of Japan and the Japanese) with nonempirical means (the use of human sacrifice). In that sense, by definition, it is a nonrational action or, more specifically, a "methodologically arational" action.[43] Second, for the realization of this idea the locus of judgment and action does not lie in the individual but in the group. The individual is supposedly chosen as a sacrifice not for his own achievement (in this case, misdemeanor) but for his ascription (his membership in the community). Third, the referent of this idea is particularistic, since the ends of the action relate only to the particular nation-state to which the actor belongs.

In its nonrationality, dependent collectivism, and particularism, this idea of death as a sacrifice for one's community shared the patterns of value characteristic of the Japanese army ideology. It did, however, deviate somewhat from the army

[41] *Ibid.*, p. 637.   [42] Sakuda, "Shi to no Wakai," pp. 62-63.
[43] See Marion J. Levy, Jr., *The Structure of Society*, Princeton, Princeton University Press, 1952, pp. 243-244.

ideology. According to that ideology, death was the final act of loyalty to the Emperor. In that sense, those who are classified under the category "Emperor" were closer in their views to the military ideology than those classified under the category "sacrifice." The principle the latter employed to give meaning to death was derived from the customs and ideas that belonged to the clan society. For that matter, that principle is more ancient even than the principle of vengeance which those classified under the category "antitrial" used, since the latter was derived from the Edo feudal period.

Belief in Immortality and Rebirth ("Immortality I and II")

The attitude toward death most frequently found among the ever committed was the belief that the spirit, even if one died on foreign soil, would return immediately to Japan to protect the fatherland (*sokoku*) or the families of the dead. According to Table 18, eighty men stated that their spirits would return to their fatherland ("Immortality I"), and forty-eight said they would return to the family ("Immortality II"). Twelve of those classified under "Immortality I" also declared that their spirits would protect their families. Thirty-six individuals in the categories "antitrial," "Emperor," and "sacrifice" asserted that their spirits would return to protect their fatherland; seventeen wrote that their spirits would return to protect their families. Thus, of the 610 who were described as ever committed, 181 expressed their belief that their spirits, after their physical death, would return to watch over either their fatherland or their families or both.

Of that number, twenty-nine acknowledged the belief defined as "Immortality I," using the cliché "to be reborn seven times to do service to my country." This hackneyed expression was derived from the story of Masashige Kusunoki (1294-1336), a loyal retainer of the Emperor Godaigo, who is said to have prophesied before his death in the battle of Minatogawa that he would be "reborn seven times to do service to my country." Masashige and his son Masatsura were frequently mentioned as heroes in national textbooks between 1898 and 1945.[44] During the war years until 1945, the Kusunoki were cited not only in the schools but also on public occasions as national heroes who exemplified the union of loyalty to the Emperor and filial piety.

[44] See Tomitarō Karasawa, *Kyōkasho no Rekishi* (*History of Textbooks*), Tokyo, Sōbunsha, 1956, pp. 280, 672-673.

Those who used this exact wording were thus repeating what we have termed "ceremonial language," which embodies the ideal pattern to which one is committed.[45]

Others among the war criminals expressed the concepts of immortality and rebirth in "daily language," which stands for the actual pattern of one's ideas and affects. A sergeant in the gendarmerie writes: "My soul [*tamashii*] will surely live in the bosom of my father. As long as the Family of Nakamura [his family name] continues, and as long as my fatherland Japan persists, my soul will continue to live."[46] This person, it is interesting to note, was baptized as a Christian while in prison. In the same message he declares that, since he has been baptized, his immortality in heaven is assured. Evidently he did not recognize the discrepancy between the Christian concept of immortality, which is universalistic, and his concept of immortality as expressed above, which is particularistic, limited in time and space to his own family and his own country and to their continuation. Many other war criminals voiced similar views which displayed a mixture of components from various religions, such as Buddhism, Shintoism, Christianity, and Japanese folk beliefs. They put logically incompatible religious beliefs together, without worrying about inconsistencies.

Here again we find examples of Levy's "nonexclusivist" attitude toward religion.[47] A corporal in the army writes: "My soul will return exactly to the spot in our backyard where I used to sing songs, looking down upon the sea."[48] An army sergeant assures his wife:

> My death, I have realized, is an eternal return to your heart. . . . As soon as my body is dead, I shall be able to live eternally in your soul. . . . You ought not to remain a widow. I sincerely hope that you will develop your new life and find happiness in it. . . . I will protect you always whatever happens to you. . . . I do not need any grave. I do not want any funeral or commemoration rituals to be performed. I am now on my way to the other world (the pure land) which assures me a happier life than you will have in this world.[49]

[45] Kunio Yanagida, "Kokugo no Shōrai" ("The Future of the Japanese Language"), *Yanagida Kunio Shū*, Tokyo, Chikuma Shobō, 1963, XIX, 31-34.

[46] *Seiki no Isho*, p. 136.

[47] Levy makes a distinction between exclusivist religion and nonexclusivist religion. See *Modernization and the Structure of Societies*, Princeton, Princeton University Press, 1966, I, 346.

[48] *Seiki no Isho*, p. 240.   [49] *Ibid.*, p. 629.

This passage exhibits a nonexclusivist religious attitude, too. The concept of "the pure land" is Buddhist, while the idea of "the eternal return" to the heart of the beloved is Western romanticism of the sort expressed in the legend of Tristan and Isolde, merged with the Japanese folk belief that one's soul will protect one's family.

Many passages can be cited to illustrate the belief in immortality and rebirth. Three will suffice here. A sergeant major in the gendarmerie states confidently:

> I am assured of rebirth. When a boy is born to my brother Toshikame, please name him Hideo after me and look upon him as you looked upon me.[50]

A lieutenant in the army asks:

> . . . how could those ex-soldiers who dedicated their lives to the Emperor and became the protective spirits of their country sleep in repose, confronted with this deplorable unconditional surrender? . . . The people who survived, for better or for worse, until the termination of the war, ought to live in the company of those spirits who sacrificed their lives for them. Several of these noble spirits must be dwelling in every Japanese survivor.
>
> All the survivors should embrace the spirit of the heroes who died for them, inherit their aspirations, and exert their best effort to reconstruct the fatherland, at the expense of their private life.[51]

An army captain confesses:

> Reading the books of some dead authors, I sometimes feel as though they were alive. In the same way I feel that after my physical death, I too shall be tied to some corner of this earth. . . . If anything remains after death, what is it like? Everybody says it is soul or spirit. Then what kind of soul or spirit will I become? I have not yet asked that question of anyone. If I did, people would laugh at me. So I thought it out myself. I now hope that wherever my spirit goes it will have power to make the melancholy joyful, to bring peace among warring men, and to restrain men from doing evil.[52]

The referents to whom and for whom the spirit is to be reborn differ in these passages. In the first, the referent is a member

---

[50] *Ibid.*, p. 386. [51] *Ibid.*, p. 308. [52] *Ibid.*, p. 409.

of the writer's own family. In the second, the reference group is the nation-state, and the purpose of rebirth is national reconstruction. The negation of enjoyment in private life for the sake of the community is stressed. Of the three, this passage comes closest to the military ideology in its particularism and in its emphasis on negative affects. In the third, the national boundary of the reference group is not specified. It can be any place "on the globe." The writer also places importance upon the function of "his spirit" as a provider of joy and peace. The third quotation thus deviates from the military ideology in its universalism and its emphasis on positive affects.

Despite these varieties of referents and functions of the spirit, there is a considerable consensus among the war criminals on the reality of the immortality of their spirits. Kunio Yanagida comments on the characteristic pattern of the Japanese belief in immortality and rebirth:

> According to Buddhism, each departed member of the family is given a *kaimyō*, Buddhist name, which is written on a tablet [of the family altar]. This suggests that, according to Buddhism, the separate individuality is retained permanently after one's physical death. According to the Japanese folk belief, however, the departed spirit of the ancestor loses its individuality and is fused into the oneness of the ancestral spirit of the family, thirty-three years after one's death. . . .
>
> The Buddhist scripture, cited by priests at the funeral, endeavors to drive the departed soul from this world as quickly as possible to the Buddhist heaven, whereas people try to have the spirit of their ancestors remain as close to them as possible permanently.[53]

Yanagida goes on to expound four features of this belief:

> First, they believed that the spirit of the dead remained on this land of Japan permanently; second, they believed that the traffic between the living and the dead was so frequent that the spirit of the dead might be invoked at any time, and not just on the special occasions of the two major festivals, *bon* and the New Year; third, they believed that the unrealized aspirations of men could be achieved after death; fourth, many of them believed that not only could the unfin-

[53] Kunio Yanagida, "Senzo no Hanashi" ("The Story of Ancestors"), *Yanagida Kunio Shū*, 1962, x, 77-116.

ished task of a dead man be carried out by his posterity, but he himself might be reborn several times, if necessary, to complete the task he had set out to perform.[54]

Yanagida points out that this belief in rebirth differs from the Buddhist concept of "the transmigration of the soul," according to which a man may not necessarily be reborn in a human form.[55] The form in which he is reborn is determined by his *karma*. Yanagida insists that the Japanese folk belief in life after death should be distinguished from Buddhism, especially in its belief in "closeness and communicability" between the dead and the living:

> We do not know how old this belief in the ancestral spirit remaining on this land of ours to protect their posterity and make them prosper may be. But it is important to note that the cosmopolitan idea of Buddhism, which preached that the departed soul would leave this land to go to some faraway place which did not belong within any national boundary, was very strange to the Japanese people. Surrounded by nations who believed the other world to be far away and cut off from them, and in spite of long years of Buddhist influence, the Japanese alone retained their belief in the closeness and accessibility of the departed spirits of their ancestors.[56]

According to Yanagida, then, solidarity between the dead and the living and the possibility of dialogue between them are the central themes of the indigenous folk belief among the Japanese. The examination of the messages of the war criminals demonstrates that these beliefs were still widely held among the generation educated before and during the war.

"Tranquility"

Table 18 shows that there were 123 men who wrote that they had attained tranquility of mind through some means or other. They were primarily concerned with the style, rather than the purpose, of death. Three major avenues to serenity of mind were mentioned. Thirty-three said that they were "resigned to their destiny (*unme*)" or "to Heaven's will [*tenmei*]"—resignation being a traditional attitude of passive acceptance of what-

---

[54] *Ibid.*, p. 120.   [55] *Ibid.*, p. 144.
[56] Kunio Yanagida, "Tamashii no Yukue" ("Where Our Soul Goes"), *ibid.*, 1963, xv, 561.

ever is imposed upon individuals by authority. Thirty-one asserted that they had found peace of mind while in prison by acquiring a religious faith like Buddhism or Christianity. Twenty-four remarked that they had achieved serenity of mind through the appreciation of everyday experience. And the remaining four persons maintained that they were consoled by the thought that they were not alone and that many of their fighting companions were already dead and others were going to die with them.

Most of these ways of achieving tranquility of mind are easily understood. Appreciation of daily experiences, however, needs to be discussed further.

A lieutenant general in the army expresses his serenity in a poem:

> Quiet is the prison
> On a rainy day;
> I was painting
> A red dahlia.[57]

A corporal in the gendarmerie composes a *haiku* verse:

> Having washed
> My prisoner's uniform
> I looked up and saw
> A solitary kite.[58]

An army colonel writes:

> Joyous is the meal time
> For the one confined
> To a cell.[59]

A corporal in the army attests to the peace of mind some of the condemned had attained: "The three officers [who were going to be executed within twenty minutes] join us in our daily exercise routine done to the accompaniment of radio music. What a splendid composure!"[60]

The war criminals left behind many poems of different kinds —the Japanese traditional short verse of *kaiku* and *tanka*, Chinese poetry (*kanshi*), and modern free verse—about natural objects and about their daily life in the prison. The meticulous execution and the intense appreciation of the minute and trivial

---

[57] *Seiki no Isho*, p. 678.
[58] *Ibid.*, p. 156.   [59] *Ibid.*, p. 94.   [60] *Ibid.*, p. 738.

details of everyday life became for some ultimate ends in themselves. In that sense, they were able to serve as a functional
equivalent for religion.[61] This sort of transformation is described
as a characteristic of the Japanese tradition of the recluse by
Shūichi Katō in his story of Jōzan Ishikawa (1584-1672).[62]

All these means—resignation, religion, the appreciation of
daily life, the feeling of solidarity—were summoned up by the
war criminals for the achievement of a manly death. A sergeant
major of the gendarmerie asserted forthrightly:

> Although I am going to be executed, I shall die with a free
> conscience. I have not injured anybody, contrary to the testi-
> mony of the trial. But don't misunderstand me, I am not
> begging you to acquit me. . . . You should observe with atten-
> tion how we face our death, and how we die.
>
> Having said this to my prosecutor, I grinned at him. He
> looked so embarrassed that it seemed he was almost going to
> cry.[63]

A sergeant in the gendarmerie was reported to have asked
the priest who accompanied him to the execution field, pointing
to the river on his way: "Where does this river flow?"[64] The
condemned man's last words may be interpreted as a sign of
the composure he had attained in the face of death. These soldiers considered this style of manly or "soldierly death" as a
method of protesting what they considered to be the unjust
deaths to which the allies had sentenced them.

5. The Not Ever Committed

"Despair" and "Regrets": The Deviant

None of the eleven persons classified under "despair" criticized
the military or Japan's war aims, although all appear to have
deviated from the Japanese army socialization in their overt
expression of despair at the thought of death. Their conduct
revealed that with them the army socialization for manly death
had failed.

A former governor attached to the occupation army wrote to
his wife to complain that she had not come to see him in prison

---

[61] Levy defines religion as "action directly oriented to ultimate ends."
See *Modernization and the Structure of Societies*, p. 948.

[62] Shūichi Katō, "Shisendōshi," *Sandai Banashi* (*A Trilogy*), Tokyo,
Chikuma Shobō, 1965, pp. 7-50.

[63] *Seiki no Isho*, p. 247.   [64] *Ibid.*, p. 155.

and confessed that he had "cried all night" in anticipation of receiving the death sentence.[65]

Six persons wrote to their own children admonishing them not to take up military life or any civil service occupation as their fathers had done. A lieutenant colonel in the army enjoined: "Don't allow our children to become civil servants or politicians. Encourage them to go into business."[66] A lieutenant colonel of the gendarmerie cautioned his children: "Do not go into any occupation where people may develop a grudge against you. For instance, money-lenders, judges, the police and interpreters working for them are such occupations."[67] A subofficer of the gendarmerie summed up his advice to his children: "As the result of my experience, I have come to the serious conclusion that it is best for us to live in peace even though we have no prestige or social status. That is the true happiness in human life."[68]

Such attitudes were entirely opposed to those which advocated vengeance on the enemies of Japan and urged the next generation to become military officers to achieve that end. Those who admitted "despair" and "regret" failed to live up to the expectation of the role prescribed for the warrior, who was expected to sacrifice himself willingly for the welfare of the state. This group can be described as desocialized with respect to the collectivistic goal orientation of the military ideology.

"Antimilitary" and "Antiwar": The Many-Layered Self, Conflicting Self, and Innovator

There were ten who criticized the military and twenty-four who denounced war, although they did not all agree in their ideas and feelings. Some tried to defend the military while at the same time denouncing war, whereas others repudiated war while subscribing to the particularistic ideology of Emperor worship and the superiority of the Japanese as an ethnic group. Thus most of those who are classified under the items "antimilitary" and "antiwar" fit the description of either the many-layered self or the conflicting self. Three out of the twenty-four listed under "antiwar" were consistent in holding peace-oriented ideas.

A subofficer of the gendarmerie who was executed in the Philippines in 1951, at the age of thirty-three, expressed his full

[65] *Ibid.*, p. 251.   [66] *Ibid.*, p. 331.   [67] *Ibid.*, p. 600.
[68] *Ibid.*, p. 412.

support for the renunciation of war and the abolition of armed forces as declared in Article Nine of the Constitution of 1947.

> We should not rearm our country in a half-baked way. Rearmament would be conducive to aggression from foreign countries, giving them excuses for armed attack on us. The allied nations would not allow us full-fledged armament. We should prevent ourselves from committing the foolish act of risking our lives for the benefit of other countries, should they engage in a war among themselves. We should strive vigorously to maintain the thoroughgoing peace and the ideal direction for the entire world and humanity as prescribed by the New Constitution. . . .
>
> We should base our relations with the rest of the world on the feeling of humanity, abandoning hatred and transcending differences in religious beliefs.[69]

According to this writer's diary, he read the Bible every day and talked often about the Church and his friends in the Church. Obviously, he was a Christian at the time. It is not clear, however, whether he was a Christian before he entered the prison or was converted to Christianity after his incarceration.

The second of the three peace advocates was a first-class private in the navy who had originally been a farmer and who was executed in Sugamo Prison in 1950, at the age of twenty-nine. His message to his sons reads:

> . . . the following is what your father most earnestly wishes to convey to his beloved sons Kōichi and Takayuki as his last words on this earth. It is concerned with the reason why your father has to die. It is not only your father who suffers in death, but your father's death is the saddest thing that could happen to your grandfather, grandmother, mother, Kōichi, and Takayuki. What is the cause of such sadness? It is war which all human beings hate. I have no time left now to explain to you what I was ordered to do by my superior officers. However, if there had been no war, there could have been no superior officers to issue orders, and consequently there could have been no incident that led to your father's execution. Moreover, without the war, all these millions of people would not have had to die on the battlefield. Without the war, families would not be grieving over their dead sons, fathers, and

---

[69] *Ibid.*, p. 577.

brothers. Therefore, your father exhorts Kōichi and Takayuki, under whatever circumstances, to oppose war for as long as you live and to teach your own sons and grandsons to oppose it categorically. And you should at the same time work toward Eternal Peace in the World which is the unanimous prayer of all mankind.[70]

The writer of this message was a Buddhist, but he believed that after death his spirit would always be with his sons to guide them so that they could abide by their father's will to oppose any war and to work for world peace.

The third opponent of war was a lieutenant colonel and navy doctor who was executed in Guam in 1949, at the age of forty-three. In his last message to his wife, he explained the incident which had led the court to sentence him to death. He had been ordered by his commander to kill two American prisoners of war, injured in a bombing raid on the prison camp by American planes. Instead of killing them, he had operated on them with the utmost care and caution possible under the circumstances in order to save their lives. Toward the end of the operation, however, the two prisoners had been carried away and slain by the doctor's subordinates under the command of his superiors. For this incident the superior officers denied responsibility during the trial and testified that the doctor was to blame. The doctor took the responsibility for slaying the prisoners, and by so doing he saved the lives of his subordinates.

I regret that those people who were in the responsible position never admitted even "a failure of supervision" of their subordinates. I am sorry that this has happened to my beloved fatherland. I had to laugh sorrowfully at myself, knowing that the way of professional warriors amounted to nothing but hypocrisy and the limitations of human rationality. It is wrong to hate everything in Japan's past. However, there are many faults which should not be repeated. . . . Is it not necessary for the Japanese people to reflect on the manner in which they became the victims of the way of professional warriors and were led into that miserable war?

Japan's defeat was inevitable. Japan lacked raw materials, was backward in science, and the character of the people had long been corrupted and blind. You should consider Japan's

[70] *Ibid.*, p. 703.

defeat as Providential and as a divine judgment, and should work joyously to contribute to the reconstruction of our new fatherland. The Japanese people should be reborn. Having come to this conclusion, I am a happy man today [on the day of execution].[71]

Previous to his entrance into the navy, he had specialized in industrial medicine. "The spirit of my late father's sisters who died prematurely, working in factories, came upon me and drove me to dedicate myself to this field."[72] He had been motivated by his aunts' premature deaths to enter into industrial medicine in order to help improve the working conditions of laborers so as not to repeat the tragedy that had befallen his aunts. In a similar manner, he now attempted to transmit to his wife and their five children the motivation to reorient themselves and to help the Japanese become independent thinkers so as not to be misled into war again.

Those who renounced the war shared with those who were committed to the military ideology the indigenous belief that their spirits would remain with their families to protect them and to guide them so that their own unfinished tasks could be achieved by the surviving generations. This traditional belief in immortality, upon which ancestor worship was based, was a major source of motivation for achievement among the Japanese in the prewar period. This orientation toward achievement was previously associated with the military ideology of honorable death for the Emperor. Some of the war criminals managed to give a new universalistic orientation to the old particularistic belief in immortality. Instead of commanding their posterity to continue in the same path of war, at least some of the war criminals tried to implant in their children intense motivations to repudiate the military ideology of their fathers' generation. They tried to accommodate their particularistic belief in immortality with a universalistic antiwar ideology. In this sense, we may characterize the last two peace-oriented individuals as representing the innovator type of personality change.

None of those who came to reject war believed that they were guilty of the war crimes of which they were convicted. Conversely, none of those who admitted that they were guilty of war crimes articulated a renunciation of war. On the whole, the International War Tribunal failed to develop in the war crimi-

[71] *Ibid.*, pp. 734-736.   [72] *Ibid.*, p. 736.

nals the awareness of guilt for "crimes against humanity" which was intended to act as the mediator of change from the war-oriented to a peace-oriented ideology. Those who arrived at an antiwar conviction did so, not through a sense of war guilt superimposed by the Tribunal, but rather through the sense of having been the victims of double injustices—injustices inflicted upon them by their superiors in the army and injustices inflicted upon them by the victors. Moreover, they not only suffered themselves but were keenly aware of the suffering that their premature deaths would cause their families. It was this sense of guilt toward their own families that led them to recant their early war-oriented ideology.

6. THE EFFECTS OF THE WAR TRIBUNAL ON SURVIVORS OF THE WAR

We may begin by assessing the effects of the War Tribunal itself as a resocializing agent for the Japanese public. The Tribunal served both functional and dysfunctional ends. That the punishment of the war criminals by the victor nations was used by the majority of the Japanese as a substitute for self-examination of their own responsibilities for the war was dysfunctional. Thus the Tribunal prevented, rather than encouraged, the process of resocialization of the Japanese by themselves.[73]

A small minority of the people voiced criticism of the International War Tribunal. A young girl of twenty-one, named Higuchi, who felt that it was not just for the victor nations to judge the defeated, started a campaign to collect signatures on a petition for the release of a certain war criminal in a prison in the Philippines. She investigated his case thoroughly and concluded that the charge against him was false. Thanks to her campaign, the man was released. To her disappointment, however, she found that he was completely absorbed in proving his own innocence of specific crimes. He had no feeling of responsibility for the atrocities committed against the natives by the Japanese military as a whole, to which he had been a party.[74]

[73] Majority opinion as expressed in major newspapers and left-wing journals favored the outcome of the Tokyo Tribunal in 1948. They created the climate of opinion which absolved the rest of the Japanese from self-examination once the war criminals had been executed. See *Nihon no Hyakunen*, I, 61-62.

[74] Shigeko Higuchi, *Hijō no Niwa* (*The Garden of Disillusionment*), 1957—cited in Osamu Kuno et al., *Sengo Nihon no Shisō*, Tokyo, Chūōkōronsha, 1959, pp. 1-6.

There was also a movie actor, Komiyama, who organized a campaign for the release of war criminals in a Filipino prison. He thought that a trial of the defeated by the victor nations could not be just, yet he did not mean to deny that the Japanese were responsible for starting the war. Consequently, he came to the conclusion that the Emperor should resign as a public confession of responsibility for the war. In 1953 he made a direct appeal to the Emperor by handing him a recommendation that he resign from the Imperial throne. Komiyama was arrested, and his advice was ignored.[75] Both Higuchi and Komiyama opposed the International War Tribunal, although they were both convinced that the Japanese were responsible for the outbreak of the war and for the atrocities committed during it.

About 1955 such critics as Ryūmei Yoshimoto,[76] Shunsuke Tsurumi,[77] and Nobuyuki Ōkuma[78] began to raise the issue of "war responsibility."[79] In his discussion of the responsibilities of the intellectual leaders of wartime Japan, Tsurumi proposed to make a distinction between "war crimes," for which punishment was inflicted on a segment of the Japanese by the victor nations, and "war responsibility," which represented the Japanese intellectuals' self-examination of their role in helping to lead public opinion in support of the war. He emphasized that the prosecution of the war criminals by the victor nations did not absolve Japanese intellectuals from examining their own responsibilities as molders of opinion. He defined one of the major tasks of self-examination to be an investigation of the way an individual yielded himself to cooperation with the government's war effort and a search for a means to safeguard himself from falling into the same path, should an analogous situation arise in the future.[80]

The functional contribution of the War Tribunal was that it established, at least theoretically, the concept of the individual

---

[75] Makoto Kamiyama, *Tennō ni Taii o Semaru Otoko* (*The Man Who Tried to Force the Emperor to Resign*), Tokyo, Daini Shobō, 1957.

[76] Ryūmei Yoshimoto, *Takamura Kōtarō*, Tokyo, Iizuka Shoten, 1957; *Geijutsuteki Teikō to Zasetsu* (*Artists' Resistance and Their Failure*), Tokyo, Miraisha, 1959.

[77] Shunsuke Tsurumi, "Chishikijin no Sensō Sekinin" ("The Intellectuals' War Responsibilities"), *Secchūshugi no Tachiba* (*In Defense of Eclecticism*), Tokyo, Chikuma Shobō, 1961, pp. 71-84.

[78] Nobuyuki Ōkuma, *Kokka Aku—Sensō Sekinin wa Dare no Monoka* (*The Evils of the State—To Whom Does Responsibility for the War Belong?*), Tokyo, Chūōkōronsha, 1957.

[79] *Nihon no Hyakunen*, i, 72-75.

[80] Tsurumi, "Chishikijin no Sensō Sekinin"—cited in Ōkuma, *Kokka Aku*, p. 273.

as the locus of decision-making, even for an individual under military orders. It also established in ideal terms the allegiance of the individual to the community of mankind to counteract the authority of governments when they order men and women to commit crimes against humanity. The victor nations which constituted the Tribunal failed to live up to these ideals, but as principles they prescribed a line of thought and action totally different from the military ideology of prewar and wartime Japan. Nobuyuki Ōkuma defined the problem of war responsibilities along this line.

> The problem of war responsibilities . . . is the problem of the discrepancy between how individuals ought to have lived and how they actually lived under modern state authority. More concretely, it is the problem of conflict between an individual's reason or conscience and the prerogatives of the state. It points to the possibility of individual refusal to fulfill the duties of loyalty to the state when the state decrees conduct contrary to his conscience. It assumes the institution of a new reference group as the object of one's loyalty as over against the nation-state to which one happens to belong.[81]

Although the International War Tribunal failed to inculcate this new concept of war responsibility into the majority of the war criminals, it did set forth an ideal goal for the resocialization of the Japanese people.

We may consider, secondly, the effects on their countrymen of the messages and letters written by the soldiers who died on the scaffold, as well as by the soldiers who died on the battlefield. Just as most of the dead soldiers and ex-soldiers believed that their souls would be in communication with the surviving members of their families and their community, so a corresponding belief was held by the survivors. Indeed, Sōsuke Mita points out that belief in the possibility of dialogue between the dead and the living constitutes the essence of the folk concept of history among the Japanese.[82]

7. Summary and Propositions

The International War Tribunal was the first formal organization established as an agency of adult resocialization in Japan

[81] Ōkuma, *ibid.*, p. 276.

[82] Sōsuke Mita, "Shisha tono Taiwa" ("Dialogue with the Dead"), *Gendai Nihon no Seishin Kōzō* (*The Mental Structure of Contemporary Japan*), Tokyo, Kōbundō, 1965, pp. 152-165.

after the defeat. As such, it had significant effects on both war criminals and the general public. The above analysis of the messages of the war criminals shows that the majority of them (87.4 percent) were ever committed to the military ideology of wartime Japan, although, for most of them, the degree of commitment decreased rather than increased after Japan's defeat and their imprisonment. Only the most highly committed ("anti-trial") professed a more intensified commitment to the war ideology than before. Among those who manifested a lesser degree of commitment ("death for the sake of the Emperor," for example), commitment was on the wane. In place of Emperor worship, the majority of the war criminals sought the meaning of death in a belief in a solidarity between the dead and the living members either of the same family or of the whole Japanese community. This indigenous belief had been put to use in the formation of the military ideology of death, according to which soldiers who fell in battle were assured of roles as gods honored in the Yasukuni Shrine. We have observed that most of the war criminals retained the indigenous faith in solidarity and communicability between the dead and the living, although they abandoned Emperor worship and belief in the Yasukuni Shrine. We have also noticed that a few of the war criminals switched the vector of ideology from a war to a peace orientation, while retaining the indigenous belief in communication between the dead and living. They not only retained the belief, moreover, but actually integrated it with their peace-oriented ideology. This indigenous belief was particularistic, in the sense that solidarity is limited to the members of one's own family, neighborhood community, or nation-state. Still, it was through this particularistic trajectory of belief that a minority of the war criminals succeeded in arriving at the universalistic concept of peace for all mankind—not through an exogenous universalistic concept of "crime against humanity" defined and imposed by the Tribunal. To that extent, the Tribunal failed to accomplish what it intended.

The above observation has some general implications for the character of the relationship between an agency of socialization and change in personality through socialization. Let us formulate some hypothetical propositions.

(1) The more the socializee recognizes the discrepancy between the ideal and the actual structures of the agency of social-

ization, the less likelihood there is of achieving the socializer's goal of socialization.

(2) The concept of the historical trajectory of industrialization as formulated by Wilbert Moore (see the Introduction, Section 2) is useful in understanding the process of change in adult personality through socialization. The concept of the historical trajectory recognizes both continuity and discontinuity of change. It assumes, on the one hand, that each society has its characteristic trajectory which is conditioned by its preindustrial legacy; on the other hand, it maintains that the trajectory is the lever through which the preindustrial society is transformed into an industrial society. In an analogous manner, when the vector of ideology of an individual changes, there is a characteristic trajectory through which the change takes place. This trajectory is rooted in the affects and ideas acquired through previous socialization, but at the same time it has the potentiality of transforming those previously acquired affects and ideas.

Thus in the resocialization of adults it is strategic to search for those specific ideas and affects in the legacy of the previous socialization which can be used as the trajectory for resocialization.

(3) The Japanese army socialization was oriented toward war and the glorification of death. In contrast, the War Tribunal was professedly oriented toward peace and respect for human lives. The analysis of the last testaments of the war criminals reveals that the majority of them made every attempt to glorify their death rather than to become respectful of human lives. To this extent, Japanese army socialization achieved its intended goal, whereas the War Tribunal failed in its attempt to bring about a reversal in the criminals' attitudes.

The war-oriented socialization for death exerted by the Japanese army depended upon predominantly negative affect socialization and upon imperfect communication. The Japanese army as the agency of socialization employed a structure of relationships which were on the whole nonrational, particularistic, functionally diffuse, intimate, dependently collectivistic, hierarchical, compulsory, secret, and exploitative. Since the Japanese army realized its goal of inculcating socializees with the ideology of glorious death, it must have discovered an effective combination of ideology, method of socialization, and structure of relationships within the agency of socialization.

The War Tribunal, in contrast, failed to inculcate its peace-oriented ideology, with its emphasis on respect for human lives, in the soldiers because it relied on negative affect socialization and a method of imperfect communication, similar to those used by the Japanese army. There were also striking parallels in the actual structure of relationships as the agency of socialization between the War Tribunal and the Japanese army. The former shared with the latter the characteristics of being predominantly nonrational, particularistic, hierarchical, dependently collectivistic, secret, and compulsory. Thus the War Tribunal did not match its ideology to an appropriate method and structure of relationships of socialization.

This observation of the relative effectiveness of socialization leads us to suggest the following three hypotheses.

In the first place, it is likely that some correlation exists between (1) the type of ideology and (2) the types of socialization and the structure of relationships within the agency of socialization. Our guess is that the war-oriented ideology, with its emphasis on the glorification of death, is correlated with a preponderantly negative affect type of socialization, with the predominant method of imperfect communication, and with the structure of relationships of the agency of socialization characterized as largely nonrational, particularistic, dependently collectivistic, hierarchical, secret, and compulsory. On the other hand, the peace-oriented ideology, with its emphasis on respect for human lives, is to be correlated with a positive affect type of socialization, with the predominant method of perfect communication, and with the structure of relationships within the agency of socialization characterized as mainly rational, universalistic, independently collectivistic, egalitarian, open, and voluntary.

In the second place, if the type of ideology one wishes to inculcate is adequately matched with the method of socialization and the structure of relationships between the socializer and the socializee, then it is more likely to produce effective results than if they are inadequately matched.

In the third place, for the resocialization of an adult with an ideology significantly different from the one previously inculcated in him, a choice of socialization method and a structure of relationships between the socializer and the socializee which differ significantly from those employed by the previous socializing agent is likely to produce more effective results than choice of a method and structure of relationships similar to those involved in the previous process of socialization.

PART TWO

FIVE

Postwar Social Change: The Eclipse of the Emperor System

THE GENERAL social change that has been taking place in Japan since the termination of the war in 1945 is characterized by three major trends. First, the Emperor system as constituted at the inception of industrialization in the 1870's has been eclipsed. Second, after World War II Japan achieved a high level of industrialization. The accelerating speed of industrialization produced heightened tensions and brought about some changes in the patterns of tension management. Third, a mass society emerged, although at the same time the structure of relationships characteristic of the traditional village community persisted.

1. THE DECLINE OF THE EMPEROR SYSTEM AS THE TRADITIONAL AUTHORITY

We shall first observe the changes in the legal and ideological aspects of the Emperor system. According to the Constitution of 1947, the Emperor was to be "the symbol of the state and of the unity of the people, deriving his position from the will of the people with whom resides sovereign power."[1] The new Constitution denied the status of the Emperor as the sovereign of the state and in its place established the principle of popular sovereignty. The inviolability of the sanctity of the Emperor, as ordained in the Constitution of 1889, was annulled. Preceding the promulgation of the new Constitution, the Emperor had renounced all claims to divinity and declared himself to be human. With the abrogation of the inviolability of the sanctity of the Emperor, the criminal offense of *lèse majesté* was abolished. Thus, for the first time since the Meiji Restoration, it became possible for the Japanese at least to discuss the operation of the Emperor system without running the risk of violating the criminal code. In the terms of the Meiji Constitution, all Japanese were defined as subjects of the Emperor; as such they did not possess any inalienable rights but only whatever rights were

[1] For a translation of the Constitution of 1947, see Arthur Tiedemann, *Modern Japan*, 2nd edn., Princeton, Van Nostrand, 1962, pp. 157-172.

bestowed upon them by the benevolent will of the Emperor. Although the old Constitution enumerated the rights of subjects, they were liable to curtailment by extra-constitutional laws and administrative practices. In reality, then, even though freedom of conscience, freedom of expression, the right of assembly, habeas corpus, and other basic rights were enumerated in the Constitution of 1889, they were actually restricted by specific laws and by the government's practice to a degree that nullified their significance. It was the new Constitution of 1947 that defined people, not as subjects of the Emperor, but as persons possessing fundamental and inalienable human rights. For the first time in Japanese history it was established in theory that people possess freedom of conscience, of expression, and of association.

Takeshi Ishida characterizes the Meiji Constitution in the following way: "The Great Japan Imperial Constitution did not function as the objective system of legal norms. . . . It had an element of moral declaration and was subject to change by concrete de facto applications."[2] In contrast, Ishida maintains, the new Constitution of 1947 was framed as a consistent system of objective norms which were expected to function as the basic legal principles of government.[3] In other words, the basic distinction between the Meiji Constitution and the present Constitution is that the former was established as a form of traditional authority and functioned as such, whereas the latter was established as a form of legal authority and was expected to function as such.[4]

Among constitutional scholars controversies concerning the

[2] Takeshi Ishida, "Meiji Kenpō Taisei kara Shin Kenpō Taisei e" ("From the Meiji Constitutional System to the New Constitutional System"), *Kindai Nihon Seiji Kōzō no Kenkyū* (*Studies of the Modern Political Structure of Japan*), Tokyo, Miraisha, 1956, pp. 296-297.

[3] *Ibid.*, p. 305.

[4] For the distinction between traditional and legal authorities, see Max Weber, *The Theory of Social and Economic Organization*, tr. A. M. Henderson and Talcott Parsons, Glencoe, Ill., The Free Press, 1947, p. 328: "In the case of legal authority, obedience is owed to the legally established impersonal order. It extends to the persons exercising the authority of office under it only by virtue of the formal legality of their commands and only within the scope of authority of the office. In the case of traditional authority, obedience is owed to the *person* of the chief who occupies the traditionally sanctioned position of authority and who is (within its sphere) bound by tradition. But here the obligation of obedience is not based on the impersonal order, but is a matter of personal loyalty within the area of accustomed obligations."

status of the Emperor and its relation to the principle of popular sovereignty are still carried on.[5] Technically, however, there is no doubt that in its legal aspect the Emperor system was transformed from a traditional into a rational system. This metamorphosis had an important bearing upon the pattern of tension management. Under the Meiji Constitution, where the people did not possess the right of assembly, there was no legal protection for groups whose structure of relationships and whose ideologies were different from or hostile to the structure and ideologies of the Emperor system itself; only those groups whose structure and ideologies conformed to the Emperor system were allowed. Under the new Constitution, however, all kinds of groups, regardless of their structures and ideologies, are tolerated—at least in theory. The legal basis for monopolism of group structures and ideologies was thus dropped, and the way was opened for a multiplicity of competing groups with different structures and ideologies.

Along with the new Constitution came a new program of socialization for school children. The Ministry of Education, the central agency of the monopolistic control of socialization in the schools, was kept intact by the American occupation authorities, but they did abolish *shūshin*, the compulsory moral education based on the *Imperial Rescript on Education*. For the adult male population, the abolition of the army meant the extinction of the major agency for the inculcation of the Emperor cult. Thus both adults and children were freed from formal indoctrination in the ideology of the Emperor system.

[5] Sōichi Sasaki and Toshiyoshi Miyazawa maintain that the political principle of the Emperor as the sovereign was abolished by the Constitution of 1947. Sōichi Sasaki, *Tennō no Kokkateki Shōchōsei* (*The Emperor as the National Symbol*), Tokyo, Kōbunsha, 1949; Toshiyoshi Miyazawa, *Kokumin Shuken to Tennō-sei* (*Popular Sovereignty and the Emperor System*), Tokyo, Keisō Shobō, 1957. In contrast, Tetsurō Watsuji and Tomoo Odaka argue that the new Constitution did not change the principle of the Imperial governance. Tetsurō Watsuji, *Kokumin Tōgō no Shōchō* (*The Symbol of National Unity*), Tokyo, Keisō Shobō, 1948; Tomoo Odaka, *Kokumin Shuken to Tennō-sei* (*Popular Sovereignty and the Emperor System*), Tokyo, Seirin Shoin, 1954. Kisaburō Yokota points out the incompatibility of the principles of the Emperor system and popular sovereignty and argues that, in order to be logically consistent, establishing popular sovereignty requires that the Emperor system be abolished. See Yoshimitsu Kasahara, "Sengo Tennō-sei no Henbō" ("The Metamorphosis of the Postwar Emperor System"), *Shisō no Kagaku*, Jan. 1966, p. 6.

In addition to these formal changes in the Constitution and in the state educational program, the shock of defeat and the subsequent behavior of the Emperor resulted in a loss of prestige for the system in the minds of many people.

Jirō Kamishima contends that people lost their respect for the Emperor as the sacred entity because he took no blame for the waging of a war fought in his name. He maintains that, if the Emperor had accepted responsibility for the war either by committing suicide or by abdicating, the prestige of the Emperor system would have been better preserved.[6] Kamishima's argument is supported by the experiences of some returning soldiers. A junior sailor who volunteered to enter the Navy at the age of fifteen bore all the hardships in the war because he literally believed that the commands of his superiors were the commands of the Emperor himself. When Japan was defeated, he expected that the Emperor would certainly commit suicide before he was to be executed by the War Tribunal. To his consternation, however, when he returned to Japan from the battlefield, he found the Emperor shaking hands with the former enemy commander. Infuriated, he wrote: "I wish I could hang the Emperor upside down on the pine tree on the hill that surrounds the Imperial Palace, and flog him with a club as hard as I was beaten up in the navy."[7] To this reaction a student-soldier who was a veteran of the war added the comment: "Actually, the ex-sailor who trusted the Emperor as the sacred being betrayed himself. He was betrayed not so much by the Emperor who was outside of himself as by the Emperor who resided within him."[8]

The negative affect of the sense of being betrayed by the Emperor and by his government was ideological disenchantment with the principle of the infallibility of the Emperor, the core of the nonrationalistic ideology of the Emperor cult.[9] That at

[6] Jirō Kamishima, "Tennō-sei to Sengo Shisō" ("The Emperor System and Postwar Thought"), Shisō no Kagaku, Jan. 1963, pp. 59-62.

[7] Kiyoshi Watanabe, "Shōnenhei ni okeru Sengoshi no Rakuchō" ("A Lacuna in Postwar History from the Point of View of a Junior Soldier"), Shisō no Kagaku, Aug. 1960—quoted in Takeshi Yasuda, Sensō Taiken: Issen Shichijūnen e no Isho (My War Experience: A Will for 1970), Tokyo, Miraisha, 1963, p. 117.

[8] Yasuda, ibid., p. 118.

[9] In the public opinion survey conducted by the Office of the Prime Minister in 1954 both in Tokyo and in Ibaragi Prefecture, there is a question pertinent to the point: "Have you had an experience of being be-

least some segment of the population publicly voiced criticism of the Emperor and discussed his responsibility for the war was proof of a growing freedom from the deep-rooted taboo against thinking rationally about the Emperor. This emancipation has provided a favorable condition for the emergence of rational ways of thinking.

The impact of defeat in the war also destroyed, at least for some part of the population, the organismic concept of the state that was one of the mainstays of the Emperor ideology. Nobuyuki Ōkuma, a professor of economics, writes about the effect of Japan's defeat on his concept of the state.

> In my mind there used to exist a concept of the state as an ideal or a norm. I even considered the state as the source of morality. My concept of it was not completely defined by the Emperor system. [But it was a broader concept of the state of which the Emperor-centered concept of the state was a subcategory.] . . .
>
> However, that concept of the state was destroyed [by the impact of the experience of Japan's defeat in the war.] We not only abandoned the idea of a National Polity peculiar to Japan. We destroyed all the idealistic elements that surrounded the concept of the state. We now try to get rid of all that transcends experience, and to be guided only by experience. When we observe everything that was done during the war by the state, we can see that they were only human actions exercised through the agencies of men, e.g., decision-making, ordering, and the execution of orders. These actions began and ended with men. And the men who occupied the upper stratum were ordinary men who were often controlled by ignorance, stupidity, and prejudice. Moreover, they were often moved by selfish motives and were helplessly partisan

trayed by your own government?" Table 22 shows the distribution of the answers.

TABLE 22
EXPERIENCE OF BETRAYAL

Betrayed by the government	Tokyo (%)	Ibaragi Prefecture (%)
Yes	43.4	31.4
No	27.8	48.1
Don't know	28.8	20.5

SOURCE: Ishida, "Meiji Kenpō Taisei kara Shin Kenpō Taisei e," p. 308.

and scheming. They were attracted and manipulated by certain powers and forces. When we look at the state from the point of view of these actions, there is nothing transcendental about the function of the state. . . . If we try to adhere to experience and to be guided only by the facts of our experience, the state is seen as an organization of power through which men control other men. There is nothing more than that in the state.[10]

Thus Ōkuma calls the destruction of all the absolutistic and transcendental concepts of the state, including the Emperor-centered concept of the state, the beginning of "the spiritual revolution" of the Japanese.

Yet many Japanese still retain strong feeling for the Emperor as a sacred entity. This attitude was dramatically exhibited in a recent incident. The journal *Chūōkōron* (*The Central Review*) published a novel entitled *Fūryū Mutan* (*A Dream Story of the Floating World*) by Shichirō Fukazawa, a onetime guitar player for musicals. The novel is a fantasy written in the style of a tall tale in which characters named "Emperor," "Emperor Dowager," "Crown Prince," and "Crown Princess" appear and use the vulgar vernacular of common people. There is one scene in which these characters are beheaded and their heads fall, making metallic sounds of *sutten kororin*. This story was interpreted by extreme rightist organizations as a personal insult to the members of the Imperial Household and a blasphemy against the Emperor system. In February 1961 a boy of seventeen, a former member of the Great Japan Patriotic Party (the boy left the group immediately before the incident), broke into the house of the publisher of the journal, killed a maid, and injured the publisher's wife.[11]

Even though the Emperor has ceased to hold actual political

[10] Nobuyuki Ōkuma, *Kokka Aku—Sensō Sekinin wa Dare no Monoka* (*The Evils of the State—To Whom Does Responsibility for the War Belong?*), Tokyo, Chūōkōronsha, 1957, pp. 42-43.

[11] Shichirō Fukazawa, "Fūryū Mutan," *Chūōkōron*, Dec. 1960, pp. 328-340. A number of articles were written about this incident in various journals. See, e.g., Taijun Takeda, "Yume to Genjitsu" ("Dream and Reality"), *Gunzō*, Feb. 1961, and Shigeharu Nakano, "Teroru wa Uyoku ni taishite Yurusareruka" ("Is the Use of Terror Tolerated to the Rightists?"), *Shin Nihon Bungaku*, Jan. 1961. See also Ryūmei Yoshimoto, "Kōgaidan—'Fūryū Mutan o Megutte'" ("An Angry Talk—Concerning 'A Dream Story of the Floating World'"), *Gisei no Shūen* (*The End of Pseudo-Systems*), Tokyo, Gendai Shichōsha, 1962, pp. 44-49, and the April 1962 issue of *Shisō no Kagaku*, which is a special edition on the Emperor system.

power and the ideology of the inviolability of the sanctity of the Emperor has theoretically been abandoned, there remain residual affective postures of the attitudes that for so long sustained the Emperor system and its ideology.

Earlier we described the Emperor system and its ideology as a composite of many layers of social systems and belief systems: militarism, constitutionalism, familism (and the village community based upon familism), and the organismic concept of the state. And now we have observed that military defeat and subsequent events destroyed militarism, constitutionalism (with reference to the Meiji Constitution), and the organismic concept of the state. We have not yet, however, touched upon familism and the village community, the bottom layer of the society upon which the Emperor system rested. We should note here, though, that the collapse of the other three—militarism, Meiji constitutionalism, and the organismic concept of the state—was important, especially insofar as it has opened the way for rationalism. The removal of these linchpins of the old society also left room for the emergence of pluralistic groups with different structures of relationships and ideologies. In our typology of the patterns of tension management in society, we call this allowance for the rise of pluralistic groups competition (synchronically) and the competitive system (diachronically).

2. MONOPOLISM, THE MANY-LAYERED SYSTEM, AND COMPETITION

Although Japan's rate of economic growth has been higher than that of most other countries in the world ever since 1900, there was a sharp decrease in industrial production immediately following the end of the war. The years 1945-1955 were years of economic rehabilitiation. Between 1955 and 1961 Japan's gross national product increased by 82 percent, in contrast to the Soviet Union's 67 percent, West Germany's 43 percent, England's 16 percent, and the United States's 15 percent.[12] Thus Japan again ranks high among the industrialized countries in economic growth, but the rate of growth is even more accelerated than in the prewar period. According to the census of 1955, 41 percent of the Japanese labor force was engaged in primary, 29 percent in secondary, and 30 percent in tertiary industries. In 1960, in comparison, the proportion of workers in primary industries

[12] Hyōe Ōuchi et al., *Nihon Keizai Zusetsu* (*Japan's Economic Statistics in Graphs*), Tokyo, Iwanami, 1965, pp. 4-5.

dwindled to 32.8 percent, while the number in secondary and
tertiary industries grew to 34.7 percent and 32.5 percent respectively. By 1960, then, the population employed in manufacturing industries had for the first time exceeded the agricultural
population. During 1967 the labor force working in primary industries decreased to 21.2 percent, that in secondary industries
to 33.3 percent; the proportion of those engaged in tertiary industries, meanwhile, increased to 45.5 percent.[13] The products
of heavy and chemical industries rose from 47.4 percent of total
industrial output in 1934-1936 to 62.3 percent in 1960.[14] These
are only a few among many indices of the high level of industrialization Japan has achieved in the postwar period, especially
since 1955.

Let us consider another index of industrialization. Simon Kuznets points out:

... the size distribution of income in the developed countries
has become less unequal during recent decades, and more

[13] For the figures for 1960, see *ibid.*, pp. 34-35. The percentage distribution for 1967 is derived from *Sōrifu Tōkeikyoku* (The Cabinet Bureau of
Statistics), *Rōdōryoku Chōsa Tōkeihyō* (*The Statistical Table of the Survey
on Labor Force*), Feb. 1968, Table 5. Table 23 supplies the percentages
of the working population engaged in different industries. Colin Clark, in

TABLE 23

DISTRIBUTION OF THE WORKING POPULATION IN INDUSTRY

Type of Industry	% of Labor Force
Primary	
Agriculture and forestry	19.3
Fisheries	1.2
Mining	0.6
Secondary	
Construction	7.3
Manufacturing	25.9
Tertiary	
Sales, finance, and real estate	21.9
Communications, transportation,	
and public utilities	6.7
Service	13.6
Civil service	3.2

his *Conditions of Economic Progress* (London, Macmillan, 1957), maintains that economic growth is measured by the greater ratio of labor force
moving into the secondary (processing) and tertiary (service) industries
from the primary (agriculture and other extractive) industries.

[14] Ōuchi et al., *Nihon Keizai Zusetsu*, pp. 80-81.

evidence for the period that goes back to the end of the nine-teenth century could be assembled to support this conclu-sion. It is possible, of course, that in some earlier periods there may have been a tendency toward greater income in-equality. In some phases of industrialization and economic growth, with rapid displacement of agricultural population and flow of lower income groups into the cities, income in-equality may have been accentuated. Furthermore, graduated income taxes and government benefits emerge only in the later phases of growth of developed countries. A plausible case can be made for a long serving in internal inequality in the size distribution of income, rising in the earlier phases of growth and declining when these turbulent phases have been passed. . . . We merely note that over the period that we are considering, the last fifty years, internal income inequality in the developed countries has probably declined.[15]

Levy states this observation in a generalized proposition: "the higher the level of modernization achieved, the greater is the possibility of approaching a perfectly unimodal distribution with adequate capital formation for maintenance and growth of productivity."[16] According to the national income distribution curves worked out by Shōkichi Endō, the income distribution in 1954 shows more equality than that of 1938 (see Graph 1). This pattern conforms to the general trend over time advanced by Kuznets, Moore, and Levy. However, if we compare the in-come distribution of 1957 with that of 1951, the former indicates more inequality than the latter, although Japan's total industrial development was higher in 1957 than in 1951 (see Graph 2). In this graph the vertical axis represents the cumulative amounts of income, and the horizontal axis represents the cumulative number of persons who fall into each income group. The as-sumption is that the more the curve approaches the 45° diag-onal line, the more equal is the income distribution.

The increasing inequality of income distribution among wage earners as compared with the rising level of industrialization

[15] Simon Kuznets, *Economic Growth and Structure*, New York, W. W. Norton, 1965, p. 167.

[16] Marion J. Levy, Jr., *Modernization and the Structure of Societies*, Princeton, Princeton University Press, 1966, I, 273. "Perhaps the most out-standing feature of income distributions in industrial societies is the nu-merical predominance of the middle-income group. The distribution, in other words, is a 'normal curve' and not bi-modal." Wilbert E. Moore, "Order and Change in Industrial Societies" (MS), Ch. VII, p. 25.

GRAPH 1. COMPARISON OF NATIONAL INCOME DISTRIBUTION
FOR THE PREWAR AND POSTWAR PERIODS[17]

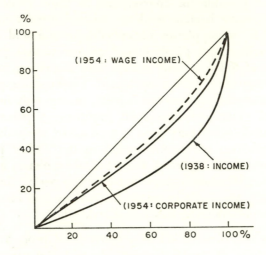

[17] This graph was based on Table 24.

TABLE 24

COMPARISON OF PREWAR AND POSTWAR INCOME
DISTRIBUTION

1938		
Income level (yen)	Number of persons (1,000)	Amount of income (10,000 yen)
Less than 1,000	41	37
1,000-1,200	331	298
1,200-1,500	341	351
1,500-2,000	300	382
2,000-3,000	227	396
3,000-5,000	208	552
5,000-10,000	129	570
10,000-20,000	51	397
20,000-50,000	23	345
50,000-100,000	6	171
100,000-500,000	3	219
500,000 more	0.3	100
Total	1,658	3,819

GRAPH 2. COMPARISON OF WAGE DISTRIBUTION FOR
1951 AND 1957[18]

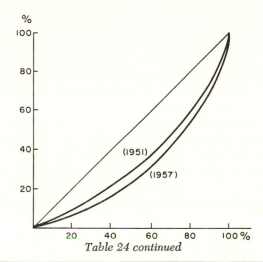

Table 24 continued

Income level (10,000 yen)	Corporation income		Wage income	
	persons (1,000)	income (10,000 yen)	persons (1,000)	income (10,000 yen)
Less than 10	37	3,091	2,035	145,711
10-20	444	73,818	2,665	391,462
20-30	912	227,110	1,575	386,122
30-40	438	150,347	693	238,313
40-50	173	76,586	311	137,863
50-70	117	67,994	215	125,006
70-100	55	45,678	84	68,162
100-200	35	46,950	43	55,269
200-500	8	24,419	5	12,823
500-more	1	11,279	0.3	2,068
Total	2,220	727,273	7,625	1,562,798

SOURCE: The income statistics for 1938 are derived from the Taxation
Bureau of the Ministry of Finance, *The Annual Report on the Statistics of
the Taxation Bureau*; the statistics for corporate incomes for 1954 are taken
from the National Taxation Office, *The Annual Report of Taxation Office
Statistics*; and the statistics of wage incomes for 1954 come from the National Taxation Office, *The Results of the Survey on the Wage-incomes of
Non-governmental Workers*. Cited in Shōkichi Endō, ed., *Nihon no Keizai*
(*Japan's Economy*), Vol. II of *Gendai Nihon no Bunseki* (*Analysis of Contemporary Japanese Economy Series*), Tokyo, Yūhikaku, 1961, pp. 225-226.
[18] The statistics of wage incomes by the differential income groups for

especially since 1955 has been a matter of concern both to Japanese economists and to the government. They attribute this imbalance to the existence of what they call "a double-structured economy." This expression was first used by Hiromi Arisawa in 1957 in a lecture to the governmental Headquarters for Productivity. Later the term was popularized through *The Economic White Paper* of the same year.[19] The double-structured economy is defined in the *White Paper* as one in which "the modernized large-scale enterprises on the one hand and the small-scale enterprises based on premodern capital-labor relationships and minute-scale enterprises and agriculture based upon domestic labor on the other are polarized, with an extremely small ratio of medium-scale enterprises existing inbetween."[20]

According to the statistics for 1955, out of the total number of industrial workers in Japan, those who worked in small-scale enterprises (with less than 99 employees) amounted to 56 percent, the workers in middle-scale enterprises (with 100-499 employees) 20 percent, and the workers in large-scale enterprises (with more than 500 employees) 24 percent. In 1963 the proportion of workers in small-scale enterprises dropped to 54.1 percent, while the number in middle-scale and large-scale enterprises slightly increased to 21.7 percent and 24.2 percent respectively. Although the percentage of the labor force engaged in small-scale enterprises is on the decline, 75.8 percent of all the industrial workers are still employed in small- and middle-scale enterprises.[21] Vast gaps in wages, working conditions, capital formation, and technology exist between the small-scale and large-scale industries. The wages of workers in domestic enterprises (with less than 4 workers) are only 59.1 percent of the wages paid to workers in the small- and middle-sized enterprises (with 5-299 workers) and only 39.2 percent of the wages paid to workers in large-scale enterprises (with

both 1951 and 1957 are derived from the National Taxation Office, *The Results of the Survey on Wage-incomes of Non-governmental Workers*—cited *ibid.*, p. 229.

[19] Hiroshi Kawaguchi et al., *Nihon Keizai no Kiso Kōzō* (*The Basic Structure of Japan's Economy*), Tokyo, Shunjūsha, 1962, p. 6.

[20] Cited *ibid.*, p. 6.

[21] Shōkichi Endō, *Sengo Nihon no Keizai to Shakai* (*The Economy and Society of Postwar Japan*), Tokyo, Chikuma Shobō, 1966, p. 56; Ōuchi et al., *Nihon Keizai Zusetsu*, 1967, pp. 36-37.

more than 300 workers).[22] With the relatively high increase in beginners' wages in the small-scale enterprises as compared with those in the large-scale enterprises, the gap in the wages between the two types of enterprise has been lessening since 1960. The most recent government statistical survey provides evidence of two distinctive trends: first, the wage gaps between the small- and large-scale industries widened in inverse proportion to the increase of the age of the workers; second, for all the age groups, the wage gaps became the narrowest in the years between 1964 to 1966. There was, however, a slight tendency toward the expansion of those gaps in 1967 in comparison with those in the preceding three years. For instance, for the age group of seventeen and below, the wage of the workers in small-scale industries was 95 percent of the wage of the workers in large scale industries in 1967 (96 percent in 1961 and 100 percent in 1966). For the age group of thirty to thirty-four, the comparable figure was 84 percent in 1967 (75 percent in 1961 and 85 percent in 1966). For the age group of fifty to fifty-nine, the workers in small-scale industries received 55 percent of the wages of those in large-scale industries in 1967 (53 percent in 1961 and 57 percent in 1966). Compared to the 1961 level, the wage gaps between the small- and large-scale industries for most of the age groups have certainly been narrowed. To acknowledge this tendency, however, is not to deny that the gaps still exist.[23]

The relationship between large-scale and small- and middle-scale enterprises is hierarchical. The large-scale enterprises exploit the lesser enterprises through subcontracting. In other words, in the double-structured economy the more modernized groups exploit the less modernized groups. This is a part of a many-layered system of tension management, which has been practiced in Japanese society since the outset of industrialization.

In the prewar period the many-layered system of tension management was exercised by three monopolistic elites—the *gunbatsu* (military clique), the *zaibatsu* (financial clique), and the *gakubatsu* (academic clique). The *gunbatsu* was actually

[22] Endō, ed., *Nihon no Keizai*, p. 111.
[23] Rōdō Daijin Kanbō Rōdō Tōkei Chōsabu (Statistical Survey Section of the Labor Minister's Secretariat), *Chingin Kōzō Kihon Tōkei Chōsa Kekka Sokuhō* (*Quick Report on the Results of the Statistical Survey of the Structure of Wages*), March 1968, pp. 1-7.

disbanded by the Occupation army and theoretically abolished by the Constitution. The *gakubatsu* escaped decomposition, at least formally, by the Occupation authorities. The *zaibatsu*, a concern organized on the basis of actual and fictitious family relationships, was theoretically dissolved by the Occupation authorities through a series of antimonopoly measures. New concerns have been formed since 1949, however. The old *zaibatsu* constituted a pyramid with a holding company at its apex in control of several major companies—for example, a bank, a mining company, a steel mill, a trading and commercial company—each having command over a number of lesser companies, which in turn had still smaller companies under their power. The stocks of the holding company were monopolized by the members of the *dōzoku* family, who held managerial positions in the companies under their control. All the stocks of the subordinate companies were owned by the members of the family.[24] Thus the old *zaibatsu* was predominantly particularistic in its recruitment of managers, predominantly secret (or closed) in its stock distribution, predominantly hierarchical in its arrangement of companies within the unit, predominantly exploitative in the relationship of the higher to the lower companies, and predominantly functionally diffuse in the sense that not only were ownership and management identified but "the family constitution" ruled everything from business management to such private affairs as family inheritance and marriage of the members of the family. In contrast, the resurgent *zaibatsu* of the postwar period is characterized by the separation of ownership and management, the dissolution of the holding company, and the dispersion of stocks among the public. In the postwar *zaibatsu* managerial positions are allocated according to achievement rather than ascription. Hence it is predominantly universalistic in its recruitment of managers, predominantly open in its stock distribution, and predominantly functionally specific in the style of execution of tasks. In place of the holding company that controls the stocks of all the companies in the unit, various major companies in the new *zaibatsu* unit mutually hold stocks of other companies, amounting in 1958 to an average of 19.0 percent of the total stocks of each company.[25]

In the postwar situation in which dispersion of stocks among the public is being practiced, ownership of 5 to 10 percent of

[24] Endō, ed., *Nihon no Keizai*, pp. 81-85.
[25] *Ibid.*, pp. 92-95.

the stocks is estimated to be enough to give a shareholder or group of shareholders control of a large company.[26] Instead of the holding company financing the capital for the companies in the unit, as in the old *zaibatsu*, capital is now financed by banks, both private and public. Instead of the *dōzoku* family members occupying the managerial positions of the companies under their control, as in the old *zaibatsu*, the managers of each of the major companies in the new *zaibatsu* hold the managerial positions of other major companies in the unit. By mutually overlapping occupation of the managerial positions, the major companies of a *zaibatsu* unit exercise monopolistic control as a unit. Thus the relationship among major companies within the new *zaibatsu* unit is predominantly egalitarian rather than hierarchical, and the tie among the major companies within the unit is less tightly knit than that of the old *zaibatsu*. Although the three chief *zaibatsu* surviving from the prewar period—Mitsui, Mitsubishi, and Sumitomo—occupy the most privileged position (for instance, the leading companies belonging to the three major *zaibatsu* rank first when loans are allocated by the major banks, both governmental and private), there are newly rising trusts and other concerns with which they have to compete. Competition among monopolistic units is consequently more intense than in the prewar period.

With the rising level of production, together with intensified competition among themselves, the new *zaibatsu* units of large-scale enterprises have resorted to the familiar pattern of tension management, the many-layered system. They have "lined up" middle- and small-scale enterprises under their control by providing them with capital and technical assistance. This policy was functional from the point of view of the big business concerns, since they thereby acquired lower cost labor. The system began to reveal dysfunctional aspects, however. By keeping the less advanced strata of workers at the lower level of wages, the system restricted the internal market for the goods manufactured by the large-scale industries. It also began to restrict technological innovation in the large-scale enterprises, because the smaller enterprises aligned with them could not adapt to their ever advancing technological level. There still persist tensions, albeit less severe than in the early 1960's, arising from the differential allocation of income and from rising ex-

[26] Kawaguchi et al., *Nihon Keizai no Kiso Kōzō*, p. 29.

pectations on the part of the lower wage earners. Thus the many-layered system, which is primarily a pattern of tension management, is still creating rather than reducing tensions.

The tensions are especially manifest among agricultural workers, most of whom belong to income groups even less well off than industrial workers. Table 25 shows the size of farm per household.

TABLE 25

SIZE OF FARM PER HOUSEHOLD

Size of Farm	1950	% of Households Occupying		
		1955	1960	1966
Small (0.5 – 1.0 chō*)	74.4	72.8	71.5	69.3
Middle (1.0 – 2.0 chō)	22.0	23.4	24.2	25.4
Large (over 3.0 chō)	3.6	4.1	4.3	5.3

SOURCE: The figures for 1950, 1955, and 1960 are from Takeo Wataya, "Nōminsō no Ryōkyoku Bunkai to Sono Igi" ("The Polarization of the Farmers and Its Implications"), Keizai Hyōron, Feb. 1962, p. 47; the figures for 1966 are from Nōrinshō Tōkei Chōsabu (Statistical Survey Section of the Ministry of Agriculture and Forestry), Nōgyō Chōsa Kekka Gaiyō (Outline Report on the Results of the Agricultural Survey), July 1967, p. 21.

* 1 chō (10 tan) = 2.45 acres = approx. 1 hectare.

In the agricultural census, farmers are classified in three categories: full-time farmers; part-time farmers I (the major part of whose income comes from farming, the minor part from nonagricultural occupations); and part-time farmers II (the major part of whose income comes from nonagricultural occupations, the minor part from agriculture). Table 26 shows the changes

TABLE 26

TYPES OF FARMING

Year	% Full-time	% Part-time I	% Part-time II
1955	34.7	37.9	27.4
1960	33.7 (−)	34.1 (−)	32.3 (+)
1963	23.9 (−)	33.9 (−)	42.2 (+)
1966	20.9 (−)	33.4 (−)	45.7 (+)

SOURCE: The percentages for 1955 and 1960 are from Takeo Wataya, "Nōminsō no Ryōkyoku Bunkai to Sono Igi," Keizai Hyōron, Feb. 1962, p. 48; the figures for 1963 from Shōzō Ōtani, "Nihon Nōgyō no Kadai (1)" ("The Issues of Agriculture in Japan"), Ekonomisuto, Jan. 1965, p. 53; and those for 1966 from Nōrinshō Tōkei Chōsabu, Nōgyō Chōsa Kekka Gaiyō, July 1967, p. 25.

between 1955 and 1966 in the composition of these three categories. It can be seen from the data provided that the proportion of both full-time and part-time I farmers is decreasing, while the ranks of part-time II farmers are correspondingly swelling. For a growing number of farmers, agriculture is becoming a subsidiary occupation. As Table 27 shows, full-time

TABLE 27

CHANGE IN TYPES OF FARMING

Size of Farm	Full-time	Part-time I	Part-time II
Small	—	—	+
Middle	—	+	+
Large	+	+	0

SOURCE: Takeo Wataya, "Nōminsō no Ryōkyoku Bunkai to Sono Igi," *Keizai Hyōron*, Feb. 1962, p. 48.

farmers are increasing only among the large farmers; among the middle farmers both part-time I and II farmers are increasing; and among the small farmers, who constitute the bulk of the agricultural population in Japan, only part-time II farmers are on the increase. Small farmers and their families simply cannot subsist on a farm of 1.25 or 2.5 acres. The Farm Economy Survey of 1962 conducted by the Agricultural Ministry estimated the minimum size of farm per household required for sustenance to be about 2 *chō* (= 5 acres).

We have already noticed that there are some gaps in wage levels among the industrial workers depending on the size of the enterprises for which they work. Between the incomes of farmers and industrial workers, similar gaps are observable. As with wage gaps among industrial workers, the income gap between the agricultural and industrial workers was the widest in 1960 and 1961. Unlike the wage differentials among city workers, however, the income difference between agrarian and urban workers has been steadily decreasing ever since 1961. The average domestic expenditure per person of the farmer was 75.8 percent of that of the industrial worker in 1960, 75.9 percent in 1961, 76.1 percent in 1962, 82.5 percent in 1965, and 84.4 percent in 1966.[27]

[27] Nōrinshō (Ministry of Agriculture and Forestry), *Nōgyō no Dōkō ni kansuru Nenji Hōkoku* (*Annual Report on the Trends of Agriculture*), 1967, p. 23.

The disparity of wages between agrarian and industrial workers, together with the fact that the majority of farm households would be below the subsistence level if they depended only on farming, explains the rapid increase in part-time II farmers, especially in the early 1960's. After 1965 labor shortages in urban industries became another incentive for farmers to take jobs outside agriculture either temporarily or permanently. The increase in part-time II farmers means that some member or members of the household have taken jobs outside agriculture either temporarily or permanently. Those who leave the village in the slack season to earn extra-agricultural income with which to supplement the family budget and then return to the village in the busy season to work on the farm are called *dekasegi* (seasonal migratory workers). This type of migratory labor has been commonly used since the inception of industrialization in the Meiji period. What is spectacular, especially since 1960 when a policy designed to promote rapid economic growth was intentionally applied to agriculture, is the increase in members of farming households who have shifted from agriculture to other industries permanently or semi-permanently, while maintaining their connections with their households in the villages. Within this shift of occupation there are various subtypes: the first consists of those who leave the village to engage in nonagricultural work, and the second consists of those who stay in the village and commute to their place of work. The first type is called *rison* (village-leavers), the second type *tsūkin* (commuters). Thus we have three types of people moving from agricultural to nonagricultural occupations: seasonal migratory workers, village-leavers, and commuters.

In February 1960 the agricultural population amounted to 34,450,000 persons, which dwindled to 28,640,000 by December 1966. Table 28 shows the numbers of the occupational shifters and seasonal migratory workers for the year 1966. As we can see from the table, although the number of occupational shifters from agriculture to other industries declined on the whole after 1963 when it was at its peak, there was some slight increase in the number of commuters in 1967 and in the number of seasonal migratory workers in 1966. Among the occupational shifters and seasonal migratory workers, there were more men than women. According to the census of 1960, 54.1 percent of the agrarian labor force was female and 45.9 percent male, an almost

TABLE 28

Occupational Shifters and Seasonal Migratory Workers

	No. (in 1966)	% Increase or Decrease Compared with Previous Year		
		1965	1966	1967 (Jan.-Oct.)
Shifters from agriculture				
to other occupations	806,800	—4.5	—5.1	—0.5
Village-leavers	383,500	—1.0	—6.6	—3.7
Commuters	423,300	—7.5	—3.7	+2.8
Seasonal migratory workers	235,300	—19.7	+2.2	—4.4

Source: Nōrinshō (Ministry of Agriculture and Forestry), *Nōgyō no Dōkō ni kansuru Nenji Hōkoku* (*Annual Report on the Trends of Agriculture*), 1967, pp. 90-91.

exact reversal of the prewar ratio.[28] Owing to the decline in the number of occupational shifters, however, the ratio of male labor in agriculture increased to 48.6 percent in 1964 and stayed at the level of 48.5 percent in 1966.[29] In the early 1960's there was a conspicuous tendency for most of the male agrarian population switching their occupations from agriculture to other industries to be below thirty-five years of age. In 1963 only 35 percent of them were above that age level, but in 1966 they amounted to 44 percent.[30] This change is partially related to the decrease in the number of village-leavers and the increase of commuters (see Table 28).

Thus in the early 1960's there emerged a general trend for the male labor force mostly under thirty-five to abandon agriculture either as village-leavers, commuters, or seasonal migratory workers, leaving behind the middle- and old-age population, mostly female, to tend to farming. Although the number of male laborers, especially those under thirty-five, abandoning agriculture is now on the wane, the general trend toward the egress of the male population from agricultural occupations persists. This situation is popularly called *san chan nōgyō* (three *chan* agriculture) because it depends on *baachan* (grandma),

[28] Hideko Maruoka's lecture at the Nōgyō Mondai Sōgō Kenkyūkai (Research Meeting on General Problems of Agriculture) held at the House of Councillors' Office Building on Dec. 12, 1964.

[29] Nōrinshō Tōkei Chōsabu (Statistical Survey Section of the Ministry of Agriculture and Forestry), *Nōgyō Chōsa Kekka Gaiyō* (*Outline Report on the Results of the Agricultural Survey*), July 1967, p. 27.

[30] Nōrinshō, *Nōgyō no Dōkō ni kansura Nenji Hōkoku*, p. 91.

jiichan (grandpa), and *kaachan* (mother). In *san chan* agriculture female labor and the labor of the older generation is dominant.

Most of the village-leavers and commuters move into the manufacturing and service industries. Table 29 shows the occupational distribution of the male occupational shifters.

TABLE 29
OCCUPATIONAL DISTRIBUTION OF MALE OCCUPATIONAL SHIFTERS

	Total Male Occupational Shifters		Those Who Have Just Finished School (1966)		Other than New Graduates (1966)
	1963	1966	Junior High School	Senior High School	
	%	%	%	%	%
Agriculture and forestry	4.0	2.6	2.1	1.0	4.9
Construction	16.3	19.7	26.3	6.1	31.1
Manufacturing	40.5	35.9	44.5	35.9	26.6
Finance, insurance, and sales	13.3	14.2	12.3	21.6	10.0
Public utilities	8.9	9.6	3.4	14.7	9.6
Service	9.8	10.7	10.8	10.2	10.3

SOURCE: Nōrinshō, *Nōgyō no Dōkō ni kansura Nenji Hōkaku*, p. 92.

This dwindling of the number of adult males in the agricultural labor force and their absorption into secondary and tertiary industries have both functional and dysfunctional consequences for the elites who control the large industries. The displacement is functional in the sense that it supplies a great fund of low cost labor. The majority of these village-leavers and commuters are nonskilled workers who are employed mainly in small-scale enterprises. On the other hand, the shift is dysfunctional in intensifying preexisting tensions and creating new strains. Since the labor force remaining on the farms was predominantly elderly and female, the relative productivity per person of agriculture decreased from 28.7 percent of that of manufacturing industries in the period 1957-1959 to 24.0 percent in 1961.[31] The increase in the number of village-leavers among the adult male population gives rise to new tensions in their families and villages. The extended absences of husbands lead to broken homes, wives become ill from overwork and the

[31] *Ibid.*, p. 16.

burden of responsibilities, juvenile delinquency increases, and the number of orphans in the villages grows. For the most productive period between the ages of twenty and forty, 64 percent of the major workers on the farm were female in 1966.[32]

The many-layered system of tension management was intended and recognized by the industrializing elites from the outset of industrialization up to the end of the war, but it was not necessarily recognized by the people at large. In the postwar era, however, especially since 1957, when the government popularized the term "double-structured economy" because the tensions arising from the system became acute, the operation of this type of tension management has been publicly recognized.[33]

3. COMMUNAL-MASS SOCIETY

William Kornhauser distinguishes four types of society: (1) "communal society" in which elites are inaccessible and nonelites are unavailable; (2) "totalitarian society" in which elites are inaccessible and nonelites are available; (3) "mass society" in which elites are accessible and nonelites are available; and (4) "pluralist society" in which elites are accessible but nonelites are unavailable.[34] Among those four, the second and fourth societies stand for two polar types. In the totalitarian society nonelites are subject to total domination by the ruling elites, whereas in the pluralist society the nonelites not only are free from the control of the elites but are encouraged to represent diverse ideas and activities. Kornhauser's typology is based upon his classification of intermediate groups which, according to his scheme, include all groups which are neither the primary group (the family) nor the state (which is inclusive of the whole popu-

[32] Nōrinshō Tōkei Chōsabu, *Nōgyō Chōsa Kekka Gaiyō*, p. 3.

[33] Comparing the analysis of postwar Japanese economy by a non-Marxist economist, Miyohei Shinohara, and a Marxist economist, Kazuji Nagasu, Hiroshi Kawaguchi concludes: "I am awakened to the fact that Mr. Shinohara, a leading economist of the modern theory school, presents an analysis of the double-structure which is amazingly identical with the analysis of the characteristics of Japanese economy which has previously been presented by Marxist scholars." Kawaguchi et al., *Nihon Keizai no Kiso Kōzō*, p. 12. It is conceivable that it was not through Marxian economists but through the influence of non-Marxian economists, who are in Japan usually called "modern theorists," that the government came to adopt the term "double-structure" and to popularize it.

[34] William Kornhauser, *The Politics of Mass Society*, Glencoe, Ill., The Free Press, 1959, pp. 40-41.

lation of a society).[35] He assumes that in communal society these intermediate groups are "strong" and "inclusive," in totalitarian society "weak" and "inclusive" in mass society "weak" and "noninclusive," and in pluralist society "strong" and "noninclusive."[36]

By "inclusive" Kornhauser means the situation in which "one group is *inclusive* of its members' lives"; by "noninclusive" he means the situation in which "no group is inclusive of its members' lives." In both mass society and pluralist society, individuals have "a multiplicity of *affiliations*,"[37] so that each intermediate group provides a place where different segments of the population meet and where competing values and ideologies confront one another. This situation is conducive both to the breaking down of compartmentalization and to the introduction of competition and the possible integration of conflicting values and ideologies.

By "strong" intermediate groups Kornhauser means groups that are autonomous and independent of control by ruling elites, and by "weak" intermediate groups he means groups under the domination of the ruling elites.[38] This category needs to be redefined. In a communal society either the central authority, the state, is nonexistent or, if it exists at all, the bond of unity among the whole population is loose. It follows that in a communal society intermediate groups are independent of the ruling elites of the state. Nevertheless, mutual constraints among primary groups are strong in communal society, and it is probable that intermediate groups are dependent upon the ties among primary groups. Thus intermediate groups are likely to be independent of the ruling elites of the state but dependent on primary group ties. We shall redefine this category by separating its two aspects. In the first the pattern variable "strong" or "weak" will pertain to the solidarity of intragroup interaction, and in the second it will pertain to the intergroup relationship of independence. We shall treat these two aspects as two separate criteria.

Solidarity is defined by Levy as "the structure in terms of which relationships among the members of a society are allocated according to the content, strength, and intensity of the relationships."[39] The degrees of "strength" and "intensity" can be

---

[35] *Ibid.*, pp. 74-75.   [36] *Ibid.*, pp. 80-84.   [37] *Ibid.*, p. 80.
[38] *Ibid.*, p. 82.
[39] Marion J. Levy, Jr., *The Structures of Society*, Princeton, Princeton University Press, 1952, p. 341.

measured in terms of the continuum between two poles: "The negative pole will be taken to mean complete antagonism— war at sight as it were. The positive pole will be taken to mean complete agreement and complete and mutual affective accord."[40] This concept of a solidarity-antagonism continuum is derived from Sorokin's definition of solidarity:

> Interaction is *solidary* when the aspirations (meanings-values) and overt actions of the interacting parties concur and are mutually helpful for the realization of their objectives.
>
> It is *antagonistic* when the desires (meanings-values) and overt actions of the parties are opposite and mutually hinder one another.
>
> It is *mixed* when the aspirations (meanings-values) and overt behavior of the parties are partly solidary, partly antagonistic.[41]

Using the concept of the solidarity-antagonism continuum, we shall define "strong" intermediate groups as those which are predominantly solidary and "weak" intermediate groups as those which are predominantly antagonistic. In communal society, intermediate groups are strong, or predominantly solidary; in totalitarian society, they are weak, or predominantly antagonistic; in pluralist society, they are strong, or predominantly solidary. In communal-totalitarian and communal-mass societies, intermediate groups are of a mixed type, partly solidary and partly antagonistic.

The aspect of independence can be defined in the following manner. A group I is independent of another group P when the structure of relationships of group I may change, in terms of the pattern variables of the structure of relationships as we have defined them, regardless of change or no change, or the direction, content, or pace of change in group P. In other words, if group I establishes its independent variability vis-à-vis group P we call group I independent of group P. If group I fails to establish its independent variability and shows a structure of relationships identical with group P's as long as there is no change in group P, or shows the identical pattern of

[40] *Ibid.*, p. 349.
[41] Pitirim A. Sorokin, *Society, Culture, and Personality: Their Structure and Dynamics*, New York, Cooper Square Publishers, 1962, p. 93.

change if a change does occur in group P, then we say that group I is dependent upon group P.

In communal society, intermediate groups are predominantly dependent on the primary groups, although they are predominantly independent of the state; in totalitarian society, intermediate groups are predominantly dependent on the state, although they are predominantly independent of the primary groups. In communal-totalitarian society, intermediate groups are predominantly dependent on both primary groups and the state. In such a society the state, intermediate groups, and primary groups are permeated by the same principles of organization, and any change in the state initiates an identical pattern of change in both intermediate and primary groups. In mass society, intermediate groups are ideally independent in the sense that their independent variability is institutionalized through the positive injunction of freedom of association either from primary groups or from the state, but actually they are dependent on the state. In communal-mass society, intermediate groups are ideally independent of both primary groups and the state but are actually dependent partly on primary groups and partly on the state. In pluralist society, intermediate groups are both ideally and actually independent of primary groups and the state. The revised classification of intermediate groups according to four basic types of society is shown in Table 30.

Japanese society before the military defeat in 1945 was a predominantly communal-totalitarian society, in that both the state and the intermediate groups were permeated by the principle of the primary group, the family. The village community, was based on either *dōzoku* or *kumi* types of the union of unit families.[42] Jirō Kamishima points out that the principles of

[42] The typology of village structure is still a controversial issue, but here we may cite two major typologies: the *dōzoku* vs *kumi* types as developed by Aruga and the *tōhoku* (northeastern) vs *seinan* (southwestern) types as developed by Tadashi Fukutake. Both of these types were derived from research carried on in various districts and, hence, are empirically derived rather than logically established types.

Aruga maintains that the *dōzoku* type of village is founded on the lord-retainer (or master-servant) relationship between the influential landlord's family, which is the main family, and the branch families composed of tenants, both related and unrelated by blood to the main family. The *kumi* type of village consists of main and branch families of more or less equal status. Aruga points out the transformability of the *dōzoku* type of village into the *kumi* type under the following conditions. First, when the main family declines in the originally *dōzoku* type of village, its relationship with its branch families becomes more like the *kumi* type. Second, in a

TABLE 30

CLASSIFICATION OF INTERMEDIATE GROUPS

| | | INTRAGROUP SOLIDARITY-ANTAGONISM | |
		Predominantly solidary	Predominantly antagonistic
		Communal society (dependent on primary groups)	*Totalitarian society* (dependent on the state)
	Predominantly dependent		
INTERGROUP INDEPENDENCE-DEPENDENCE			
	Predominantly independent	*Pluralist society* (Ideally and actually independent of both primary groups and the state)	*Mass society* (Ideally independent of both primary groups and the state, but actually dependent on the state)

village where a number of equally influential *dōzoku* groups exist, the relationships of those groups can be characterized as of the *kumi* type. (Kizaemon Aruga, "Nihon no Ie" ["The Japanese Family"], in *Nihon Minzoku*
[*The Japanese Race*], ed. Nihon Jinrui Gakkai [The Japanese Anthropological Association], Tokyo, Iwanami, 1959, pp. 161-184.)

Fukutake's classification of village types is based primarily on the characteristics of the system of production. The northeastern type of village exhibits: (1) relatively low productivity in agriculture and an undeveloped
state of industry in the neighboring areas—conditions which make each village community more or less self-contained and allow only a low degree of
social mobility; (2) a relatively high degree of dependence among the villagers on communal organizations in carrying out their agricultural production, as well as in their recreational pursuits—a condition which makes them
amenable to community controls in their daily activities and attitudes toward
life; and (3) a predominantly hierarchical system of ranking families within
the village. The superordination-subordination relationship between the landlords and small peasants in such a village assumes a collectivistic rather than
an individualistic pattern. Fukutake points out that the "upper circle" of
the village, the landlords or the main families, are "able to manipulate the
village community in their own interests in return for some benevolent
[*onjōteki*] aid for the villagers" without arousing a feeling among the
middle- and lower-rank peasants that they are being exploited. (Tadashi
Fukutake *Nihon Sonraku no Shakai Kōzō* [*The Social Structure of the Japanese Village*], Tokyo, Tokyo Daigaku Shuppankai, 1959, pp. 74-75.)

In contrast, the predominant type of village in the southwestern part of
Japan exhibits: (1) a relatively developed state of industry and a higher

organization in the village community were Shintoism, gerontocracy, familism, hierarchical organization of status, and self-
sufficiency. The basic patterns of the belief system of the villagers were: religious beliefs in the fusion of gods and men

---

degree of differentiation in the occupational structure in the adjacent areas—
conditions which make it possible for the villagers to leave the village to
take jobs in the cities or to stay in the village and take jobs as a side occupation and which make it likely that landlords will acquire higher education
and move out of the village to become absentee landlords; (2) in proportion
to the increase of geographical and social mobility of village members, and
also of the penetration of a money economy into the village, an increase in
the private ownership of previously communally owned properties such as
forests and greater independence of the villagers from communal organizations and control; and (3) the likelihood that, where landlords do not live
in the villages and have no direct contact with the villagers and where
some of them are money-lending landlords with no hereditary status to act
as a base for a master-servant relationship with the villagers, the village will
consist of more or less independent farmers with equal status. (*Ibid.*, pp.
75-77.)

Masao Gamō, combining these two typologies with the results of empirical
studies made by Kunio Yanagida and other sociologists and anthropologists,
has constructed a tentative typology of the overall structure of village communities in Japan. According to his scheme, the northeastern type, defined
by the hierarchical relationship of the main and branch families, and the
southwestern type, defined by the nonhierarchical relationship of the main
and branch families, are the two major types. The first type is subdivided
into the *dōzoku* type and the pseudo-family (master-servant) type; the
second type is subdivided into the *kumi* type and the age-group type. Gamō
attempts to relate the structural type of the village to the structural type of
the unit families within the village. He maintains that in the northeastern
type of village the unit families are predominantly extended families,
whereas in the southwestern type village the unit families are predominantly
nuclear families. Among the former the right of the paterfamilias is strong
and the status of the wife low; among the latter the right of the head of the
family is relatively weak and the wife's status comparatively high. In the
former type the patrilineal relatives have priority over matrilineal relatives;
in the latter the reverse is the case. In the former type cadets are strongly
discriminated against in relation to the eldest son, whereas in the latter type
there is relatively little discrimination between them. In the former primogeniture is the rule with allowance for inheritance by the eldest daughter,
whereas in the latter primogeniture is the rule with allowance for ultimogeni-
ture. In the former there is no system of retirement, and, consequently,
different generations are likely to live under the same roof; in the latter the
system of retirement prevails, so that married sons may live independently
from their parents. (Masao Gamō, *Nihonjin no Seikatsu Kōzō Josetsu* [*An
Introduction to the Life Structure of the Japanese*], Tokyo, Seishin Shobō,
1960, pp. 15-75.)

Geographically speaking, the villages in the northeastern part of the
Japanese mainland (*tōhoku*) exemplify a predominantly *dōzoku* type of
structure, while the villages in the southwestern part of Japan (*seinan*),
the areas around Kyoto in the eastern part (*kanto*) of the mainland, the
areas around Tokyo, and Shikoku Island represent the *kumi* type. (*Ibid.*,
p. 75.)

and the cyclical rhythm of *hare* (fine weather = festivals) and *ke* (cloudy weather = ordinary work day), which was primarily based on the rhythm of agricultural production; belief that hard work is reciprocated by rewards; belief that obedience earns protection; the idea that decision-making should be based on the unanimous consent of all the members of the group which the decision concerns; and an intolerant attitude toward outcasts and other outgroup members.[43] When the villagers migrated to the cities, they carried with them both the village structure of relationships and its belief system. And they retained them in the cities, although both the structure of relationships and the belief system underwent certain metamorphoses.[44]

Thus the structure of relationships brought from the native villages came to constitute "the secondary village" or "the fictitious village" within the cities.[45] In the primary (that is, native) village the members were united by the worship of the common *ujigami* (which meant primarily the family god and later the village god), and their unity was constantly reinforced through participation in recurrent festivals, which in one way or another were connected with the *ujigami* shrine. In comparison, there were two major ties uniting the members of the fictitious villages. The first was their common origin in a native village or prefecture. The association of members coming from the same prefecture is called *kenjinkai*. The most powerful such association in the early Meiji period was the Yamaguchi-*kenjinkai*, which was the basis for the Chōshū-*batsu*, which itself was the most influential body within the military clique, *gunbatsu*. The second tie consisted of *dōsōkai*, the alumni associations of universities and schools, which were the basis for the *gakubatsu*. Kamishima maintains that the new middle class developed as the fictitious village according to the *dōsōkai* type of union, whereas the old middle class was structured according to the *kenjinkai* type of union. He argues further that the switch from the old to the new middle class was initiated in the 1880's when the Meiji Government issued education ordinances and promulgated local autonomy systems.[46] It was not until after the Russo-Japanese War (1904-1905) that the new middle class

---

[43] Jirō Kamishima, *Kindai Nihon no Seishin Kōzō* (*The Mental Structure of Modern Japan*), Tokyo, Iwanami, 1961, pp. 24, 42.

[44] *Ibid.*, p. 172.   [45] *Ibid.*, p. 28.   [46] *Ibid.*, pp. 175-176.

actually emerged.[47] Whether it was old middle class or new middle class, it transported the structure of relationships and the system of beliefs peculiar to the primary village community to the cities. According to Kamishima, the structure of relationships and the system of beliefs peculiar to the primary village community as well as to the fictitious village in the city were the sources of the legitimacy of the Emperor system from the Meiji Restoration until the end of World War II.[48]

In contrast, we can characterize postwar Japanese society as a predominantly communal-mass society, in that syndromes of both communal and mass society coexist. Trends toward mass society had already been set in motion during the prewar period. For instance, the rise of the new middle class subscribing to the principle of achievement through university education, in place of the old middle class based upon the principle of ascription through family status, meant an increase in the accessibility of the elites. Actually, however, the proportion of those who acquired higher education was still rather small—1.6 percent of the productive age population (fifteen to fifty-nine years old) in 1935. It was only after the war that compulsory education was extended from six years to nine years, resulting in an increase of those who received higher education to 5.5 percent of the productive age population in 1960.[49] Universal manhood suffrage was instituted in 1928, but it was not until 1946 that both men and women became eligible to vote at the age of twenty. The mass communication media developed extensively during the 1920's and 1930's. Still, its development has been most spectacular in the postwar period. In ownership of television sets Japan ranks second only to the United States.[50] The circulation of daily newspapers per 1,000 persons was 384 in Japan in 1959, ranking it third in the world after England and Sweden.[51] The

[47] Kazuo Ōkōchi, *Nihon no Chūsan Kaikyū* (*The Middle Class in Japan*), Tokyo, Bungeishunjū Shinsha, 1961, pp. 21-29.

[48] *Ibid.*, pp. 22-24.

[49] Monbushō Chōsa-kyoku (Research Bureau of the Ministry of Education), *Nihon no Seichō to Kyōiku* (*Japan's Growth and Education*), Tokyo, 1963, p. 57.

[50] In 1961 the percentage of households owning sets was 89.0 for the United States vs. 63.0 for Japan. See Ōuchi et al., *Nihon Keizai Zusetsu*, pp. 216-217. In 1967 the figure for Japan was 83.1 percent (quoted from the survey of television and radio recipients' fees conducted by Nihon Hōsō Kyōkai [The National Broadcasting Association] in March 1968).

[51] Yano Tsunetarō Kinenkai, ed., *Nihon Kokusei Zue* (*Japanese Census in Graphs*), Tokyo, Kokuseisha, 1961, p. 4111.

circulation of popular weekly journals reached 12,000,000 per week in 1959[52] and was quadrupled in the following year.[53] The rapid diffusion of the mass communication media is making the nonelite ever more amenable to the control of ruling elites.

The Constitution of 1947 institutionalized freedom of association, thus establishing tolerance of various intermediate groups with multiple structural principles and value orientations. On the surface, then, contemporary Japanese society looks like a model mass society. At the bottom, however, the primary village community and the fictitious village within the city are still preserved. We have already pointed out the growing migration of the agrarian population to the cities. Most of these people go into unskilled work such as manufacturing, construction, and services. There are major status distinctions among manual workers at present, who are classed as either regular workers, temporary workers, or contractual workers. Most of the regular workers in large-scale industries belong to unions, whereas the temporary workers and contractual workers who work side by side with the regular workers in large-scale industries are excluded from union membership. The contractual workers are not paid directly by the company for which they work but by their labor boss (*oyakata*), who makes a contract with the company. The traditional *oyabun-kobun* (the boss-and-henchmen) relationship persists among the contractual workers. The most typical contractual labor relationship is found among construction workers.[54] Most of the regular workers in small- and middle-scale factories do not have unions, and pa-

---

[52] Survey conducted by the Office of the Prime Minister—cited in Naoyuki Arai, ed., "Sengo Jānarizumushi Nenpyō" ("A Chronological Table of the Postwar History of Journalism"), *Shisō no Kagaku*, Feb. 1965, p. 102.

[53] Sōboku Yamada, "Jānarizumu towa Nanika" ("What is Journalism?"), *ibid.*, p. 9.

[54] For an extensive empirical survey and analysis of the construction workers and their labor relationships, see Shōzō Uchiyama, *Kensetsu Rōdōron* (*Theory of Construction Labor*), Tokyo, Hōsei Daigaku Shuppan Kyoku, 1963, Vol. I. This book also has a chapter on the comparative study of construction labor in the United States and Japan. The government statistics for 1966 reveal that, except for those who have just graduated from schools, construction ranks at the top of the industries into which male village-leavers and commuters enter. A total of 31.1 percent of them entered that line of work in 1966, and 37.8 percent of those who were thirty-five and above moved into that occupation. (*Nōrinshō, Nōgyō no Dōkō ni kansura Nenji Hōkoku*, p. 92.) If we included the seasonal migratory workers, the percentage of those who accept employment in construction jobs would be even higher.

ternalistic labor relations prevail among them. And it is these less modernized areas of the labor market that most of the village-leavers, commuters, and seasonal migratory workers enter.

Unless the income gap between the agrarian population and the urban workers is overcome, some segment of the former will continue to leave the village to take jobs in the cities either temporarily or permanently. This trend has a disruptive effect upon the primary village community, but at the same time it strengthens the fictitious village relationships within the city by the constant renewal of the communal pattern of relationships and of the belief systems. As long as the double-structured economy endures, the intermediate groups organized after primary groups will tend to reproduce themselves. That is tantamount to saying that, as long as the many-layered system of tension management survives, communal and mass societies will coexist.

The traditional authority of the Emperor system is declining as a predominantly communal-totalitarian society is being transformed into a predominantly communal-mass society. However, as long as the communal pattern is perpetuated, even if partially, the affective and ideological posture which was conducive to the ideology of the Emperor system in its original formulation will remain dominant, at least among some part of the population.[55]

[55] See Keiichi Matsushita, "Taishū Tennō-sei Ron" ("Mass Emperor System"), Chūōkōron, April 1959, and its criticism by Hirosumi Abe in "Gendai Tennō-sei no Mondaisei" ("The Problems of the Contemporary Emperor System"), Rekishi to Gendai, Dec. 1964. See also Yoshimitsu Kasahara, "Sengo Tennō-sei no Henbō" ("The Metamorphosis of the Emperor System After the War"), Shisō no Kagaku, Jan. 1966, pp. 7-12.

SIX

The Circle: A Writing Group among the Textile Workers

1. THE INDIGENOUS SOURCES OF CIRCLES

Circles are small, voluntary, informal groups organized for educational and recreational activities. The circle movement is defined by Shunsuke Tsurumi as "a movement that aims to develop the universalistic principles [of values, ideas, action, and relationships] that accompany modernization through particularistic means indigenous to Japanese society."[1] It was after 1951, when the San Francisco Peace Treaty was concluded and the military occupation came to an end, that the circles began to emerge. They are formed either as groups on their own or as subgroups of large formal organizations such as labor unions, youth organizations, and parent-teacher associations. Their activities cover a wide range—singing, dancing, dramatics, photography, moviemaking and criticism, mountain climbing, reading, discussion, writing, etc. Some groups combine more than one of these activities. We shall restrict our study, however, to circles oriented primarily toward writing, because it is easier to trace the process of personality change in the members through their own writings than through other media. Owing to their informality and anonymity, it is extremely difficult to make a precise estimate of how many writing circles now exist throughout Japan. According to a study made in June 1965 by a librarian at Nihon University, where the mimeographed copies of the pamphlets produced by the writing circles are kept, there are 1,500 separate series of pamphlets containing some 6,000 issues.[2]

[1] Shunsuke Tsurumi, "Hōkoku—Taishū no Shisō: Seikatsu Tsuzurikata, Sākuru Undō" ("Report on People's Thought: Life-Composition and the Circle Movement"), in Osamu Kuno et al., Sengo Nihon no Shisō (Postwar Japanese Thought), Tokyo, Chūōkōronsha, 1959, p. 112.

[2] Tatsuhisa Matsuura, "Sākuru-shi no Seiri Chūkan Hōkoku" ("An Interim Report on Circle Pamphlets"), Shisō no Kagaku, June 1965, p. 85. These pamphlets and books were collected by a group of members of the Institute of the Science of Thought, who have been reviewing the circle pamphlets each month since January 1956, first for Chūōkōron and later for Shisō no Kagaku.

The rise of writing circles among adults as a means of self-reeducation was first stimulated by the publication of a collection of compositions written by high school pupils in a mountain village, edited by their teacher Seikyō Muchaku. *Yamabiko Gakkō* (*Echoes from a Mountain School*) appeared in 1951 and subsequently became a national best-seller.[3] This work was based on the native educational crusade called the "life-composition" movement (*seikatsu tsuzurikata undō*) that dates back to 1918. The indigenous character of the method and content of the education described in *Echoes from a Mountain School* attracted much attention, especially at the end of military occupation by foreign powers.

Rokurō Hidaka attributes this interest to the general change in the value orientation of Japanese society from militarism and fascism to pacifism and democracy which occurred immediately after the military defeat. Democracy, which is theoretically grounded on voluntarism, was actually superimposed on the Japanese by compulsion from occupation authorities. The discrepancy between the content of the values changed and the method by which they were changed was dysfunctional for the majority of the people, since they looked upon democratic values as ideals given to them, rather than as things they had earned on their own. Many school teachers, for example, have had great difficulty in applying the content and method of the new education imported from America directly to the Japanese situation. For that reason, perhaps, the search for an indigenous method and content of resocialization was launched first by school teachers.[4] *Echoes from a Mountain School* was one of the outstanding works to come out of this search. It has had a marked influence on postwar patterns of adult socialization.

The writing circles borrowed their group structures and the methods and content of their socialization from two major pre-war legacies of indigenous patterns of socialization: on one hand, the traditional agencies of socialization called *wakamono-gumi* (young men's groups) and *musume-gumi* (young women's

[3] Seikyō Muchaku, ed., *Yamabiko Gakkō*, Tokyo, Seidōsha, 1951. The most recent edition was published by Yuri Shuppan in Tokyo in 1957. In this essay I shall use this recent edition. An English version of the book is entitled *Echoes from a Mountain School*, tr. Kimura Michiko, Tokyo, Kenkyūsha, 1954.

[4] See Rokurō Hidaka, "Seikatsu Kiroku Undō" ("Life-Record Movement"), *Kōza Seikatsu Tsuzurikata* (*Lectures on Life-Composition*), Tokyo, Yuri Shuppan, 1963, v, 285-287.

groups) common in village communities during the Tokugawa period, and, on the other, the life-composition movement initiated by a group of school teachers before the war and developed by the postwar generation of school teachers.

During the Tokugawa period the sons of the samurai were educated at *han* (fief) schools, while the children of common people were educated at *terakoya* (temple schools). Schools of the first type concentrated on inculcating the knowledge necessary for the administrative positions normally held by the sons of samurai; the second type emphasized the practical skill in reading, writing, and arithmetic required by commoners' children. The *kumi*, unlike the schools, were peer groups.[5] In them young adults between the ages of about fifteen and thirty were trained for adult roles in their village communities. There they learned, among other things, the history of the village, the genealogy of the families in the village, the festival rituals and dancing, occupational skills and competence, the proper etiquette of social intercourse between men and women, the facts of sex, and the proper decorum of the young toward their elders. The young men and women dwelled in separate lodging places. The communal living of each group constituted the major part of its training. The young men visited the young women's lodging places during the evenings where they would talk together while engaged in their night work, the men, for example, weaving straw shoes and the women sewing. This gathering provided the opportunity for men and women to get to know each other and to choose their own mates. When a couple decided that they wished to marry, their respective groups would approve the match and argue its merits before the parents. Rarely could the parents resist the pressure even if they were opposed to the marriage.

The *kumi* members were independent of the authority of their *han* (fief) administration and of the *bakufu*, the central government. But they were not totally independent of the village com-

[5] For the exposition of *wakamono-gumi* and *musume-gumi*, see Kunio Yanagida, "Meiji Taishō Shi" ("A History of Meiji and Taishō"), *Yanagida Kunio Shū*, Tokyo, Chikuma Shobō, 1963, xxiv, 295-299; *idem*, "Konin no Hanashi," *ibid.*, 1963, xv, 43-53; Tarō Nakayama, *Nihon Wakamono Shi* (*A History of the Youths in Japan*), Tokyo, Nichibunsha, 1958. *Kodomo-gumi* (children's group) was found not only among farmers' children but also among samurai children. In the case of Aizu-*han* it was called *asobi* (a play group). See Moriichi Katsuta et al., *Nihon no Gakkō* (*Schools in Japan*), Tokyo, Iwanami, 1964, pp. 40-44.

munity or of the primary groups, except in the specific matter of the choice of a mate. Their adult roles were defined for them according to the tradition of the village community, and the members of the *kumi* were obliged to follow these traditional patterns. The training itself, however, was not carried on by the village elders but by the young adults themselves. In this limited sense, the *kumi* type of socialization was autonomous from the authorities of the village community. Both *wakamono-gumi* and *musume-gumi* persisted in villages until about the end of the Russo-Japanese War (1904-1905), when the state-controlled agency, *seinendan* (the youth organization), took over socialization of young adults.[6]

The postwar writing circles inherited some aspects of the traditional type of peer-group socialization: primary concentration on learning adult roles; autonomy, in the way of learning, from authorities outside of the state, of the village community, and of the primary groups; combination of learning with the recreation; and emphasis on the positive affect socialization of sharing and maximizing enjoyment and excitement among the members of the group.

Life-composition was a method of education initiated by school teachers who endeavored to develop rational, independently collectivistic, and voluntaristic types of ideas and action among their pupils at the time when education was controlled by the state for the inculcation of the predominantly nonrational, dependently collectivistic, and compulsory ideology of the Emperor system. The first attempt was made by a primary school teacher, Keinosuke Ashida (1873-1951), who advocated that children be encouraged to choose their own subject matter in writing compositions rather than forced to write on the stereotyped and uniform titles given by the teacher, as prescribed by the curriculum laid down by the Ministry of Education. In his book *Tsuzurika Kyōju* (*The Teaching of Composition*), published in 1913, he emphasized that composition based on freedom of choice of subject matter and freedom of expression was a potent means of developing individuality and initiative in children.[7] In 1919

6 See Katsuta, *ibid.*, p. 45; Nagano-ken Shimo Ina-gun Seinendan Shi Hensan Iinkai, ed., *Shimo Ina Seinen Undō Shi* (*A History of the Movement of the Youth Organization in Shimo Ina*), Tokyo, Kokudosha, 1960, p. 16.

7 See Takajirō Imai and Mitsushige Mineji, *Sakubun Kyōiku* (*Composition Education*), Tokyo, Tōyōkan, 1957, pp. 26-33; Keinosuke Ashida, *Keiu Jiden* (*Autobiography*), Tokyo, Kaigensha, 1950; Shunsuke Tsurumi,

a journal of children's literature, *Akai Tori* (*The Red Bird*), was launched by a novelist and children's story writer, Miekichi Suzuki (1882-1936). In this journal Suzuki set aside a column to which children were asked to contribute their compositions and poems, for which Suzuki himself would supply commentary. Suzuki encouraged the realistic and vivid description of the experiences of the children in their daily lives. The journal was discontinued in 1929 but was revived in 1931. It finally went out of existence with Suzuki's death in 1936.[8]

Mitsushige Mineji, a prewar leader of the life-composition movement, credits Suzuki with two contributions to the development of the movement. First, Suzuki and his journal cultivated among children the attitude of learning from the observation of facts and from their own experiences, rather than from the formal textbooks provided by the state. Second, he recognized dialects, the everyday language of common people, as legitimate tools of expression.[9] This last point needs to be emphasized. We have already observed that the prewar socialization both at schools and in the army stressed the importance of meticulous citation of the *Imperial Rescript,* which represented the most ceremonial of all the ceremonial languages. The styles of the language in which textbooks were written and in which belles lettres were composed also represented various kinds of ceremonial language. In accordance with the curriculum prescribed by the Ministry of Education, children were required to copy the samples of those various kinds of ceremonial language as their exercises in composition.

As opponents of this system, both Ashida and Suzuki endeavored to destroy the fetishism of ceremonial languages among teachers and children alike and to establish in their place a new attitude of respect for the everyday language of the common people. We have already contrasted ceremonial language as the vehicle for expressing the ideal pattern of one's thought, feel-

---

"Nihon no Puragumatizumu—Seikatsu Tsuzurikata Undō" ("Japanese Pragmatism—the Life-Composition Movement"), in Osamu Kuno and Shunsuke Tsurumi, *Gendai Nihon no Shisō* (*Contemporary Japanese Thought*), Tokyo, Iwanami, 1956, pp. 72-115; "Ashida Keinosuke Nenpu" ("A Chronological Table of Keinosuke Ashida"), *Kokugo Kyōiku* (*Japanese-Language Education*), No. 31 (July 1961), pp. 179-184.

[8] For a study of Miekichi Suzuki and his journal, see Nihon Jidō Bungakukai (The Japanese Association of Children's Literature) ed., *Akaitori Kenkyū* (*A Study of* The Red Bird), Tokyo, Komine Shoten, 1960.

[9] Imai and Mineji, *Sakuban Kyōiku*, pp. 58-66.

ings, and action with everyday language as the instrument for expressing the actual pattern. The chief merits of the life-composition method as initiated by Ashida and Suzuki were the introduction of the vernacular as the proper mode of expression in education and the advocacy of the direct expression of children's lives, feelings, ideas, and actions. It was left to the teachers of the postwar period to recognize the discrepancies between the ideal and actual patterns of life and thought as the proper subject matter of education through life-composition. Although Keinosuke Ashida and Miekichi Suzuki were not associated directly with one another, the former initiated the idea that freedom of expression among children should be respected, while the latter propagated this idea among the wider reading public.[10] Both men, moreover, were representative of the general democratic trends of the Taishō period (1912-1926). During these years various short-lived attempts were made to develop humanistic and democratic types of education to counteract the state-controlled education based on militarism and nationalism.[11] Thus the works of Ashida and Suzuki belong to the initial period of the life-composition movement.[12]

The second period of the movement began around 1929 with the appearance of the journals *Tsuzurikata Seikatsu* (*Composition Life*) published in Tokyo by teachers from various dis-

[10] *Ibid.*, p. 29.

[11] In 1917 a private school, Seijō Shōgakkō, was established in Tokyo as an experimental school in Japan by Masajirō Sawayanagi, who advocated that education promote the development of the creative and critical faculties of children. In this school, instead of the state-made textbooks, textbooks written by the teachers of the school were used. These "home-made" textbooks had a great impact on various other schools. At this school ceremonies on national holidays such as the Emperor's Birthday (*Tenchōsetsu*) and National Foundation Day (*Kigensetsu*) were abolished. Similar experimental schools emerged both in Tokyo and in other parts of Japan. See Katsuta et al., *Nihan no Gakkō*, pp. 205-218.

[12] Miekichi Suzuki criticized the group of teachers who called their work the life-composition movement and kept himself aloof from them. It cannot be denied, however, that *The Red Bird* and Miekichi Suzuki inspired many teachers who later became leaders of the life-composition movement. See Imai and Mineji, *Sakuban Kyōiku*, pp. 75-76. For instance, Michita Suzuki, who later became a leader of the movement, wrote about the deep impression he had received from Miekichi Suzuki's lecture given in a northern city, Sendai, where Michita Suzuki taught school. "I was greatly inspired. I was impressed by his [Miekichi Suzuki's] contention that the aim of teaching composition is not to make children write belles lettres but to let them write human records of their own lives." Chūdo Kan, "Akai Tori no Seiritsu to Hatten" ("The Establishment and Development of *The Red Bird*"), in Nihon Jidō Bungakukai, ed., *Akaitori Kenkyū*, p. 17.

tricts, *Hoppō Kyōiku* (*Northern Education*) published in Akita Prefecture in the northeastern part of Japan, and *Kokugojin* (*The Japanese Language Teacher*) published in Tottori Prefecture in the central part of Japan.

There were three noteworthy features of this second phase of the movement. First, its prime movers were primary and secondary school teachers scattered all over the country. The local groups of teachers in the northeastern districts, in Hokkaidō, in the northern inland districts, and in Tottori Prefecture in the central area were especially strong. A group of teachers in Tokyo acted as a center of communications among the autonomous local groups instead of imposing its own ideas on them. Their deep local roots of these groups, the multiplicity of ideas expressed within them, and the absence of any central hierarchical authority distinguished the life-composition movement from most of the new intellectual movements since the inception of the modernization of Japan. Practically all of the new intellectual movements were launched by a group of intellectual elites educated at universities either in Tokyo or abroad, and their central organizations in Tokyo disseminated their ideas to other cities, towns, and villages. The life-composition movement in its second phase was the first intellectual movement that emerged simultaneously from various localities and was initiated by nonuniversity graduates.[13] The relationships among different local groups, including the one in Tokyo, and among individual members in each group was predominantly egalitarian, independent, voluntaristic, and open. These characteristics of the groups distinguished them from the structure of the Emperor system, which was predominantly hierarchical, dependent, compulsory, and secret.

The second feature of the movement was that, without recourse to any specific preestablished system of rational ideas, the teachers who organized the groups managed to foster rational ways of thinking among children whose lives were circumscribed by relationships and modes of thought and behavior that were largely nonrational. Under the impact of financial crisis in 1927 and world depression in 1929, aggravated by bad harvests, the rice-producing villages in the northeastern part of Japan suffered acute poverty, especially during the years from 1927 to

---

[13] Most of those teachers were the graduates of normal schools. For the spread of the movement among different localities, see Imai and Mineji, *ibid.*, pp, 106-109.

1934. Even in normal times these areas were the poorest and least modernized of any districts in Japan. The teachers in these villages found that the content of the state textbooks was remote from the existential situation of the peasant children. For instance, the textbook used in compulsory moral education taught children to greet their parents in the morning with the most polite form of "good morning" (*ohayō gozai masu*), sitting on the *tatami*-matted floors and bowing most deferentially. The children who had been thus instructed at school actually practiced the proper decorum on wooden floors with no *tatami* mats, to the consternation of their parents. The parents regarded their children's behavior as an insult to their destitute way of life, since they themselves had never lived in a social situation where this form of greeting would have been correct.[14] The teachers were not satisfied with the method of composition advocated by the editor of *The Red Bird*, feeling that he was more interested in improving children's literary style than in improving their living conditions.[15] Nor did the teachers find the dogmatic Marxism advocated by the intellectual elites of the Communist Party relevant to day-to-day classroom teaching in their remote villages.[16] Thus the teachers could find no ready-made theory or method of education suitable to their purpose, which was to develop a rational way of thinking and acting among children who lived in the midst of a nonrational environment.

One of the methods they constructed out of their own teaching experiences was called "composition based on investigation." As advocated by Ichitarō Kokubun, this method emphasized the importance of allowing children to define the problems of their daily lives by themselves, of observing facts and analyzing the origins and solutions of the problems, and of cooperating with their teachers and with one another in finding answers to them even if they were of a personal nature.[17] This approach encouraged rational attitudes among children, since both the means and the ends of solving actual problems were

[14] This was an episode told to the author by one of the teachers who taught in a village in Tōhōku (northeastern) district in the prewar days.

[15] Imai and Mineji, *Sakuban Kyōiku*, pp. 83-84.

[16] Tarō Ogawa and Ichitarō Kokubun, eds., *Seikatsu Tsuzurikatateki Kyōiku Hōhō* (*The Life-Composition Method of Education*), Tokyo, Meiji Tosho, 1955, p. 91.

[17] Ichitarō Kokubun, "Shiraberu Tsuzurikata no Shuppatsu to Sonogo" ("The Beginning of Composition Based on Investigation and Its Aftermath"), 1934—quoted in Imai and Mineji, *Sakuban Kyōiku*, p. 113.

empirical and the children were encouraged to test the validity of the proposed means of achieving the ends envisaged. This approach fostered independently collectivistic attitudes among children, for each member of the class was expected to think on his own and at the same time was invited to cooperate in solving problems.

The third notable aspect of the second phase of the life-composition movement was the institution of mimeographed collections of compositions called *bunshū*. Usually a *bunshū* was compiled by the teacher of a particular class with the cooperation of the pupils. Each *bunshū* had its own title and was issued either monthly, quarterly, biannually, or at some other regular interval, depending on the aim of the individual teacher. The *bunshū* served various functions. It was used as a homemade informal textbook to be read and discussed by children in a composition class. At a time when education was officially based on unidirectional communication from teacher to pupils, the *bunshū* served to promote mutual communication between teacher and pupils and among pupils themselves, thereby promoting a sense of solidarity in the classroom. *Bunshū* were exchanged among teachers of different schools in various districts, as well as among teachers in the same school. Thus, through the exchange of *bunshū*, the teachers established an informal communications network of their own and strengthened their solidarity at a time when the sole formal communication teachers had was a one-way line from the Ministry of Education, the policy-making center of state-controlled education. According to an educational journal published in 1936, there were about one hundred and twelve representative *bunshū* circulating among teachers in that year.[18]

The life-composition movement in its second phase was an educational movement consisting of voluntary and informal groups of teachers resisting state-controlled formal education. It was a unique movement in that the content and method of education deviated from the state-controlled system and the structure of the groups departed from the structure of relationships characteristic of the Emperor system. After the outbreak of the Sino-Japanese War in 1937, the teachers who were promoters of the life-composition movement were gradually purged

---

[18] According to the list of *bunshū* published in *Kyōiku—Kokugo Kyōiku* (Education—Japanese-Language Education), Feb. 1936, there were 112 titles. On the basis of this list, Table 31 was worked out.

TABLE 31

DISTRIBUTION OF BUNSHŪ

Area	No. of bunshū
Hokkaidō	10
Tōhoku Chihō (northeastern district)	20
Kantō Chihō (eastern district)	25
Chūbu Chihō (central district)	14
Kinki Chihō (near metropolis district including Kyoto, Nara, and Ōsaka)	17
Chūgoku Chihō (central inland district)	15
Shikoku Chihō	1
Kyūshū Chihō	5
Korea	3
Manchuria	1
China (Japanese school in Shanghai)	1
Total	112

SOURCE: Shunsuke Tsurumi, "Nihon no Puragumatizumu," p. 99. See also Imai and Mineji, *Sakuban Kyōiku*, pp. 142-144.

from their teaching posts. Some three hundred were arrested and thrown in prison in 1940, and a number of them died there.[19]

The third phase of the life-composition movement was initiated by Seikyō Muchaku and his class of forty-three pupils at a high school in Yamamoto village in Yamagata Prefecture. While inheriting the prewar legacies of both the *kumi* type of socialization and the life-composition method, they added something new to them. Muchaku's method was similar to the latter insofar as he cultivated rational, voluntary, and independently collectivistic ways of thinking among his pupils by encouraging them to write about their own life experiences in their everyday language and to discuss in the group the actual problems presented in their writings. But he did not stop there. He oriented this writing and discussion method toward the redefinition of his pupils' present roles as sons and daughters of peasants and their future roles as adults in the village community. His method was akin to the *kumi* type of socialization in that he emphasized the learning of future adult roles in the village community but

[19] See Ichitarō Kokubun, ed., *Ishi o mote Owaruru Gotoku* (*To Be Driven Away as Though with Stones*), Tokyo, Eihōsha, 1956. This is a collection of essays written by fourteen teachers who participated in the life-composition movement in the prewar period about their experiences of purge, arrest, and imprisonment.

departed from it in that he advocated the redefinition rather than the mere acceptance of those roles as traditionally pre-scribed. Muchaku so organized his class that, in effect, it became a clearinghouse for the tensions of his pupils as they searched for new definitions of their roles.[20]

After the military defeat there was a general switch in the policy of education in public high schools. During the war years a typical high school principal addressed his pupils at the open-ing ceremony thus: "A high school is the place to learn how to die honorably for the sake of our country, and for the sake of the Emperor."[21] In contrast, Tōzaburō Satō, the valedictorian of his graduating class at Yamamoto High School in 1951, de-clared: "At our high school we have learned how tremendously important human life is, and how to live it worthily."[22] The ideal of postwar education was to inculcate in children a desire for a better life instead of training them to be prepared for the worst —namely, their own death. In the course of teaching social studies, Muchaku found various discrepancies between the ideal and actual patterns of the social structure. He encouraged his pupils to write about their actual life experiences and to compare with the ideal pattern of life described in their textbooks. Then he promoted discussion in the class to redefine the roles of peasants in such a way that they would work to bridge the gap between the actual and the ideal.

His method is illustrated in the handling of the problem faced by one of his pupils, Kōichi Eguchi. Kōichi was in his second year at the high school when his widowed mother died, leaving behind her Kōichi, his younger brother and sister, and his grand-mother of seventy-four. His family owned only three-quarters of an acre, on which they grew tobacco. Kōichi, as the eldest son, had to assume sole responsibility for supporting his family,

<hr>

[20] William J. Goode describes the family as "the main center of role allocation" for adults and children. He writes: "it also becomes a vantage point from which to view one's total role system in perspective. . . . Thus it is from this center that one learns the basic procedures of balancing role strains." See his "A Theory of Role Strain," *American Sociological Review*, xxv, No. 4 (Aug. 1960), 493. It is our contention that the circle is the functional equivalent of the family as "a role budget center" where the family fails to function as such, either for lack of communication among its members, long absence of some members of the family, or other reasons. This point will be developed in the chapters on the family.

[21] Kunio Shiratori, *Mumei no Nihonjin* (*The Anonymous Japanese*), Tokyo, Miraisha, 1961, p. 189.

[22] Muchaku, ed., *Yamabiko Gakkō*, p. 250.

working in the field, drying and pressing tobacco leaves, marketing them, and buying the necessary provisions for the family. At the suggestion of his teacher, he made up a schedule of his farm work and realized that he scarcely had time to attend school, although he thought it was vital for him to finish at least high school. He discovered that, on the income from the three-quarters of an acre of land plus a welfare allowance, his mother, confronted by accumulated debts, had found it impossible to make ends meet. His mother had worked hard, had borne her burdens quietly and died. But Kōichi learned at school that, according to the new Constitution, every Japanese was entitled to live "a healthy and happy life." He wanted to finish high school so that he could learn a new role for an adult peasant and work to improve his life. Kōichi was playing a double role: full-time farmer supporting a family and student under an obligation to complete his education.

Kōichi spelled out his dilemma in writing, outlining his schedule of farm work and the precise amount of his family budget. The teacher displayed Kōichi's writing to the class, and after discussion his classmates decided to help him with his farm work after school and on weekends so that Kōichi would be able to attend school. The teacher himself moved from another hamlet to Kōichi's village in order to be able to participate in the project.[23] The conflict of roles a member of the class had faced was at least temporarily alleviated by the help of his classmates, who in their turn learned a possible pattern of management of their own problems.

The enduring effect that Muchaku's teaching exerted on his pupils was partly due to the establishment of a mainly positive affect type of socialization in an environment where negative affects predominated. Most of the forty-three children's compositions collected in *Echoes from a Mountain School* describe the poverty of their peasant families. Left to themselves, the children might have succumbed to distress, anxiety, and shame. But in the classroom discussion they were encouraged to take the roles of others so that the distress and anxiety of one child could be shared by the others, who would try to alleviate his burden, as they had done for Kōichi. Enjoyment and excitement were also shared by all the members of the class, particularly when the

[23] See Kōichi Eguchi, "Haha no Shi to Sonogo" ("Mother's Death and Its Aftermath"), *ibid.*, pp. 14-29. This composition won the Minister of Education Prize in 1955.

time arrived for the annual excursion, for which the members of the class worked to save money so that everyone could go.[24] Both in distress and in enjoyment Muchaku stressed mutuality and the sharing of experiences. His method of socialization was based primarily on the model of perfect communication.

The postwar writing circles of adults inherited this pattern of socialization of school children, an amalgamation of the traditional *kumi* type of socialization and the life-composition method. We shall examine one type of circle, a writing circle consisting of a group of female workers in a textile mill.

2. A WRITING CIRCLE IN A TEXTILE MILL: TOWARD THE INTEGRATION OF THE ROLES OF PEASANT DAUGHTER AND INDUSTRIAL WORKER

Productivity in the textile industry as a percentage of productivity in all manufacturing industries declined from the prewar average of 32.8 percent (1934-1936) to 12.3 percent in 1960.[25] The proportion of female workers in the textile industry, however, is still higher than in any other sector of manufacturing. In most textile mills they make up 80 percent or more of the total labor force.[26] According to a survey undertaken by the Labor Ministry in 1951, 66.9 percent of these women textile workers were of agrarian origin.[27] The same survey shows that their average age was 19.6 and their average period of service two years and three months.[28] About 80 percent of them lived in the dormitories attached to the factories.[29] Most of these workers had left

[24] Same Eguchi, "Sugikawa Seoi" ("The Job of Cedar Bark Transportation"), and Miharu Abe, "Ryokō no Kotonado" ("On the Excursion and Other Matters"), *ibid.*, pp. 72-77, 103-107.

[25] Hyōe Ōuchi et al., *Nihon Keizai Zusetsu* (*The Japanese Economy in Graphs*), Tokyo, Iwanami, 1965, pp. 80-81.

[26] See Rōdōshō Fujin Shōnen Kyoku (Women and Minors' Bureau of the Labor Ministry), *Fujin Rōdō no Jitsujō* (*The Conditions of Women Labor*), Tokyo, 1961, p. 25. According to the report made by Nihon Bōseki Dōgyōkai (The Spinning Manufacturers' Association), the average ratio of female workers in the factories under the management of the nine major spinning companies in Japan was 86.2 percent for 1947. See Seiji Keizai Kenkyūjo (Political and Economic Research Institute), *Fujin Rōdō no Kihon Mondai—Sengo Bōshoku Kōjō no Jittai Chōsa* (*The Basic Problems of Female Labor—A Survey of the Postwar Spinning and Weaving Factories*), Tokyo, Chūō Rōdō Gakuen, 1948, p. 1.

[27] Rōdōshō Fujin Shōnen Kyoku, *Bōseki Kōjō no Joshi Rōdōsha*, Tokyo, 1951—cited in Chitose Shimazu, *Joshi Rōdōsha—Sengo no Menbō Kōjō* (*Women Workers—Cotton Spinning Mills in the Postwar Period*), Tokyo, Iwanami, 1953, p. 172.

[28] *Ibid.*, pp. 176-177.

[29] Seiji Keizai Kenkyūjo, *Fujin Rōdō no Kihon Mondai*, p. 2.

their agrarian villages immediately after completing their compulsory education. Often they went back to their native villages to marry farmers. This general pattern of migration among female textile workers made them the potential connecting links between agrarian and urban ways of life. They could play a vital role in integrating the values, norms, and actions of peasants and those of industrial workers.

We can study the impact of factory life on workers of agrarian origin from the point of view of labor commitment.[30] The process of labor commitment of workers of agrarian origin, like the process of adult socialization, involves the relationship between two sets of values, norms, ideas, and overt actions. The workers come into factories as young adults or as adults with values, norms, ideas, and overt actions acquired previously in the village community. It is likely that most of them are precommitted to the village way of life. It can be assumed, then, that the possible processes of labor commitment among them will be describable according to the types of personality change we have already schematized (see Chapter One, Section 3. We shall therefore redefine the six general types of personality change in terms of the processes of labor commitment.

Let us assume that a person is early in his life committed to V (the set of values, norms, ideas, and overt actions characteristic of the village community) and at a later time is exposed to I (the set of values, norms, ideas, and overt actions characteristic of the industrial system). The types of labor commitment can then be summarized in the following way.

Ever committed. The ever committed person subscribes to at least some part of V but no part of I. He is uncommitted from the point of view of the industrial system.

Reversely committed. The reversely committed person empties himself of V and replaces it with at least some part of I. From the point of view of the industrial system, he is fully committed—at least for as long as he is in the factory.

Deviant. The deviant is committed neither to V nor to I. From the point of view of the industrial system, he is totally uncommitted and may be called an "outright deviant."

Many-layered self. The many-layered self retains some part of V while adopting some part of I and thus compartmentalizes

[30] For the definition of labor commitment, see Wilbert E. Moore and Arnold S. Feldman, eds., *Labor Commitment and Social Change in Developing Areas*, New York, Social Science Research Council, 1960, pp. 1-4.

them. From the point of view of the industrial system, he is semi-committed and can very well be an "external conformist."

Conflicting self. The conflicting self retains at least some part of V but at the same time is drawn to I and is conscious of the conflicts within himself between V and I. From the point of view of the industrial system, he is semi-committed and ambivalent.

Innovator. The innovator sifts out parts of both V and I in relation to the goal he himself has chosen and integrates at least some of each of V and I to create a new pattern. From the point of view of the industrial system, the innovator is fully committed. He may bring about changes both in the industrial system itself and in the village community system.

The writing circle we shall study was composed of workers in a factory in a town near Ōsaka, one of four owned by a wool textile company employing altogether 5,000 workers. The writing circle numbered about fifty members, mainly women. These female textile workers were exposed to four different socializing agencies—their families, management, their labor union, and their circle. We shall begin by examining the influence the first three of these agencies exerted on the workers.

Female textile workers in the prewar period were generally members of at least two groups—their families and the company where they worked. In the postwar period another group affiliation was added—the labor union. These three major groups function as agencies of socialization, each prescribing a specific role for its members. A female worker in a unionized industry has at least three roles to play—as a daughter, as a laborer, and as a trade unionist. We shall seek first to determine what is involved in these three role prescriptions.

The Family: The Role of a Daughter in Relation to her Peasant Parents (representing the core of the agrarian way of life for a female textile worker)

Historically, since the beginning of textile mills in the 1870's, female textile labor has been described as "family budget supplementary labor." According to the classical works of Moritarō Yamada and Yoshitarō Hirano published in the 1930's, there existed "a vicious circle between the high land-rent of tenant farmers and the semi-slave-like low wages of the industrial workers" who were the sons and daughters of those tenant farmers.[31] The land tax reform of 1878 required that 30 percent of the crop produced per *tan* be paid to the government as a land tax and 38 percent to the landlord as land rent, leaving only 32 percent to the tenant farmer.[32] In the 1890's, 45.1 percent of the farmers were tenant farmers, cultivating an average of about one acre of land, and thus about half of the farming population in Japan were then living on approximately 30 percent of the crop yielded by about 1.2 acres of land. Jikei Yokoi, a prominent critic of those days, commented: "A tenant farmer cultivating only one acre is not a farmer. . . . It is obviously impossible to feed five mouths from one acre of land."[33]

Female textile workers in the prewar period were recruited mainly from the families of these petty tenant farmers. They were expected to send their remittances home in order to supplement the deficits of their parents' budgets. These circumstances gave employers an excuse for keeping their wages below subsistence, since they were not expected to support themselves but only to supplement their families' budgets. The below subsistence wages, in their turn, made it impossible for the female workers to become fully committed to their work. Even after the land reform of 1946, under which most of the tenant farmers became owner-cultivators, the prewar pattern of family budget supplementary labor persisted among female workers. In 1952, 90 percent of the female textile workers still sent remittances home, amounting on an average to 30 percent of their monthly wage ($20.60). Of these women 41.5 percent acknowledged that they were working to supplement the family budget, and 29.5 percent said that they were working to save for wedding expenses; only 13.1 percent declared that they were working to support themselves.[34]

[31] Yoshitarō Hirano, *Nihon Shihonshugi Shakai no Kikō* (*The Structure of the Capitalist Society of Japan*), rev. edn., Tokyo, Iwanami, 1959, pp. 95-96.

[32] *Ibid.*, p. 28.

[33] Jikei Yokoi, "The Shaking of Agrarian Foundations," *Taiyō*, iii, No. 2 (1897), 210—quoted *ibid.*, p. 85.

[34] Shōbei Shioda, "Zenkoku Seni Sangyō Rōdōkumiai-dōmei" ("The National League of Textile Workers' Unions"), in Kazuo Ōkōchi, ed., *Nihon Rōdō Kumiai Ron* (*Essays on Labor Unions in Japan*), Tokyo, Yūhikaku, 1954, pp. 285-286. The family budget supplementary system is not limited to textile workers but encompasses all working women in Japan. According to a survey conducted in 1948 by the Women and Minors' Bureau of the Ministry of Labor, 68.1 percent of the 1,705 women working in various industries in Tokyo replied that they were working to supplement their family budgets. See Rōdōshō Fujin Shōnen Kyoku, *Fujin to Shokugyō*

In her role as a daughter of peasants, a female worker was not expected to be a fully economically independent person. Her earnings were not considered to belong entirely to her but were regarded as an integral part of the total family income.[35] This concept of a family income in which the individual contribution is not distinguishable was derived from a pattern of agricultural production where the family members worked as a unit with no sharp identification of the amount of labor performed by individual members. Since the land belonged to the family, the fruits of the labor of each individual person accrued to the family as a whole, represented by the head of the family.

Although the view of female labor as family budget supplementary labor has an agrarian origin, it is related to the more general principle of *on* and repayment of *on*. According to the principle of *on*, the daughter is indebted to her parents for her birth and nurture, and she is expected to pay back her immeasurable debts to them. To give her parents as much of her earnings as they wish is the major part of the role prescription of a daughter of a peasant.

In this context the parent-daughter relationship was predominantly nonrational, particularistic, functionally diffuse, intimate, dependently collectivistic, hierarchical, compulsory, secret, and exploitative.

The Company: The Role of an Employee in Relation to Management (representing partially the industrial way of life for a female textile worker)

Since the inception of the textile industry, management has been a staunch advocate and ingenious inventor of paternalistic labor policies. One of these was the dormitory system. In the dormitories fifteen to twenty girls were housed in one room with twenty *tatami* mats. The female employees were under the

---

(*Women and Occupations*), Tokyo, 1948, p. 11. According to the survey made by the author in 1948, 74.2 percent of the 350 female workers in textile, machine, communications, finance, chemical, and transportation industries and in civil service were family budget supplementary workers. See Kazuko Tsurumi, "Seikatsu Kiroku Izen—Hataraku Fujin no Ishiki Chōsa" ("Before Entering Life-Record Movements—An Attitude Survey of Working Women"), *Seikatsu Kiroku Undō no Nakade* (*An Essay on the Life-Record Movement*), Tokyo, Miraisha, 1963, pp. 7-16.

[35] In the prewar days there existed a type of indentured labor among textile workers. Under this system the company recruiting agent paid advance money to the parents, and the daughter had to work "to pay back" the money given to her parents.

care of surrogate mothers, elderly women who kept daily records of their charges' comings and goings and who also taught sewing, cooking, and other domestic arts and skills. The company managers were father substitutes. The young women were subject to restrictions in their freedom to go out and were pressured to work hard and punished for failure to live up to the standard of production set by the management; sometimes violence was used and was justified in the name of *oyagokoro* (parental benevolence). In each room of the dormitory, newcomers were taught to call their senior roommates "elder sister"; some of the seniors were subforewomen in the factory. Thus a fictitious family relationship was imposed by the management on the girls, one which kept them under twenty-four hours' surveillance by agents of the management. There were also "uncles," who were recruiting agents stationed in the native villages of the working girls. They carried remittances and messages from the girls to their parents. In this way the female workers were also kept under the remote control of their own parents through these human pipelines.[36]

After the war, legislation was passed to protect the workers. For instance, the Labor Standard Act of 1947 states: "Employers must not interfere with the freedom of the private lives of laborers who live in the dormitory." Promoting self-government in the dormitory, the Act declares: "Employers must not interfere with the election of any of the officers of the dormitory, including the chairman and the room heads." According to the law, the workers should participate in making and revising the rules necessary for maintaining orderly dormitory life.[37] Thus in theory the dormitory system was democratized, and autonomy and privacy for the workers in their dormitory life were established.

[36] For the prewar conditions of the female textile workers, Wakizō Hosoi's *Jokō Aishi* (*A Tragic History of Female Workers*), Tokyo, Kaizōsha, 1929, is a most prominent classical work on the subject. For the history of female silk mill workers, see Mitsuhaya Kajinishi et al., *Seishi Rōdōsha no Rekishi* (*A History of Silk Mill Workers*), Tokyo, Iwanami, 1955. For a report, based on interview materials covering three generations of textile workers, concerning their changing working conditions and attitudes, see Kazuko Tsurumi, "Onna Sandai no Ki" ("A Record of the Three Generations of Women Workers"), *Seikatsu Kiroku Undō no Nakade*, pp. 98-129.
[37] "Rōdō Kijun Hō" ("The Labor Standard Act"), in Hiroshi Suekawa, ed., *Kihon Roppō* (*The Six Basic Laws*), Tokyo, Iwanami, 1962, Ch. X, Articles 94-96, p. 771.

But in practice, by a variety of means, management still restricts the lives of the workers in the dormitories.[38]

The persistence of the dormitory system and of the fictitious family relationship between the company and the workers in the textile industry is related to the whole attitude of the management toward the female workers. The management does not expect them to stay long in the factory. The head of a spinning plant expressed this view of the management:

> Owing to the increasing use of machines in the textile industry, there is little need for highly skilled female labor. Actually a female worker develops her skill to a high level in three years, reaches her peak after five years, and her efficiency comes down after that. . . . Therefore, from the point of view of the company, except for the male workers whose labor is required for the most skilled operations, we do not want our workers to stay too long. Four to five years of service is enough from female workers.[39]

The management does not expect a lifetime commitment to the industrial system from female workers as it does from male workers. It expects them to be committed workers, but only for a limited period—from the time immediately after the completion of their compulsory education until marriage. They are expected to be hard-working, efficient, and docile workers with a short-term commitment. Emphasis on the fictitious family relationship and on learning practical domestic skills in the dormitory reinforces this managerial policy.

The management-labor relationship in the postwar period in general is ideally rational, universalistic, functionally specific, avoidant, independently individualistic, and hierarchical, although a degree of compulsion, secrecy, and exploitation remains. In theory at least some degree of voluntariness, openness, and reciprocity is emphasized in modern labor management. Owing partly to the persistence of the fictitious family

[38] In 1952 the League of All Textile Workers' Unions issued a statement that it was the duty of the labor unions to work toward actual democratization of the dormitory system in the textile industry. Shimazu, *Joshi Rōdōsha*, pp. 170-171.

[39] *Ibid.*, pp. 174-175. The quoted interview took place in 1937. However, the author quotes a statement made by a member of the labor-management section of a textile company, expressing exactly the same view to her during her field research in the early 1950's.

relationship, however, the actual pattern of the management-labor relationship in the textile industry still tends to be predominantly particularistic, functionally diffuse, intimate, dependently collectivistic, compulsory, secret, and exploitative.

*The Labor Union: The Role of a Rank-and-file Member in
Relation to Union Leaders (representing partially the industrial
way of life for a female textile worker)*

There are two major federations of labor unions in the textile industry. The first is the Zensen Dōmei (National League of Textile Workers), consisting in 1960 of 442,000 workers, 64 percent of whom were women. The second is the Seni Rōren (Federation of Textile Workers' Unions), consisting in 1960 of 32,000 members, 80 percent of whom were women.[40] Zensen encompasses mainly cotton and wool workers, whereas Seni is composed of silk workers. The former is affiliated with the Zenrō Kaigi (National Labor Congress), which represents the right wing of the Japanese labor movement. The latter is affiliated with the Chūritsu Rōren (Independent Labor Unions' League). The group of workers we shall study here belongs to the former.

Although the majority of workers in the textile industry are women, very few women are elected to be officers in their unions. According to the survey conducted by the Women and Minors' Bureau of the Ministry of Labor in 1951, in the twenty-five factories where 85 percent of union members were women, only 16 percent of the union officers were women. One out of five male union members was elected to office, compared with only one out of forty-three female union members.[41] Women's participation in union activities is thus still relatively low. There are various reasons for this anomaly. First, as long as they are short-term workers (as prescribed by the management) rather than career workers, they cannot be vitally interested in the efforts to improve long-term working conditions, which constitute the major activities of the unions. Second, most of the male union leaders usually use a stereotyped jargon, the "ceremonial language" of the unions, which is remote from the everyday language of the rank-and-file laborers and thus creates a difficulty in communication for the female workers. Third, there is for women a stigma attached to labor union activities in general

[40] See Rōdōshō Fujin Shōnen Kyoku, *Fujin Rōdō no Jitsujō*, p. 134. The statistics are for the year 1961.
[41] Shimazu, *Joshi Rōdōsha*, pp. 230-231.

and specifically to speaking out in public. The present writer has asked in the course of her research among textile workers why few women spoke up in any of the public meetings held in the factory when there were any men present. The women replied that they would be considered unfeminine if they spoke in public, and they feared that they would thereby lose their chances of marriage, which were already slight because of the great preponderance of women in textile factories.

The labor union ideally expects all its members, both male and female, to be fully committed to the industrial system on a long-term basis. The role of a union member is to be conscious of his or her rights and duties as a full-fledged, self-supporting worker. It is difficult for family budget supplementary workers to have that attitude, and they are therefore usually indifferent to union activities and subservient to the union leaders when called upon to act, as in the election of officers or voting on resolutions.

The ideal pattern of the relationship between rank-and-file members and leaders of the labor union is rational, universalistic, functionally specific, independent, collectivistic, intimate, hierarchical, voluntaristic, open, and reciprocal. Owing to the difficulties mentioned above, however, the actual pattern of the relationship between female rank-and-file members and union leaders tends to be predominantly particularistic, dependent, individualistic, compulsory, secret, and exploitative.

The Circle: Toward the Redefinition of the Roles of a Female Worker and a Peasant Wife and Mother

The foregoing description shows the general circumstances within which female textile workers lived in the postwar period. The condition of the female workers in a wool factory of about 1,000 workers situated in a city near Ōsaka was similar. In this factory there emerged a writing circle of some fifty women and three men. Most of the young women had come from villages along the Ina valley in Nagano Prefecture immediately after they graduated from high school. Those who finished school around 1950 had been exposed to two conflicting ideologies. They had been indoctrinated with militarism in the primary schools during the war and with democratic principles at high school after the war. When they entered the factory, they were exposed to the kind of conflicting demands from the management, from the labor union, and from their own parents outlined

above. How to meet these conflicting demands and how to cope
with the discrepancies between what they had learned at high
school and what they actually encountered in the factory were
difficult problems for these girls.

At first they gathered together in their leisure hours for singing, chatting, reading, and writing group diaries under the leadership of Yoshirō Sawai, who was then on the executive committee
of the labor union. The circle was formed as a subgroup of the
union. When *Echoes from a Mountain School* was published in
1951, Sawai recommended the book to the circle. The girls found
that their family backgrounds were very similar to those of the
children in the mountain school, and they were impressed by
the children's endeavors to improve their lot. They began to
write about their own families in the villages, as simply and as
frankly as the children had in their compositions. Twenty-two
essays were collected and mimeographed in the first issue of
their *bunshū,* entitled *My Family.* The common theme of these
writings was the necessity of making remittances to their families.
Michiko Tanaka, who had finished only compulsory education
and whose family of seven owned less than two acres of land,
wrote:

> With the help of the remittance I have been sending home
> since April, my younger sister entered senior high school. To
> tell the truth, I did not want to send money home. Who wants
> to sacrifice herself by sending money to her family when she
> herself could not afford even to buy the book she wants?
> However, my determination not to send money home was
> undermined when I went back there during the New Year's
> holidays. In our house, I found the *tatami* mats as worn out
> as ever, the kitchen, which we had planned to remodel, left
> as it always had been, and the sliding screens, with their paper
> torn and patched. I saw nothing but signs of poverty in our
> house, and that made me promise my parents that I would
> send them a monthly remittance. My younger sister looked
> terribly sorry for me. So I wrote to her and encouraged her to
> write to me giving the news of her school life. In reply, I
> received a letter from her: "Our parents told me not to write
> to you about school lest that might disturb you. Since there
> is nothing very much to tell you outside of my experience at
> school, you will receive fewer letters from me." I do hope my

sister will feel more relaxed and learn what is necessary for the improvement of our future lives as farmers' wives.[42]

Harumi Shiga's father died in the war, and her mother and elder brother worked on the farm, which consisted of 0.84 acres of paddy field and 0.84 acres of dry field. She, too, expressed reluctance to give up her earnings:

> Even the barn is inside our house. The ceiling is low and the pillars lean a bit to the west. A large fireplace is dug in the floor in the center of the room so that the smoke circulating in the room makes the sliding screens constantly sooty. The Shinto altar in the simply made alcove is so sooty that we cannot read the words on the tablets. The red Dharma doll has turned black. This must be a very old peasant house. . . .
>
> In a letter from home they said they had our house repaired. I expected it to be in better shape. However, to my disappointment, when I returned home in April, I found only the verandah slightly improved.
>
> "It cost us two thousand yen," my mother said, as though it had been a great extravagance. I gave her two thousand yen which was all I had then. Later, my mother wrote to me and told me to send more money for repairs to the store house. I got angry, thinking that my family was too demanding. Maybe they cannot help it.
>
> I answered my mother that I have to live my own life. What is my own life? I have never described to my family in a detailed way how I and my friends live in the factory.
>
> As a matter of course everybody wants to live in a nice house, to wear pretty clothes, and to eat good food. That is why, I think, we are trying hard and we should try harder.[43]

In the prewar days it was taken for granted that the girls' wages belonged not to themselves but to their parents. But these girls, who had received a postwar education and had learned that each individual has fundamental human rights including the right to one's own earnings, could not acquiesce in the traditionally prescribed role of a daughter duty-bound to support her poor peasant parents. Besides, their labor union's definition

---

[42] Michiko Tanaka, "Ie no Hitotachi" ("My Folks"), in Junji Kinoshita and Kazuko Tsurumi, eds., *Haha no Rekishi* (*History of Mothers*), Tokyo, Kawade Shobō, 1954, pp. 21-22.

[43] Harumi Shiga, "Watashi no Ie" ("My Family"), *ibid.*, pp. 42-43.

of a living wage showed that they could not live on what they earned, even without sending money home. According to the labor union's wage demands, there was no allowance for remittances to be sent home. The women workers learned, as members of the union, that ideally they were independent of their parents and their parents of them. Actually, however, as members of peasant families, they knew that their parents were poor and that they had to help them. Through writing and discussion in the circle, each girl came to realize that her own family was not the only poor one, that almost all the other girls' families were poor also, and that the problem of remittance was therefore common to all of them. They realized that it was the poverty of peasants that created the conflict between the ideal role of a member of the labor union and the actual role of a daughter of a peasant family.

They knew that most of them would eventually return to villages to be peasant wives. They felt that the only practical way for them to cope with the problem of poverty in the agrarian village was through a redefinition of the role of a wife and mother of an agrarian family. In order to achieve such a redefinition, they thought, it was necessary to know concretely what was involved in their traditional role. And the best method of learning that was to study the lives of their own mothers. Thus they agreed to write the biographies of their mothers. Forty-one biographies were collected and mimeographed in their second *bunshū*, entitled *My Mother*, in March 1953. Shortly thereafter some members of the circle read an essay written by a historian, Tadashi Ishimoda, who pointed out the importance of the role of mothers in the modern history of China and Korea. He also described the deeper influence his "feudal" and self-sacrificing mother exerted upon him and his work, compared to that of his "progressive" and self-centered father who had "modern" ideas. And he concluded: "The work and action of sons is always sustained by the sacrifice and sufferings of their mothers."[44] Inspired by this essay and other essays written by historians about this time, Sawai, the leader of the circle, suggested that the biographies of their peasant mothers might become a partial documentary basis for a history of common Japanese women. This time about ninety women and a few men participated.

[44] Tadashi Ishimoda, "Haha ni tsuite no Tegami" ("A Letter on the Mother"), *Rekishi to Minzoku no Hakken* (*The Discovery of History and Nation*), Tokyo, Tokyo Daigaku Shuppankai, 1952, pp. 346-370.

Those who had already written biographies expanded and revised their writings by interviewing their mothers when they returned home for a vacation or by asking their mothers questions by letter. Thus the third *bunshū, A History of Mothers*, was produced toward the end of the same year.[45]

Hisako Suzuki wrote about her mother, who was then fifty-three:

> When my mother had finished third grade in primary school, she left school to work in a silk mill. She gave her parents all the meagre wages she received at the factory, and her parents then returned a small sum for pocket money. When she was seventeen, she got pleurisy from overwork. Hard-working as she had been, she did not have money to see a doctor, so she took up Tenri-kyō [a folk religion] to cure herself. After her recovery she married my father. She told me that she had never met him until the day of their wedding. My father's house was also poor, and the mother-in-law was noted in the village as a strong, hard-working woman. For my mother who had been sick and had never worked on the field, it was a very difficult life. She says she did not even have a place in the house where she could be alone even when she wanted to cry.
>
> When I used to cry when my mother scolded me, she said: "It is good that you can cry now. When a woman gets married, she cannot afford to cry. If she cries in her bed, she is found out. If she cries in a toilet, her mother-in-law complains that she is in the toilet too long. If her face shows that she has been crying, her mother-in-law gossips about her with the other old women over their cups of tea. If she cries in front of her own parents when she is allowed to visit them once a year, she is scolded by her parents for being immature. It is good that you can cry now."
>
> Although my grandmother was a severe mother-in-law, she was very nice to us, her grandchildren. She also spent seventy-two years of as hard a life as my mother lived. . . .
>
> My mother used to tell me: "Do whatever your employers tell you to do. Be a good girl, and be recognized as a good

[45] For a detailed account of the development of the circle, see Yoshirō Sawai, "Noro Noro to Ayundekita Nakamatachi—Haha no Rekishi o Kaku made no Koto" ("The Group That Walked Very Slowly—Until We Wrote *History of Mothers*"), in Kinoshita and Tsurumi, eds., *Haha no Rekishi*, pp. 132-162.

girl by them." So I entered the factory thinking that it is best to work hard and be quiet. The first *Bon* [in July] after I entered the factory, the labor union demanded a lump sum for the workers. The managers said "no," but after many sessions of collective bargaining they paid us the lump sum we had demanded. This was an entirely new experience for me. If we had kept quiet when the managers refused to give us the extra pay we demanded, we would have got nowhere. For the first time I realized that, if we made no demands, the company would never increase our pay on its own accord, even if its profits increased.[46]

When the mothers' biographies were read and compared by the circle members, it was clear that there were some common themes in their mothers' lives. They were all more or less unhappy. The sources of their unhappiness were the existing structure of agricultural production and distribution, the war that deprived them either temporarily or permanently of their husbands or sons, and the extended family system under which the wife had to live with her parents-in-law whether or not her husband was alive. The most important from the point of view of the young girls was that, according to the traditional family system, their mothers' marriages had been arranged by their parents and were not based on love of the partner. In the group the young women also pointed out that, although all their mothers were very hard-working and self-sacrificing for their own families, they were extremely competitive in relation to other families and never tried to cooperate with others outside of their own families to improve the common lot. In keeping with the traditional village norms, they believed that hard work is to be rewarded by a good harvest and that obedience is to be rewarded by protection. They were resigned to what they called their fate and told their daughters to be obedient to their superiors and to be resigned to their lot as well. The daughters sympathized with their unhappy mothers and had tremendous respect for their perseverance in the face of their hardships; but, since their attitude of absolute obedience to their own parents, their parents-in-law, and their husbands had brought them unhappiness, they began to try not to be so blindly submissive

[46] Hisako Suzuki, "Onna no Mondai—Haha to Watashi no Baai" ("The Problem of a Woman—Case Studies of My Mother and I"), *ibid.*, pp. 115-119.

to their superiors. Because their mothers' attitude of resignation kept them perpetually poor, they began to search for a better way of coping with their environment.

The young women concluded that the most practical first step to becoming "happier mothers" than their own mothers was to try to select their own mates on a basis of mutual understanding and love. Three pairs of fortunate lovers emerged out of the circle. This apparently happy result became a great stumbling block for the circle, however. There were only three eligible young men in the circle, not counting the leader, Sawai. Each of these three men was liked by three or four girls, who were naturally brokenhearted when they realized that the men were committed to one particular girl. The leader, Sawai, was handsome, intelligent, well-informed, kind, understanding—he had all the qualities that young girls adore. Whatever difficulties of a personal or collective nature arose, the girls consulted him, and he always put their problems before the group for discussion. Although he had many admirers in the circle, he never committed himself to any of them; instead, he treated them all as good friends. His attitude toward the girls was a stabilizing factor in the circle, especially in this critical period when the girls who had been successful in "catching" the men were the targets of the others' jealousy and antagonism. The majority of the girls blamed the three pairs of lovers for being so involved in each other's company that they neglected their obligations to the group. When they discussed the matter with Sawai, he suggested they bless the lovers instead of accusing them. "We have always tried to share our joys and sufferings," he said. "From this point of view, if any two persons in our group fall in love, don't you think it is only reasonable that we should congratulate them?" The girls agreed that Sawai's reasoning was correct.

The girls discussed the best way to congratulate the couples and devised a new ritual which they called *kokeshi okuri* (presentation of a pair of *kokeshi*—wooden folk-art dolls). They planned a picnic outing to a nearby mountain. Thirty-five members gathered on the mountain. They boiled rice on the campfire, ate their supper of rice and tinned tuna, and sang. During a pause in the singing one of the girls began to speak: "As all of you very well know, we have three pairs of lovers among us. We want to congratulate them today." Producing three boxes, she continued:

We should like to give them each a present. Since we did not have time to consult all of you regarding the choice of our gift, six of us have decided on *kokeshi* dolls. We are giving a pair of dolls to each pair of lovers—the man to keep a female doll and the woman a male doll. Please put these dolls where you can see them often. Whenever you look at these dolls, we hope you will think of us, your friends in the circle, and try to nurture your love within the life of the group for the benefit of yourselves and of the whole group.[47]

Soon the circle began to expand to draw in male workers of other industries in the same town. They went on picnics, sang, read, and wrote together. Out of these joint activities there emerged more pairs of lovers who were engaged and eventually married. The group worked out a wedding party ritual that expressed what they wanted to say about marriage.

It is interesting to note that these new festivals, such as the presentation of *kokeshi* dolls, were used to strengthen positive affects in the group—specifically, the sharing and maximization of joy and excitement—and to reduce negative affects—namely, jealousy and distress. In the traditional peer-group socialization in the village, participation in festivals was an important part of the learning of adult roles. The circle inherited this traditional emphasis, but the content and form of the festivals were innovations.

There was a correlation between participation in the activities of the circle and participation in various labor union activities. A case of mishandling of the union fees by the chairman of their union was brought to light, and a vote of no-confidence in the chairman was proposed. The vote was not called for at the meeting at which it was scheduled, however. A member of the circle commented on this fact at the meeting and questioned why criticism of the union leadership had been hushed up. Her diary was read, according to the usual practice, by the dormitory mother during her inspection tour of the rooms of the workers. The dormitory mother admonished the girl: "You have a wrong idea in your head. Let me put you right." To this the girl

[47] Yoshirō Sawai, "Bōseki no Musume kara Hyakushō Musume e" ("From Textile Workers to Peasant Daughters"), in Seiichi Isono, Junji Kinoshita, Kazuko Tsurumi, Rokurō Hidaka, and Hideko Maruoka, eds., *Nakama no Naka no Renai* (*Love in the Group*), Tokyo, Kawade Shobō, 1956, pp. 174-180; Akio Miyake and Michiko Tanaka, "Atarashii Aijō" ("New Love"), in Kinoshita and Tsurumi, eds., *Haha no Rekishi*, pp. 122-130.

replied: "You don't have to do that. I am responsible for my own ideas and conduct."[48] In the past female workers had been very much afraid of the dormitory mothers and the management that stood behind them, and the workers easily succumbed to this kind of pressure. Fearlessness in upholding what they thought right was a new attitude that emerged from the activities of the circle, with its emphasis on independence of judgment for each individual member.

In September 1953 the Zensen Dōmei proposed to leave the Sōhyō (General Council of Labor Unions), the federation of left-wing labor unions. The labor union in the circle's wool factory was split into two factions. When the union meeting was held to make their policy decision, registered voting delegates were prevented by their foremen from attending the meeting. But a few of these managed to attend the meeting as observers, and one spoke up, protesting:

> Our union delegated us to attend the meeting, and our superiors told us we could attend the meeting if we so wished. However, my superior warned me: "Now that you are married, you had better not meddle with the labor union." In any case, my job is important for me, and I do not want to be negligent in my duty to my employer. However, I thought it was also my duty to attend the meeting and express my opinion.
>
> But I was not able to do so. I was not given a certificate as a representative. I came here, but there was no seat for me. I looked around the delegates and have found, to my surprise, that many of the representatives here today are not the ones nominated by our union. . . . Is this the way a democratic labor union should operate?"[49]

No action was taken.

The next year when the Zensen Dōmei supported a strike of the Ōmi silk mill workers who were rebelling against inhuman treatment by the autocratic owner of the factory, the members of the circle took the lead in helping the strikers with their picketing.[50] Thus they showed that they were loyal to the policy of the

[48] Kazuko Tsurumi, "Shufu to Musume no Seikatsu Kiroku" ("The Life Records of Mothers and Daughters"), *Seikatsu Kiroku Undō no Nakade*, pp. 81-82.

[49] *Ibid.*, pp. 82-83.

[50] Isono et al., eds., *Nakama no Naka no Renai*, pp. 56-82.

Zensen, whenever they thought their policy was right from the standpoint of workers. But they could not follow their policy blindly.

Their increasing participation in labor union activities was accompanied by some change in their attitude toward work. In 1954 Sawai was discharged from the company,[51] and the members of the circle who had hitherto been dispersed in various sections were grouped together into a special section isolated from other workers. To the surprise of the management, the group of circle members proved to be more productive than other workers, and the foremen of other sections began to understand why they were so productive. According to the girls' own explanation, it was simply more pleasant to work with the friends they knew and liked best.[52]

In slack periods it was the usual practice of textile companies to curtail production and discharge workers temporarily. In February 1958 some workers in the factory, including many of the members of the circle, were laid off temporarily and had to apply for unemployment insurance. The girls succeeded in extracting a tacit promise from the management that they would be rehabilitated within six months. (Six months is the limit on the payment of unemployment insurance benefits.) While they were back in their native villages, they kept up communication with their friends remaining in the factory in order to strengthen their sense of solidarity. They were rehired precisely six months later.[53] Previously, once textile workers had been sent back to the villages, they seldom tried to return to the same factory. They resigned themselves either to staying at home until they got married or to looking for jobs in smaller factories, which meant lower wages. By their persistent efforts to return to their factory, the circle members proved themselves to be fully committed industrial workers, in comparison with the female textile workers

[51] Sawai applied for a few days' holiday by saying that he wished to go home to meet a candidate for marriage. When holidays were granted, instead of going home, he attended a meeting of school teachers who were interested in the life-composition method of education. This the company claimed was a breach of promise, and they discharged him. In response, he sued the company through the local court and defended himself by claiming that he was entitled to freedom of conduct during the vacation legally granted. It took him three years to win his case in court. Although he won, the company did not rehire him. He became a full-time union organizer.

[52] Isono et al., eds., *Nakama no Naka no Renai*, pp. 182-183.

[53] *Ibid.*, p. 184.

of the past, who had been either noncommitted or semi-committed.

Some fifteen years have elapsed since most of the women entered the factory in 1950. By now almost all of them have left the factory and are married, some living in cities but most in the villages along the Ina valley. When they left the factory, they promised one another that they would meet every five years. On the third day of January 1965 the first reunion was held in Ina, and thirty-four persons—the circle members, their husbands, and children—attended. There they conversed and compared notes on married life. Their discussion centered on how the ideal role of a mother as redefined by them while they were in the factory coincided, or did not coincide, with the actual role of wife and mother in a peasant family. Although they had not been able to live up to the ideal, they claimed that there were great differences between their present families and their parents' families. It had been almost unthinkable in their mothers' generation for the wives of peasant families to leave their houses during the days of the New Year's festival, the most important holiday in Japan. But many of them had managed to attend the meeting. They agreed that, in order to have their ideas accepted by their husbands and parents-in-law, they had first had to work hard to prove to the family that they were "good-for-something." By their hard work in day-to-day life they had gained permission to attend the meeting. They recalled that the agrarian women of their mothers' generation had also worked hard or even harder but that they had still not been allowed to go out, especially on the holidays. Now not only were the younger women able to go out, but some of their husbands accompanied them, and a few even invited their wives' friends, both male and female, to come to their homes after the meeting to stay overnight with them. One of the circle members commented: "It was very rare in the past for a peasant family to receive the wife's friends during the New Year holidays. It was utterly impossible to receive her male friends on any occasion. It is still not usually done."[54] The relationship of these young wives with their husbands is now changing from one predominantly hierarchical, avoidant, secret, and exploitative to one predominantly egalitarian, intimate, open, and reciprocal. Unlike their mothers, most of them were married on the basis of mutual consent, even

[54] From a mimeographed record of the meeting held on Jan. 3, 1965, in Ina.

if the marriages could not strictly be said to have arisen out of love.

Most of the circle members belong to young wives' groups in their respective village communities. They have introduced the method of writing, reading, and discussion into these groups and have tried to transform the traditional village peer groups into circles through which young wives might cooperate for the improvement of their material lives and their family relationships. Some of the women have continued working in small factories in nearby towns, where they had initiated collective bargaining procedures to secure better wages and were trying to organize unions.

Through their family and village life they are consciously acting as integrators of the roles of peasant and industrial worker and at the same time as mediators of intergenerational changes. We can characterize them as innovators in their development of labor commitment and innovators of small-scale social change in their personality development.

3. Some General Observations

From the experience of the writing circle of the textile workers, we can draw some hypothetical generalizations.

What is the place of affects in the process of redefinition of one's role? One of the women workers said: "Our mothers worked hard and persevered in resignation to their fate. We shall inherit from them their propensity for hard work and their perseverance, but we shall use them to improve our lot instead of succumbing to it."[55] The peasant mothers in their hard-working and self-sacrificing existence showed their capacity to invest intense affects, both positive and negative, for a long duration of time. This high level of density of affects, according to their daughters, were the assets they wished to inherit. They felt they were capable of redirecting the vector of affects toward objects different from those to which their mothers had directed theirs, while keeping intact the high level of affective density which their mothers had achieved.

The following is a conversation between a daughter and her mother who had lost her husband in the war:

In the autumn festival there was a preview of the war movie called "The Sands of Iwō Jima." After my mother saw this,

[55] Tsurumi, "Onna Sandai no Ki," p. 126-127.

she repeated: "How disgusting, how disgusting." So I re-
torted: "Mother, you are disgusted with the war. So am I.
Don't you think it is all right for me to do something to prevent
a war?"

My mother replied despairingly: "What's the use? I wish
another war would start and we would all be bombed to
death!" I felt sorry that my mother was so hopelessly crushed
by her misery.[56]

In this passage the mother's attitude toward the war reflects a
type of perverted negative affect termed by Max Scheler *ressentiment*.[57] The mother perversely claimed to direct intense positive
affects toward death and negative affects toward life. This
twisted reaction stemmed from her accumulated experience of
thwarted wishes and hopes. The daughter, in contrast, was not
a victim of *ressentiment*, since her negative affects against war
had been continuously released by her participation in activities
to prevent war sponsored by the labor union and her circle. The
intense and enduring negative affects of the mother were transmitted to the daughter, but the daughter changed their direction
and attempted to point them instead toward what Scheler called
"authentic values"—not toward death but toward a better life.

In traditional society, in the intergenerational transmission of
role models, the level of density and the vector and objects of
affects were generally kept together and intact. In a rapidly
changing society, however, the density of affects may well become separated from their original vector and objects; it is also
more likely to be transmitted than the latter, if any characteristics of affects are transmitted at all.

The children of a mother with low density of affects are likely
to play their roles throughout their life cycles with low density
of affects. The children of a mother with high density of affects

[56] Harumi Shiga, "Haha no Koto" ("About My Mother"), in Kinoshita
and Tsurumi, eds., *Haha no Rekishi*, p. 77.

[57] "*Ressentiment* denotes an attitude which arises from a cumulative
repression of feelings of hatred, revenge, envy and the like. When such
feelings can be acted out, no *ressentiment* results. But when a person is
unable to release these feelings against the persons or groups evoking them,
thus developing a sense of impotence, and when these feelings are continuously re-experienced over time, then *ressentiment* arises. *Ressentiment*
leads to a tendency to degrade, to reduce genuine values as well as their
bearers." Max Scheler, *Ressentiment*, Glencoe, Ill., The Free Press, 1961,
p. 23.

tend to play their roles throughout their life cycles with high density of affects.

Our data are concerned only with the transmission of the role of mothers. Generalization is not complete, however, until we examine the place of the affects of fathers in the transmission of the role of fathers to their sons. We should also examine the effect of the density of mothers' affects in the transmission of the role of fathers to their sons, as well as the effect of fathers' affects in the transmission of the mothers' role to their daughters.

From what we have observed of the writing circle of the textile workers, it may be possible to derive some general notion also of the structure of a circle. To some extent the circle we have been studying bears a structural resemblance to the peasant family and the company. With both it shares the characteristics of functional diffuseness, intimacy, and collectivism. At the same time, it has in common with the ideal structure of the labor union the characteristics of rationalism, universalism, independence, collectivism, voluntarism, openness, and reciprocity. We should note, of course, that this analysis of the structure of the circle is peculiar to this particular circle and may not be applicable to all circles.[58]

Japanese observers recognize certain minimum requirements for a circle. Its size should be sufficiently small so that a face-to-face relationship can be established among all its members. It is by definition informal. The relationships among its members are rational, voluntary, egalitarian, and open in communication, and the criterion of participation is voluntaristic. Outside of these minimum requirements there is no preestablished structure for a circle. Each circle is somewhat different in its structure. That structure evolves gradually and is dependent on the type of role strains that are being managed within the circle and the types of group affiliations its members have outside the circle, to say nothing of the idiosyncrasies of each member. Only in a society where freedom of association is ideally established can circles with differing structures proliferate.

As an agency of socialization, the circle stands in marked

[58] E.g., a writing circle called "Yamanami no Kai" ("A Group of Mountains") led by Kunio Shiratori, an ex-soldier and senior high school teacher, emphasizes the function of discommunication rather than communication among its members. The structure of this circle, consisting of young men and women of heterogeneous occupations and social origins, is very different from that of the circle of the female textile workers. See Kunio Shiratori, *Mumei no Nihonjin.*

contrast to the army, as examined in previous chapters. The circle is predominantly solidary and is independent in its structure from the state, whereas the army is predominantly antagonistic and dependent on the state. The common factor that the circle shares with the army is relative dependence in its structure on the primary group—the family and the village community. The circle as an intermediate group is solidary enough and independent enough of the state to serve as a vehicle for bringing about a pluralist society, if it proliferates. On the other hand, the structure of the circle, as exemplified by the textile workers' writing circle, is similar in some respects—in intimacy and functional diffuseness, for example—to the structure of primary groups and is not totally independent of the latter. In this sense, if circles such as the one we have described in this chapter proliferate, then they may serve as intermediate groups for the communal-pluralist, rather than the pluralist, society. Nevertheless, as we have suggested, the structure of each circle is subject to variation, provided that it fulfills the minimum requirements. And it is possible that circles which are solidary and independent of both the state and primary groups may emerge and proliferate. It suffices here to point out the emergence of intermediate groups independent of the state that serve as the effective agencies for the resocialization of adults. This situation clearly distinguishes the pattern of adult socialization after defeat from the pattern before defeat.

SEVEN

The Family: The Impact of the War on Women

WHAT has been the impact of the war and of defeat in the war upon the roles of women in Japan? Are they now actually different from what they were before and during the war? And, if so, to what extent have they changed?

This chapter makes an attempt to answer these questions in a very limited scope. It tries to analyze the processes of role change and, through it, the processes of personality change of Japanese women as mothers and as wives. Our attention will be focused on the family, rather than on the place of work or any other social system, as the major context within which adult women's role changes take place. The reasons for choosing the family as the focus are threefold. First, the overwhelming majority of adult women are married and live with their families. According to the census of 1965, only 1.3 percent of women aged fifty and above are single, whereas 53.2 percent of them are married and live with their spouses and 45.5 percent have been married but separated from their spouses either by death or by divorce.[1] For the majority of adult women, then, the roles of mother and wife are the most vital roles they play in life. Second, we assume that any change in those roles is decisive in changing the personality of these women. Third, our assumption is that the family is the most strategic agent of adult socialization for the married women whose most vital roles are played in its context.

• The importance of the family as an agent of socialization throughout an individuals' life cycle is supported by some basic assumptions about the peculiar function the family serves for the management of an individual's role strains. Levy holds that the family is the concrete structure in which all the roles of an individual, including those within that structure, are interrelated with one another and that there are no other concrete structures in any society in which this occurs as extensively as it does within the family.[2] Owing to this strategic position the family occupies

[1] Rōdōshō Fujin Shōnen Kyoku (Women and Minor's Bureau of the Labor Ministry), *Fujin no Genjō* (*The Present Situation of Women*), Fujin Kankei Ippan Shiryō, No. 61 (March 1967), pp. 2-3.

[2] Marion J. Levy, Jr., "Aspects of the Analysis of Family Structure," in

in an individual's life, Goode asserts that the family is "a role budget center."[3]

● The strategic position of the family as a role budget center becomes more crucial in a rapidly changing society than in a more stable society, for the following reasons.

● First, in a stable society the ideal role within the family is singularly and relatively clearly defined for the position a person occupies. Individual difference arises out of the degree of commitment to, or the degree of deviance from, that ideal role. In a rapidly changing society, however, it is likely either that the ideal role is not clearly defined or that more than one ideal role emerges for the same position an individual occupies. If the ideal role is not clearly defined, it is up to the individual to make up the definition of her own role. If conflicting ideal roles are given to the individual, it is up to her to choose which ideal role she would actually perform or to redefine the role in order to accommodate the existing conflict. In any case, in a rapidly changing society the individual is required to choose her role or to redefine it in order to perform her role adequately.

✦ Second, in a traditional society the role-set of a person within a family is hierarchically structured in such a way that a conflict between the roles that pertain to the position an individual occupies is minimized. For instance, if the role of a daughter-in-law conflicts with that of a wife, the former takes precedence according to the principle that the rule of descent is prior to conjugal relationship. However, in a transitional society, where discrepancies exist between the ideal pattern of the conjugal family and the actual persistence of the traditional family, role conflicts are likely to be felt to be acute by individual actors within the family. Such a tension is difficult for an individual to resolve within the family. It sometimes requires her to seek aid in an extra-familial group, where persons with similar problems compare notes to work out some new patterns of management of the role strain. In such a case, that particular extra-familial group may become a temporary role budget center for the intra-familial role strain.

Third, in a rapidly changing society children are likely to receive school education drastically different from the kind their

Ansley J. Coale et al., eds., *Aspects of the Analysis of Family Structure*, Princeton, Princeton University Press, 1965, p. 30.

[3] William J. Goode, "A Theory of Role Strain," *American Sociological Review*, xxv, No. 4 (Aug. 1960), 493.

parents received. Under such circumstances the parents' competence as the socializers of their children becomes problematic, while children may take an active role in resocializing their parents. This situation may cause role strain for the parents and may sometimes lead to intergenerational conflict between parents and children, unless some change in the concept of the role of a mother or a father may be worked out to manage the conflict.

. Fourth, as the level of industrialization increases, it is likely that extra-familial groups will proliferate. The more extra-familial groups there are, the more various will be the roles prescribed to an individual who belongs to multiple groups. The more roles an individual has to assume, the more role strains and conflicts are liable to be produced. The multiplication of extra-familial group affiliations for adults in a modernized society is likely to increase, rather than decrease, the importance of the family as the role budget center for adults.

• A few words need to be said about the source materials used in this chapter. They consist of personal documents composed in various writing circles by both agrarian and city women all over Japan. Out of the many such documents written by common men and women about their own lives, we shall here select only those which reveal in detail the processes of change over time of the authors' ideas and attitudes. The life records we use are of two kinds: those of peasant wives living in villages, on the one hand, and those of the wives of salaried men and industrial workers living in cities, on the other.

1. A Married Woman's Role Sequence through the Life Cycle of the Family: General Trends

According to the Civil Code of 1947, the traditional patterns of the *ie* (unit family) and the *dōzoku* (union of families) systems were ideally abolished. Actually, however, they persist in various forms. There is, for instance, a tendency for some unit families to develop into extended families, even if they begin with the size of a conjugal family. We shall here deal only with this form of persistence of the traditional family to the neglect of other forms, since this is most germane to the question of the role sequence of married women in their life cycles.

Takashi Koyama points out that there was a general tendency toward cyclical change of family patterns before the Meiji Restoration. He arrived at this conclusion by examining the family records of certain villages over a period of sixty years from 1802 to 1861. He classified families into seven forms (A, B, and C are variations of the nuclear family, D, E, F, and G of the extended family):

A. One person household
B. Families of husband and wife only
C. Families of husband, wife, and unmarried child
D. Families of husband, wife, married child, and/or grandchild
E. Families of husband, wife, parents, and/or grandparents
F. Families of husband, wife, child, and parents
G. Families including collateral kindred[4]

There are two major types of the "family life cycle," according to Koyama. The first is the life cycle of "the modern conjugal family," which is characterized by the normal process: A → B → C → B → A. The second is the life cycle of "the patriarchal extended family," which is characterized by the normal process: G → F → C → D → F → G.

In both types of the family life cycle, extended or conjugal, the form C (with husband, wife, and unmarried child) appears as a transient stage, and the existence at one point of time of a nuclear family does not necessarily mean that it persists as such through cyclical changes over time. This proposition still holds true to some extent in the postwar period. According to a survey conducted from 1956 to 1957 by the Society for the Study of Family Problems, 58 percent of the families in the mountain village sections of Tokyo metropolitan areas and 79 percent of the families in the apartment house districts of Tokyo were classified as nuclear families (A, B, C).[5]

A survey conducted in 1961 and 1962 by the Women and Minor's Bureau of the Labor Ministry determined that, of the 905 households in agrarian villages all over the country, 40 percent were nuclear families and 60 percent extended families. It also pointed out that there was a high correlation between the age of the wives of the family heads and the family type. There were more extended families among the households with the wives in their twenties and thirties than among the households

[4] Takashi Koyama, *The Changing Social Position of Women in Japan*, UNESCO, 1961, p. 35.
[5] Koyama, *Study of the Modern Family*, 1960—cited in Takeshi Nakano, "Recent Studies of Change in the Japanese Family," *International Social Science Journal*, UNESCO, XIV, No. 3 (1962), 533.

with the wives in their forties. The extended type increases again among the households with the wives in their fifties.[6] The same bureau carried out research in 1964 on 2,792 families of workers, both white- and blue-collar, in cities and found that only 26.5 percent of the workers lived with their parents, whereas 68.3 percent did not. There is a similarity, however, in the pattern of cyclical changes between farmers' and working men's families. The families with the husbands in their thirties show the highest percentage of those living with their parents in both cases.[7] These empirical findings indicate that there still exist in the postwar period two types of the life cycle of a family—conjugal and extended. They also point to the fact that the extended type is more persistent among farmers than among city workers.

The ideas that the family has a life cycle like a person and that there are two types of family life cycle suggest that there are two possibilities of role sequence for married women. If a woman belongs to a modern conjugal family, her role sequence will be: a. wife (B) → wife – mother (C) → wife (B) → widow (A). If a woman is a member of an extended family, her role sequence will be: b. wife – daughter-in-law – sister-in-law (G) → wife – daughter-in-law – mother (F) → wife – mother (C) → wife (or widow) – mother – mother-in-law and/or grandmother (D).

These two types of role sequence lead to different role conflicts and strains peculiar to them. First, in both cases, conflict between the role of the wife and that of the mother is predictable. With type b, conflicts between the roles of the wife and the daughter-in-law and between the roles of the mother and the daughter-in-law are also probable.

Second, in type a, theoretically there is always only one adult married woman within the family, whereas in type b, at least in some stages in the life cycle of the family, there are two or more than two adult married women in the family. In the former case, the wife becomes the *shufu* (the headwife, or the manager of the household affairs) on the day she is married. In the latter case, however, the wife has to wait for some years to assume the position of the headwife if her mother-in-law is still alive and

---

[6] Rōdōshō Fujin Shōnen Kyoku, *Nōka Fujinseikatsu ni Kansuru Ishiki Chōsa* (*An Opinion Survey on the Life of Agrarian Women*), Tokyo, Finance Ministry Printing Office, 1962, pp. 19-20.

[7] Rōdōshō Fujin Shōnen Kyoku, *Kinrōsha Katei no Shōhi Seikatsu Suijun ni Kansuru Ishiki Chōsa* (*An Opinion Survey on the Consumption Level of Working Men's Families*), Tokyo, Finance Ministry Printing Office, 1964, p. 11.

able to hold that position. The right to the management of domestic affairs is symbolized by *shamoji* (a rice ladle), and it is an important ritual of passage for a daughter-in-law to receive the ladle from her mother-in-law and to take over the position of the headwife. This ritual is called *shamoji watashi* (handing over the ladle).[8] How many years the wife has to wait until she accedes to the role of the headwife depends upon the local customs and upon the individual family. It is up to the mother-in-law to decide when her daughter-in-law should inherit from her the right of household management. Until then, the mother-in-law trains and prepares her son's wife for prospective headwifeship. In the prewar days, for both city and agrarian women, the interval between their marriage and their assumption of the role of headwife was the important adult socialization period equivalent to the period of conscription for men. After the war, shortened though the interval has been, the period of apprenticeship for headwifeship still exists, especially for agrarian women.[9] The role of the wife without the rights of management of domestic affairs but under obligation to discharge household chores under the direction of her mother-in-law usually brings with it certain strains for the wife. This is a problem peculiar to the women who go through the role sequence of type *b*.

Third, for the middle-aged women, the two types of the role sequence posit different anticipatory problems of old age. For the women in type *a*, how to prepare themselves to live alone with or without their husbands is a problem of anticipatory socialization. The major concern of the women in type *b* is how to prepare themselves to play the role of a mother-in-law without

---

[8] See Yasuo Hashiura, *Minkan Denshō to Kazokuhō* (*Folklore and Family Law*), Tokyo, Nihon Hyōronsha, 1942, pp. 61-64. Noboru Niida has made a brilliant comparative study of the status of *shufu* in traditional China and medieval Germany. He points out that both in China and in Germany *shufu* was called "the key holder" (*t'ai-yao-shih-de* in Chinese and *Schlusselgewalt* in German), which is equivalent to "the ladle holder" (*shamoji-tori* or *hera-tori* in Japanese) in Japan. See Noboru Niida, *Chūgoku no Nōson Kazoku* (*The Agrarian Family in China*), Tokyo, Tokyo Daigaku Tōyōbunka Kenkyūjo, 1952, pp. 242-310.

[9] According to the Women and Minors' Bureau survey conducted from 1961 to 1962, only 72 percent of women married for less than five years, 75 percent of those married for five to ten years, and 86 percent of those married for ten to fifteen years were *shufu*, while 99 percent of the women married for twenty-five to thirty years were *shufu*. After thirty years of married life, the percentage of women still holding the role of *shufu* declines to 91 percent. *Nōka Fujin Seikatsu ni Kansuru Ishiki Chōsa*, p. 21.

the right of headwifeship, regardless of whether they are widowed or not.

Fourth, there is a problem of widowhood for the women in both types *a* and *b*, but in different forms. Usually, widowhood arrives in old age in the life cycle of most women. The war, however, cast a large number of both agrarian and urban women into premature widowhood. Many of them found themselves widows, unprepared. To become a widow without being prepared causes a strain in itself. For women who live in a nuclear family, being widowed means having to assume the role of father to their children, if they have any. Women who live in an extended family have to cope with role conflicts between themselves and their daughters-in-law or the sisters-in-law, not to speak of having to bear the strain of acting as a substitute father. The recent trend of agrarian men leaving their homes to work in cities for a long period of time is producing a problem for women analogous to premature widowhood. The wives left at home, although they have husbands, are for all practical purposes widows, at least for the time being.

In our substantive analysis we shall discuss the role conflicts peculiar to the extended type of family life cycle mainly in reference to peasant women and the role strains characteristic of the conjugal type mostly in reference to the wives of working men in cities. This way of approaching the matter does not, however, preclude the possibilities of city wives having the role conflicts characteristic of the extended family and vice versa.

2. Hypotheses Concerning the Types of Family and Women's Role Change

Our hypothesis should be made clear at the outset. It pertains to the pattern of the family and the pattern of role change.

Size is only one way of classifying families. They may be classified also according to the internal structure of relationships. The norm of the traditional samurai extended family expects solidarity between parents and children to be more enduring and intense than solidarity between husband and wife. The following description of the solidarity structure of the traditional Chinese family applies equally to the norm of the traditional Japanese family:

> The primary orientation of the married couple was toward the production of children. The husband did not choose his

wife nor she him. . . . In addition, the wife was expected to
care for her husband's household and raise his children. . . .
In the third place, the wife was in the family to serve her husband's parents. In the fourth place, she owed her husband
complete obedience though she was expected to give priority
to his parents' commands. Also, she was expected to promote
the welfare of the family in any way required of her. Only
as a remote and subsidiary consideration was she cast in the
role of a companion to her husband, and any overt show of
affection on his part for her was viewed as a definite break of
good taste.[10]

We assume that there is a high correlation between the level
of density of positive affects invested in a relationship and the
degree of the effectiveness of that relationship in ideological
socialization. If a woman invests her love and interests more
intensely and enduringly in her relationship with her husband
than in any other relationships, then her husband is likely to become the strategic agent of her ideological socialization. Under
such circumstances her role as a wife is the strategic role for her
ideological socialization. If she invests her love and interests
more intensely and enduringly in her relationship with her children than in any other relationships, then her children are likely
to become the most effective agents of her ideological socialization. Under such conditions her role as a mother is the strategic
role for her ideological socialization. If a woman invests equally
intense and enduring love and interests in her relationships
with her husband and in her relationships with her children,
then these relationships probably have an equal effect on her
ideological socialization. In this event the roles of a wife and a
mother are equally strategic to her ideological socialization.

Ideally speaking, in the traditional extended family the
relationship between the mother and her children is more intense and enduring than her relationship with her husband. In
contrast, the ideal pattern of the modern conjugal family
places more emphasis on the solidarity between the husband
and wife than on the solidarity between the mother and her
children.

On the basis of our assumption about the correlation between
the degree of intensity of positive affects invested in a re-

[10] Marion J. Levy, Jr., *The Family Revolution in Modern China*, Cambridge, Harvard University Press, 1949, p. 175.

lationship and the effectiveness of that relationship in changing one's ideological postures, we may hypothesize as follows:

(1) If the traditional extended type of relationship persists within a family, then the children are likely to be more effective agents of the ideological socialization of their mother than her husband. On the other hand, if the modern conjugal type of relationship exists within a family, then the husband is likely to be more effective in the ideological socialization of his wife than her children.

(2) If the traditional extended type of relationship persists within a family, it is likely that the role of a mother changes more rapidly and more profoundly than the role of a wife, if any change occurs at all. If the modern conjugal type of relationship exists within a family, then the role of a wife is likely to change more rapidly and more profoundly than the role of a mother, if there is any change.

(3) We may apply the foregoing hypotheses to measure the degree of actual persistence of the traditional pattern of family relationships. If the ideal pattern of the modern conjugal family is prevalent, and yet some women may still be more influenced by their children ideologically than by their husbands, then we may suspect that the traditional pattern of family relationships actually persists. If wives are influenced by their husbands and husbands by their wives more effectively than by their children in ideological socialization, then we may contend that the modern conjugal family pattern of relationships is actually prevalent to that extent. If the husbands and children are equally effective in the ideological socialization of the women who are their wives and mothers, then we may hold that their family patterns are actually either in transition or of mixed forms.

The statistical data show, as already mentioned, that there are more extended type of families by size in agrarian villages than in cities, where the majority of the families are of the nuclear type by size. Therefore, we may expect that among city women changes in the role of a wife will be more rapid and more conspicuous than changes in the role of a mother, whereas in villages the converse will be true.

Keeping these hypotheses in mind, we shall make a comparative analysis of the case histories of middle-aged women, in cities and in villages, who lived through the fifteen years of war from 1931 to 1946 and who have written about their experiences of the war and the period following.

3. The Roles of Mothers and Wives during the War: Case Studies

Before we discuss postwar changes in the roles of women, we shall first see how women actually played the roles prescribed to them during the war years.

The Mother of a Soldier

Just as men were trained to die for the sake of the Emperor, so women were taught to dedicate their sons willingly to the Emperor and to his country. A primary school textbook produced by the government in 1910 told the story of "A Sailor's Mother," based on an incident that happened during the Sino-Japanese War of 1894-1895. The mother sent a letter to her son, who was then serving as a sailor on a warship. The letter read:

> I was informed that you neither went into action during the Battle of Toyoshima nor rendered any distinguished service on the tenth of August during the attack on Ikaiei. Your mother deeply regrets. For what purpose have you gone to the war? Is it not for the sake of repaying *on* to the Emperor by consecrating your own life to him? Everybody in the village is very kind to me by always telling me: "Since your only child is gone to the war, you must need help. Please don't hesitate to ask us for help." Whenever I see any of them, I am ashamed of my cowardly son. It really breaks my heart to think of my son not having accomplished any feat. Every day I visit Hachiman Shrine to pray that you may distinguish yourself in a battle. . . ."[11]

This story continued to be included in the state-made textbook and exerted influence on the formation of the affective and ideological postures of men and women until the end of the Pacific war. The letter reveals what is entailed in the ideal role of the mother of a soldier (or a sailor). Intense and enduring negative affects of self-sacrifice are a prominent feature. A self-sacrificing mother demands her son to sacrifice himself to the Emperor. The letter expresses a strong conviction that the public welfare of the state symbolized by the Emperor takes precedence over the private well-being of oneself and one's son.

[11] Quoted in Tomitarō Karasawa, *Nihonjin no Rirekisho* (*The Curriculum Vitae of the Japanese People*), Tokyo, Yomiuri Shinbunsha, 1957, pp. 141-142.

Concealed beneath this attitude, however, is a brand of egotism, not of the individual, but of one's own family. The mother tells her son to die gloriously for the sake of the Emperor because she wishes him to distinguish the family name so that her family may become prestigious in the eyes of the members of her community. She wishes her son to compete with the sons of other families for the honor of his family name. This amounts to family egotism, and we call such an ideological posture individualism from the point of view of the family as a unit. Another ideological posture is absolute obedience to the "group mind" represented by the head member of the system to which one belongs. The individual is not expected to make a decision of his own separate from that of the group of which he is a member. This ideological posture we call dependence. The sailor's mother, when she tells her son to distinguish his family name, does so representing her family, not making the decision uniquely her own. In this sense, her basic ideological posture is characterized as in the main dependently individualistic.

We shall now examine how this ideal role of a patriotic mother was observed by soldiers' mothers during World War II.

Many of the Japanese mothers felt a conflict between the ideal and actual roles of the mother of a soldier. The twenty-two mothers who gathered in a small group discussion in a local community center in Iwate Prefecture in 1961 found out for the first time that they had shared in common the habit of talking to pebbles during the war.

> "They said that if we pick pebbles on the riverside, wash them, offer them to gods and pray, a soldier may be saved from getting a corn on his foot. Hearing this, I used to pick pebbles every day, cleaned them and offered them to our family altar and prayed to our ancestral gods."
> "Yes, indeed. Washing the pebbles, I used to talk to them: 'Feel better with your feet, don't you? I shall clean your feet, so that you may sleep well.'"
> "Aye, aye. Those pebbles I put into my bosom, embraced them talking to them, 'Now let's go to sleep together.'"[12]

Now that the war has come to an end with Japan's defeat and women are encouraged to speak up, those mothers who lost their

[12] Tokushi Obara, ed., *Ishikoro ni Kataru Hahatachi* (*The Mothers Who Talked To Pebbles*), Tokyo, Miraisha, 1964, p. 20.

sons in the war are able to say in public: " 'For what purpose did I have to let my son die, now I really wonder' " and " 'We certainly have been deceived.' "[13]

The conflict these peasant mothers experienced between the ideal role of a patriotic mother imposed upon them by the state and the role they actually performed of an intensely loving mother was not recognized by them as a conflict of norms but rather as a conflict of emotions. They deeply loved their sons and were severely distressed by their being sent to war. They wished their sons to return home safely, but they were almost sure that their sons would die on the battlefield. Besides, they were extremely afraid of what might happen to them if their actual feelings became known to their neighbors. In order to solve this acute emotional conflict, they resorted to the magical action of purifying, communicating with, and sleeping with the pebbles. And all these rituals were performed in secrecy and kept secret for almost twenty years after the end of the war.

Speaking out in public about their sufferings during the war is a first step toward the redefinition of their roles. Still, they have not yet defined their new roles in so many words. They say that they have realized that "they were deceived," but they do not say by whom they were deceived. They say that they do not wish to repeat the experience of being involved in a war, but they do not say by what change in the concept of their roles it is possible not to repeat it.

The Wife of a Soldier

We shall see how the ideal role of a soldier's wife based on the ideology of the traditional samurai family was actually played by the war widows among peasant women in a village in Iwate Prefecture which contributed 125 soldiers from 93 families and counted eleven widows among its population by the end of the war. The life stories of the nine widows who still live in the village are collected in the book entitled *He Never Returned.*[14] None of the nine women has yet remarried. They have overtly conformed to the ideal role of a soldier's wife by serving their parents-in-law, refusing to be remarried, and working extremely hard to raise their children. Their personal

---

[13] *Ibid.*

[14] Keiichi Kikuchi and Ryō Ōmura, eds., *Anohito wa Kaette Konakatta* (*He Never Returned*), Tokyo, Iwanami, 1964.

and intimate accounts of their lives nonetheless reveal some conflicts among the various roles they actually have had to assume.

First, under war conditions the traditional norm was enforced obliging husbands and wives not to show their affection for each other. Actually, though, the war situation which separated a man from his wife and exposed both of them to the danger of death enhanced, rather than mitigated, the intensity of the love they felt for one another. Ideally, the wives of soldiers were expected to encourage their husbands to die bravely on the battlefield; in reality, they wished them to return home soon and in good health, and at least some of them said so to their husbands when they were alone.

Second, there is a discrepancy between how war widows should ideally be treated by their neighbors and how they have actually been treated. As the wives of soldiers who have died for their country, they have every reason to expect their countrymen to treat them with honor and respect. The truth is, however, that they have been ridiculed and often humiliated as ordinary widows are by their fellow villagers.

One woman relates that, when men got drunk, they would tease her by saying, "You must be lonesome. I shall come to console you tonight." Then one evening, after she had gone to bed, she heard a loud noise outside as though a pile of firewood were falling and someone were trying to break in. Another war widow, who tells a similar story, claims she used to sleep with a sickle in her bed to protect herself from a possible intruder.[15]

Practically all the nine war widows describe experiences when they were ridiculed and humiliated by the villagers and forced to seek seclusion away from both men and women in the village in order to shield themselves from gossip and threatening remarks. It was only after the war, and not until recently, that the war widows came to compare notes among themselves. During the war they were isolated even from one another. They lived without communication outside of their own immediate families.

Third, within the family their duties have been so burdensome that it has become almost impossible for them to carry out successfully their roles as mothers to their children. As long as their parents-in-law live, they are duty bound, as the major and

15 *Ibid.*, p. 41.

often as the sole breadwinners of their families, to feed them and serve them. Under the strain of working terribly hard to make a living for their parents-in-law, their children, and themselves, under the constant pressure of being watched and ridiculed by their villagers, and in their isolation and loneliness, the war widows have felt themselves becoming tough, perverse, and embittered. The children of some of the war widows have criticized their mothers for lacking the tenderness of heart and gentleness of manner which they expect of them. According to wartime norms, the primary objective for war widows is the bringing up of the children entrusted to them by their deceased husbands. But actually, owing to the overdemanding duties they have had to fulfill and under the role strains peculiar to widowed women, it has often been extremely difficult for them to fulfill their essential duties as a mother adequately. Thus war widows have been placed in a position which defeats the primary purpose of their own existence.

Fourth, these war widows were usually married in their early twenties, some even sooner. Thus they were young when they gave birth to their children and still relatively young when they finished raising them. In the traditional extended family, after the children are grown up, usually at least one of the married sons stays with his mother so that the mother may have the roles to play in her old age of mother-in-law and grandmother. But now many young men and women go to work in cities either temporarily or permanently, leaving their mothers alone in the village. This trend is especially upsetting for war widows, many of whom are still in their forties when they have finished raising their children and serving their parents-in-law. Even when they live with their married children, widows are apt to feel lonesome, particularly as a result of the changing ideology of the family. The young daughters-in-law who have received postwar education more often than not do not wish to take orders from their mothers-in-law in the matters of household management and of child-rearing, and the latter are consequently left with the sense of being out of a job. Yet the widowed mothers feel themselves still too young to be disengaged from all the obligations within and without their families. Mrs. Obara, whose deceased husband was a charcoal maker, confides her present problem:

The war widows were expected to sacrifice themselves for the sake of their children, keeping intact the prestige of their dead husbands.

When our children are grown up and the most difficult days are over, people say to us, "you must be relieved." I married my daughter rather early, since I thought it would be better to have a man in the house so that we might be respectable. Now that a grandchild is born, outwardly I look as though I have no trouble.

No one knows our real feelings better than the women like us, the war widows. Now that we are getting old and having our children married, we long for our deceased husbands more than ever.

The other day I happened to step into the neighborhood of our charcoal oven in the mountain and saw a pile of wood blackened and decaying into a mount of mold. I felt my life was like that pile of wood decaying instead of being made into charcoal.[16]

Hisa Obara, who is now forty-five, put up a small retail shop in the village to bring up her only son and to support her mother-in-law. She worked hard to send her son to a university. She gave him money to make a long trip during the winter vacation, but he did not write to her as often as she expected him to.

Fifteen long days elapsed after he left for his trip before he wrote to me for the first time. I thought then that this sort of thing will occur again and again from now on, which would do me in, if I don't do anything on my own to find some purpose in my life other than just longing for my son. I thought of cultivating some hobby to quiet myself.

A child cannot be a child forever. When he grows up, he has got to enter a world different from his childhood environment.

Getting old, and being distressed, I long for my deceased husband more than ever. I am sorry for him that he who should have lived long and done well died so prematurely. Compared to him, I ought to feel grateful for the very fact of living as long as I do.

It is very lonesome for a human being to live alone. From now on, I wish to make many friends and to live together with

16 *Ibid.*, pp. 20-21.

them encouraging one another. I wish to reeducate myself by studying or cultivating some hobbies with my friends.[17]

Most of the war widows come to feel a void in their lives when they reach middle age and seek to fill it by finding new roles for themselves in which they can reinvest the intense and enduring positive affects for their husbands, long pent up while they were busy. This void in the role of women will be studied further and a theory to account for it developed in the following chapter with reference to the postwar role of women in their old age.

The Mother of Evacuated Children: The Ideal and Actual Roles of School Children

On June 30, 1944, the war cabinet decided to evacuate primary school children from the third to the sixth grades from the city of Tokyo to protect them from air raids. Those children who could not depart with their families were required to evacuate collectively under the supervision of their schools.[18] This policy was applied eventually to other major cities considered to be possible targets of bombing.

Recollected from the standpoint of mothers in the cities, air raids and the evacuation of their children were the two most painful and "unforgettable" of all their war experiences. Tsuruko Kurosu, the wife of a glass blower, working in a small factory in Tokyo, writes about her experience of sending her nine-year-old son, Toshio, and her six-year-old daughter, Mieko, to their school evacuation center at Yunohama in Yamagata Prefecture, then sixteen hours' train ride from Tokyo. After the great air raid in Tokyo in March 1945, she went to visit her children at the evacuation center.

Upon arriving, she was surprised to find Mieko, who used to be plump, so skinny that her bones showed at her elbows and knees. When she asked her own children as well as her neighbors' children whether they wished to go back home, they answered in unison: "It is better here than in Tokyo. We can eat polished rice every day, and besides there is no air raid here. So we do not wish to go home."

[17] *Ibid.*, pp. 108-109.
[18] See Gekkōhara Shōgakkō, ed., *Gakudō Sokai no Kiroku* (*The Records of School Children on Evacuation*), Tokyo, Miraisha, 1960, pp. 389-401. This book contains the government documents concerning the evacuation of the school children of the metropolitan area.

On the following day, however, Mrs. Kurosu came upon evidence that life at the center was not as pleasant as the children had said it was. Early in the morning the daily exercise began. The children were made to run around the seashore, but some of them looked pale and fell on the sand after one or two rounds. Toshio looked embarrassed when he asked his mother to wash his underwear which was full of lice. His underpants were soiled with feces. Later he explained to his mother that the children here were so hungry that, whenever they went to the mountain to get firewood, they also searched for berries, nuts, and whatever looked edible. They often suffered from diarrhea as a result. If their teachers discovered that they had diarrhea, they would not be given any food, which was scanty to begin with. Toshio, fearing the punishment, had hidden his soiled underpants for a long time at the bottom of his suitcase.

Mrs. Kurosu also observed that the children at the center, including her own, did not usually move around or make noise when they were left alone. They just sat quietly, playing cards or chess. But the teachers and their children, she found, moved around more vigorously and made more noise than the ordinary pupils. The teachers' children looked as though they weighed more and were healthier than the ordinary children. She was told by some children that they had been scolded when they peeped into the rooms where their teachers were eating rationed butter and tinned food, which the pupils were not allowed to have although they were entitled to them.

Before Mrs. Kurosu left for Tokyo, the children of her neighbors one by one came to her and secretly handed her letters for their parents, asking Mrs. Kurosu to tell their parents to come and call for them. They explained to her: "We cannot say in public that we wish to go home, because someone might tell our teachers, who would punish us for saying so."

Both Toshio and Mieko came to the station to see their mother off, but they disappeared before the train departed. Mrs. Kurosu saw from the window of the train, which began to draw away, Toshio trying to hide himself from view in an alley, crying with his arms crossed covering his face. Mrs. Kurosu writes that she would never forget how she felt at that moment.[19]

[19] Tsuruko Kurosu, "Gakudō Sokai" ("The Evacuation of School Children"), in Kazuko Tsurumi and Kikue Makise, eds., *Hikisakarete: Haha no Sensō Taiken* (*To Be Torn Apart: Mothers' War Experiences*), Tokyo, Chikuma Shobō, 1959, pp. 146-161.

Although she had not done much writing since her primary school days, Mrs. Kurosu began to record her reflections on the war experience of herself and her family because she thought it was an important part of the history of her own family to be bequeathed to her children. After she finished writing, she discussed her war experience with mothers who had had similar experiences. She came to realize that an isolated mother could not possibly protect even her own children once the war had broken out, however hard she might try. So thereafter, she said, she hoped to cooperate with other mothers to give their children a better environment in which to grow up.[20]

The Mother of a Child Who Died in Hiroshima

A great number of men, women, and children died when the atomic bombs were dropped on Hiroshima on August 6 and on Nagasaki on August 9, 1945.[21] Toshie Fujino, a victim of the

[20] See Kazuko Tsurumi, ed., *Empitsu o Nigiru Shufu* (*The Housewives with Pencils in Their Hands*), Tokyo, Mainichi Shinbunsha, 1954, pp. 29-31.

[21] The number of deaths caused by the atomic bombs in Hiroshima and Nagasaki is still an extremely controversial subject. So we shall juxtapose some of the figures made public since 1945.

The Hiroshima Prefectural Office reported to the Internal Affairs Ministry in September 1945 that the estimated number of deaths, including those who had been missing, was more than 110,000 persons. It admitted, however, that this total did not include military personnel. (Shinbunsha Chūgoku, ed., *Hiroshima no Kiroku* [*The Record of Hiroshima*], Tokyo, Miraisha, 1966, p. 13.)

In November 1945 the Hiroshima Prefectural Police Headquarters listed 78,150 dead, 9,428 vitally injured, 27,997 lightly injured, and 13,983 missing. It, too, admitted that these figures did not cover military personnel. (*Ibid.*, p. 14.)

The American Medical Association reported in July 1946 that in Hiroshima 80,000 had died, 40,000 were injured, and 80,500 needed immediate medical treatment; the corresponding figures it gave for Nagasaki were 40,000, 25,000, and 50,000. (*Ibid.*, p. 21.)

In August 1949 Mr. Hamai, then the mayor of Hiroshima, announced in a program of the American Broadcasting Company: "I was responsible for the distribution of food immediately after the bombing, and that is why I was in a vantage point for estimating the death toll. On account of the atomic bomb, 30,000 soldiers and between 28,000 and 30,000 laborers died. But the government did not include them in its announcement of the overall death toll in Hiroshima. Including those soldiers, laborers, and others who died later on account of the atomic bomb, the death toll in Hiroshima, according to our estimate, amounted to more than 240,000." (*Ibid.*, p. 43.)

In January 1950 the ABCC, the research and clinic center established by the Americans in Hiroshima, made public the results of its research. It estimated the victims of the atomic bombs to be 84,810 in Hiroshima and 79,707 in Nagasaki. (*Ibid.*, p. 49.)

These estimates were refuted by a group of Japanese physicists, medical doctors, political scientists, and economists on the research committee of

atomic bomb herself, lost her youngest son on the sixth of August.

Mrs. Fujino was born in 1904 in the city of Wakayama and graduated from a girls' high school. Her marriage to a government-employed communications engineer was arranged by her family, and she saw him only once ceremoniously before she was married. She reflected upon her married life during the war:

> The twenty years of my married life have been a long, long period of servitude. I tried to do my best to serve my husband, mother-in-law, and sisters-in-law, who did not acknowledge half of what I served them. I felt myself caught up by the love of my four children for me, just as an insect was caught in a spider's web. . . . I have made up my mind to efface myself for the sake of this family and to live solely for the love for my four children to bring them up well. With that single purpose in mind, I endured all the hardships, always gnawing my lips, so to speak.[22]

Despite her disappointment in her husband that came early in her married days, she tried to play the traditional roles of daughter-in-law, sister-in-law, and wife faithfully. After the family experienced the atomic holocaust in Hiroshima in 1945, when she lost her youngest son, her husband got tuberculosis and had to retire from his post as a civil servant. It was during the period of acute shortage of food that she had to take care of her sick husband, who spit up a basinful of blood from time to time. In order to feed him fresh milk and greens, she raised a goat and cultivated vegetables in her garden. She worked hard to tend to her wayward husband until at least he said she looked like "a *Kannon* [goddess of mercy]" to him.

Mrs. Fujino writes that, for the thirty years of her married life to her husband, she felt her communication with him had never been complete or satisfactory. It was, however, toward

---

the Japan Anti-Nuclear Bombs Association. They published *A Report on the Victims of the Nuclear Bombs* in July 1961 which put the death toll caused by powerful radioactivity at approximately 200,000, including military personnel, in Hiroshima, and 120,000 in Nagasaki. (*Ibid.*, p. 149.)

Thus the estimates of total fatalities, according to various sources, range from 78,150 to more than 240,000 for Hiroshima and from 40,000 to 120,000 for Nagasaki.

[22] Toshie Fujino, "Ashi Ato" ("Footsteps"), in *Ashi Ato*, Tokyo, Dōin Gakuto Engo Kai (Society to Aid the Mobilized Students), 1960, p. 191.

the very end of his life that she began to tell him all that she had never told him before and that she came to be able to talk in a joking mood.

Not more than ten days after her marriage, she had found a postcard addressed to her husband from his girl friend. The girl wrote that she was afraid she might be forsaken now that he had been married. Having read the card, Mrs. Fujino left it at the doorstep of their house until her husband came home and pretended that she had not seen it. Mrs. Fujino told her husband that she had been suffering from this incident ever since.

Her attitude toward her husband's girl friend was typical of the role of a traditional wife, who was expected not to show jealousy toward her husband's affairs with other women.

There was yet another source of her disappointment in her husband. He, the engineer, used to scold her for her lack of knowledge of mathematics and mechanics whose principles, he maintained, should be applied to the organization of the kitchen and of the garden. Her husband's constant criticism of her made her extremely self-conscious, even when she went through such daily routine motions as placing a teacup in front of him on the table. For her part, she felt sad that he did not share with her an artistic appreciation of life and literary taste. While her husband was sick, she met a man who taught her how to compose *haiku* poems. She felt she could communicate to him better than she could to her husband. She thought to herself "how happy we could have been, had we been man and wife." When she received a letter from his wife informing her of his death, she wrote a poem:

> Mourning for my friend,
> At the fireside I wept,
> In the kitchen I wept.[23]

She never told her husband about her feeling for this man, who happened to be her husband's friend. And she remained, at least in her overt actions, faithful to her husband until his death. But she did not weep for him when he died:

> During my husband's funeral, I did not show tears to the mourners. On the seventh day, after the special Buddhist service for my deceased husband was over, I was informed

[23] *Ibid.*, pp. 277-278.

that my married daughter Suzuko was in travail at the hospital. I hurried to the hospital, leaving the house to a helping hand. . . . I stayed in the hospital that night. For the first time after my husband's death, I wept in the hospital bed. It was not because I was sorry for my deceased husband that I wept. I wept because I felt sorry for myself. Tears came to console myself for having managed to endure thirty long years of servitude.[24]

Mrs. Fujino's relationship with her husband was typical of the conjugal relationship in a traditional family. It was predominantly hierarchical, avoidant, exploitative, compulsory, and closed in communication for most of their married life. In contrast, her relationship with her children, especially with her youngest son, was intimate and intense. It often happens that a wife who has been married in a traditional way into a traditional family turns out to be disappointed in her husband and finds her emotional compensation instead in love for her children.

Mrs. Fujino's husband was transferred from Wakayama to Hiroshima during the war, and a hundred days before the atomic bombs were dropped the mother took her two daughters and her youngest son to join her husband in Hiroshima. The eldest son then was at the Military Academy and was not living with them. The mother describes her youngest son, Hirohisa, then thirteen years of age, with a deep affection she does not show in her description of her husband. On the eve of the bombing of Hiroshima, the mother and her son were sitting on the balcony.

Hirohisa sat pensively on the floor resting his chin on his knees, looking up at the sky. "What is in your mind?" I asked him. "Mother, my elder brother will soon die, won't he? If he dies, what would you and father do? When I come to think of it, I feel so sad that I cannot bear it." Then he continued, "Perhaps I may become a doctor, so that I might cure my brother, should he be disabled in the war. I wish I could make him happy. Is it not a good idea, Mother?" How considerate is this boy of mine! It made me happy to see him so deeply affectionate, although I was afraid that he was a bit sissy. . . . The boy added, "Why do we have to have a war? I hope they will stop it immediately. Why can't we live in peace, with the Americans sending us Japanese what we need, and with the

24 *Ibid.*, pp. 307-308.

Japanese sending to the Filipinos what they need. The whole world then can be one nation. . . . If anybody should wish still to make a war, the people on this planet could unite to make a conquest of the moon. . . ."

"Mother, there is something I cannot possibly understand. What on earth is the Emperor doing? Even if the Emperor wins the war, having made so many of his soldiers die, could he take the vast territory that he might win to the other world when he himself dies? Even the Emperor could not help dying, and dying alone, could he? Why is it, then, that he has not said, 'stop the war'? I wonder why the Japanese have to die for the sake of the Emperor? I for one do not wish to die for the sake of the Emperor. I do wish to live long so that I may fulfill my duties of filial piety. Am I an unpatriotic Japanese to think in this way?" . . . I became worried about my son, suspecting that his teacher might be a communist. So I said to him, "Hiro, don't write what you really think, when you write your composition. What would you do if a policeman came to get you?"[25]

The dialogue between the mother and son reveals that their relationship was predominantly open in communication, intimate in affection, reciprocal in the sense that their communication was on the basis of mutual give and take, and voluntary in the sense that there was no compulsion on either side. Mrs. Fujino suffered from discommunication with her husband until the last days of her thirty years of married life, while she enjoyed an almost perfect and mutual communication with her thirteen-year-old son. This disparity reveals that she was much closer to her son in her emotional as well as intellectual life than to her husband.

On the morning after this dialogue took place, her son was at his school, which happened to be in the center of the bombardment area. Both mother and father went in search for him, but he was never found. After her husband's death and long after her son's death, Mrs. Fujino was offered a proposal for remarriage. But she turned it down. She said she could afford to refuse remarriage, since she had a widow's allowance as the wife of a deceased civil servant. Besides, she writes, "how could I forget the memories of thirty years with my late husband? No, actually my soul seems not to be held back by my deceased husband, but

[25] *Ibid.*, pp. 166-167.

it seems to be embraced tightly by my son who has been lost under the atomic bomb."[26]

After the war it was the dead son that influenced her ways of thinking more strongly than her husband, who had also been a victim of the atomic bomb.

> I feel that my son sacrificed himself to end the war. I can console myself by thinking that my son's death saved the lives of many other young people. However, when I read in the newspapers about nuclear experiments, I become very sad. I long for peace single-heartedly so that the death of our children may not be wasted. The image of my dead son makes my wish for peace ever stronger.[27]

4. Motivations for the Redefinition of the Role of Women after the War

Mismatch between Affection and Ideology

These accounts of the wartime experiences of mothers and wives reveal that their performance of their roles during the war produced in them an accumulation of intense and enduring negative affects of distress, fear, humiliation, and anguish. It is quite conceivable that the recollection of these intense negative affects during the war came to be clearly associated with the negative affects of hatred and disgust against the war itself and against the roles they were prescribed to play during it. The majority of mothers and wives felt a mismatch between their positive affects toward their children or husbands, on the one hand, and the ideological postures involved in their prescribed roles, on the other. The discrepancies between their actual and ideal roles, as disclosed in their intimate accounts of their wartime experiences, are the testimonies of the recognized dissonance between their actual affective postures and the ideological postures imposed upon them.

As a hypothesis we propose that those whose affective postures and ideologies are adequately matched are less likely to change their ideologies in response to changes in external circumstances, whereas those whose affective and ideological postures are inadequately matched are more amenable to ideological changes.[28]

[26] *Ibid.*, p. 309.
[27] *Ibid.*, p. 267.
[28] I owe this hypothesis to Silvan S. Tomkins, *Affect, Imagery, Consciousness,* New York, Springer, Vols. I and II, 1962 and 1963, and also to Daniel

Since our cases of the mothers and wives show relatively high degrees of dissonance between their affective and ideological postures during the war, it is likely that they were highly vulnerable to change when they were exposed to new ideologies and new situations after the war.

We may raise another hypothetical point concerning affects and ideologies in the change of roles. Usually, change in affective postures is less rapid than change in ideological postures. A corollary to this generalization is that one's level of density of affects is likely to persist despite change in one's ideological postures. Those women who invested intense and enduring negative and positive affects of suffering and love in order to perform their roles as mothers and wives contributing to the war effort will quite probably maintain their high level of density of affects in performing their new roles as mothers and wives in the pursuit of peace, if their ideological orientation changes. In contrast, those women whose affective involvement in the war was casual and transient may be involved in the pursuit of peace after the war but only as casual and transient observers. It is not possible to give any conclusive evidence to test these hypotheses within the limits of the present work, since almost all our samples represent those women who were emotionally, intensely, and enduringly involved in the war either negatively or positively and since we have practically no personal documents written by the women who were only casual observers of the war. But we can at least use them as explanatory, if not predictive, hypotheses to account for the existence among middle-aged women of enthusiasm in their search for new definitions of their roles as mothers and wives in the postwar period.

The War Responsibilities of "Ignorant Mothers"

The question of the war responsibilities of ordinary mothers was first raised by Harue Suda, who wrote:

> I have come to realize how sad it is to be ignorant. . . . Ignorance itself may not be a vice, but it leads us to commit a crime without our intending to. Those who make use of others' ignorance for their advantage are of course guilty. But we cannot deny the guilt of those who are ignorant enough to be used by them. . . .

J. Levison, "Idea System in the Individual and in Society," in George K. Zollachan and Walter Hirsch, eds., *Exploration in Social Change*, Boston, Houghton Mifflin, 1964.

We are responsible for the making of the war because we were ignorant enough to obey our leaders blindly and to be induced to cooperate wholeheartedly with them.[29]

Kikue Makise, in her early fifties, the wife of a journalist in Tokyo, refers to the criticisms made by some children about the records of the war experiences written by their mothers:

One of the mothers in our writing group told us that her children now in their twenties who were educated at primary or secondary school during the war shed tears when they read the mothers' writings on their war experiences. However, one of her children who was born after the war and is now in the first grade at the secondary school commented: "You mothers tried to escape and went around searching for food only after the air raid began. Why didn't you do something before the war actually started? You looked like fools who knew nothing about the coming of the war." . . .

Many of us had conflicting attitudes within ourselves. As loyal subjects of the Emperor, we thought it was prestigious to send our sons and husbands to war. But at the same time and at the bottom of our hearts we did not want them to go. Why, then, did we let our love for our sons and husbands succumb to our sense of loyalty to our country?

I entered the primary school immediately after the Sino-Japanese War [1894-1895]. In those days, most of the children wished to become soldiers, and I felt sorry to be a girl and not to be able to become a soldier. . . . I still remember that every morning we recited the *Imperial Rescript on Education.* I still can recite such chapters from our primary school text-books as "The Mother of a Sailor," "Kiguchi Kohei, the Trumpeter," and "Raise Your Gun, My Grandson Ichitarō."[30] We unquestioningly accepted what was taught at school. We were not supposed to ask why when the myth of gods and goddesses was taught as an integral part of our national history. The children who simply believed in what the elders told them were the exemplary pupils. School education nurtured the mind to accept the wars that the government had made ever since the Sino-Japanese War. The high school children today do not know this shameful history of our school education.

[29] Tsurumi and Makise, eds., *Hikisakarete*, pp. 58-59.
[30] These stories exemplified the national paragons of brave soldiers and their patriotic mothers and grandmothers.

That is why they do not know why their mothers were blindly driven into the last war. It was the education that produced the ignorant mothers.[31]

By reflecting upon and writing about their war experiences, the members of a writing circle in Tokyo came to realize that they were ignorant and that their ignorance was the result of the state-controlled education imposed upon Japanese students since the Meiji period.

A member of another writing circle in Nagoya commented at its symposium on war experiences:

> While I was writing about my war experience, I compared what I am now with what my mother was during the war and found a vast difference between us. My mother was in her forties then, and she was kept utterly ignorant of what was going on in society. Now that I am a mother, I am placed in a different situation from that in which my mother was then. In my case, I can study if I will. Under these circumstances today, it would be an injustice to my own children were I to keep myself ignorant and be drawn into a war again.[32]

These city women who belong to different writing circles discuss the function of ignorance in reference to their war experiences. They point out that the ignorance of the majority of people was functional from the point of view of the government leaders for the purpose of waging the war. But it was dysfunctional from the point of view of the women who lost their sons and husbands in the war. It was also dysfunctional for the mothers who had to suffer from the lack of food with which to feed their children and who were forced to be separated from their evacuated children.

There are some important observations to be made concerning the women's discussion of their own ignorance. First, the issue of the war responsibilities of those who were led into the war was raised by ordinary housewives, who themselves were led into it and suffered from it. The military and political leaders were tried by the International War Tribunal as war criminals. The wartime intellectual leaders were criticized after the war by intellectuals belonging mostly to the younger generation. The

[31] Tsurumi and Makise, *Hikisakarete*, pp. 227-229.
[32] Izumi no Kai, ed., *Shufu no Sensō Taikenki* (*The Records of the Housewives' War Experiences*), Nagoya, Fūbaisha, 1965, pp. 231-232.

criticism of these leaders, then, came from others. In contrast, the question of the war responsibilities of the mothers was broached by the mothers themselves. Thus the war guilt of the mothers was admitted on a voluntary basis, whereas the leaders' guilt was imposed upon them on a compulsory basis.

Second, their concept of war responsibilities is deeply tied up with their role as mothers. They feel they have an obligation to bring up their children in the best possible environment. But, because they were ignorant and were led into the war, they failed to provide their children with an environment physically, emotionally, and intellectually adequate for their growth and maturation.

The Fear of Discommunication with One's Own Children

A survey was made in 1966 by Shunsuke Tsurumi, Akira Yamamoto, and Hideo Kitamura on intra- and extra-familial communication in six major cities in Japan, including Osaka, Kyoto, Nagoya, and Yokohama. According to their findings, the married women in all these cities converse most and enjoy their conversation best with their own children. The percentages of the women who converse most with their children and enjoy them best increase as the women get older, reaching their peak at the age level of the fifties. The percentages of the women who converse most with their husbands and enjoy them best reach their peak at the age level of the thirties and drop conspicuously at the age levels of the fifties and sixties.[33]

The results of the survey indicate that there exists a persistent tendency, more than twenty years after the war, for intimacy between the mother and her child to be stronger than that between the wife and her husband. It proves that the majority of women consider it more important to be able to communicate with their children than with their husbands, at least among the generations of women educated and perhaps married before or during the war.

A peasant mother of forty in a village near Atami writes:

Sometimes I am caught with a fear, while working busily on the field. My fear is about myself getting behind my own

[33] Shunsuke Tsurumi et al., *Rokudai Toshi to Shimin: Bunkado Chōsa Hōkokusho* (*The Six Major Cities and Their Citizens: A Survey on Their Cultural Levels*), a pamphlet published under the auspices of Shitei Toshi Kikaku Chōsa Jimu Shukansha Kaigi (Council of the Planning and Research Directors of the Major Cities), Kyoto, 1966, pp. 19-24.

children. My children are growing up in every respect every day, while we mothers are working hard from dawn to twilight, tending to our orange orchards. Feeling agitated, I try to read books after supper is over and the dishes are washed. However, my hard day of work makes me sleepy before I finish only a page. . . . Occasional rainy days are my days of education. But being left alone, I may become a frog in the well and cannot expand my perspectives. I really hope to get together with other mothers to study with them so that I may catch up with my children.[34]

There exist gaps in knowledge as well as in ways of thinking between the mothers who were educated before and during the war and their children who are receiving postwar school education. For instance, the children now study, in social studies, the new Constitution which many prewar-educated mothers have never read. Even at the primary school level the mothers find it difficult to understand their children. Moreover, they are afraid that the gap in communication with their children will increase as their children grow up if they do nothing about their own ignorance of what their children are learning.

Ignorance, the mothers find, is dysfunctional because it hinders their communication with their children, whom they expect to be their best talking companions. The sense of discommunication with their husbands usually does not disturb them so much since, as the above-mentioned survey shows, discommunication with their husbands is more or less taken for granted, especially by the women.

The recognition of ignorance by the women has two aspects: first, ignorance about the war and, second, ignorance about postwar education. Both types of ignorance pertain primarily to their roles as mothers and are related to their love for their children. It is this recognition of their own ignorance and its dysfunction that primarily motivates these mothers to join various extra-familial groups and organizations in order to expand their perspectives. And it is participation in multiple group activities that helps them to redefine their roles.

[34] Kayoe Umehara, "Dō Shitara Yoide Shō" ("What Should I Do?"), *Watashitachi no Seikatsu to Iken* (*Our Lives and Opinions*), a collection of life records of the members of the PTA's in the city of Atami, edited and published by the City Board of Education of Atami, 1956, p. 134.

EIGHT

The Family: The Changing Roles of Women as Mothers and Wives

1. REDEFINITION OF THE ROLE OF MOTHER AMONG MIDDLE-AGED CITY WOMEN

Mrs. Awata: Conflicting Self

In 1954 there emerged in Tokyo a small writing circle called Hinata (meaning "sunny"), consisting of some twenty women, mostly the middle-class wives of salaried professionals.

In March 1956 the Hinata group invited a professor of law to give a lecture. The members of the circle wished to study the new Constitution, since constitutional revision was one of the issues in the coming election for the House of Councillors. The lecture on the Constitution stimulated their interest in political issues. At that time the government and the majority party, the Liberal Democratic Party, attempted to pass legislation to make membership on boards of education appointive instead of elective, as initiated under the occupation. Institution of an appointive system would mean an increase in governmental control over school education. The mothers who wrote about their war experiences, being extremely sensitive to the effects of state-controlled education on themselves and on their children, became concerned about this attempted revision of the educational system.

Some of the mothers began to read newspapers more intently than before, and some even joined mothers from other groups and PTA's, in an effort to collect signatures against the passage of the legislation. It was a new experience for these mothers to stand on the street and talk to strangers to solicit their cooperation. And, although the legislation was passed, this marked the beginning of their further participation in public affairs.

Again, in 1957, when the government tried to impose a teachers' efficiency rating system in all public schools as another means of strengthening its control over education, some of the mothers in the writing circles took part in the campaign against its enforcement.

While these campaigns were going on, Mrs. E., a woman of

fifty, withdrew from the Hinata group, leaving behind a message that explained why she had to quit:

> After all I was not up to attending the meeting today. . . . It was raining all day, and besides I had a mountain of chores to do at home. . . . I ended up not going, knowing that I was wrong not to go. . . . Thanks to my staying at home, however, my closets were tidied up and two pieces of quilts were padded with cotton. If I always stay at home, rooms are tidy and food and clothes are well looked after, which will make my family happy. However, while we enjoy our small happiness within the family, I get worried about what's happening outside of it. I know the latter generally counts more than the former. Still, it is difficult for me to push myself to participate in public affairs.[1]

Yasuko Awata, in her forties, a college graduate and the wife of a scholar, was one of the leaders of the Hinata group. She was active in the PTA's of the schools her two children attended and was quite caught up in the various campaigns on educational issues. Mrs. Awata admits that a conflict similar to the one described by Mrs. E. existed among the rest of the members in her group, including herself.

> . . . Thus conflicts arose between our desire for "small happiness" and our participation in public activities. Within us, housewives in the uptown residential section, there still persists deep attachment for "small happiness" or "happiness in a hidden corner," which has been inculcated in us through the traditional education for women to be "good wives and wise mothers." Even those of us who have come to think seriously about public affairs are still obsessed by it. Perhaps our inability to get over our obsession is due to the fact that we are in a position to live comfortably without going out of our homes to participate in social activities. Sometimes our participation in social activities gets us into trouble, and we feel we would be better off without public involvement. Of course, all of the members of our circle, including myself, cherish "small happiness." . . . On the other hand, if we allow ourselves to be immersed only in our own "small happiness,"

---

[1] Yasuko Awata, "Shufu no Mezame to 'Chiisana Kōfuku' " ("The Awakening of Housewives and Their 'Small Happiness' "), Shisō, No. 424 (Oct. 1959), p. 132.

we become worried and disturbed by the feeling that we are not fulfilling our duties. Then we are at a loss, not knowing how to manage this conflict. . . . This unmanageable conflict within ourselves arose not only between our attachment to "small happiness" as over against our participation in social activities but also out of our reassessment of what we had taken for granted as "small happiness." In any case, up until five years ago, we were all solely preoccupied by our own "small happiness" as isolated individuals. But through our five years' work in various groups, we came to get at least a wider perspective from which to reexamine what our "small happiness" consists of.[2]

Three years after Mrs. Awata wrote this essay, she became involved in a big campaign for the expansion of senior high school facilities in Tokyo. The years from 1947 to 1949 were called the period of the "baby boom," when the sudden increase of marriages after the termination of the war produced a sudden growth in the birth rate. By 1963 the children of that generation were ready to enter senior high school. If the classroom capacities of the senior high schools were kept at the size they were in 1962, approximately fifty to sixty thousand applicants would not be able to enter any senior high schools, and the number of rōnin (off-school students) would thereby be greatly increased.[3] Mrs. Awata, who had a son entering senior high school at just that time, thought it was her responsibility to cooperate with the mothers who had sons of her own son's age in solving this problem of the shortage of schools and their inadequate capacities. She joined a large organization called the Citizens' Council, which was established specifically to cope with this issue, and she worked hard for it during practically the whole year.

The reasons for her decision to disengage herself from all her public activities, which she made after the campaign was over, were twofold. In the first place, while she was working for the big Citizens' Council, she had encountered many unpleasantnesses and humiliations coming, not from the side of those against whom her campaign was directed, but from those she had expected to be her friends. It was easier to fight against

[2] Ibid., p. 134.
[3] According to the survey made by the Municipal Office of Education, cited in Tomin Kyō Dayori (A Newspaper Put out by the Citizens' Council on the Problems of Entrance into Senior High Schools), Sept. 1, 1962.

suppression exercised by one's enemy, she felt, than to bear injustices done to her by her own friends.[4] Thus she was disgusted with involvement in any large-scale social and political movements.

The second reason for her disengagement concerned her son. She had joined the movement originally to help bring about enlargement of the capacities of senior high schools, because she thought it was good for her own son as well as for the other boys of his age. Owing to her involvement in activities outside of her family, however, she neglected her son, who had been suffering from infantile asthma, and did not see to it that he was properly fed while he was working hard for his entrance examination for senior high school, and as a result the boy suffered tremendous nervous strain and fell ill. His mother, naturally enough, felt guilty for having failed to take proper care of him in this most critical period of his life.

Ideally and in the long run, Mrs. Awata still believes that, in order to bring up her own children in an environment suitable for their education, a mother should cooperate with others to make the environment better. Actually and in the short run, however, the very act of engaging in social and political movements leads a mother to neglect her own children, who require her constant and attentive care. Thus Mrs. Awata was faced with the dilemma whether to stick to the ideal role of a mother as redefined by herself and her fellow mothers in the writing groups or to revert to the old concept of that role.

Mr. Awata from the beginning encouraged his wife to participate in social and political activities. From a theoretical standpoint both of them agree that a wife should be independent in her judgment and thinking. But independence, both ideally and actually, is also a source of some new tensions between husband and wife. Mrs. Awata has come to be disillusioned in political movements while her husband has not. They have developed different assessments of political and other affairs.

Mrs. Awata now gives private lessons in English and belongs to a group studying English literature. Through her tutoring and her study she tries to cultivate her own field of work and

---

[4] From an interview with Mrs. Awata on July 27, 1964. According to Levy's *Six Laws*, "that segment of the community with which one has the greatest sympathy as a liberal inevitably turns out to be one of the most narrow minded and bigoted segments of the community." Marion J. Levy, Jr., *Levy's Six Laws*, MPH, Princeton, 1966.

to make herself really independent from her husband in her way of thinking. Her disengagement from public activities is the expression of her acutely felt emotional and ideological conflicts.

Mrs. Kawasaki: Reversely Committed

Kikue Kawasaki, in her late fifties, is the wife of a local civil servant and the mother of six children. Throughout the war her second son, who was in the Military Preparatory School, had the strong conviction that Japan would win the war. She had never doubted herself that Japan would be victorious, and so she was completely stunned by the news of the unconditional surrender. On April 10, 1946, for the first time in her life, she cast a ballot at the election of members of the Parliament.

> Previously, I absolutely trusted the government and never dreamed of criticizing it. However, since Japan's defeat we have been exposed to the fact that the government had lied to us so blatantly that it compelled me to change my mind about the government one hundred and eighty degrees.
>
> I made up my mind on my own accord to choose a candidate who would truly represent our feeling that we should never fight again. Thus I voted for a Socialist Party candidate.[5]

The feeling that she had been deceived served as the turning point of her ideological posture from the support of the war policy of the government to the search for peace. Her initial move toward peace was expressed in her venture to vote for the Socialist Party in the first election. During the days of acute shortage of food immediately after the war, she took her children to stay with her husband's brother, who was a farmer in Kyūshū. There she helped with the farm work until the day of her childbirth. The baby died three days later. Her bereavement over the loss of her baby became associated in her mind with the hard life she had to lead because of the war and made her more determined than ever to search for peace. In the meantime, her husband had been transferred from Mishima in Shizuoka Prefecture to the prefectural office in Nagasaki, and with her children Mrs. Kawasaki moved there in 1949 to join her husband.

[5] Kikue, Kawasaki, "Akao Buraku" ("Akao Village"), *Seikatsu o Tsuzuru*, Nagasaki Seikatsu o Tsuzuru Kai, No. 6 (1965), p. 12.

In 1953, when her fourth son was in the fourth grade, an educational program for parents was initiated at his school. The program came to be called Mothers' Class, and Mrs. Kawasaki was elected its chairman. In June 1955, when the first Mothers' Congress was held in Nagasaki, she attended the meeting. After the meeting was over, she joined a group of women who visited Chieko Watanabe, then twenty-four, a victim of the atomic bomb, who had been lying in bed with the lower half of her body maimed. The wives of fishermen, day laborers, and salaried men who visited Chieko on that day were so deeply moved by her and her mother, who kept a small wooden-clog shop, that they decided to form a writing circle among themselves in order to help Chieko and other girl victims of the atomic bomb like her. Mrs. Kawasaki offered to serve as the secretary of the group. These series of activities indicate that she was becoming more and more active in peace movements.

Toward the end of 1956 she was visited by a stranger who introduced himself as a member of the staff of the local bureau of investigation, who inquired what they discussed at the regular meetings of her writing circle.

. . . he said: "It is all right for you to study. But you ought not to go so far as to discuss who makes the war. . . ." For the moment I was flabbergasted, but at the next moment I got angry. "The war" is the name of the devil for us. Is it not our legitimate right to wish that it will never happen again? If there be anyone who tries to make a war, that one is the enemy for us all. Why do we have to abstain from discussing such matters and from inquiring into the truth of the matter? I could not understand what he was really driving at. However, I did not have the courage to protest to him on the spot. . . . The man asked me, "Will you please give me a part of the membership list?" After a moment of hesitation, I handed the list of our circle membership, reasoning that our circle is not a secret society. . . .

Being encouraged by many of our friends, I wrote a letter to the editors of a major newspaper, entitled "We are free to discuss." It caused greater excitement than we expected, and we received many letters of endorsement and encouragement. The local newspaper also took up the matter, which developed into such a public stir that the chief bureau of investigation publicly admitted that it had gone too far.[6]

The unpleasant encounter with the bureau of investigation did not discourage her in her commitment to the cause of peace. On the contrary, it drove her into activities involving even greater risks. In the following year, for instance, she attended the Meeting to Study Education for Peace held under the auspices of the City Teachers' Union. After the meeting she joined a demonstration for peace.

> I marched arm in arm with my eldest daughter, who became a high school teacher that year, joining the line of the teachers whom we knew. It was the splendid first experience of demonstration in my life as in the life of my eldest daughter. I felt, pulsating from the arms linked with those of our friends, the great sense of solidarity with the people with whom we share the common cause.[7]

After the demonstration she participated in a campaign against various educational measures initiated by the government in order to increase state control over school education. In 1958 her husband became sick and had to stay in bed for three years. Her second son, after graduating from Tokyo University, had gone to the United States to study as a Fulbright scholar. Having returned to Japan, he also fell ill, at about the same time his father was recuperating. During this period Mrs. Kawasaki busied herself attending to two sick persons in the family. These family worries did not detain her from her public activities, however. She got involved actively in the campaign for the expansion of facilities for the senior high schools, mainly because she was worried about her fifth son, who was then a junior high school student.

Mrs. Awata followed a zigzag course in changing her ideological posture. In contrast, Mrs. Kawasaki changed her ideological posture once at the time of the termination of the war and never returned again to her previous stance. Moreover, her commitment to the cause of peace, having once replaced her previous commitment to the war, intensified cumulatively with the repeated triads of the initial "resonance [to the ideology of peace] and risk taking, punishment and suffering, increased density of

6 *Ibid.*, pp. 19-20.
7 *Ibid.*, p. 20.

positive affect and ideation, resulting in increased risk taking."[8]

But why had Mrs. Kawasaki intensified her commitment in the face of various occasions of suffering and distress? It is characteristic of her writing to emphasize the step-by-step influence of her children on her and not to mention her husband's doings and thinking, except once when he became ill. The second son is mentioned most often. It was he who converted from commitment to the war policy of the militarists to the cause of peace after the war. He was sick in bed when the demonstration opposing the Security Treaty was staged in 1960. He told his mother then: "Although I cannot join the demonstration, I have given my signature to protest against the Security Treaty." The eldest daughter encouraged her mother to join a peace demonstration. The daughter later married her brother's classmate at Tokyo University, who was active in peace movements. Her fourth son, now a student of Kyoto University, is very active in protest demonstrations against the American atomic submarines that have called at Japanese harbors. It was, then, the constant encouragement and support of these children of her own that led her to declare twenty years after the termination of the war: "We shall never let our own sons, all the sons in Japan, go to the war!" As long as any of her children perseveres in his or her commitment to peace, Mrs. Kawasaki is not likely either to lower the level of her commitment to peace or to return to her previous ideological posture of detachment.

2. REDEFINITION OF THE ROLE OF WIFE AMONG MIDDLE-AGED VILLAGE WOMEN

According to the statistics for 1968, the labor force engaged in agriculture and forestry dwindled in that year to 19.3 percent of the total working population.[9] This constituted a marked decrease in farm labor compared to the prewar period: in 1930, for instance, farmers made up 48.4 percent of the entire labor force.[10] Another conspicuous difference is that 54 percent of those

[8] Silvan S. Tomkins, "The Psychology of Commitment," in *Affect, Cognition, and Personality*, eds. Tomkins and Carroll E. Izard, New York, Springer, 1965, p. 158.

[9] Sōrifu Tōkei Kyoku (Statistics Bureau of the Office of the Prime Minister), *Rōdō Chōsa Tōkei-hyō—Sokuhō* (*Labor Statistics Table—Quick Report*), Feb. 26, 1968, Table 3.

[10] The census of 1930—quoted in Hideko Maruoka, *Nihon Nōson Fujin Mondai* (*Agricultural Women's Problems in Japan*), Tokyo, Yakumo Shoten, 1948, p. 31.

engaged in agriculture in 1966 were women,[11] a reversal of the prewar ratio, which in 1932 stood at 49 percent women to 51 percent men.[12]

According to the Women and Minors' Bureau survey of 1964, 55.7 percent of the wives of factory and office workers investigated were not gainfully employed. Of those who were gainfully occupied, only 18.2 percent of the total of both groups had full-time jobs, while 2.4 percent worked part time, 5.7 percent were self-employed, and 11.3 percent were engaged in domestic work. Among the entire population of married city women regardless of their husbands' occupations, only 15 percent were gainfully employed on a full-time basis. In contrast, according to the survey of the same bureau undertaken from 1961 to 1962, 98 percent of the farmers' wives questioned worked on the farm, while 1 percent were engaged in occupations other than farming, leaving only 1 percent not gainfully employed.[13]

There has been a noticeable change in the role of farmers' wives in the postwar era, especially during the 1960's. Hard working as they were, peasants' wives before the war served only as part of the labor force and did not have any say in the planning and management of agricultural production. The Women and Minors' Bureau research in 1962 revealed some decided changes in this respect. Of the entire sample of women surveyed, 67 percent were the major workers on their farms. More of the part-time farmers' wives were major workers (78 percent) than the wives of full-time farmers (64 percent). Of those wives engaged in farming, 11 percent were the major decision-makers in crop planning, while 71 percent at least participated in decision-making; 10 percent of them assumed responsibilities in selling their products, while 61 percent at least shared such responsibilities. The percentage of participation in farm management was consistently higher in various categories of decision-making among the wives of part-time farmers than among those of full-time farmers.[14]

We shall examine how this altered situation has affected the role of the farmers' wives. Owing to the shortage of male labor

[11] Sōrifu Tōkei Kyoku, *Rōdō Chōsa Tōkei-hyō*, Table 3.

[12] Maruoka, *Nihon Nōson Fujin Mondai*, p. 36.

[13] Rōdōshō Fujin Shōnen Kyoku (Women and Minors' Bureau of the Labor Ministry), *Nōka Fujinseikatsu ni Kansuru Ishiki Chōsa* (*An Opinion Survey on the Life of Agrarian Women*), Tokyo, Finance Ministry Printing Office, 1962, pp. 34-35.

[14] *Ibid.*, pp. 34-37.

in agriculture, there has been a marked decrease in farm productivity. An expert on agrarian problems suggests that, to prevent any further decline, men should remain in their villages and work on the farms. If that course of action is impossible, then the wives should devise some form of cooperative farming.[15] The first alternative would be extremely difficult to implement, since male farmers have switched to other occupations because they have found that they could not make both ends meet by farming. But the second suggestion would be hard to carry out, too, owing to the competitive attitudes that exist among individual families in a village. The saying *tonari no kurō wa kamo no aji* ("the neighbor's suffering is the taste of a duckling"), which continues to circulate in villages, shows how prevalent this competitive attitude still is.

The following is a case in which a woman did achieve this difficult task of creating a cooperative form of farming and, at the same time, changed her role from that of a farmer's wife dependent on her husband and her parents-in-law to that of an independent wife-farmer.

Mrs. Yagi and Her Neighbors: Innovators of a Small-Scale Change

Masako Yagi, who was born and brought up in a city, came to her husband's native village in Hiroshima Prefecture during the war to live with her husband, her three-year-old son, her parents-in-law, and her grandmother-in-law. Her husband's family operated a middle-sized farm with 1.2 *chō* (about 3 acres) of rice field and 1.5 *tan* (about 0.25 acre) of dry field. Her husband accepted a teaching job at the village primary school, leaving the farm work to his wife and to his parents.

Mrs. Yagi began her apprenticeship in farming under the direction of her parents-in-law. At first the father-in-law managed the farm, hiring outside help to do the heavy work. As he grew old and retired from active oversight of the farm, Mrs. Yagi had to learn to run the farm with hired hands, who were not dependable, since they also began to desert farming for more lucrative work. To add to her troubles, death deprived Mrs. Yagi of the aid of her grandmother-in-law, who had taken care of her eldest son and the three younger ones, born in successive years after her arrival in the village. Her mother-in-law, who was getting

[15] Ryōzō Takahashi, *Otō o Kaese* (*Give Me Back My Daddy*), Tokyo, Ie no Hikari Kyōkai, 1965, p. 141.

on in her years, handed Mrs. Yagi the right of management of the household affairs to boot. Thus the days of apprenticeship as a daughter-in-law were over for Mrs. Yagi ten years after the termination of the war. She was now expected to play the roles of the mother of her four children, of the wife who had the right of headwifeship, and of a full-fledged farmer taking sole responsibility for the family's farm.

Both the eldest and the second sons declared that they did not wish to be farmers but wanted to enter universities instead. The two younger ones were not yet old enough to help their mother. Thus she was left alone not only to manage the farm but to do all the heavy labor by herself.

Being hard pressed, Mrs. Yagi decided to try an entirely new method. Some years after the war the wives of her four neighbors began to cooperate among themselves in the planting of rice and wheat on their farms. Their farms were more or less equal in size and smaller than Mrs. Yagi's farm. Mrs. Yagi wished to be admitted into the cooperative rice-planting group. So she asked her neighbors to come and meet at the village center. At that gathering she suggested that they should put all of their farm work on a cooperative basis instead of just the rice- and wheat-planting, as they had hitherto been doing. Her neighbors agreed, but there remained the problem of how to settle the distribution of wages.

Among the five families in the cooperative farming group, the husbands' occupations differed. My husband is a salaried man, the husband of the Shimoya family is a painter, and the Matsudaya's and the Nishi's husbands are stone breakers working on a construction project, while Takenoshita's husband is the only man who is engaged in farming on a full-time basis. But he has just recovered from his illness and cannot do much work at the moment at least. . . . There was no problem in fixing the wages equally among the families according to the work the women did. However, we thought it would not be just to give men who could go out and earn more cash money than women a wage equal to that paid to the women. . . .

In the end we reached an agreement that we women would do as much work as we could, asking our men to earn cash money outside of farming as long as possible until the really busy season in farming arrived. The wage for women, we have decided, is 40 yen [360 yen = 1 dollar] per hour plus

40 yen for a meal for every four hours' work. How much more should be added to the men's wage will be fixed according to the kind of work they do. Usually, for both men and women, the working hours are from eight in the morning until five in the evening, and we shall have an hour off for lunch, half an hour for tea, and twenty minutes' rest each for the morning and the afternoon.

Thus we solved, for that year at least, the problem of labor shortage, and I looked forward to a new experience of participating in a cooperative farming project.

My mother-in-law was also pleased to be freed from the chore of preparing meals for the hired hands everyday.[16]

There are some points of interest pertinent to our problem of changing women's roles in this description of the development of a cooperative farming project. Cooperative farming is originally rooted in the old practice of *yui* in village communities. However, there are some differences between the new pattern of cooperative farming that Mrs. Yagi's group has evolved and the traditional form of *yui*. In the first place, the traditional form was the "mutual aid or labor exchange" practiced usually in the busy seasons only.[17] Cooperative farming, in contrast, is a form of mutual aid on a year-round basis. Second, *yui* rested on the traditional extended family system, consisting of the main and branch families, whereas cooperative farming involves a group of nonrelatives. The families that participated in *yui* were hierarchically arranged; those engaged in cooperative farming organize themselves on the egalitarian principle. Third, in the *yui* system it was the headman of the main family that decided about the organization and the working conditions of labor, whereas in cooperative farming it is the wives who have the greatest voice in determining not only their own wages but even the men's. Fourth, within the traditional *yui* the exchange

[16] Masako Yagi, "Kyōdo Kōsaku Made" ("How I Joined Cooperative Farming"), *Chihō* (*Our Local World*), a circle pamphlet, ed. Tomoe Yamashiro, Miharashi, No. 1 (Dec. 1962), p. 22.

[17] "*Yui* usually means mutual aid or labor exchange. . . . This presupposes the existence of independent farmers, with their own labor organizations. In ordinary times, their own labor system is enough to take care of their farms. In the busy seasons, however, they need more labor than their own, and thus they helped themselves, taking their turn to work upon their respective farms." Kizaemon Aruga, *Nihon Kazokuseido to Kosaku Seido* (*The Japanese Family System and Tenancy*), Tokyo, Kawada, 1943, pp. 655, 659.

of labor was not mediated by money, but within Mrs. Yagi's group the exchange of labor is put on a contractual basis in which the wages are precisely fixed per hour according to the kind of labor performed. Thinking in terms of figures and numbers has thus been introduced into the life of a farmer's wife, contributing to turn her previously predominantly nonrational way of thinking and acting into predominantly rational modes of thought and action.

Book-keeping Movement among Women in the Agricultural Cooperatives

Mrs. Yagi's experience in cooperative farming is not an isolated case but one among many experiments emerging all over Japan. In 1961 there were 3,178 cooperative farm groups; the number increased to 5,614 in 1965 and slightly decreased to 5,512 in 1967. Of this latter total 7.7 percent are operated on a completely cooperative basis, as Mrs. Yagi's group is, while 92.3 percent of them use cooperative arrangements only partially. Out of the 393 cooperative farming groups newly established from February 1966 to February 1967, 214 comprise five households or less.[18]

That women play a major part in promoting cooperation in farm management and production is illustrated by the reports presented at the Tenth Annual National Convention of the Readers of the *Ie no Hikari* (*Light of the Family*), the organ of the Women's Section of the National Association of Farmers' Cooperatives, held in February 1968. The proceedings of the convention consist of thirty-five reports, each representing one of the different prefectures in Japan. Only one of the thirty-five reporters is male, a farmer twenty-two years old; the rest are agrarian women, of whom two are in their twenties, seventeen in their thirties, thirteen in their forties, and two in their fifties. Practically all of them hold the position of responsibility for the management of their farms as well as for their family budget. Out of the thirty cases reported by these women, twenty-seven are concerned with how they improved their agricultural production and income through cooperation with other women in their respective villages. And, of those twenty-seven cases, nine

[18] Nōrinshō Tōkei Chōsabu (Statistical Survey Section of the Ministry of Agriculture and Forestry), *Nōgyō Chōsa Kekka Gaiyō* (*Outline Report on the Results of the Agricultural Survey*), July 1967, pp. 43-45.

specifically deal with a group book-keeping movement, while the rest relate the experiences women had combining a book-keeping movement with cooperative farming.

The book-keeping movement is aimed at cultivating the habit of modern book-keeping among women, with the help and guidance of the Women's Section of the National Association of Farmers' Cooperatives. Women have organized their own groups in various districts to learn to keep separate and itemized accounts of household expenditures, on the one hand, and the costs of production and income from the farm, on the other. This book-keeping practice has enabled women to grasp the facts of domestic life and farm work for the first time in terms of figures. It also has encouraged them to turn farming into a planned economy. They have come to draw up budgets for future family spending and, in order to meet increased levels of expenditure, have devised new schemes for diversified farming instead of repeating the traditional patterns of crop rotation. The practice of modern book-keeping has thus implanted in agrarian women the basic attitude of rationality. The book-keeping movement promoted under the leadership of the Women's Section of the National Association of Farmers' Cooperatives is unique in that it has fostered open communication among women living in the same hamlet. Five to ten women in a hamlet gather once a month to compare one another's books to make monthly tabulations of their own costs of living and to discuss how to eliminate waste and improve their financial situation. Mrs. Yakushiji of Ehime Prefecture reports:

At first the idea of making one's family budget public was repugnant to many of us. As we went along, however, we gradually overcame our sense of resistance and realized how fortunate we were to be able to discuss our problems together in a group of friends. We discussed how to dissolve antagonism between a mother-in-law and a daughter-in-law over money matters. We also talked about various problems that we had hitherto suffered alone. Our discussion developed from private affairs to social problems, and thus our housekeeping account books served as a very useful means of opening up our eyes to larger problems than just domestic affairs. Had we been left to ourselves, we could not have made monthly tabulations. It was the group that enabled us to break through the hard crust of conventionalism and to improve our living.[19]

The group book-keeping movement that is developing among agrarian women contributes toward overcoming competitive attitudes among families and cultivating a spirit of cooperation and collectivism.

The trend for wives to become independent and responsible farmers has given rise to some changes in their roles within and without the family. The Women's Section of the National Association of Farmers' Cooperatives cites some instances of change in the status of women owing to their emergent position as full-fledged independent farmers. One of the changes is that women have become interested in group studies on scientific farming and have begun to have their say not only on matters of farming but also on various public matters in the village.

> Wives report that they have self-confidence in rice-cultivation now that they have formed a study group. . . . [One of them says] "Previously, I made foolish mistakes while I obeyed what my husband told me to do. Since I came to attend the study group and have studied on my own, my husband has begun to listen to me. Not only that, he began to consult with me on planting plans." . . .
> The chairman of the Farmers' Cooperatives in Fukugama said: "The village women's industriousness in their study of scientific agriculture shows the development of their consciousness as professional farmers. . . . Those women who have begun to study and work on their farms on their own have shining bright eyes, which distinguish them from those who still work under the direction of their husbands. They have stepped forward to become farmers who use not only their bodies but their brains too. The independence of women as professional farmers is also tied up with the general trend toward their control of the family purse [to hold the family purse means to have the right of management of the household economy]. From now on, women should lighten their burden by

[19] Ie no Hikari Kyōkai (Association of the *Ie no Hikari*) *Dai Jukkai Zenkoku Ie no Hikari Taikai Keiken Happyō Kai Shiryō* (*Proceedings of the Tenth Annual National Convention of the Readers of the* Ie no Hikari), 2 vols., Feb. 6, 1968. For a detailed analysis of the data from the proceedings, see Kazuko Tsurumi, "Kazoku ni okeru Fujin no Yakuwari Henka" ("Women's Role Change in the Family"), *Shisō*, May 1968, pp. 746-766.

putting their farming on a cooperative basis and at the same time by mechanizing their farm labor."[20]

3. Redefinition of the Role of Mother-in-Law among Agrarian Women in Their Old Age

In the life of a mother-in-law in an extended family there are two different periods. In the first period she is fully occupied in the management of household affairs and the training of her daughter-in-law as the prospective head-wife of the family. The second period begins at the time she transfers the right of management of household affairs to her daughter-in-law. When she thus retires from the role of overseer of household affairs, she also passes on the duty of training her granddaughter-in-law, if there is any, or the prospective one, if there is an unmarried grandson in the family. We can very well assume that by this time all of her own children are grown and she is freed from the duty of bringing them up. The mother-in-law in this second stage, then, no longer fulfills any major functions within the family, except for such a minor one as taking care of her grandchild, if there is any, while its own mother is out working in the field.

In the traditional extended family, which is based on the principle of gerontocracy, the old men and women are respected and feared *qua* old persons, even if they do not have legitimate roles to play within the family. Among the younger generation of their sons and daughters-in-law, however, reverence for old age *qua* old age is fading, unless the old people are performing some useful function within the family. Retirement, the old custom of the traditional extended family, is actually the process of disengagement from all major duties previously held in the family. In that sense, retirement is the situation which ideally creates role-void with reference to one's own family. Yet, as long as the tradition of gerontocracy persists, old men and women will not actually feel their retirement as role-void. Role-void creates tension when those who have lost their legitimate roles feel themselves deprived of the attention and care they expect from the significant others. Role-void is thus a form of relative deprivation with reference to the pattern of relationships that existed in the past but exists no more. It is a type of role strain

[20] Zenkoku Nōkyō Fujin Soshiki Kyōgikai (National Council of Agricultural Women's Organizations), *Kome to Nōson Fujin (Rice and Village Women)*, Tokyo, 1959, pp. 114, 116-117.

that occurs when the system to which one belongs undergoes drastic change in its structure of relationships. It also occurs, as the example of the war widows shows, when a member of the system whom one expects to play an important role is prematurely taken away.

Cumming and Henry characterize old age as the period of disengagement, by which they mean "decreased interaction between the aging person and others in the social systems he belongs to," resulting in "decreased involvement with others and his increased preoccupation with himself."[21] Disengagement entails a decrease in the number of one's roles and the degree of one's involvement in them, until one's legitimate functions approach a zero point, which we call role-void. It is our contention, however, that the old person who is disengaged from his previous roles may be reengaged in some new roles, thus reviving involvement with a new set of persons or with the same set of persons in ways different from those in which he has previously been involved. Thus we agree with Cumming and Henry that growing old is a process of disengagement, but at the same time we hypothesize that there is a possibility for old persons to enter upon new roles bringing them into contact with new sets of persons in order to manage the strain arising from the sense of role-void.

We shall test this hypothesis by studying the cases of mothers-in-law who have attended the old folks' school organized by Bunjō Kobayashi, a Buddhist priest who is chairman of the community center in a village in Nagano Prefecture. He describes how a group of old women came to see him one day and complained about their daughters-in-law, an experience which prompted him to open up a school for them and their male counterparts.

> "Indeed, when we were young daughters-in-law, the only occasion on which we were allowed to go out was either on the Girls' Festival on the third day of March or after the autumn harvest to pay a visit to our own parents. [But nowadays, our daughters-in-law have too many outings!]
>
> "In our days, there was not a single daughter-in-law who was allowed to read a newspaper. We were too busy to do so. In contrast, nowadays there is radio to listen to anytime,

[21] Elaine Cumming and William E. Henry, *Growing Old: The Process of Disengagement*, New York, Basic Books, 1961, pp. 14-15.

and, besides, farm work is much easier than it was in our days. [We worked much harder than daughters-in-law today usually do!]

"Since the establishment of the community center, which organizes a special school for young daughters-in-law, they have come to look so superior that they are not afraid of us, the old mothers-in-law, anymore. [We used to fear and respect our mothers-in-law above anybody else!]

"Everything has been changed nowadays. They tell us that, since these are the days of democracy, they are entitled to ignore old folks like us." . . .

The complaints of the old women went on almost without end. I felt, listening as they talked, that they were truly lonesome.[22]

The old women asked the priest to provide opportunities for them to study things new and changing, so that they might be able to communicate with the younger generations. One of the old women said:

"Indeed, we are not satisfied with ourselves being old-fashioned. We know we ought to change. However, we old folks do not know what is going on today. We, therefore, always talk about the good old days which we know best. That is why we are being criticized for being old-fashioned, which annoys us. Why don't you tell us new stories. We shall be glad to come and listen to you, having our daughters-in-law make us some nice picnic lunches. You may say that you would teach the young ones, from whom we old folks should learn. No, that doesn't work. Since within our families it is the old folks who are expected to know better than the young, we would lose face should we ask them to teach us anything. Be nice to us old folks, and you will find us swarming to you and studying with you as hard as the younger folks. Please teach us new things."[23]

These words moved the priest, who first organized a week-long group tour to Kyoto for them and a discussion group after the tour, which developed into a school for old folks called Rakusei Gakuen (Enjoyment-of-Life School). It was launched

[22] Bunjō Kobayashi, *Rōjin wa Kawaru* (*Old Folks Change*), Tokyo, Kokudosha, 1961, pp. 8-9.
[23] *Ibid.*, pp. 9-10.

in May 1954 with eighty-six men and women beyond the age
of sixty. By 1961 the number of students had swelled to two
hundred and fifty. They gathered at the Kōkyūji Temple at least
once a week to attend lectures, to discuss their own personal
problems, to sing and dance, and to participate in other group
activities. Out of these group studies and recreation there have
emerged some observable changes among the old people, practically all of whom were farmers.

First, they have begun to overcome the communication gap
and to establish mutual contact with the persons of younger
generations within and without their own families. The Rakusei
School invited a distinguished poetess to give a lecture before
the old people. The poetess, impressed by their enthusiasm for
learning new things, wrote four songs especially for the Rakusei
students. A composer wrote music for these songs, and the old
people thus acquired happy and modern tunes of their own.[24]
When the old folks were given the scores of their new songs,
they were puzzled, since none of them was able to decipher the
musical notes. The priest-teacher told them to ask their grandsons and daughters to teach them how to read the music. The
younger people became interested and taught their grandparents how to sing these songs. Singing together made their
relationships more intimate than before. Meanwhile, the young
people and the old folks began to compare notes on what they
learned and did at their respective schools. This exchange transformed not only the content of the conversation between young
and old but the pattern of communication as well, from one-way
to two-way communication.[25]

The occasional visits to the primary and secondary schools in
the village by the Rakusei School group also contributed to
mutual understanding between the old and younger generations, not only within their own families but also outside of
them.[26]

Out of the increased communication and interaction between
the old and younger generations arose a suggestion made by
one of the old women at the Rakusei School to the effect that
a public holiday should be instituted for the younger generation
of farmers in the village. She made the following proposal in
their regular meeting at her school in July 1958:

[24] *Ibid.*, pp. 67-74.   [25] *Ibid.*, pp. 89-90.
[26] *Ibid.*, pp. 159-163.

"Today I should like to make a proposal. Thanks to the folks [meaning their sons or daughters-in-law] who now take the major responsibilities for our farm work, we are able to enjoy ourselves and to study at our school. So I hope that these young folks will take a good rest at least once a month. If you agree with me, I should like to ask our priest-teacher to declare such a holiday for all the working villagers." . . .

Listening to this speech, the chairman of the Community Center summoned the district chiefs and the leaders of the youths' and women's organizations to consult about the public holiday from farm work. The youth organization made a public opinion survey whose result showed that 86 percent of the villagers agreed to have such a holiday. On September 23 the first holiday was observed. The fact that the proposal came from the older generation, I believe, helped the introduction of such a holiday without any serious opposition. In any case, the monthly holiday has been appreciated by the farmers ever since.[27]

Second, the old folks have begun to find new roles outside of their families and to gain enough confidence in themselves so that they can be socially useful in performing these new roles.

At our school we held a study meeting to look for some socially useful work that may be fulfilled by old men and women. We decided that the old women would stitch dusters while the old men would weave straw sandals and that we would donate them to schools, nursery schools, and the public offices in our neighborhood. Subsequently, five hundred dusters and fifty pairs of straw sandals were collected and distributed, which were very much appreciated.[28]

They have also contributed to the public welfare of the village life in various ways, by weeding the banks of the village main street, for example, or by cleaning up the gardens of the temples and shrines, distributing wastepaper baskets at bus stations to keep them tidy, petitioning the ward office for the construction of a public dumping place in place of letting people throw their refuse into the river, and so on. Trifling as some of these activities may seem, they are noteworthy considering that the Japanese people traditionally tend to be meticulously clean in their

[27] *Ibid.*, pp. 90-91.
[28] *Ibid.*, p. 98.

own domiciles, while they are inclined to put up with a very low standard of sanitation in public places. It is interesting to observe that these old men and women, through their constant labor to keep the public places in the village clean, are attempting to resocialize the rest of the villagers to the new standard of public cleanliness. Thus they call their activity of distributing wastepaper baskets at the bus stations their "moral education" of the villagers.[29]

Third, these old men and women, who had been isolated from one another, confining themselves in their own families, have now come to realize that they can only overcome their private grievances by engaging in collective actions. A year after the Rakusei School was opened, some old men and women complained that they were always hard up for pocket money. According to a survey made of the 572 old men and women in the village, 28 percent of them earned enough for their own personal expenses, while 55 percent had to ask for pocket money from their sons or daughters-in-law, who usually could not afford to give them enough, even if they wished to. The old men and women then studied the old-age pension systems in the Western countries and decided that they should demand a similar system from their own government. So they drafted a petition for the establishment of social welfare legislation for old people and sent it with their signatures to the Parliament, to political parties, to the Welfare Ministry, and to other agencies. Five years later an old-age pension system was introduced in Japan.[30]

Fourth, owing to the above-mentioned changes from discommunication to increased communication with the younger generations, from the sense of the lack of legitimate roles to the discovery of new roles, and from detachment from public activities to engagement in them, the affective postures of the old persons have also undergone change. Kobayashi, the priest-teacher, reports that not only have they stopped complaining and grumbling but their facial expressions have become brighter and they now laugh a lot.

In many villages I encounter the expressionless faces of old men, who look as though they were sure to lose something if

[29] Information about these activities based on interviews with Reverend Kobayashi and some of his disciples at the Rakusei School on August 18, 1964.
[30] Kobayashi, Rōjin wa Kawaru, pp. 34-37, 113-118.

they laughed. It is the old men with such faces that darken the family life for the rest of its members. . . .

Among the students of Rakusei School, there were some such rigid faces at the beginning. . . .

Nowadays [seven years after the founding of the school] the old folks at our school laugh a lot. The lecturers who come to visit our school always comment that "the old people here look unusually bright-eyed." Many people ask us, "Is there any secret to keep old men and women always smiling as they do here?" But I cannot answer this question with a few words. Many factors have been accumulated to change their facial expression, I suppose.[31]

Among those many factors, the priest-teacher counts the technique of stepping out of the family as the prime one underlying the change from predominantly negative to predominantly positive affective posture.

In agrarian villages, old people hardly have an opportunity to step out of their own families. Being stuck to their families, the old people inevitably work up nervous tension. From this point of view alone, old folks' schools are necessary not only for the sake of the old people themselves but also for the sake of the younger people.[32]

A daughter-in-law writes about the change in her mother-in-law's attitude toward her, on account of the latter's change of habit from confinement in the house to engagement in various groups and meetings outside the family circle:

My mother-in-law is seventy-nine years old. While she was young, she worked so hard that she could spare no time to attend any school sports, parents' meetings, women's club meetings, movies, or theatres. When my eldest son entered school, I wished to go to his school to visit his class at work. But my old-fashioned mother-in-law refused to let me go, saying "You don't have to visit your child's school every month." I always regretted that I could not go. I have not been allowed to go to any women's club meetings, to PTA meetings, or to the community center until very recently. . . .

When a movie came to our district, I asked my mother-in-

[31] *Ibid.*, pp. 92-93.
[32] *Ibid.*, p. 96.

law to go and see the show. . . . I encouraged her to go, saying "It is free of admission, mother. You had better go with
our neighbor." Finally, and for the first time, she went.
Since then she attends the movies whenever they come to
our district hall. . . .

Nowadays, whenever we receive an invitation, she asks me,
"is that an invitation for a movie again?" She now looks forward to the movies. I also encourage her to go and attend
lectures. She now goes to school sports on her own accord
and has come to understand what the PTA and women's
clubs are all about. She now encourages me to visit my son's
class at work, to attend PTA meetings, and even to go to the
public library to borrow books. I am very much impressed
by the change that has come over my once old-fashioned
mother-in-law.[33]

Rakusei School is not a solitary experiment in the resocialization of old people. There are now similar schools and study
groups for old people all over the country, mainly in agrarian
villages. These experiments indicate, as the priest-teacher
maintains, that old people may change their patterns of both
ideological and affective postures provided they are exposed
to adequate agents of resocialization. They also reveal that a
characteristic pattern of change for old people in extended families is the process of disengagement from familial roles, followed
by reengagement in newly discovered roles outside of the
families, resulting in changes in the structure of relationship
of the old persons with the members of the younger generations
within their families.

We can characterize the process of the personality change of
the old folks at Rakusei School as the innovator type of a small-
scale change. Many of the socialization devices that are used
at the school are based on traditional customs of the village
community. The temple school itself was originally patterned
after the style of popular schools in the Tokugawa period.[34]
Excursions for old men and women are not uncommon in the
village community, where various group tours used to be arranged under the name of kō, which originally had some religious meanings. Free labor on behalf of the community, such

[33] Kenji Maruyama and Kensuke Ikeda, eds., Inadani ni Tsuzuru (Voices
from the Ina Valley), Tokyo, Ie no Hikari Kyōkai, 1965, pp. 75-76.
[34] For an exposition of the temple school, see R. P. Dore, Education in
Tokugawa Japan, Berkeley, University of California Press, 1965, Ch. VIII.

as mending roads and cleaning shrine gardens, was also cus-
tomarily practiced by various *kō* groups.[35] The traditional *kō*
group tour for old folks was merely a pastime activity for disengaged men and women. At Rakusei School trips stimulate
desire for novelty among the old and thus motivate them to
reengage themselves in new roles. The venerable custom of free
labor on behalf of the community was traditionally defined for
each group of persons in the village. At Rakusei School each
act of public service is initiated by some individuals and performed voluntarily by each person. It thereby promotes independent judgment and decision-making on the part of each
member of the group, rather than keeping them dependent on
the group to prescribe to them what they should do.

The unique combination of the old institutions and customs
with new ideas and orientations seems to have contributed to the
success of resocialization of the old folks at Rakusei School in
producing the innovator type of personality change among
them.

4. CONCLUSION

Granting that the choice of our samples is arbitrary, we can
still draw some generalizations from the analysis of the case histories of those city and agrarian women we have studied.

(1) According to the statistical survey, there are more extended families remaining in the villages than in the cities.
The results of our analysis of personal documents, on the other
hand, show that among city women the role of a mother changes
more rapidly and more decisively than that of a wife, whereas
among agrarian women the role of a wife changes more rapidly
and more decisively than that of a mother, at least for the respective groups of middle-aged women. These seeming discrepancies can be explained on the basis of our analysis in the following manner.

In the first place, both the city women and the agrarian women
whose personal documents we have studied are those who were

---

[35] *Kō* is the group formed primarily for religious or economic purposes
combined with recreational activities. *Ise Kō* is the most famous among such
groups specially organized for taking trips. *Michi Bushin Kō* is the road-
mending group. See Tarō Wakamori, ed., *Nihon Rekishi Jiten* (*Encyclopaedia of Japanese History*), Tokyo, Jitsugyō no Nihonsha, 1952, pp. 172-
173; Kōta Kodama, *Kinsei Nōmin Seikatsu Shi* (*History of the Life of Farmers in the Near-Modern Period*), Tokyo, Yoshikawa Kōbunkan, 1960, pp.
249-250.

married either before or at least during the war. Almost all of their marriages were arranged, in accordance with the traditional practice. Even if the present size of some of their families places them within the category of a nuclear family, that fact alone does not necessarily mean that the structure of relationships within their families is that of the modern conjugal family. It is quite conceivable that traditionally married couples do not easily change their structure of relationships despite the legal changes and the increasing attention being given the ideology of the modern conjugal family in the mass media. That the role of a mother changes more conspicuously and more rapidly than the role of a wife among city women confirms, rather than contradicts, this conception of the traditional married couples in cities. That pattern can very well be taken as an indication of the persistence of the structure of relationships of the traditional extended family among city women, despite the outward appearance of the size of the modern conjugal family.

On the other hand, in spite of the prevalence in the villages of the extended family measured in terms of its size, the actual structure of relationships within agrarian families, we want to suggest, is closer to the conjugal type than it appears to be.

In the second place, among agrarian women the most decisive change occurs in the occupational role of wives. It is not so much their solidarity with their husbands that is primarily responsible for their role change as the circumstances that require them to be independent of their husbands. The majority of married agrarian women are engaged in farming full-time, whereas the majority of married women in the city either are not gainfully employed at all or are gainfully employed only part-time. Most of the married women in the city are still full-time wives or mothers. This fact suggests that the precedence of change in the role of a wife over that in the role of a mother is less a characteristic of the pattern of the agrarian family than it is of the pattern of the family in which wives are gainfully employed full-time and the wives' earnings are at least equally as important as their husbands' earnings in support of the family. If this is the case, then an increase in the number and percentage of the city wives who have full-time jobs can be expected to bring about a radical alteration in the pattern of role change among city women.

The number of married women in cities who seek full-time employment is definitely on the rise. They cannot catch up for some time to come, however, with their counterparts in the villages with respect to the ratio of those who are gainfully employed on a full-time basis. And, as long as this gap between the married women of the cities and those of the villages remains, we can predict that this seemingly paradoxical situation will persist: among agrarian families there will be more emergence actually of the modern conjugal type of relationship and less persistence actually of the traditional extended type of relationship than among the families of the salaried men and industrial workers in the cities; conversely, among the latter there will be more persistence actually of the traditional extended type of relationship and less emergence actually of the modern conjugal type of relationship than among the former.

(2) Among city women we have observed one case in which a woman disengages herself from social and political movements whenever she encounters difficulties and another case in which a woman intensifies her commitment to peace movements whenever she suffers from the consequences of her risk-taking. Both descending commitment and ascending commitment to the cause of peace for those women depend upon the ideological postures of their children, rather than upon those of their husbands. The mother who intensifies her commitment to peace is sustained and encouraged by her children who are active in antiwar movements. The mother who disengages herself from public activities has children who either are not interested in, or are opposed to, their mother's social and political involvement.

From these observations we may elicit the hypothetical proposition that, wherever the traditional extended type of family relationship is actually predominant, the ideological postures of the children rather than those of the husbands ultimately exert more decisive influence on the ideological postures of the married women. Analogously, we may hypothesize that, wherever the modern conjugal type of family relationship is actually predominant, the ideological postures of the husbands rather than those of the children ultimately exert more decisive influence on the ideological postures of the married women.

If among urban families traditional extended type of relationships are actually persistent, then we may study the ideological postures of the children in order to predict the direction of ideological change their mothers will take. If at least one of her children is committed to the antiwar campaign, the mother, who has been previously indoctrinated to support war, is likely to replace her previous commitment with a new commitment to peace, and she may increase the degree of her commitment as her child becomes more and more deeply committed to the new ideology. Under such circumstances her personality change is likely to take the reversely committed form. If none of her children is interested in any public affairs, or if they are even hostile to their mother's being engaged in social movements, it will be extremely difficult for the mother to sustain her interest and continue her activities in social and political movements, even if she is already deeply involved. Under such circumstances her personality change may take the form of either the many-layered self or the conflicting self. If her children have been and still are committed to war, in spite of the change in the general trend from war to peace, then it is likely that the mother will not change her previous commitment to war, and indeed she may even intensify it. In such a case, her personality change may take the form of ever committed to the previous ideology.

It follows, then, that children's ideological postures exert more influence on their mothers within the traditional extended family than within the modern conjugal family. We may formulate this conclusion into a hypothetical proposition: the importance of the ideological postures of the younger generation is greater in deciding the ideological postures of the women of the older generation in a society where the pattern of the traditional extended family actually persists than in a society where the pattern of the modern conjugal family is actually predominant. This hypothesis might explain partially, as we think it does, the relative weight that the student movements carry in such traditional societies as prerevolutionary China, present-day Korea, and Japan today.

(3) With regard to the hypotheses about role-void and the process of reengagement, our substantive data are rather scanty. These data suggest at least that there is a possiblility of reengagement in newly defined roles for persons of old age. How enduring and how far-reaching this change is we do not yet know. These data do, however, provide some indications that socialization can continue throughout one's lifetime and that change of both ideological and affective postures in one's old age is possible, if difficult.

In order to make our hypotheses more fruitful, we should collect and compare the personal documents of old people in both cities and villages, in different occupations, and in different patterns of families.

PART THREE

NINE

The Student Movement: Its Milieu

THE ANALYSIS of the student movements in this and the succeeding chapters is based on interviews with one hundred students of universities in Tokyo undertaken during May and
June 1962, two years after the campaign against the revision of
the Japanese-American Security Treaty. Since the focus of this
essay is on the student movement in 1960, it is already somewhat
dated. We believe, however, that it still has a significant bearing
on the understanding of the student movement as it exists today,
for the following reason. In 1960, when the movement was at its
peak, there emerged for the first time in the history of the Japanese student movement a potent political organization independent of the Communist Party of Japan or of any other country.
This organization initiated some new patterns in the student
movement in Japan both with respect to the ideo-affective postures of its leaders and with respect to the structure of relationships within the group. In this respect, an analysis of the student
movement as it existed in 1960 provides a strategic point of reference with which the student movement now, and probably in
the future, can be compared and contrasted. By use of such a
yardstick, one may obtain a fuller understanding of the current
student movement than could be achieved by studying it in
isolation.

Our interviews were conducted by means of a questionnaire
consisting of one hundred and three inquiries, most of which
were amenable to statistical handling. Simple yes-and-no answers fitted for statistical analysis have been tabulated to show
some general trends.[1] The rest of the data were used for the

[1] From July 1961 to June 1962, with a research assistantship provided me
by the Center of Japanese Studies of the University of California, I worked
with Professor Lewis S. Feuer (now of the University of Toronto) on a
sociological investigation of student movements in Japan. I owe this survey
of student movements to him and to the University of California with which
he was then connected. In drafting our questionnaire, I consulted with some
leaders and ex-leaders of the student movements in Japan. Messrs. Satoshi
Kitakōji, Takeo Shimizu, Kenichi Kōyama were the most helpful among
them. I also learned much from discussions I had with Professor Rokurō
Hidaka and Mr. Morimitsu Ozaki of Tokyo University.
After the draft questionnaire was prepared, Professor Feuer asked for the
comments of some of his colleagues. Invaluable suggestions made by Profes-

explanation of the history of the student movements and for the description of individual life-histories of the students. The overall purpose was to put the close-up views of the student movements in the general context of the postwar universities in Japan and to draw intellectual portraits of some of the leaders of the movements, comparing them with their fellow students who were not involved in the movements and also with the communist intellectuals of the 1930's.

1. WHAT IS A STUDENT MOVEMENT?

A student movement is defined by its participants as a sustained, concerted action undertaken by a group or groups of students opposed to the existing system or systems of power. Sumihisa Kuroha, erstwhile leader of the Anti-Mainstream Zengakuren (the Japanese abbreviation for the National Federation of Student Self-Government Associations), has analyzed the student movement as follows:

> The overwhelming majority of the participants in student movement are of petty-bourgeois origin. Yet the student movement is not oriented toward the materialistic interests of that class. The student movement is a social and political movement whose participants join, not from the motives of materialistic interest, but from ideological and idealistic motives. Among students considered as a social stratum, there exists a wide variety of philosophical and political attitudes which neither reflect the social origins of individual students nor provide an atmosphere conducive to the emergence of a unitary political movement. However, their scientific knowledge, their youthful sense of justice, and their heroic spirit arouse them in periods of crisis to fight as a unit for ideals of radical social change against the reactionary ruling class. Especially when their own nation suffers foreign oppression, student movements tend to become activist. That is why student movements are

sor Juan J. Linz, Dr. Abraham Halpern, and Professor Charles Y. Glock, as well as Professor Feuer himself, were most gratefully incorporated into the revised final form of the questionnaire. The actual interviewing was carried out by Miss Sadako Yokoyama and myself.

In the process of programming and computation, Professors F. F. Stephan and C. E. Helm of Princeton University provided indispensable aid. Dr. Yungshik Chang, now of the University of British Columbia, helped me with punch-card processing. Mr. Joel High of the Computer Center of Princeton University undertook the actual work of computation and tabulation.

relatively stronger in colonial states and in countries where democracy is not fully developed than elsewhere; for students in such countries are more likely than in other countries to have their aspirations and ideals thwarted.[2]

Thus a student movement, as defined by its participants, is an agency for producing change in the existing social environment. Any social change has two distinct aspects, one relating to the ideological content of the change and the other relating to the structure of relationships within the change-producing agent. The salient feature of the postwar Japanese student movement is that at least some of the student groups have recognized the importance of making the structure of relationships within their own groups different from the structure characteristic of other groups to which they are hostile. This distinguishes it from the prewar student movement under the control of the Communist Party.

The postwar student movement was born out of three traumatic experiences: Japan's defeat in the war, the sense of being betrayed by the older generation, and a disillusionment with the Communist Party as a leader of revolutionary movements in Japan. Disappointment among active members of the student movements in the Communist Party grew from a variety of grounds. Here it suffices to point out two major shifts of policy within the Communist Party.

After the termination of the war, the communists set out to make the party appear lovable to the people. In 1952, however, they decided to prepare for guerrilla warfare and encouraged the construction and use of Molotov cocktails, especially in remote villages and provincial towns. This shift in party policy followed two years of internal confusion caused by Cominform criticism of the milder activities which the party had previously pursued. The Sixth Party Conference in July 1955 marked the second change in party policy. It recommended legalism, rather than the use of violence, as the best means of accomplishing revolutionary changes. Party members were instructed to solicit cooperation from the masses of people by helping them achieve their everyday demands, instead of alienating themselves from the masses by resorting to such violent tactics

[2] Gakusei Undō Kenkyūkai (Study Group of Student Movements), *Gendai no Gakusei Undō (Contemporary Student Movements)*, Tokyo, Shinkō Shuppan, 1962, p. 16.

as had previously seemed right. The new strategy was forced upon rank-and-file members of the party without much discussion of the matter. To many student members, it came "like a thunder out of the blue sky."[3] Actually, it was pressure from Moscow (where the process of de-Stalinization was in progress under the leadership of Khrushchev) that led to the Japanese party to abandon its previous strategy.[4]

It was characteristic of the Japanese Communist Party that it should change policy and tactics under pressure from foreign communist parties without giving its own rank-and-file members any opportunity to discuss the question. Members who tried to voice criticism of the new party line with any real vigor were punished with expulsion from the party. In fact, seventy-two Zengakuren leaders were purged from the party in 1957 between June and the end of the year.[5]

These events led student leaders to suspect that the Communist Party, which had been the staunchest opponent of the Emperor system ever since the inception of the party in the 1920's, actually shared some basic patterns of values and relationships with the very system against which it had been fighting. For instance, just as the Emperor system was founded on belief in the sanctity of the Emperor, so the Communist Party asserted the basic infallibility of the party despite changes from time to time in the party line (nonrationalism). Similarly, just as the Emperor system hindered the development of independent judgment by individuals, so the party encouraged dependence rather than independent thinking (dependence). And just as the Emperor system was built on the principle of secrecy in communication, so the party operated on the principle of closed communication (secrecy).

Since 1956, a year after the Sixth Party Conference, the Zengakuren has become a policy-making agent for the promoters of student movements, entirely independent of the Communist Party.[6] Its leaders have striven to form a group whose structure

[3] Motoi Tamaki, *Nihon Gakusei Shi* (*A History of the Japanese Students*), Tokyo, Sanichi Shobō, 1961, p. 232.

[4] For a postwar history of the Japanese Communist Party, see Kōken Koyama, *Sengo Nihon Kyōsantō Shi* (*A History of the Communist Party in Postwar Japan*), Tokyo, Haga Shoten, 1966; Robert A. Scalapino, *The Japanese Communist Movement 1920-1966*, Berkeley, University of California Press, 1966.

[5] Koyama, *ibid.*, p. 229.

[6] *Ibid.*, p. 227.

of relationships differs from that of both the Emperor system and the Communist Party. They have also sought to resocialize themselves and other members in their groups to the end that each of them may become a locus of independent judgment and action, though simultaneously committed to revolutionary objectives (independence).

Satoshi Kitakōji, a former chairman of the Zengakuren who was expelled from the Communist Party, stated in a symposium that one of the most important aspects of the student movement is its furtherance of the process of forming a new selfhood.

> ... we students are faced with the problem of "how we should live." It was so before the war, and so is it after the war.
>
> Our generation is full of possibilities. Our destinies have not yet been decided. Neither are we yet burdened with material interests of bread and butter. We as youth and as a nascent intelligentsia are strongly inclined to search for ways in which to connect an individual's way of life and society's mode of existence. It is, therefore, extremely important to recognize the student movement as the process of the formation of selfhood that might meet this universal problem of the intelligentsia and at the same time to identify it as a political movement.[7]

Search for a new selfhood (*shutaisei*) is not limited to the leaders of student movements. Robert Lifton emphasizes that search as one of the main characteristics of all the students, leaders and nonleaders alike, whom he interviewed. He translates *shutaisei* as "subjecthood," in the literary sense, and interprets it as the combination of "selfhood" and "social commitment."[8]

Vague and elusive as it is, concern for *shutaisei* among both leaders and nonleaders of the student movement reveals that the movement seeks to change not only the existing social structure but also the very persons who are involved in the movement. Members of student groups are also aware that, in order to resocialize themselves within those groups, the structure of their relationships must not be the same as that of the organizations

[7] Satoshi Kitakōji et al., "Gakusei Undō no Genjō to Tenbō" ("The Present Situation and the Future Prospect of Student Movements"), *Shisō no Kagaku*, No. 62 (May 1967), p. 22.

[8] Robert Jay Lifton, "Youth and History: Individual Change in Post-War Japan," in *The Challenge of Youth*, ed. Erik H. Erikson, New York, Doubleday, 1963, p. 274.

to which they are opposed. Thus we can define the student movement in postwar Japan as, ideally, an agent for the resocialization of young adults.

2. SAMPLES

The samples in our survey are limited to one hundred students (including three ex-students) drawn mainly from three universities in the Tokyo area—Tokyo University, Chūō University, and Keiō University. We are far from claiming that our samples are representative of all university students in Japan. On the other hand, in selecting the universities and the individual students, our major concern was to acquire a fairly balanced distribution between students who were active in the student movements and those who were not and between universities known to be strong in such activities and those known to be weak.

Tokyo University, a national university, consists of two units, one located in Hongō and the other in Komaba. All the freshmen and sophomores and those students majoring in liberal arts are enrolled in the Komaba school; juniors and above in the departments other than liberal arts attend the Hongō school. Each branch has an independent student body, with characteristic traits of its own. The student bodies of both Komaba and Hongō are affiliated with the Zengakuren, and they are considered to be very strong. There is a general tendency in Japanese universities for freshmen and sophomores to be more active and interested in student movements than the upperclass men, who usually retire from political activity to avoid the stigma of radicalism when they are hunting for jobs. Tokyo University is no exception. Relatively speaking, Komaba is the more politically alive of the two campuses. The students' self-government association of Chūō University, a private institution, had once been, but at the time of our research was no longer, affiliated with the Zengakuren. The students there, especially those who attend the evening session, were nevertheless thought still to have a strong political orientation. Keiō University, another private institution, had never been associated with the Zengakuren and was felt not to be much involved in politics.

The individual students themselves we classified into three categories: (A) those who were interested and active in student movements; (B) those who were interested but not active; and (C) those who were neither interested nor active. Both the student section of the university administration and the student self-government association of each university helped us to select students in equal numbers from these categories. In our tabulation we assigned each of the students interviewed to one of those three categories by combining his answers to the following two questions: "Are you interested in the student movement?" and "Are you active in the student movement?" Those who answered "very much interested" or "fairly interested" to the first question and "very active" or "fairly active" to the second were classified in the "activist" category A. Those who answered "very much interested" or "fairly interested" to the first question and "little active" or "not at all active" to the second were classified in the "interested" category B. The "apathetic" category C comprises those who replied "a little interested" or "not at all interested" to the first question and "a little active" or "not at all active" to the second. Although we sought to get equal numbers of subjects in each category from each one of the four university-units (Komaba, Hongō, Chūō, and Keiō), the actual distribution turned out to be unequal.

We chose twenty-one students from each university-unit—hence, eighty-four in all. Then we selected leaders and ex-leaders from different factions of the student movement on the inter-university level. Thus we finally arrived at the distribution of samples according to the three categories shown in Table 32.

As this table reveals, the activists are overrepresented in our samples, while the apathetic are underrepresented. In our

TABLE 32

DISTRIBUTION OF UNIVERSITY STUDENTS BY
ATTITUDE TOWARD THE STUDENT
MOVEMENT (ATSM)

	Chūō	Tokyo (Hongō)	Tokyo (Komaba)	Keiō	Others	Finished	Total
A (activist)	10	10	12	9	4 (Waseda 2) (Kyoto 1) (Kyōiku 1)	2	47
B (interested)	6	11	5	6	1 (Waseda)	1	30
C (apathetic)	6	6	5	6	0	0	23
Total	22	27	22	21	5	3	100

analysis we shall try to counterbalance this unequal apportion-
ment by taking the percentage distribution within each category
and comparing these percentages across categories. Throughout
our present study the classification of our subjects into these
three categories is fundamental, since we are interested in locat-
ing continuity and discontinuity between leaders and nonleaders
of the student movement. In the following pages we shall refer to
the attitude toward the student movement by using the abbreviation ATSM. In reference to ATSM, A stands for the activists, B
for the interested, and C for the apathetic. A few words need to
be said about the representation of different factions of the student movement existing at the time of the survey. The leaders of
the Democratic Youth League, the student organization affiliated
with the Communist Party at Hongō, were approached, but
they politely refused to cooperate. They said they could not
cooperate with a survey subsidized by an American university. We regret that our samples are biased to the extent that the
Democratic Youth League is not represented either at Hongō
or on the interuniversity level, while the rest of the factions,
wherever they exist, are represented at each university, as well
as on the interuniversity level.

Our samples include six female students out of a total of one
hundred students. This is slight underrepresentation in the light
of government statistics for the year 1962, when women constituted 15.4 percent of the student population of all Japanese
universities.[9]

3. FAMILY

Did the place of birth, father's occupation, and parents' education affect their sons' and daughters' attitudes toward the
student movement?

First we must note that the differences among the three types
of students with respect to their birthplace were minimal. A
majority of all three groups came from big cities rather than from
small towns and villages. Among the activists, though, the ratio
of those who came from small towns was higher than among
either the interested or the apathetic. Another recognizable
difference was that the percentage of those who were born
outside of Japan was higher for the interested and for the activists than for the apathetic. The areas counted as outside of

[9] Monbushō (Ministry of Education), *Waga Kuni no Kōtō Kyōiku* (*Higher
Education of Japan*), Tokyo, 1964, p. 87.

Japan were Manchuria, China, Korea, and Formosa, territories which Japan either colonized or invaded during World War II. Although our evidence is not conclusive, it is interesting to conjecture whether the impact of childhood experience in either colonial or invaded countries might sensitize an individual to social tensions.

There were, however, some noticeable differences in the family background of the three types of students. The distribution of the activists and the interested among the families of managers and officials, proprietors of small-scale business, and professionals was fairly even. But the overwhelming majority of the apathetic were from proprietors' families, with only a low percentage of them from the families of managers and officials and still fewer from those of professionals.

Since we did not ask the students how much money their parents earned, we cannot correlate the level of parents' income with the students' attitudes. But we may, in this connection, note two other related factors. First, 23.4 percent of the activists and the 16.6 percent of the interested had lost their fathers, whereas more than 95 percent of the apathetic had fathers still living. Second, as Table 33 shows, over half of the activists worked either to supplement their living expenses or to support themselves, whereas most of the apathetic depended solely on their fathers' incomes.

TABLE 33
SOURCES OF INCOME BY ATSM

	A		B		C		Total
	No.	%	No.	%	No.	%	
Living expenses provided by:							
Solely parents	15	(31.9)	11	(36.6)	18	(80.8)	44
Parents plus my work	23	(49.5)	14	(46.6)	4	(17.3)	41
Solely scholarship	0		1	(3.3)	0		1
Scholarship plus my work	3	(6.3)	3	(10.2)	1	(1.9)	7
Solely my work	4	(8.5)	1	(3.3)	0		5
Support parents	2	(3.8)	0		0		2
Total	47	(100.0)	30	(100.0)	23	(100.0)	100

Did those students who worked actually need to have worked? Our survey as it stands does not prove there to be a correlation between student work and a parental level of income relatively lower than that of those parents whose children do not work. However, there are some surveys which confirm that such a correlation exists.

Surveys have been conducted annually since 1949 by Tokyo University on the economic condition of its students, both in Hongō and in Komaba. According to the Tokyo University report, before the war about 80 percent of the students came from families that could afford to provide their tuition and living expenses completely. This situation changed radically after the war. In 1959, 23 percent of the students worked because it was "absolutely necessary," and 40 percent worked to improve their financial situations, leaving only 37 percent not working who were supported completely by their parents. According to a survey carried out in that same year by the Ministry of Education, 63 percent of the students in government universities and 33.8 percent of private university students all over Japan were gainfully occupied part time.[10] Both surveys indicate a def-

[10] The following table shows the result of the survey undertaken by the Ministry of Education in 1959.

TABLE 34

OCCUPATIONS OF FATHERS OF UNIVERSITY STUDENTS

Father's Occupation	Day School Students (%)	Night School Students (%)
Technical work	6.8	8.6
Teaching or other profession	14.2	6.5
Medicine or pharmaceutics	4.5	0.6
Management or administration	25.7	20.3
Clerical work	19.6	21.8
Sales	3.0	3.3
Agriculture, forestry, or fishing	13.2	15.8
Craft or labor	3.0	7.1
Unemployed	3.3	1.9
Other occupation	6.7	14.1

SOURCE: Monbushō, *Shingaku to Ikuei Shōgaku* (*University Education and Scholarships*), Tokyo, 1961, p. 32.

Tokyo Daigaku Gakuseibu (Student Section of the Administration of Tokyo University), *Sengo ni okeru Tōdaisei no Keizai Seikatsu* (*The Economic Life of Tokyo University Students After the War*), Tokyo, Tokyo University, 1960, pp. 27, 122-123.

inite correlation between the level of income of the parents and the undertaking by students of part-time employment.[11]

If we apply these findings to the results of our survey, we may state that there is a general tendency for the apathetic to come from families of relatively higher income levels than either the interested or the activists.

The correlation between the father's occupation and the son's or the daughter's interest in student movements seems to be partially a function of the level of education required for the occupation of the father. Table 35 shows that more of the fathers of the interested had reached a higher level of education than the fathers of the activists and that more of the activists' fathers had attained a higher level of education than the fathers of the apathetic. Moreover, the percentage of those who were sons or daughters of professionals and technical experts, whose occupations require relatively high levels of education, was higher for the interested and for the activists than for the apathetic. In contrast, the majority of the apathetic came from the families of small-scale business proprietors, whose occupation does not require a high level of education.

As far as the mother's education is concerned, however, there

TABLE 35

FATHER'S EDUCATION BY ATSM

	No Education No.	Elementary No. %	Senior High School No. %	University No. %	DNK No. %	Total No. %
A	0	5 (10.8)	10 (21.2)	32 (68.0)	0	47 (100.0)
B	0	2 (6.7)	5 (16.7)	22 (73.3)	1 (3.3)	30 (100.0)
C	0	3 (13.1)	8 (34.8)	12 (52.1)	0	23 (100.0)
Total	0	10	23	66	1	100

[11] According to the Tokyo University survey, after the war about 50 percent of the students of that university came from salaried men's families, whereas before the war only 30 percent did. The increase in students engaged in part-time jobs is attributed to this increase of the salaried men's families in the social origin of the university students. (*Sengo ni okeru Tōdaisei no Keizai Seikatsu*, pp. 44-45.) The Ministry of Education survey contains a table which shows that the lower the level of income of their parents, the lower the amount of money the students actually receive from them for their living expenses as well as for tuition. (*Shingaku to Ikuei Shōgaku*, pp. 53-60.)

seems to have been no noticeable difference among the three
types of students (see Table 36).

TABLE 36

MOTHER'S EDUCATION BY ATSM

	No Education No. %	Elementary No. %	Senior High School No. %	University No. %	Total No. %
A	0	7 (15.0)	32 (68.0)	8 (17.0)	47 (100.0)
B	1 (3.3)	7 (23.3)	17 (56.8)	5 (16.6)	30 (100.0)
C	0	4 (17.4)	13 (56.5)	6 (16.1)	23 (100.0)
Total	1	18	62	19	100

Can it be, as these data apparently indicate, that the level of
the father's education has some bearing on his children's interest in student movements, while the level of education of the
mother is irrelevant? If we assume that such a disparity does
exist, how can we account for it?

We may interpret these relationships first by referring to the
relative ratios of communication between the father and his
child and between the mother and her child.

We asked the students if they talked with their fathers and
mothers about personal economic problems, family matters,
love, study, and politics. The answers were tabulated to show
communication with the father and with the mother separately.
From this table we worked out what we call the ratio of communication (the numbers of positive answers divided by the
numbers of the fathers and mothers alive and relevant) for each
of the five subject matters and for each of the three types of students. The results are displayed in Table 37. From this table
we can derive some observations about trends in children-
father and children-mother communication.

(1) Both for the activist and for the interested, the average
communication ratio with the father was higher than it was for
the apathetic. This difference might be traced in part to the
relatively high level of education the fathers of the activists
and of the interested had received. If the university education
of the father is directly related to the high average ratio of
communication with him, the interested should have shown the
highest average ratio of communication with their fathers.
The table, however, reveals that the activists, whose fathers oc-

TABLE 37

RATIO OF COMMUNICATION WITH
FATHER AND WITH MOTHER BY ATSM

Subject	A		B		C	
	With Father %	With Mother %	With Father %	With Mother %	With Father %	With Mother %
Economy	60.0	80.2	64.0	73.7	50.0	77.2
Family	82.8	84.4	68.0	92.5	59.0	72.7
Love	28.5	44.4	16.0	33.3	13.6	40.9
Study	54.2	37.7	60.0	51.8	63.6	45.4
Politics	80.0	66.6	60.0	66.6	40.9	31.8
Average	61.1	62.6	53.6	63.5	45.4	53.6

cupied the second rank in the level of education, were ahead of the other two groups in this respect. The table also shows that politics was the subject of discussion in which the activists' communication ratio with the father most surpassed that of the interested and the apathetic. The activist was the person most committed to political affairs. Thus we may conjecture that the high or low ratio of communication with the father is inversely related not only to the high or low level of the father's education but also to the high or low level of the son's or the daughter's commitment to the subject.

(2) Comparing the ratios of communication with the mother with those of communication with the father on such matters as personal economic problems, family matters, and love, we see that the former were consistently higher than the latter for all three of the groups. On the other hand, the ratios of communication with the father were higher than those with the mother for all three groups on the subject of study and for the activists and for the apathetic on the subject of politics.

As far as communication with the mother is concerned, the mother's level of education does not seem to have been relevant. This finding might be explained by referring to the kinds of subject matter regarding which the ratios of communication with the mother were consistently higher than the ratios of communication with the father. These subjects are predominantly private and pertain primarily to affects. A high level of education is not necessarily required for understanding these matters. In contrast, study is the only subject the discussion of which requires a relatively high level of education. And this was the only subject, out of the five items tested, in which communication with the father was consistently higher for all three groups. For politics, however, correlation between the level of education and the ratio of communication is not decisive. Perhaps it is because discussion about politics is not entirely cognitive and, hence, does not depend so much on the level of education as discussion of study.

TABLE 38

AVERAGE RATIO OF COMMUNICATION

Subject	With Father %	With Mother %
Economy	58.6	77.6
Family	71.9	84.0
Love	20.7	40.4
Study	58.6	43.6
Politics	63.4	57.5
Average	54.6	60.2

(3) Table 38 shows that the average ratio of communication with the mother for the entire set of samples was higher than that with the father. This general tendency from the point of view of the children corresponds to the general pattern of communication from the points of view of their parents. According to a survey made in six major cities in Japan on married men and women's communication style, women beyond the age of forty converse most and enjoy conversing best with their own children, whereas men beyond forty converse most with their wives without enjoying conversing with them and converse less with their children than with their wives without enjoying conversing with the children as much as their wives enjoy conversing with their children.[12]

Putting the results of our survey together with those of this survey, we may conclude that, from the points of view of both the parents and their children, there is a general trend suggesting that mother-children communication is greater in quantity

[12] Shunsake Tsurumi et al., *Rokudai Toshi to Shimin: Bunkado Chōsa Hōkōkusho* (*The Six Major Cities and Their Citizens: A Survey on Their Cultural Levels*), published under the auspices of the Shitei Toshi Kikaku Chōsa Jimu Shukansha Kaigi (Council of Planning and Research Directors of the Major Cities), Kyoto, 1966, pp. 19-24.

than father-children communication and that, at least from the standpoint of the mothers, communication with their children is the most enjoyable of all kinds of communication. The degrees of enjoyment, it should be noted, may not be equal for the mother and her children. The latter may enjoy conversing with their fathers better than with their mothers, even if they converse less with the former, and they probably enjoy conversing with their friends even better than with their own parents. Still, the high degree of enjoyment on the part of mothers conversing with their children is important. We assume that the investment of positive affects is a key contributing factor in the formulation or reformulation of values and ideas. If our assumption holds, then we may postulate that children are more likely to change their mothers' ideas and values than their fathers'.

This process of change does not work the other way around, however. We asked the students: "Is there someone—a friend, a teacher, girl (or boy) friend, member of your family, etc.—who contributed strongly to turning you to the ideas you presently hold? Who specifically?" Sixteen out of the one hundred persons interviewed specified their parents. Eleven mentioned their fathers and four said both father and mother, but only one pointed to his mother alone. Although students in general converse more with their mothers than with their fathers, the mothers' influence on the students' ideas is much weaker than the fathers' influence on them. If the mother is more affected by her children than her children are by her, the mother-children relationship turns out to be like a one-sided love affair. And this kind of relationship seems to occur more pronouncedly in times of rapid social change than in times of relative stability with respect to the norms of the family and of society at large.

(4) Just as the average communication ratios with the father were higher among the activists and the interested than among the apathetic, so those with the mother were also higher among the former two groups than among the last. On the subject of politics, communication ratios with the mother were 66.6 for both the activists and the interested, whereas the comparable ratio for the apathetic was 31.8. It was with respect to this subject that the difference of communication ratios with the mother between the apathetic and the others was most pronounced. This fact leads us to speculate that this is the area where those who are engaged or interested in student movements are most prone to exert influence on their mothers. For

these students, their mothers are fit targets for "enlightenment" in political thinking.

4. UNIVERSITY

In 1963 there were 270 universities (with 762,749 students) in Japan. Japan ranked third in the world, preceded only by the United States and Soviet Russia in the proportion of university students in the total number of the young men and women of their age group. University students in 1963 amounted to 15.6 percent of the total population of their peers. In 1935, in contrast, only 2.45 percent of the population of the ages between 18 to 21 had received higher education.[13]

In prewar days university education was more likely to be given to the sons of the privileged class than in the postwar period. The marked increase after the war in the percentage of students working their way through college, which we have already noted, is a clear indication of this change.

Despite the rapid rise in the number of universities and the enlargement of their capacities, however, competition for entrance to the universities is very stiff indeed in postwar Japan. That a college education is the key to the attainment of higher positions with higher income is shown by various surveys. Makoto Asō, who investigated the curriculum vitae of those registered in *Jinji Kōshinroku* (*Who's Who in Japan*), points out that since 1948 elitist positions have been occupied increasingly by university graduates. In 1957, 80.5 percent of those registered in *Who's Who* had received higher education.[14] According to a survey made by the Central Labor Committee for the year 1960, wages of university graduates were double those of elementary school graduates at the time of retirement.[15] And, as the Model Wage Table made public in 1961 by the Tokyo Chamber of Commerce showed, the average wage for a man aged fifty-five with a university degree is 12,000 yen more per month than that of a man with a senior high school education.[16]

There is also a rigid stratification among university graduates themselves as far as status is concerned. The top positions in

---

[13] Monbushō, *Waga Kuni no Kōtō Kyōiku*, pp. 32-35, 196, 276-277.

[14] Makoto Asō, "Kindai Nihon ni okeru Eriito Kōsei no Hensen" ("The Changing Composition of the Elites in Modern Japan"), *Kyōiku Shakaigaku Kenkyū*, No. 15 (1960)—quoted in Moriichi Katsuta and Toshio Nakauchi, *Nihon no Gakkō* (*Schools in Japan*), Tokyo, Iwanami, 1964, p. 156.

[15] Quoted in Katsuta et al., *ibid.*, p. 161.

[16] Quoted in *Mainichi Shinbun* (*Mainichi Newspaper*), Feb. 11, 1962.

government, politics, and academic life are generally occupied by the graduates of national universities, Tokyo University (formerly Tokyo Imperial University) being at the apex of the pyramid. Of the teaching staffs of Tokyo University and Kyoto University, 90 percent are graduates of the universities in which they hold positions.[17] Among the members of the House of Councillors elected in 1962, the majority of the Conservative Party members were graduates of national universities, while the majority of Socialist Party members were graduates of private universities. Those with only primary school education were conspicuously absent from the ranks of the conservatives; among the socialists there were a few.[18]

Thus career prospects are more or less determined, first, by whether one goes to a university at all and, second, by the status of the university from which one graduates. On the whole, national universities such as Tokyo and Kyoto are more prestigious than most private universities. And they offer the additional advantage of having much lower entrance fees and tuition than private universities.[19]

Given these conditions, applicants tend to rush either to the national universities or to the relatively prestigious private institutions, and competition for acceptance is therefore severe. Students who fail to get into the institution of their choice the first time around often try more than once to gain admission to the desired university. This practice produces a large educational reserve army, consisting of the *rōnin* (off-school students). According to Ministry of Education statistics, 35.6 percent of university entrants in 1959 were off-school students.[20] Tokyo University, where competition for admission is stiffest, reported that 4.7 percent (116) of those who passed the entrance examination of that institution for 1962 were found to have neurotic symptoms. Psychiatrists wondered whether the cause was not

[17] Michio Nagai, *Nihon no Daigaku (The Japanese University)*, Tokyo, Chūōkōronsha, 1965, p. 102.
[18] Michio Nagai, "Habatsu to Yūmono" ("What We Call Cliques"), *Mainichi Shinbun*, July 26, 1962.
[19] In 1962, 90 percent of the students who entered national universities paid less than the average of 30,000 yen, including examination and entrance fees, whereas more than 90 percent of those who entered private universities paid more than the average of 50,000 yen. Of these, 35 percent paid more than 100,000 yen to enter private universities. Monbushō, *Daigaku Nyūgakusha Jittai Chōsa (A Survey of University Entrants)*, 1962—quoted in Nagai, *Nihon no Daigaku*, p. 103.
[20] Monbushō, *Shingaku to Ikuei Shōgaku*, p. 30.

the constant pressure of a highly competitive system of entrance examinations, beginning even with the nursery school and continuing through elementary, middle, and senior high school up to the university itself.[21]

The nerve-wracking competition of the entrance examinations, together with the generally accepted notion that the university diploma, especially one from a prestigious university, counts more in getting jobs than personal merit, gives rise to attitudes toward university education that are peculiar to postwar Japan. The officially announced entrants to universities for the year 1962 totaled 86,200 persons. The number of students actually admitted, however, amounted to 142,133, which exceeded the official tally by 1.75 times.[22] The explanation for this disparity is that neither the university administrations nor the students anticipate regular attendance by all the registered students at all times. Poor class attendance as well as poor classroom performance is more or less taken for granted. Since the university entrance examination is the last in a long series of school entrance examinations and since the status of the university matters more in landing a job than individual achievement, a sudden sense of relaxation overcomes those who have succeeded in getting into the university of their choice, even if it is only their second or third choice. Once in a university students encounter very little competition.

With this brief sketch of the general characteristics of postwar Japanese universities as a background, we shall now turn to our own survey.

Of the one hundred persons we interviewed, six were freshmen, twenty-two sophomores, twenty juniors, forty-five seniors, four graduate students, and three graduates. Categorized by their major courses of study, seven were in humanities, sixty-eight in social sciences, eight in natural sciences, sixteen in engineering, and one in medicine. To the question "Are you satisfied with classroom lectures?," only one (a graduate student in medicine) replied that he was completely satisfied. Eighteen replied that they were fairly satisfied, forty-five little satisfied and thirty-one dissatisfied; five gave no answer. In other words, 76 percent of the students interviewed were either little satisfied or completely dissatisfied with classroom lectures. As for

[21] Tomio Tezuka, "Daigakusei no Seishin Shōgai" ("The Mental Disturbances of University Students"), *Mainichi Shinbun*, May 27, 1962.
[22] Nagai, *Nihon no Daigaku*, p. 6.

the sources of dissatisfaction, forty-seven stated that the content of the lectures was poor, fourteen that the method of teaching was poor, eleven that school facilities were poor, and three that their teachers' attitudes were poor.

At each university from which the students we interviewed came, lecture classes contain some four to six hundred students, and microphones are used. The privilege of attending seminars (consisting usually of twenty to sixty members) is limited; at the Law School of Tokyo University, for instance, only two hundred students out of six hundred are able to take part in seminars. Thus communication with professors either in or out of the classrooms is, for the majority of students, mostly a one-way affair.

Relatively speaking, there is closer intercommunication between students and teachers in the senior high schools than between students and professors in the universities. Table 39 shows the relative frequency of communication with teachers at senior high schools and at universities on different subjects.

TABLE 39
COMMUNICATION WITH TEACHERS

(Answers to the question: "Have you discussed with your teachers the following subjects?")

Subject	With Senior High School Teachers			With University Teachers		
	Yes	No	No Answer	Yes	No	No Answer
Economic problems	21	79	0	15	84	1
Family	24	76	0	9	89	2
Love	23	77	0	13	86	1
Study	73	27	0	46	53	1
Politics	54	46	0	42	57	1

Students enjoy the most active communication with their fellow students on both study and politics. Eighty-four out of the one hundred interviewed said that they talked most with their friends about study, while seventy-seven talked most about politics. Friends included student autonomy companions, study circle friends, upperclassmen, and classmates.

Considering that the majority of the students are not satisfied with their classroom instruction and cannot get to communicate with their professors, poor class attendance is not surprising. Only sixteen of the one hundred said that they were always present and twenty-eight usually present, whereas forty were often absent and sixteen always absent. Thus the majority of the students interviewed cut their classes either often or always.

Where do students study, if they study at all, outside of the classrooms? University libraries are not usually well equipped —another source of the complaints of those we interviewed. Rather, it is in informal groups, such as study circles, that many students learn on their own. Eighty-two out of the one hundred interviewed were engaged in some kind of extracurricular group activities. There were fifty-two varieties of study and hobby circles to which the students we interviewed belonged. We shall make a list of some of these groups, since their names are revealing of the students' interests (the number of persons interviewed who belonged to each circle is given in parentheses): Social Science Study (9), Student Newspaper (6), Historical Study (3), Study of Constitution (3), Reading (3), Study of Philosophy (3), Chinese Studies (3), Catholicism (2), Accounting (2), Dialectics of Nature (2), Literature (2), Sociological Study (2), Technology and Society (2), Labor Movements (2), Defense of Peace and Democracy (2), Chorus (2), International Relations (1), Agricultural Problems (1), Dialectical Materialism (1), Mathematics (1), Esperanto (1), Outcast Problems (1), English Speaking (1), Russian Language (1), Social Psychology (1), Painting (1), Orchestra (1).

Students complained that their professors tried only "to impart knowledge without stimulating us to think." They were dissatisfied because their classroom lectures were "far removed from actual problems and [had] nothing to do with them." Besides, they said, "the choice of courses is so limited that we cannot take what we really wish to." Study groups organized by students dissatisfied with formal lectures are therefore the functional substitutes for classroom lectures. In these study groups the lively discussion which very seldom occurs in classrooms takes place.

There were marked differences in preference in group membership among the activists, the interested, and the apathetic. Of the activists, 72.3 percent belonged to some study circles, 6.4 percent to sports clubs, and 4.2 to both kinds of groups. Of the interested, 60 percent were affiliated to study circles and 16.6 percent to sports clubs. In contrast, 60.8 percent of the apathetic were members of sports clubs, and only 26 percent were members of study circles, while 4.4 percent belonged to both. Study circle membership was thus highest among the activists, followed next by the interested. There seems to be a high correlation between study circle membership and interest and activity in student movements. Student movements, in other words, are the extension of study group activities; there what has been learned and thought within study groups is put into practice.

A senior of Tokyo University at Hongō suggested that there is a motivational link between students' discontent with formal teaching, on the one hand, and the rise of student movements, on the other:

> In spite of the fact that our classes are as small as twenty in number, there is something in the atmosphere of the classroom that discourages discussion with our professors, who give us lectures as though they were disregarding our presence. Those who are really interested in study are compelled to study on their own. We studied very hard to get into this university. But, now that we are in, we are utterly disappointed with what we are given by the university. This leads us, I guess, to direct our energy into student movements.

How well did the activists perform academically as compared with the interested and the apathetic? Tables 40 and 41 show the self-estimates made by the students interviewed on the basis of their school records and their class attendance.

Combining the data presented in these two tables, we can observe some general tendencies. On the whole, the interested were the best students both in class attendance and in school grades; the activists cut their classes most frequently, while still maintaining the average academic standing; and the majority of the apathetic, though they attended their classes regularly, had the lowest marks of all the groups. There seems to be some correlation between the degree of interest in student movements and the number of students who repeat. Of the activists, 40.8 percent said they had repeated a year at least once, and 26.6 percent of the interested admitted having done so too, whereas only 8.1 percent of the apathetic had ever repeated. Students call repeating *ryūnen* (to remain in the same year) rather than *rakudai* (failing), since *ryūnen* often signifies an act of volition

TABLE 40
School Records by ATSM

	Excellent No. %	Very Good No. %	Average No. %	No Good No. %	No Answer No.	Total No. %
A	2 (4.2)	11 (23.4)	26 (55.3)	8 (17.1)	0	47 (100.0)
		27.6 (above average)				
B	2 (6.6)	11 (36.6)	12 (40.0)	5 (16.8)	0	30 (100.0)
		43.2				
C	1 (4.3)	9 (39.1)	8 (34.7)	5 (21.9)	0	23 (100.0)
		43.4				
Total	5	31	46	18	0	100

TABLE 41
Class Attendance by ATSM

	Always Present No. %	Usually Present No. %	Often Absent No. %	Always Absent No. %	Total No. %
A	6 (13.7)	9 (18.7)	23 (48.9)	9 (18.7)	47 (100.0)
		32.4		67.6	
B	4 (13.3)	13 (43.4)	9 (30.0)	4 (13.3)	30 (100.0)
		57.7		43.3	
C	6 (26.0)	6 (26.0)	8 (34.7)	3 (13.3)	23 (100.0)
		52.0		48.0	
Total	16	28	40	16	100

and is consequently more respectable than *rakudai*, which is passive and stigmatized. Many student movement leaders deliberately repeat in order to be able to continue their activities in such movements.

5. Zengakuren

The history of the student movement since 1945 can be divided into six periods: (1) the period 1945-1948 of spontaneous and sporadic movements for the democratization of separate schools and universities; (2) the emergence in 1948-1953 of the Zengakuren as the overall organization of student movements; (3) "the dark days" of 1952-1955 when the movement was controlled by the "leftist adventurism of the Communist Party"; (4) the period 1956-1958 of reconstruction and the rise of the Bund; (5) the anti-Security Treaty struggles of 1959-1960; and (6) the period of schism after 1960. To make a long story short, we shall here concentrate only on the fourth and the fifth periods.

The Leaders of the Bund

In October 1956 the Japanese government tried to survey farm lands in the town of Sunagawa as a first step toward procuring certain areas adjacent to the American military base which were needed for its expansion. The farmers, owners of those farm lands inherited from their forefathers, protested. Labor unions, farmers in other parts of the country, teachers, writers, professors, Buddhist priests, and housewives came to Sunagawa to support the local farmers in their fight against expansion of the American military base. It became a national issue. Students under the leadership of the Zengakuren sat down with the farmers on the farm land to prevent the intended survey. The students were in the front row of the demonstrators and led the fight against expansion of the military base which, in the event, saved from procurement those farms whose owners objected. This success gave self-confidence to the student leaders. Minoru Morita, then a student at Tokyo University and a member of the executive committee of the Zengakuren, testifies that the Sunagawa incident was a turning point for the student movement. The leaders of the Zengakuren, most of whom had hitherto been under the influence of the Communist Party, came to be so overtly and so strongly critical of the party that they formed themselves into an independent communist group.[23]

It was the suppression of the Hungarian revolt by the Soviet army (an event which occurred only ten days after the big clash in Sunagawa between the students and the police) that initiated the change in the climate of opinion among student leaders. Thereafter they became more and more skeptical about authoritarian control by communist parties, whether from Moscow, Peking, or Tokyo.

[23] From the author's interview with Morita on July 6, 1962.

The years succeeding the Sunagawa clash and the Hungarian rebellion and ending with the formation in late 1958 of the Bund (the Communist League) saw rapid and radical ideological transformations among the leaders of the Zengakuren. These were the years "when student activists as a group read and thought most deeply and with the utmost concentration" in search of new theories.[24] Three major factions were observable in this stage of theoretical groping. First, there were those student leaders who stayed loyal to the Communist Party; this group, at the time of anti-Security Treaty struggle, came to be known as the Anti-Mainstream Zengakuren and later organized itself into the Zenjiren. The second faction, the Structural Reformists, regarded Khrushchev's critique of Stalin as insufficiently radical; in their effort to carry that critique still further, the Reformists came upon Togliatti's theory, which became their guiding philosophy. The third faction sought to attack Stalinism in the most devastating manner. It later split into the Revolutionary Communist League (the Kansai organization led by Shiokawa) and the Bund (the Communist League founded by Shima and other student leaders purged from the Communist Party). Shiokawa was chairman of the Zengakuren from December 1958 to June 1959, when the Bund managed to acquire two-thirds of the seats on the executive committee and elected Karōji of Hokkaidō University to the chairmanship. Thereafter the Bund took control of the Mainstream Zengakuren, which conducted the anti-Security Treaty fight under its leadership.

What was the Bund? What did it stand for? On what specific points of doctrine did it differ from the Communist Party?

In May 1958 at the Eleventh Plenary Meeting of the Zengakuren, 120 universities with 300 student self-government associations and 300,000 student members were represented. It was the postwar peak of Zengakuren membership.[25] At this gathering a group of Communist Party members occupied the stage and presented a false charge that some of the Zengakuren executive committee members, including Morita, had usurped the funds of the Japanese Anti-Nuclear Bomb Council. This move precipitated a violent conflict between the Communist Party and the

[24] *Ibid.*

[25] See Norio Tamura, "Sengo Gakusei Undō-shi Nenpyō" ("The Chronological Table of the History of the Postwar Student Movements"), in the Appendix of Akio Ōno's *Zengakuren Keppūroku* (*The Blood and Wind Record of the Zengakuren*), Tokyo, Nijusseikisha, 1967, p. 271.

Zengakuren representatives, which culminated in a large-scale purge of Zengakuren leaders from the Communist Party. Among those who were expelled from the party in 1958 were Kōyama, then chairman of the Zengakuren, Shiokawa, who succeeded Kōyama, Shima, and Morita. Morita tells of the event:

> We tried to convince the party headquarters that we were not guilty of the false charge which they had fabricated and that we were supported by the majority of the students who were present at the meeting. The party, however, insisted that it was an iron law of the party that the members of the lower echelons ought to obey those of the higher ranks in the party and that the party members were not allowed to criticize publicly what had been decided by the Central Committee of the party. We were thus expelled from the party under the pretext that we denied the sanctity of the Central Committee of the Communist Party by challenging its false charges against us in public. Thus the party maintains its monolithic organization and its claim to be the only vanguard party of the working class. It was this concept of the omnipotence of the party and its infallibility that we challenged.
>
> When I was purged from the party, I personally did not suffer from a sense of alienation. But as a group those of us purged had to struggle against the charge that to stop being a member of the Communist Party was a betrayal of the working class.[26]

Shima, the central figure in founding the Bund, describes the initial aims of this short-lived but intensely active organization.

> It was during the demonstrations against the Police Duty Bill[27] in October 1958 that we made up our minds to form the

[26] From the author's interview with Morita.

[27] In October 1958 the Kishi cabinet proposed to the Diet the revision of the Police Duty Bill. The alleged purpose of the revision was to extend the range of police intervention into situations "where it is obvious that public welfare and order are engaged" or "where there is recognizably emergent danger to human life, body, or property." But the labor unionists, students, and ordinary citizens, both men and women, felt that their fundamental human rights—freedom of assembly and freedom of speech—might be endangered under the pretext of protecting "public welfare and order." Mass demonstrations against the proposed revision of the law were sponsored by labor unions, the Zengakuren, cultural and learned societies, women's organizations, farmers' organizations, and peace groups, until finally the revision was shelved. Rekishigaku Kenkyūkai (Association for the Study of History), ed., *Sengo Nihonshi* (*A History of Postwar Japan*), Tokyo, Aoki Shoten, 1965, III, 192-194.

Bund. We then felt an acute need for an organization of our own to conduct our fight against reactionary measures such as the Police Duty Bill and the Teachers' Merit-Rating System enforced in 1957[28]

The primary motivation for the formation of the Bund was the desire to build up a revolutionary group that was distinctive from the Communist Party. The major rallying point in our thought was antiauthority. We were opposed not only to the Japanese Communist Party but also to the international communist organizations, including the International Federation of Student Organizations. We were also critical of Trotskyite groups such as the Revolutionary Communist League.

It took us one whole year to formulate our own platform. Although Marxism provided our rallying point, we attempted to include non-Marxist ideas in our program. In other words, we attempted to create a revolutionary movement with revolutionary ideas but freed from Marxism as a rigid monolithic ideology.

[28] Ehime was the first prefecture to enforce the Teachers' Merit-Rating System in April 1957. Toward the end of the same year the Conference of Chairmen of the Prefectural Boards of Education made public its tentative program for a Teachers' Merit-Rating System, based on the Ehime plan. Under this system all public school teachers were to be classified into five grades according to their efficiency in carrying out their duties. The items on which the teachers were to be rated included such subjective matters as "whether they have the right educational conviction" and "whether they teach their pupils with enthusiasm." Moreover, the principal of each school was entrusted with sole authority to estimate the efficiency of all the teachers in his school. Promotion and salary increases were to be based upon the marks given by the principal to each teacher. This system was criticized for the subjective nature of the method and standards of rating teachers' performances. The critics charged that the principal could wield his power to eliminate teachers he did not like and to favor those he liked, regardless of their merit; in any case, they argued, merit cannot be measured in such an arbitrary manner. It was also feared that the enforcement of this system might be another step toward strengthening government control over public education, which had already begun in 1954 with the substitution of appointive boards of education for elective boards. According to this Teachers' Merit-Rating System, the teachers' work was to be rated by the principals, whose work was in turn to be rated by the boards of education appointed by the prefectural governers, who were responsible to the minister of education on educational matters.

Despite strikes, protests, and demonstrations staged by the Japan Teachers' Union and by university students, the Teachers' Merit-Rating System was enforced all over Japan, except in Kyoto and Ōita Prefectures, in 1958. See *Nikkyōso Jūnenshi* (*Ten Years of the Japanese Teachers' Union*), Tokyo, Nihon Kyōshokuin Kumiai, 1958, pp. 389-398.

Just when our program was completed, we were confronted with the anti-*anpo* campaign. [The Japanese-American Security Treaty in Japanese is "Nichibei Anzen Hoshō Jōyaku." It is usually called by its abbreviated form of *anpo*.] While resisting the Security Treaty, we began to ask ourselves whether and how we could create a revolution in Japan.

In March 1960 I observed the coal miners' strike in the Miike Mine.[29] I was so deeply impressed by the intense scenes of their valiant fight that I could not get over them. It led me to think that a revolution is not made, it is something that *simply happens*. Yes, it happens because people are aroused to the occasion by witnessing a heartrending scene. Thus, I thought, what we should do was to present to the public a moving image that would crystallize into one moment the true meaning of the situation. This was why we broke through the Diet gates on November 27 and June 15. It was the most dramatic means of symbolizing the reclamation of the Diet, which had been beyond the reach of the people, on behalf of the people whose representative it should have been.

However, just when the anti-*anpo* campaign was going on, we had to contend with an internal split in our organization. An organization is doomed if it cannot function fully in the face of a great occasion. In effect, the Bund was defeated by the established ideology of Marxism, the very thing which we had attempted to overcome. Therein lies, I have to admit, our own immaturity as *thinkers* [author's italics].[30]

---

[29] The Miike branch of the Mitsui Coal Mining Company announced the discharge of 2,210 miners in August 1959, as a part of the program of rationalization of the mining industry. When the union refused to accept this large-scale layoff, the company again sent discharge orders to 1,297 miners. In January 1960 the company declared a lockout of the mine; the miners protested by staging a strike, which lasted until July 1960. With the support of Sōhyō, it proved to be the biggest strike in postwar Japan, with 2,905,000 persons involved and 600,004,800 yen extended on the campaign.

During the campaign, the union was split into two parts; the "second union" was supported by the company, while the "first union" consisted of those who were determined to fight to repeal the discharge order. In March a member of the first union was assassinated in public while picketing.

The anti-Security Treaty campaign and the Miike coal miners' strike went on at the same time, and many students who were active in the anti-Security Treaty campaign visited Miike to support and to encourage the "first union" members. They felt that the Miike strike and anti-Security Treaty demonstrations had a common enemy, namely, "the Japanese monopoly capitalist power." Rekishigaku Kenkyūkai, ed., *Sengo Nihonshi*, IV, 57-62, 106, 197-205.

[30] From the author's interview with Shima on July 29, 1962.

What was the program of the Bund? The constitution of the Communist League declares its aim to be the establishment of "a new revolutionary political party, dissociated from the leaders of the communist movements and carrying out an uncompromising fight against them." It undertook the task of "reviving and creating true Marx-Leninism"; in so doing, the members were "guaranteed complete freedom of discussion, although they were called to unity in action."[31] The meaning of "true Marx-Leninism" was explained in an essay entitled "In Quest of The Theory of Alienation." It proposes to study and develop the theory of alienation as evolved by Marx in his earlier work, *Philosophical and Economic Manuscripts*, and as expanded later in the *Sacred Family, Theses on Feuerbach*, and *Capital*. The basic blunder of Stalinism, according to this essay and others, is its utter neglect of this most important part of Marx's theory. Stalinism is also criticized for its insistence on "revolution in one country," which "inevitably distorts communism into nationalism."[32]

At a later stage in the campaign the Bund, originally a loosely knit organization drawing on both Marxist and non-Marxist ideas, moved toward the tactics of "revolution with violence." Morita observes:

> In April and May 1960 there emerged within the Bund a catchword: "Be ready for an armed conflict." At the same time the Bund, which originally had been intended to be a transitional body, came to be regarded as a full-fledged vanguard party, the central agent for the promotion of a revolution. Such an adventurist idea hampered the development of a lucid and precise way of thinking when it was most needed and thus prepared for the final dissolution of the organization immediately after the campaign.[33]

We shall now examine the attitudes of rank-and-file students during the Anti-Security Treaty campaign and their relationships with the leaders of the Zengakuren.

[31] *Kyōsanshugi* (*Communism*), No. 2 (April 1, 1959), p. 83.
[32] Shigeru Mori, "Sogairon no Tankyū" ("In Quest of the Theory of Alienation"), *ibid.*, No. 5 (Oct. 1, 1959), p. 54.
[33] From the author's interview with Morita.

The Students' Attitudes toward the Anti-Security Treaty Campaign

Of the one hundred students we interviewed, eighty-two said that they had joined anti-*anpo* demonstrations, although only seventy-two were university students during those days. Some students, in other words, participated in the demonstrations even as senior high school students or as *rōnin* (off-school students).

TABLE 42

UNIVERSITY STUDENTS AT THE TIME OF ANPO;
ANPO DEMONSTRATORS BY ATSM

	Were You a University Student?			Did You Join the Demonstrations?		
	Yes No. %	No No. %	Total No. %	Yes No. %	No No. %	Total
A	36 (76.5)	11 (23.5)	47 (100.0)	47 (100.0)	0	47 (100.0)
B	22 (73.3)	8 (26.7)	30 (100.0)	24 (80.0)	6 (20.0)	30 (100.0)
C	16 (69.5)	7 (30.5)	23 (100.0)	11 (47.8)	12 (52.2)	23 (100.0)
Total	74	26	100	82	18	100

Table 42 shows that, among both the activists and the interested, those who joined demonstrations outnumbered those who were university students at the time of the demonstrations. As for the apathetic, although their rate of participation in the demonstrations was the lowest (and the number of those who were university students at that time the least), it is noteworthy that eleven out of the sixteen who were university students at the time of *anpo* joined the demonstrations.

Since our samples of the apathetic were extremely small, we cannot take this to be conclusive evidence. But we can at least say that some of those who were neither active nor interested in the student movements walked side-by-side with the students who were generally interested or active.

Table 43 presents the distribution of the answers to the question "What do you think was the meaning of the anti-Security Treaty demonstrations?" Opposition to the Security Treaty and expression of antiwar sentiment ranked the highest among all three groups. It is interesting that only two out of forty-seven activists replied that the demonstrations were an expression of

TABLE 43

THE MEANING OF THE ANTI-SECURITY TREATY
DEMONSTRATIONS BY ATSM

(More than one item counted per person)

	A (47)	B (30)	C (23)	Total (100)
Opposition to Kishi	15	3	8	26
Prevention of Eisenhower visit to Japan	3	0	0	3
Expression of anti-American sentiment	2	0	3	5
Opposition to Security Treaty	26	15	8	49
Expression of antiwar sentiments	21	18	5	44
Defense of the Constitution	8	8	0	16
Opposition to Japanese imperialism	0	0	0	0
Don't know	2	2	3	7
Others	12	8	1	21

anti-American sentiment, while three out of the twenty-three apathetic (one of whom did not join the demonstrations at all, and another of whom joined them only once) described them as anti-American demonstrations. Certainly the majority of active participants in the Mainstream Zengakuren regarded the protests, not as directed against the United States, but very clearly as aimed at the Japanese government in power. This orientation distinguishes the views of the Mainstream Zengakuren from those of the Anti-Mainstream faction, led by the Communist Party, who identified American imperialism as the major target of attack and who in fact demonstrated against Eisenhower's press secretary, James Hagerty, when he arrived at Haneda Airport on June 10.

The waves of demonstrations continued every day after May 19, reaching a climax on June 15 when some demonstrators (mostly women) were attacked by right-wing extremists and more than sixty persons were injured. Shortly after this incident students under the leadership of the Mainstream Zengakuren broke through the Diet gate to hold a protest meeting inside the gate. There were about eight thousand students massed before the front gate, seven hundred of whom succeeded in passing through, whereupon the mechanized police force launched a counterattack. The unarmed boys and girls were assaulted with truncheons by helmeted police. A girl student at Tokyo University, Michiko Kanba, was found dead after the mêlée. Later that evening some four thousand students again entered the Diet gate to hold a meeting in protest over Miss Kanba's death from police violence; but labor unionists and other demonstrators who surrounded the Diet were urged by leaders of the Communist Party and the National Congress for Prevention of the Security Treaty Revision to go back home and not to enter the Diet gate in support of the students. At this point, with truncheons and tear gas, the police again attacked both the students and some of their instructors who had come to the scene in an attempt to negotiate on behalf of wounded students. During that single evening more than one thousand students and other citizens were injured; 182 students were arrested.

We have already mentioned that, toward the end of the anti-*anpo* campaign, some of the Bund's leaders were contemplating a "violent revolution." But it should be noted that not a single politician, authority, or policeman was actually killed or injured either by students or by other demonstrators. On the contrary, it was a student who was killed and students, their professors, and other citizens who were attacked and wounded. Even if a "violent revolution" and an "armed conflict" were considered by some of the student leaders, they never really intended to use violence against persons, however vehemently they opposed such persons' policies. Thus it can be claimed that the Bund in practice established the principle of nonviolent civil disobedience.[34] This method clearly distinguished the Bund from those to whom it was opposed.

Table 44 lists the answers given by the one hundred students interviewed to the question "What ends should the demonstrations have achieved?" The majority of the students interviewed, regardless of the differences in their attitudes toward student movements, answered that the aim of the demonstrations was to block ratification of the Security Treaty. The ends of forcing dissolution of Parliament, establishing a coalition cabinet of

[34] Shunsuke Tsurumi, "Nemoto kara no Minshushugi" ("Democracy at the Grass-Roots"), *Secchūshugi no Tachiba* (*In Defense of Eclecticism*) Tokyo, Chikuma Shobō, 1961, pp. 121-135.

TABLE 44

THE ENDS THE DEMONSTRATIONS
SHOULD HAVE ACHIEVED BY ATSM

(More than one item counted per person)

	A (47)	B (30)	C (23)	Total (100)
To block ratification of the Security Treaty	29	16	9	54
To force dissolution of Parliament	8	11	1	20
To force Kishi's resignation, to establish another liberal-democratic cabinet	0	2	3	5
To establish a socialist cabinet	4	3	1	8
To establish a coalition cabinet of those opposed to the snap-vote	8	4	0	12
To cause a revolutionary change in the socio-economic system	6	4	0	10
To stop Eisenhower's visit to Japan	0	1	0	1
To defend the Constitution	4	7	4	15
Don't know	0	1	5	6
Others	8	4	2	14

those opposed to the snap-vote (including Anti-Mainstream factions of the Liberal Democratic Party), and defending the Constitution were all primarily concerned with democratic principles and procedures, rather than with the ideological direction of the change which they wished to bring about through demonstrations. In contrast, establishing a socialist cabinet and causing a revolutionary change in the socioeconomic system were related to the ideological direction of the change, rather than to democratic procedures. It should be noted that, even among the activists, achieving a revolution through the anti-Security Treaty demonstrations was not the goal of the majority. As far as our survey indicates, more persons among the activist and the interested groups than among the apathetic were concerned about the crisis of democratic procedures which, left unprotested, might have led the nation again into the path of a war.

Another point to be noted is that there were many who stated their own definitions of the ends of the demonstrations—eight among the activists, four among the interested, and two among the apathetic. Let us enumerate some of the goals these students defined in their own terms. Activists gave the following goals, other than those listed in the questionnaire: "to create a political crisis"; "to establish a new left, independent of either the Communist or the Socialist Party"; "to protest against rearmament"; "to protest against monopoly state capitalism"; and "to expose the Communist and Socialist Parties' betrayal of the people whom they allegedly served." An interested student maintained that he joined the demonstrations "as a form of self-expression"; another admitted that he attended the demonstrations because he "wished to oppose anything and everything." An apathetic student joined the demonstrations while still in senior high school "so that the content of the Security Treaty might be rewritten in such a way as not to involve Japan in the danger of war." He added that "it is not nice to spoil the Japanese relationship with America."

Limited as our sampling was, it still reveals the multiplicity of motives and objectives which combined to produce a torrent of concerted actions all directed against the Security Treaty revision.

Most of the students interviewed stated that the demonstrations were partly successful and partly unsuccessful. Obviously, they were a failure in the sense that they did not prevent the Security Treaty from coming into effect. But they did have two major beneficial results. Some of the students interviewed stressed that the demonstrations constituted "the greatest popular movement since the war" and that "democratic consciousness" and "the recognition of the importance of the rules of democracy" were "driven home to the participants." Others interviewed emphasized the complete debunking of "the sanctity of the Communist Party" as the major unintended consequence of the June demonstrations. Until then, at least among Japanese intellectuals, the Communist Party had enjoyed a sacred status founded on the staunch and uncompromising opposition of the communists (albeit a minority of them) to the militarists and fascists during the war, when most intellectuals allowed themselves to suffer "thought-conversion." But during the anti-

Security Treaty demonstrations the conduct of the Communist Party (as well as that of many other political parties and large-scale political organizations) ended the myth of party infallibility and so freed the minds of intellectuals from the taboos upon thinking and acting against and beyond what the party had authorized. Such freedom already existed among the student leaders who had formed themselves into the Bund before the anti-*anpo* campaign was launched. It was only through the anti-Security Treaty demonstrations, however, that the death of the myth finally became evident to the vast majority of the people, including intellectuals. Just as the sanctity of the Emperor was eclipsed by Japan's defeat, the sanctity of the Communist Party (opposed to the Emperor system) was "unboned" by the Zengakuren students, who took the initiative in fighting against all established systems. Ryūmei Yoshimoto, an independent poet respected by the Zengakuren students, rates very highly the effectiveness of the anti-*anpo* campaign, which, as he sees it, has brought "death to all the make-believe institutions" of which the most colossal was the Communist Party.[35]

When the campaign ended, there were three factions within the Bund—the Fighting Flag, the Transmission of a Revolution, and the Proletarian Correspondence. The first argued that students alone could not achieve a revolution, that instead they should concentrate their efforts upon forming themselves into a vanguard of the working class. The second insisted that students as students could bring about a political change and that they should fight more vigorously to prevent the emergence of an Ikeda Government in succession to the Kishi administration. The third, violently opposed to both of the other two factions, strove to maintain the leadership of the Zengakuren. By the beginning of 1961 these factions had all disappeared: some of their members simply deserted the Bund or its factions, and some even changed their affiliations to organizations outside the Bund (such as the Revolutionary Communist League) with which the Bund had once exchanged the most violent polemics. Thus the leaders of the Bund destroyed the organization they had created. At the Fifteenth Plenary Meeting of the Zengakuren, held in August

[35] Ryūmei Yoshimoto, "Gisei no Shūen" ("The End of the Make-Believe Institutions"), in Yoshimoto et al., *Minshushugi no Shinwa: Anpo Tōsō no Shisōteki Sōkatsu* (*The Myth of Democracy: The Intellectual Generalizations of the Anti-Security Treaty Campaign*), Tokyo, Gendai Shichōsha, 1960, pp. 43-76.

1960, Satoshi Kitakōji of Kyoto University was elected chairman. The ensuing period was characterized as a time of reshuffling of groupings within the Zengakuren.

Why was the Bund dissolved at the very time it had completed so big a campaign? Opinions differ about the major factors that led to its collapse. Morita has observed that, during the final stages of the anti-*anpo* demonstrations, the leaders began to compete among themselves for supreme command of the organization because they began to consider that the Bund was a *great* organization waging a *great* battle. This kind of internal struggle for power was just that weakness for which the Bund's leaders had most severely criticized the Communist Party. When an organization is eroded by the same disease as that which marks the system it most opposes, that organization, says Morita, is sick unto death.

Another explanation has been given by Michiko Shibata. Toward the very end of the series of demonstrations, so many of the leaders of the Bund were arrested that rank-and-file members were left without any orders or direction from above. This predicament encouraged the rank and file actually to exercise that freedom of discussion which was enshrined in the constitution of the Bund. When the Bund's original and immediate objective (to prevent ratification of the Treaty) was frustrated, the freedom of discussion—originally meant to strengthen the organization's internal solidarity—functioned in such a way as to produce real disunity among those whose opinions differed. Thus, in a way, the Bund went bankrupt for lack of time in which its bold new principles might have matured.[36]

Conflicting as these two interpretations seem on the surface, both agree that the Bund was launched as a fresh pioneering experiment to construct a group whose structure of relationships differed both ideally and actually from the structure of relationships in those other groups to which it was opposed.

The Zengakuren at the time of the anti-*anpo* campaign consisted of groups of thinkers or would-be thinkers who attempted to reconstruct their organization on entirely new principles quite distinct from those prevalent in the established organizations of both the right and the left. As complete a flop and as short-lived as their organization, the Bund, turned out to be, it still remains a valuable social experiment not only in the history

[36] Michiko Shibata, "Bundo no Seiritsu" ("The Emergence of the Bund"), *Shisō no Kagaku*, May 1964, p. 66.

of student movements but also in the minds of those who made the attempt. Morita, in his interview with the writer, claimed that the student leaders of those days of the Zengakuren's "re-nascence" are still the most independent thinkers yet to have emerged among student leaders of the postwar period.

Those Zengakuren leaders identified common elements in the structure of relationships of Stalinism, on the one hand, and that of the Emperor system, on the other. They also recognized, out of their own bitter experiences with the Japanese Communist Party, that the internal structure of that party had been eroded by principles characteristic of the Emperor system. That was why, we may conjecture, the student leaders took anti-Stalinist criticism more seriously than did the leaders of the Japanese Communist Party; for they regarded de-Stalinization as identi-cal with de-Emperorization. They were working to eradicate the Emperor system from their own organizations and to eman-cipate their own ways of thinking and feeling from the taboos of Emperor ideology.

Thus they set themselves the difficult task of creating new organizations completely independent both of any state power (such as the Soviet Union, the People's Republic of China, or Japan) and of any existing high-powered organization (such as the Communist Party in any of those countries). They en-deavored to make their own organizations rational, universalistic, independently collectivistic, egalitarian, reciprocal, voluntary, and open—in other words, radically different from the structure of relationships that characterized the Emperor system.

In the succeeding chapters we shall examine what new sets of ideo-affective postures emerged from the student movements of those turbulent times.

TEN

The Student Movement: Group Portraits

THERE are four major questions to be considered in this chapter. First, what are the ideological postures characteristic of the generation of student activists who took the lead in the anti-*anpo* campaign of 1960? Second, what are their characteristic affective postures? Third, how do their characteristic ideo-affective postures compare with those of students of their own generation in general? Fourth, how do their ideo-affective postures differ from those of their predecessors, the communist intellectuals of the 1930's?

1. IDEOLOGICAL POSTURES

Prevalence of Interest in Marxism

Among Japanese students in general there is a widespread interest in Marxism. Table 45 sets out the pattern of the answers

TABLE 45
INTEREST IN MARXISM BY ATSM

Interest in Marxism	A		B		C		Total
	No.	%	No.	%	No.	%	
Very much	37	(78.7)	23	(76.7)	3	(13.0)	63
Fairly	7	(14.7)	6	(20.0)	3	(13.0)	16
A little	2	(4.2)	1	(3.3)	9	(39.3)	12
Not at all	1	(2.4)	0		7	(30.4)	8
No answer	0		0		1	(4.3)	1
Total	47	(100)	30	(100)	23	(100)	100

received to the question "Are you interested in Marxism?" Even among the apathetic the majority were at least "a little interested." During the 1930's the Japanese Communist Party was illegal and Marxist literature was labeled as subversive; mere possession of such literature could be grounds for arrest. Now, however, the Communist Party is a full-fledged legal political party, and Marxist documents are available at any bookstore. Those who are interested may read them in public without risking the danger of being arrested. This change partly accounts for the widespread interest in Marxism among the postwar generation of students.

To the question "To which of the following ideas do you feel *most sympathetic* now?" fifty-six out of the one hundred subjects interviewed chose Marxism alone or in combination with some other ideology or ideologies. Although ninety-one expressed interest in Marxism, only fifty-six counted Marxism as a system of ideas to which they felt sympathetic. And yet Marxism was the most frequently chosen ideology of all the systems of ideas given as alternatives (see Table 46). The ideologies listed in our questionnaire were Marxism (M), Non-Marxist Socialism (NMS), Liberalism (L), Humanism (Hu), Pragmatism (P), Anarchism (A), Nihilism (Ni), Existentialism (E), Nationalism (Na), Idealism (I), Hedonism (He), Ideology-free (IF), and Others (O).

TABLE 46

FREQUENCY OF THE IDEOLOGIES CHOSEN BY ATSM

(More than one item counted per person)

Ideology	A (47) No. %	B (30) No. %	C (23) No. %	Total (100)
M	38 (80.4)	16 (53.3)	2 (8.6)	56
NMS	3 (6.3)	10 (33.3)	3 (13.0)	16
L	4 (8.5)	3 (10.0)	11 (47.8)	18
Hu	11 (23.4)	14 (46.6)	7 (30.4)	32
P	5 (10.6)	6 (20.0)	1 (4.3)	12
A	4 (8.5)	6 (20.0)	0	10
Ni	5 (10.6)	6 (20.0)	0	11
E	9 (19.1)	11 (36.6)	1 (4.3)	21
Na	1 (2.1)	1 (3.3)	2 (8.6)	4
I	2 (4.2)	4 (13.3)	3 (13.0)	9
He	3 (6.3)	2 (6.6)	6 (26.0)	11
IF	3 (6.3)	6 (20.0)	5 (21.7)	14
O (Pacifism)	1 (2.1)			1
(Catholicism)		1 (3.3)	1 (4.3)	2
(Plutolatry)			1 (4.3)	1

Since there was a widespread interest in Marxism among our subjects and since Marxism was their first choice among all the ideologies listed, we can legitimately center our analysis on the type or types of Marxism they held. It is our major concern here to find out whether there is any difference in the approaches to Marxism taken by the prewar intellectuals and by postwar students, as we observe them in 1962. If there is any difference, what are the distinctive ideo-affective postures of the postwar students?

A Monolithic Approach to Marxism: The Prewar Style

Shunsuke Tsurumi has noted four aspects of the Marxism adhered to by Japanese communist intellectuals since the establishment of the Communist Party in Japan in 1922. First, they grasped dialectical materialism as a deductive system, to the utter neglect of an inductive approach. They accepted it as a monolithic and total system, in which one could not examine propositions separately to test their tenability with reference to specific empirical data without running the risk of having one's loyalty to the party questioned. Second, the Communist Party was a predominantly secret system in that its members refused intercommunication with groups holding other ideologies. Third, when communism was introduced to peoples among whom a universalistic concept of truth or justice had been prevalent, in the form of Christianity as in Western countries or in the form of a belief in heaven as in China, communism was likely to be accepted as a universalistic system of ideas. When it was introduced to Japan, where a particularistic tribal religion—Emperor worship—had been prevalent among the people, it managed to maintain its posture of universalism while fighting against the Emperor system. Fourth, the Japanese Communist Party was established by a group of radical intellectual elites, and the party operated illegally and in isolation from the people. This strategy made it difficult for the communist intellectuals to understand the indigenous and deep-rooted sentiments of the masses.[1]

The prewar communists' approach to Marxism can be characterized in the following manner. It was, to begin with, predominantly nonrational, for the Marxist intellectuals of those days accepted dialectical materialism as a total and infallible theoretical system. According to them, once one admits the basic postulates of Marxism to be true, all the propositions deduced from them must be necessarily true. To deny or even to doubt any single postulate or proposition within the system was therefore

---

[1] Shunsuke Tsurumi, "Nihon no Yuibutsuron—Nihon Kyōsantō no Shisō" ("Materialism in Japan—The Thought Pattern of the Japanese Communist Party"), in Tsurumi and Osamu Kuno, *Gendai Nihon no Shisō* (*Contemporary Japanese Thought*), Tokyo, Iwanami, 1956, pp. 30-70.

to call in question the entire system. The prewar approach to Marxism was also predominantly secret, since it inhibited the holders of the the ideology from communicating with those who entertained different ideas; an eclectic approach was prohibited. The approach was predominantly dependent in that the members of the Communist Party were expected to be faithful followers of the party line, and independent judgments, criticisms, and initiatives on the part of the individual members were discouraged. It was, finally, predominantly universalistic. This universalistic attitude was functional insofar as it upheld them in their fight against the particularistic ideology of the Emperor cult. But it was dysfunctional to the extent that it alienated them from the masses, imbued with the particularistic ideology, for whom the communists allegedly fought. We may characterize such an attitude as above-the-people universalism.

In comparison to this predominantly nonrational, secret, dependently collectivistic, and universalistic approach to Marxism on the part of the Marxist intellectuals of the 1930's, the attitude our subjects took toward the same ideology is more eclectic.

An Eclectic Approach to Marxism: The New Style

Table 47 displays the complete list of the varieties of ideologies, both Marxist and non-Marxist, and the combinations of them chosen by our subjects. According to this table, forty-five

TABLE 47

Ideologies Chosen by the Students by ATSM

	Ideology	A	B	C	Total
M 1.	M	24	3	1	28
L 1.	L	3	0	4	7
M 2.	M-Hu	5	1	0	6
NMS 1.	NMS	1	1	2	4
Hu 1.	Hu	1	3	0	4
IF 1.	IF	0	1	3	4
M 3.	M-Hu-P	1	1	0	2
M 4.	M-A-N-E	1	1	0	2
NMS 2.	NMS-Hu-I	0	2	0	2
L 2.	L-Hu	0	1	1	2
Hu 2.	Hu-Na	1	0	1	2
M 5.	M-NMS	0	1	0	1
M 6.	M-P	1	0	0	1
M 7.	M-O (Pacifism)	1	0	0	1
M 8.	M-Ni	0	1	0	1
M 9.	M-A-Ni	0	1	0	1

(Table 47 Continued)

	Ideology	A	B	C	Total
M 10.	M-A-I	0	1	0	1
M 11.	M-Ni-E	1	0	0	1
M 12.	M-P-E	0	1	0	1
M 13.	M-E-He	1	0	0	1
M 14.	M-NMS-Ni-E	1	0	0	1
M 15.	M-Hu-I-He	0	0	1	1
M 16.	M-P-A-E-IF	1	0	0	1
M 17.	M-A-Ni-E-IF	0	1	0	1
M 18.	M-NMS-L-Hu-P	0	1	0	1
M 19.	M-A-E-IF	0	1	0	1
M 20.	M-Hu-P-A-Ni-E-Na-I-He-IF	0	1	0	1
M 21.	M-NMS-L-Hu-P-A-Ni-E-He-IF	0	1	0	1
M 22.	M-NMS-L-Hu-P-A-Ni-E-Na-I-He-IF	1	0	0	1
NMS 3.	NMS-L	0	0	1	1
NMS 4.	NMS-Hu	1	0	0	1
NMS 5.	NMS-Ni-IF	0	1	0	1
NMS 6.	NMS-Hu-E-I	0	1	0	1
NMS 7.	NMS-Hu-Ni-E	0	1	0	1
L 2.	L-He	0	0	1	1
L 3.	L-Na	0	0	1	1
L 4.	L-Hu-IF	0	0	1	1
L 5.	L-E-I-He	0	0	1	1
L 6.	L-I-He-O (Plutolatry)	0	0	1	1
Hu 3.	Hu-IF	1	0	0	1
Hu 4.	Hu-Na-He	0	0	1	1
Hu 5.	Hu-He	0	0	1	1
Hu 6.	Hu-P-He	0	0	1	1
Hu 7.	Hu-P-E-IF	0	1	0	1
A 1.	A-E	1	0	0	1
E 1.	E	0	1	0	1
E 2.	E-O (Catholicism)	0	1	0	1
O 1.	O (Catholicism)	0	0	1	1
Total		47	30	23	100

out of one hundred held one and only one ideology, while the rest chose a combination of two or more than two ideologies. The latter attitude we call an eclectic approach to existing ideologies. Fifty-six were sympathetic to Marxism, but one half of those who supported Marxism also supported some ideology or ideologies other than Marxism. Thus at least half of those who were sympathetic to Marxism possessed eclectic attitudes toward Marxism.

Some of our subjects professed self-contradictory combinations of ideologies—for example, the combinations that include both Marxism and non-Marxist socialism (M 5, M 14, M 18, M 21, M 22) and those that include more than one ideology and an "ideology-free" stance at one and the same time (M 16, M 17, M 19, M 20, M 21, M 22, NMS 5, L 4, Hu 7).

Those who combined Marxism and an ideology-free position might have justified themselves by arguing as follows. According to the Marxist definition, an ideology is a "false consciousness," a conception of reality distorted by virtue of the class interest of its holder.[2] Since Marxism is a "true reflection" of reality, it amounts to an ideology-free position. This argument does not apply to the above-mentioned cases, however, since all of them include some idea system or systems which are defined from the Marxist standpoint as distorted pictures of the world. But there is still another argument proposed by Marxists. As formulated by Marx and Engels, Marxism is an ideology in the sense that it is based on the interest of the proletarian class, and it is *the only ideology* that enjoys the status of a "scientific theory" of the existing society, for the very reason that the proletariat is in a position to foresee the future course of history in its first approximation and to bring it to fruition.[3] Thus, whichever argument one uses, the attempt to combine Marxism and an ideology-free stand with other non-Marxian social theories can be shown to lead to the pitfall of self-contradiction.

It should be noted that most of the students interviewed were serious readers of Marxist literature and could be expected to know what was orthodox Marxism and what was not. Those who

[2] For the Marxist definition of ideology, see Karl Marx and Friedrich Engels, *German Ideology*, in *Marx and Engels: Basic Writings on Politics and Philosophy*, ed. Lewis S. Feuer, New York, Doubleday, 1959, pp. 247-248. For the history of the concept of ideology, see Karl Mannheim, *Ideology and Utopia*, New York, Harcourt, Brace, 1940, pp. 49-67. The definition of ideology used throughout the present work is Silvan Tomkins's (see pp. 22-23).

[3] The position that Marxism is an ideology, since it has a class basis, and is at the same time the only ideology that is compatible with the scientific theory of the existing society is propounded by Engels in *Socialism: Utopian and Scientific*. This point is emphasized by a former Zengakuren leader, Ichiyō Mutō, in his recent essay, "Marukusushugi to Atarashii Kakumei Shutai" ("Marxism and the New Selfhood of Revolution"), *Shisō no Kagaku*, No. 67 (Oct. 1967), pp. 2-15.

deviated from the orthodox Marxist standpoint did so self-consciously rather than haphazardly. Their eclectic approaches toward various ready-made ideologies could in general be interpreted as an indication of a revolt against established authority in the world of thought, whether on the left or on the right wing. They might also be attributed to the general feeling, prevalent among the postwar generation of students, of a mismatch between their affective postures and the ready-made ideologies. The combinations of thought systems, some of which seem self-contradictory from orthodox standpoints, might very well have been indications of their dissatisfaction with the established ideologies and of their determination to try to work out some new patterns of ideas which would be more congenial to their basic affective postures than those already familiar.

The search for a new synthetic pattern of ideas was especially conspicuous among those who supported Marxism. Out of the forty-eight varieties of ideological points of view listed in Table 47, twenty-two are variations of Marxist stands, including Marxism alone. There are seven combinations, held by thirteen subjects, in which Marxism is united with Humanism, with or without other ideologies. There are ten combinations, held by ten persons, in which Marxism is joined to Existentialism, together with other systems of ideas. And there are eight combinations, held by eight students, in which Marxism is allied with Nihilism, with or without other idea systems. These three varieties—Marxism with Humanism, with Existentialism, and with Nihilism—occur more frequently than combinations of Marxism with any other systems of thought.

There is another indication of an eclectic approach to Marxism. As already noted, fifty-six of the one hundred professed to be sympathetic to Marxism. But there were even more than fifty-six who agreed with some specific propositions made by Marx. Seventy in all replied that they thought "the theory of history as a class struggle" was correct; another seventy accepted "the theory of contradictions of capitalism"; forty-five believed in "the inevitability of the advent of socialism"; and forty-seven subscribed to "the theory of the dictatorship of the proletariat." Thus we can see eclectic approaches to Marxism both among those who supported Marxism and among those who did not.

We shall examine more closely the attitudes of those who supported Marxism. To the question "What do you think of Marxism?" these students answered as indicated in Table 48.

TABLE 48

OPINIONS ON MARXISM

Correct as a system	43
Wrong as a system	1
Some part right, some part wrong	12
Total	56

It seems that most of the students supported Marxism as a total system. However, in response to the questions concerning the tenability of each of the four basic propositions of Marxism mentioned above, we got somewhat different results. Twenty-eight out of the fifty-six replied that all four propositions are right, twenty-six answered that some are right but that some are either wrong or doubtful, and two disagreed with all four propositions. This result reveals that, although the majority of those who supported Marxism said they accepted Marxism as a total system, in fact at least half of them did not actually agree with all the basic propositions of Marxism. The discovery of this anomaly is interesting. One possible interpretation is that, while many still thought ideally that a Marxist must accept Marxism as a mono-lithic system, they were actually testing each separate proposition empirically. Some of them explained that they disagreed because of empirical data observable in the contemporary world situation.

2. MOTIVES

We asked our students which of the following factors—persons, events, reading, or emotional motives—was (or were) most important in turning them to the ideas they presently held.

TABLE 49

MOST DECISIVE FACTORS IN CHOICE OF IDEOLOGICAL STAND BY ATSM

(More than one item counted per person)

Factors	A (47) No. %	B (30) No. %	C (23) No. %	Total
Persons	6 (12.6)	7 (23.3)	5 (21.7)	18
Events	27 (57.4)	16 (53.4)	12 (52.2)	55
Emotional motives	4 (8.5)	1 (3.3)	2 (8.6)	7
Reading	15 (31.9)	11 (36.6)	0	26
Others	3 (6.3)	0	4 (17.2)	7
DNK	1 (2.4)	2 (6.6)	3 (13.0)	6
DNA	0	0	1 (4.2)	1

From Table 49 we can see that events had the greatest influence upon our subjects' ideological stands, with reading second and personal influence and the emotional motives following in that order.

Events

What concretely is meant by the influence of "events"? To answer this question, we shall divide our subjects into three categories: those who chose Marxism, those who chose non-Marxist socialism (those who held Marxism and non-Marxist socialism were classified under Marxism), and all those who chose neither Marxism nor non-Marxist socialism. Table 50 shows the concrete events that helped turn our students to the ideas they held at the time we interviewed them.

TABLE 50

CLASSIFICATION OF EVENTS, CIRCUMSTANCES, OR EXPERIENCES THAT
CONTRIBUTED TO ADOPTION OF PRESENT VIEWS

(More than one item counted per person)

Events, Circumstances, Experiences	No.
Marxism (56)	
Participation in demonstrations	
Against *Anpo*	18
Police Duty Bill	7
Teachers' Merit Rating System	4
Education laws	2
Subversive Activities Prevention Law	1
Expansion of Sunagawa Military Base	2
Miike miners' strike	1
Nurses' strikes	1
Total	36
Impact of social events	
Korean War	3
Red purge	2
Bloody May Day incident	2
Court trials of the Matsukawa incident	1
Twentieth Communist Party Convention	1
San Francisco Peace Treaty	1
Chinese Communist Revolution	1
Postwar social events in general	1
Total	12

(*Table 50 Continued*)

Events, Circumstances, Experiences	No.
Influence of education	
Preuniversity education	4
Preuniversity extracurricular activities	3
University education	1
University extracurricular activities	2
Total	10
Family influence	
Family poverty	2
Revolt against *ie* system	2
Father's death	2
Father's detention	1
Family atmosphere conducive to Marxism	1
Revolt against mother's expectations	1
Total	9
Personal experience	
Discrimination against as a Korean	1
Work during off-school years	1
Suicide committed by friend during off-school years	1
Self-criticism of the ideas one held during the war	1
Hard life in the postwar period	1
Year repeated at university	1
Brokenheartedness	1
Revolt against Christian background	1
Total	8
Religious influence	0
None	3
Non-Marxist socialism (11)	
Participation in demonstrations	
Against *anpo*	3
Impact of social events	
Cold war	1
Anpo	1
Reactionary government policies	1
Dropping of atomic bombs by United States	1
Total	4
Influence of education	
University education	1
Family influence	

(Table 50 Continued)

Events, Circumstances, Experiences	No.
Father's retirement	1
Illegitimate child	1
Total	2
Personal experience	0
None	1

Ideological stands other than Marxism and Non-Marxist socialism (33)

Participation in demonstrations	
Against *anpo*	3
Teachers' Merit Rating System	1
Total	4
Impact of social events	0
Influence of education	
Preuniversity education	3
University extracurricular activities	2
Total	5
Family influence	
Family atmosphere congenial to ideas held	6
Sister's death	1
Decline in family business	1
Total	8
Personal experience	
Love affair	2
Success in entrance exam	1
Work since senior high school days	1
Total	4
Religious influence	
Church	1
Catholic school	1
Total	2
None	9

Among those who supported Marxism, participation in demonstrations was cited most often as the decisive factor in winning them over to that ideology; among those who were sympathetic to non-Marxist socialism, the impact of social events was felt by most to have had the greatest influence; and among those who were inclined to liberalism and other nonsocialist ideas, the largest number admitted that there were no specific social or personal events that had turned them to their current ideas. Family influence in the formation of one's ideological stand was strongest of all among the third group.

Of the fifty-six subjects who supported Marxism, only eleven checked reading alone as the most important factor in their adoption of that standpoint. The nine others for whom reading was an important factor mentioned it in combination with "events" or with "persons." Thus only 17.8 percent of those inclined to Marxism turned to that ideology through reading alone.

In this respect the postwar students differed from their prewar counterparts. Table 51 sets forth the results of a survey undertaken by the Ministry of Education in 1931 concerning "the causes of student interest in left-wing ideologies." According to

TABLE 51

Causes of Students' Interest in Left-Wing Ideologies

Cause	No.	%
Influence of reading left-wing theories	105	35.59 ⎫ (49.49)
Influence of proletarian arts and literature	41	13.90 ⎭
Influence of left-wing friends among students	38	12.88
Doubt about the present social situation	37	12.54
Influence of a school campus contaminated by left-wing ideas	17	5.76
Influence of left-wing lectures and speeches	11	3.73
Discontent with education	9	3.05
Influence of left-wing movements off campus	9	3.05
Influence of the family contaminated with left-wing ideas	6	2.04
Doubt about existing religions	5	1.69
Counterreaction against criticisms of Marxism	4	1.36

Source: Monbushō, *Gakusei Seito Sakei no Genin ni kansura Tōkeihyō*, 1931—quoted in Tomitarō Karasawa, *Gakusei no Rekishi* (*A History of Students*), Tokyo, Sōbunsha, 1965, p. 232.

this survey, most of the prewar students (49.49 percent) became interested in Marxism through reading books, in social
science (35.59 percent) and in literature (13.90 percent).
During the 1930's the Peace and Order Preservation Law and
other legislation prohibited people from participating in demonstrations against government measures. Moreover, the Communist Party was illegal then, and Marxist literature was labeled
as "subversive." An approach to Marxism primarily through
reading and in secret seems to have been related to the way in
which the prewar students held Marxism as a deductive system
of thought.

In contrast, the majority of the postwar students, as far as our
survey reveals, became interested in Marxian ideas primarily
through engagement in social movements, protesting against
government measures which they judged detrimental to their
basic values, the values of "peace and democracy" guaranteed
by the Constitution of 1947. The postwar students encountered
Marxism through actions guaranteed as the legal rights of any
Japanese citizen. They behaved in a spirit of self-assertion, exercising constitutional rights which they took for granted.

We may characterize the approach to Marxism prevalent
among the postwar students as Marxism primarily through
engagement, in contrast to that among the prewar students as
Marxism primarily through detachment. This distinction applies
to the way one encounters the ideology. A person who has encountered Marxism through detachment may later become
engaged in some social or political movements as he becomes
committed to that ideology. But the manner in which the initial
resonance with an ideology takes place seems to be important
in coloring the way in which its content is interpreted by the
person who holds it.

We may point out hypothetically that Marxism approached
through detachment and with the negative affective postures of
fear and terror tends to be held as a monolithic and closed
system, whereas Marxism approached through engagement and
with the positive affective postures of joy and excitement is likely
to be held as a relatively open system of ideas tolerant toward
eclectic combinations and unorthodox interpretations.

Reading

The second important influence on our students' ideological
commitments was reading. Even though the initial resonance

with Marxism for the majority of subjects resulted from their participation in demonstrations, they admitted that reading also contributed to the change in their thinking. More than half of those who specified the period said they had encountered Marxist literature initially by the end of their senior high school days. What books and authors attracted them to Marxism? Table 52 lists the ones they mentioned. This list of authors and titles

TABLE 52

BOOKS AND AUTHORS THAT INFLUENCED STUDENTS

Author	Title	No.	Total of Each Author
Marx	Communist Manifesto	13	
	Correspondence	1	
	German Ideology	2	
	Introduction to the Critique of Political Economy	1	
	Philosophical and Economic Manuscripts	1	
	Various Works	4	22
Lenin	Imperialism	1	
	Left-Wing Infantilism	2	
	State and Revolution	3	
	The Strategy of the Social Democrats in Democratic Revolution	1	
	What Should Be Done?	5	12
Mao Tse-tung	New Democracy	1	
	Problems of Strategy in Revolution in China	1	
	Theory of Conflict	3	
	Theory of Practice	4	
	Various Works	2	11
Engels	Family, State, and the Origin of Private Property	1	
	Socialism: Utopian and Scientific	2	
	Various Works	3	6
Trotsky	Eternal Revolution	1	
	History of the Russian Revolution	1	
	Revolution Betrayed	1	
	What Comes Next?	1	4
Stalin	Dialectical Materialism and Historical Materialism	1	
	Foundation of Leninism	3	4
Lukacs	From Existentialism to Marxism	1	

(Table 52 Continued)

Author	Title	No.	Total of Each Author
	Theory of Class-Consciousness	1	
	Theory of Organization	1	3
Sartre	Nausea	2	2
Rolland	Jean Christoph	2	2
Katsumi Nishiguchi	Yamasen	2	2
Sholokhov	And Quiet Flows the Don	2	2
Huberman	What Is Socialism?	2	2
Hyman	Democracy, Fascism and Communism	1	1
Fromm	Escape from Freedom	1	1
Rousseau	Social Contract	1	1
Weber	Protestant Ethics and the Spirit of Capitalism	1	1
Hua Ko	The May Fourth Movement	1	1
Kropotkin	An Appeal to Youth	1	1
Takiji Kobayashi	Novels	1	1
Camus	The Stranger	1	1
Gide	A Trip to the USSR	1	1
Wilson	The Outsider	1	1
Saneatsu Mushakōji	Novels	1	1
Castro	My Cuba	1	1
Huberman and Sweezy	Cuba	1	1
Noboru Shirozuka	Feuerbach	1	1
Goethe	Wilhelm Meister	1	1
Dostoyevsky	The Brothers Karamazov	1	1
Kazuo Hirotsu	Matsukawa	1	1
Gorō Hani	History of the Japanese People	1	1
Togliatti	Various Works	1	1
Du Gard	Les Thibault	1	1
Rilke	Martha	1	1
Kōzō Uno	Various Works	1	1
Nehru	Autobiography	1	1
Dunham	Various Works	1	1
Not specified		8	8

shows that a wide variety of books helped persuade students to support Marxism. Marxisms of different schools and different countries are represented, and even authors critical of Marxism or of the Communist Party are included. Thus eclectic and open attitudes are manifest in the varieties of books students mentioned as having influenced them at the turning points of their intellectual lives.

Our students, both Marxists and non-Marxists, held non-conformist attitudes toward established models in living and in thinking. In reply to our question "What statesmen do you respect?" Forty-one out of the one hundred said "none," and three gave no answer. In response to the question "Is there anyone whom you respect?" twenty-four replied "no," and fourteen gave no answer. Still, the percentages of those who mentioned no one whom they respect, neither statesman (43 percent) nor any other person (38 percent), are not very high compared to the results of surveys of university students conducted in 1938. According to those surveys, 37.4 percent of the 2,713 students of Kyoto University did not name anyone whom they respected; 60.7 percent of the 247 students of Niigata Medical College gave none; and 70 percent of the 682 students of Tokyo Commercial University mentioned none.[4]

One marked contrast between postwar students and wartime students that comparison of our survey with these earlier surveys brings out is the difference in the kind of persons mentioned. The wartime students specified, among others, Takamori Saigō, Shōin Yoshida, Maresuke Nogi, Masashige Kusunoki, Hideyo Noguchi, Heihachirō Tōgō, Shigenobu Ōkuma, Nichiren, Goethe, Beethoven, Christ, Tolstoy, and Hitler, most of whom are either national heroes who appear in the public school textbooks or famous classical figures practically everyone knows. In contrast, the post-war students named a vast variety of persons, both distinguished and obscure, ancient and contemporary, national and foreign, chosen out of their reading as well as out of their everyday experiences. The following is a complete list of the individuals they mentioned (with frequency of citation): Schweitzer (8), Marx (7), Lenin (7), Beethoven (3), parents (2), Yukichi Fukuzawa (2), Madame Curie (2), F. D. Roosevelt (2), Hirokazu Kuroda (2), Sartre (2), Christ (2), Churchill (2), Russell (2), Gramsci (2), Castro (1), Michelangelo (1), Goethe (1), Trotsky (1), Ryūmei Yoshimoto (1), Senroku Uehara (1), Takauji Ashikaga (1), Engels (1), senior high school teacher (1), Montaigne (1), Hideyo Noguchi (1), Risaburō Hiroike's father (1), Senji Yamamoto (1), Hajime Kawakami (1), mother (1),

---

[4] "Senjika Gakusei Seikatsu Chōsa" ("Surveys of the Life of University Students during the War"), *Nihon Hyōron*, May 1939, pp. 359-382.

Confucius (1), Malraux (1), Masao Maruyama (1), Lincoln (1), Yutaka Taniyama (1), Tadao Yanaihara (1), younger sister (1), Gauguin (1), Itsurō Sakisaka (1), Nietzsche (1), Kōzō Uno (1), Weber (1), Schliemann (1).

Persons

We asked the students if there was someone—a friend, a teacher, girl (or boy) friend, member of their family, etc.—who had played a large part in moving them to adopt the views they held. Among those sympathetic to Marxism, we discovered, the peer group had had the greatest, and the family the least, influence. As for teachers, those in senior high schools had exerted the strongest influence; no student mentions the influence of a university teacher. This pattern of personal influence in the Marxist students' intellectual lives differs considerably from the pattern for the apathetic students, among whom Marxism was least popular. Within this group those who denied any personal influence outnumbered those who admitted the influence of family members, and the latter in turn were more numerous than those who cited the influence of teachers or friends. In other words, compared to the activists and the interested, the apathetic students were the most dependent on their families in intellectual matters, just as they were economically the most dependent upon their parents.

Emotional Motives

We asked our students to what emotional motives their present ideological stands were related. Table 53 summarizes the answers given by the fifty-six subjects who favored Marxism.

The absence of motivation related to "religious feelings" requires some explanation. Among the one hundred students interviewed there were only five Buddhists, four Protestants, and three Catholics; eighty-eight subjects professed no religion at all. The percentage of religious believers in our survey is nevertheless higher than the one revealed in the survey undertaken by Sophia University in 1966 of 3,686 university students, male and female, in Tokyo. Only 7.6 percent of the male subjects interviewed in that survey professed some religion, 3 percent being Christians and 4.6 percent Buddhists, Shintoists, and believers in the new religions such as Sōkagakkai. The same survey shows that some 70 percent of the sample held the opinion "that religion is absolutely unnecessary to anyone who has strong confi-

TABLE 53

EMOTIONAL MOTIVES RELATED TO MARXISM

(More than one item counted per person)

Emotional Motive	No. of Students	Type of Affect (P = positive) (N = negative)
Inferiority complex	3	N
Humanistic feelings	23	P
Religious feelings	0	
Sympathy for the suffering	8	P
Revolt against the older generation	12	N
Quest for success	2	P
Antiestablishment sentiment	21	P or N
Others (specified by students)		
Peace sentiment	2	P
Quest for truth	4	P
Mistrust of oneself	1	N
Mistrust of the Japanese	1	N
Assertion of human desires	1	P
Sense of responsibility	1	P or N
Sense of guilt for being a member of the privileged class	1	N
Quest for happiness	1	P
Desire for freedom of expression	1	P
Total	82	

dence in himself, possesses a powerful personality, and has determined will power."[5] Finally, of the fifty-six subjects of our survey who supported Marxism, only two—a Buddhist and a Protestant—admitted any religious affiliation. With so few adherents of religion among these samples of the student population, it should not be surprising that we did not find any students who related their ideological stands to religious feeling.

The emotions listed are divided into positive and negative affects. There are some emotions, such as "antiestablishment sentiment," that cannot be defined either as positive or as negative, since classification depends on whether desire for novelty or anger against the establishment is stressed. Leaving out those which are ambiguous, we count a total of forty-two positive affects and eighteen negative affects. This result may be taken as an indication that, for postwar students, Marxism is related

[5] Fernando M. Basabe et al., *Japanese Youth Confronts Religion*, Tokyo, Sophia University, 1967, p. 95.

more to positive affective postures than to negative affective postures.

Since no study has been made of emotional motives related to Marxism among prewar students, we cannot make a precise statistical comparison. Karasawa offers us some help, however, in his *History of Students*, where he provides a list of environmental factors which led students of the 1930's to adopt left-wing ideologies. Based on the reading of personal records written by 286 students and edited by the Ministry of Education, his list includes such emotional motives as "discontent with school education," "competition with schoolmates," "poverty and spiritual malcontentment with family life," "humanistic feelings," "doubts about religion and idealistic philosophies," "spirit of revolt," "curiosity and adventurism." Karasawa emphasizes that motives springing from humanism and a sense of justice are especially pronounced in their writings.[6] If that is so, there may be no great difference between the emotional motivation of postwar Marxist students and their prewar counterparts. We cannot be certain about this point, however, until we analyze the personal documents of the prewar leftist students statistically and in more detail.

There is another point worth noting here. According to Table 53, only one Marxist student specified his emotional motive as a "sense of guilt for being a member of the privileged class." This was a more prevalent emotional motive for the left-wing students in the 1930's. Karasawa observes that in the prewar period there were relatively more left-wing students among the sons of wealthy and upper-class families than among the poor.[7] In those days only well-to-do families could afford to send their sons to universities. In contrast, as we have already seen, in postwar Japan more families of moderate means send their sons and daughters to universities. At the same time, most of the activist and interested students work to help finance their university education. For the majority of these students, then, collective guilt consciousness for being members of the privileged class is no longer a problem; they do not consider themselves privileged enough to feel guilty. If there is any radical difference between the emotional motives of postwar Marxist students and those of their prewar counterparts, perhaps the rarity of a guilt complex

[6] Tomitarō Karasawa, *Gakusei no Rekishi (A History of Students)*, Tokyo, Sōbunsha, 1965, pp. 235-249.

[7] *Ibid.*, pp. 231-232.

among the former is one of the most conspicuous. If this collective guilt complex of the prewar intellectuals was a prevalent source of negative affective postures related to Marxism, the majority of the postwar generation of radical students are free of that type of negative affect.

3. AFFECTIVE POSTURES

To learn what affective postures prevailed among our subjects, we focused our attention on their career preferences and their choices of ways of life for the twenty-year period after their graduation from college.

First we asked the students what they wished to do immediately after they finished school. Their answers are summed up in Table 54.

TABLE 54

OCCUPATIONAL OBJECTIVE AFTER GRADUATION BY ATSM

Occupational Objective	A	B	C	Total
Graduate student	13	6	4	23
Accountant, pharmacist	0	0	3	3
Teacher, researcher	7	3	1	11
Engineer, technician	1	0	0	1
Businessman, nongovernmental white-collar worker	7	2	11	20
Civil servant	2	4	2	8
Mass communications employee	4	3	2	9
Lawyer, doctor, professor	4	5	0	9
Free-lance writer	0	1	0	1
Political activist	5	1	0	6
Industrial worker	1	0	0	1
No answer	3	3	0	6
DNK	0	2	0	2
Total	47	30	23	100

The activist group distinguished itself from the apathetic group in three respects. In the first place, many more activists than apathetic students planned to go on to graduate schools. Furthermore, a considerable number of the activists intended to engage in revolutionary activities, whereas none of the apathetic students expressed any such desire. Finally, those who expected to enter some occupation requiring a university education immediately after finishing college were more numerous among the apathetic (82.6 percent) than among the activists

(53.2 percent). In all three respects, the interested group fell in between these two groups.

Characteristically, the generation of the activists who have gone through the experience of the anti-*anpo* campaign tends to split into two parts that diverge in seemingly opposite directions immediately after graduation—on the one hand, toward immersion in study with at least a temporary withdrawal from the political arena and, on the other, toward even greater commitment to political activities. These two tendencies, contrary as they may seem on the surface, have evidently sprung from the same source—the sense of defeat prevalent among the activists who led the anti-*anpo* campaign. They were not able to prevent the Security Treaty from coming into effect, although they fought against it with all their strength. Moreover, they lost one of their best fellow students in the struggle, and many who participated in the demonstrations were injured, some disabled, by police truncheons. These misfortunes only sharpened their already acute sense of failure. The effect on some was to lead them to an awareness of the inadequacy of their knowledge and analysis of the actual situation, both national and international, and thus to more serious studies than they had hitherto undertaken. Other activists reacted by attributing the failure of the anti-*anpo* campaign to the inadequacy of existing political organizations, in which students were alienated from the majority of the workers. These activists felt an urgent necessity to devote themselves to the formation of new revolutionary organizations among workers.

Next, we asked our students what they wanted to achieve by the time they reached the age of forty. Table 55 lists their goals and the number of students aspiring to each.

Comparing views on future occupations among the three groups, we can discern some tendencies peculiar to each. To the activists the life of a professional revolutionary seemed most attractive; the interested viewed the career of a professional as the most desirable of all; and among the apathetic the managerial position in business was the most popular occupation. For members of the Communist Party, a "professional revolutionary" was a person who worked full-time for the party. However, almost all the activists interviewed had been purged from the Communist Party or had never been affiliated with it. So, for them, to be a "professional revolutionary" meant to work for a new organization or to attempt to organize one of their own.

TABLE 55
Desired Achievement by Age Forty by ATSM

Desired Achievement	A	B	C	Total
Accountant, pharmacist	0	0	3	3
Teacher, researcher	2	0	0	2
Engineer, technician	2	0	0	2
Managerial position in business	3	3	7	13
Civil servant	0	3	1	4
Administrative position in civil service	0	0	1	1
Mass communications employee	0	0	2	2
Managerial position in mass communications	2	3	2	7
Professional (lawyer, professor, architect, writer, doctor)	7	9	2	18
Professional revolutionary	10	1	0	11
Managerial position in business + political activities	3	0	0	3
Professional + political activities	9	2	0	11
Industrial worker + political activities	1	0	0	1
Member of parliament and cabinet minister	2	1	1	4
Shop owner	0	0	1	1
Housewife	0	0	2	2
Any occupation that provides a living	0	1	0	1
Just to live pleasantly	0	0	1	1
Rather be dead	0	1	0	1
Worried	0	1	0	1
No answer	6	5	0	11
Total	47	30	23	100

But it would have been extremely difficult for them to make a living if their only source of income were from political activities. Thus there arose another, and perhaps more realistic, approach to political involvement—combining some remunerative occupation with political activities. Of the activists, three preferred to hold a managerial position in business while carrying on political activities at the same time, nine wished to combine a profession with political activities, and one chose to be an industrial worker while engaged in political activities. There were two activists who intended to become statesmen on left-wing tickets. We classified all of those who had future plans to continue political activity in one way or another as politics-oriented in their choice of careers. Twenty-five activists out of forty-seven (53.1 percent) were politics-oriented in this sense, whereas only four such persons out of thirty (13.3 percent) were to be found among the interested, and only one out of twenty-three (4.3 percent)—who wished to be a statesman, probably on the conservative ticket—among the apathetic. These comparative figures indicate clearly that the activists were by far the most politics-oriented.

The favorite choice of the interested was the occupation of an independent professional—lawyer, doctor, professor, writer, architect, etc. Nine out of thirty (30 percent) of the interested preferred professions, compared with seven out of forty-seven (14.8 percent) of the activists and two out of twenty-three (8.6 percent) of the apathetic. Thus we can describe the interested as professions-oriented in their career preference.

Among the apathetic those who declared a managerial position in business most to their liking outnumbered all who made other choices. If we add to this number the single individual who wished to become a shop owner, we then find eight out of twenty-three (34.7 percent) of the apathetic preferring business as their career, in contrast to three out of forty-seven (6.3 percent) of the activists and three out of thirty (10 percent) of the interested. Thus the apathetic were the most business-oriented of the three groups in their choice of prospective occupations.

Summing up, we can characterize the activists as politics-oriented, the interested as professions-oriented, and the apathetic as business-oriented in their career preferences.

The third question we put to the students asked them to judge how confident they were of achieving the goals they had set themselves? The activists, we discovered, were the most self-confident of the three groups, followed by the apathetic and then the interested.

From the responses to our next query we learned that there was a consensus among the three groups concerning the qualities necessary for the attainment of their goals. All three ranked "hard work" as the most important quality and "health" a close second, since it enables one to work hard.[8] All three groups were

---

[8] In Section 3 of Chapter Five it was shown that the conviction that hard work is reciprocated by rewards was one of the basic beliefs of the people in the traditional village community in Japan. It is interesting to note that

achievement-oriented in their evaluation of the means to attain their goals.

The replies to our fifth question revealed that the activists, the interested, and the apathetic shared a predominantly positive affective posture, notwithstanding the diversity of their ideological postures. Table 56 shows the answers our subjects gave to the question: "What way of life do you want to pursue, at least for twenty years after you graduate?" (Items a to f were provided to the students as alternatives from which to choose.)

TABLE 56

PREFERRED WAY OF LIVING FOR TWENTY YEARS AFTER GRADUATION BY ATSM

Way of life	A No. %	B No. %	C No. %	Total No.
To defend the capitalist system and to pursue my own happiness	0	1 (3.3)	10 (43.5)	11
To pursue my own happiness, without any interest in the system	1 (2.15)	0	3 (13.0)	4
To always pursue my own happiness whatever happens to the system	0	3 (10.0)	5 (21.7)	8
To work to change the system and at the same time to pursue my own happiness	24 (51.0)	13 (43.4)	4 (17.2)	41
To defend the capitalist system, even at the expense of my own happiness	2 (4.2)	0	0	2
To work positively to change the capitalist system, even at the expense of my own happiness	11 (23.4)	6 (20.0)	1 (4.6)	18
Other (My own happiness lies in working to change the social system; were I to give up my revolutionary activities, I would feel empty and unhappy)	8 (17.1)	3 (10.0)	0	11
Do not know	0	3 (10.0)	0	3
No answer	1 (2.15)	1 (3.3)	0	2
Total	47 (100.0)	30 (100.0)	23 (100.0)	100

Among the apathetic 43.5 percent identified the maintenance of the capitalist system with pursuit of happiness in their private lives, and 34.7 percent were interested solely in the pursuit of happiness regardless of the social system under which they lived. Thus 78.2 percent of the apathetic were inclined to a positive affective posture. Among the interested 43.4 percent expressed a desire to work to change the system and at the same

---

a similar belief in hard work still persists among the postwar generation of students, at least up to the time of our survey in 1962.

time to pursue their own happiness, and 10 percent made statements to the effect that their own happiness lay in working to change the existing system. Altogether, 53.4 percent of the interested preferred to identify their own happiness with revolutionary activities. Among the activists, finally, 51 percent said they intended to work to change the system and at the same time to pursue their own happiness, and 17.1 percent devised answers of their own in which the accent fell on identification of political commitment with one's own happiness. Thus we can say that 68.1 percent of the activists associated commitment to a revolutionary cause with positive affects of enjoyment and happiness.

The disposition to identify revolutionary activities with a negative affective posture was far less prevalent than identification with a positive affective posture among both the activists and the interested. Only 23.4 percent of the activists and 20 percent of the interested wanted to work positively for the change of the capitalist system, even at the expense of their own happiness.

The commitment of the communists of the 1930's to revolutionary movements was tied up with predominantly negative affects of self-sacrifice, suffering from imprisonment and torture, and fear of death (see Chapter One, Section 5). In contrast, the majority of student activists today, as revealed in our 1962 survey, associate their political commitment primarily with positive affects of joy, excitement, and happiness. It is not that these postwar student activists have no experience of negative affects. Far from it, for they have witnessed the premature death of some of their fellow students in demonstrations, and many of them have been at various times injured, arrested, imprisoned, expelled from schools, and purged from the Communist Party. Yet, in spite of these agonizing experiences, the generation of student activists who participated in the anti-*anpo* campaign of 1960 maintain a predominantly positive affective posture and insist on the identification of a career as a revolutionary with predominantly positive affects.

Our sixth and final question sought to elicit information about our subjects' attitudes toward sex. We found that the activists and the interested were more liberal than the apathetic in their attitudes toward sex.

A majority of the apathetic (61.1 percent) displayed conservative attitudes: 21.7 percent would not condone sexual relations without the prospect of marriage and 39.4 percent would not permit sexual relations before marriage. In contrast, the activists and the interested for the most part preferred more liberal sexual attitudes. The relatively liberal attitude of approving sexual relations only with the person one loves was endorsed by 53.1 percent of the activists and 63.3 percent of the interested. The most liberal attitude—favoring enjoyment of sex as much as one wishes—was favored by 14.8 percent of the activists and 3.35 percent of the interested. Altogether, 67.9 percent of the activists and 66.65 percent of the interested supported liberal attitudes toward sex.

Borrowing Feuer's classification of basic ethical attitudes, we may characterize the postwar generation of student activists as hedonistic revolutionaries, in contrast to the leftist intellectuals of the 1930's, who may be called ascetic revolutionaries.[9]

This classification is useful for our analysis since it covers the two factors that constitute the basic difference between the communist intellectuals of the 1930's and the student activists who took the lead in the anti-*anpo* campaign of 1960. First, the sense of collective guilt that played a central role in motivating the former to become communists rarely entered into the decisions of the latter to become revolutionaries. Second, we have reason to suspect that the former invested predominantly negative affects, the latter predominantly positive affects, in revolutionary activities.

We have already observed in the first section of this chapter that, unlike the communists of the 1930's, students today maintain a predominantly rational, independent, and open attitude toward Marxism. We might hypothesize, then, that hedonistic revolutionaries, whose affective postures are predominantly positive, tend to interpret their revolutionary ideology in a predominantly rational, independent, and open manner, whereas ascetic revolutionaries, whose affective postures are predominantly negative, tend to approach their revolutionary ideology in a predominantly nonrational, dependent, and secret way.

[9] Feuer distinguishes between hedonism and asceticism thus: "Basically, an ethic is hedonist when it is free from a sense of primal guilt; a hedonist outlook is characterized by an absence of internalized self-aggression. 'Good' can then be defined in terms of the person's spontaneous likings and desires. The Calvinist ethic, in which the asceticism of the sixteenth and seventeenth centuries was expressed, was founded by contrast on an assertion of the primacy of guilt. . . . The Calvinist ethic was permeated with hatred of the body, hatred of the senses and pleasure. Man's desire for pleasure had brought his fall; austerity, frugality, self-denial were good because they mortified the fount of man's sin." Lewis S. Feuer, *The Scientific Intellectual*, New York, Basic Books, 1963, p. 8.

ELEVEN

The Student Movement: Individual Portraits

AMONG the six factions in existence at the time of our survey, we shall concentrate our attention here on three—the National Committee of the Revolutionary Communist League, the Structural Reformists, and the Socialist Student League. These three groups are independent of the Communist and Socialist Parties, but at the same time they all claim to be Marxist. From each of these three factions two leaders will be selected for close scrutiny of their intellectual histories. We shall first trace their development from their childhood experiences, particularly after their entrance into primary school, up to the time they enrolled at universities. Our study of their earlier experiences will be centered on preuniversity education, since the change from education based on the Emperor cult to one based on the Constitution of 1947 was the major and most overt transformation in the pattern of socialization in the postwar period. In this part of our study our attention will be focused mainly on the effects of preuniversity education on the formation of the affective postures of our subjects. Second, we shall inquire into the ideological postures of the leaders which are characteristic of each of these three factions to see if there is any discernible difference between these postures. Third, we shall discuss the factors that contributed to the departure, in varying degrees, of their ideo-affective postures from those of the communist intellectuals of the 1930's.

1. EFFECTS OF PREUNIVERSITY EDUCATION:
AFFECTIVE POSTURES

The National Committee
of the Revolutionary Communist League

Satoshi Kitakōji, a student at Kyoto University, was born in 1936 in Kyoto, the eldest son of a high school teacher. His father is now a ward assemblyman, on the communist ticket, in the city of Kyoto. Our subject entered a primary school during the Pacific war.

Looking back upon his primary school days, he describes himself as having been "a boy fascist" who believed in Japan's

victory in the war and was extremely upset by the news of the
mass suicide of Japanese soldiers on the Pacific islands. He had
been evacuated to a village near Kyoto during the war, and he
did not return to the city until two years after the termination
of the war, when he was in the fourth grade. Then he was exposed to the "new education." His first reaction to the changed
atmosphere of his school was favorable. He thought "democracy
is a splendid thing," since it enabled him and his classmates to
argue against the formerly overbearing upperclassmen. Thus
for him democracy meant an emancipation from oppressive
influences. He switched smoothly from fascism to democracy.
When he entered high school, he organized a Junior Red Cross
—an action that sprang, he says, from the humanistic and democratic spirit acquired in his primary school days. At this stage
he was vaguely interested in communism, because he felt that
it was congenial to his humanistic feelings.

In his senior high school days Kitakōji had two experiences
which led him to become a communist. First, as editor of the
student newspaper at his school, he had to cope with the school
principal who attempted to suppress freedom of expression
from time to time. The second, and more decisive, factor was
the Asahigaoka High School incident of 1954. Three teachers of
that school, including his father, were transferred by order of
the City Board of Education to other schools, on the grounds
that they had been practicing "tendentious education" (implying
communist-inclined education). The education provided at Asahigaoka Senior High School had been taken up in the parliamentary hearing on some twenty cases of "tendentious education" from all over the country. These cases were used by the
Liberal Democratic Party to promote the passage of legislation
to prohibit public school teachers from engaging in political
activities and thus to "neutralize" public school education. The
parents who supported "Asahigaoka education," as practiced
by the three teachers and their colleagues, organized a group
to study the Constitution of 1947 and the Fundamental Law of
Education based on the Constitution. Through these studies
they reached the conviction that the teaching at Asahigaoka
High School was in accord with the spirit of the Constitution
and the Law of Education.[1]

[1] Kazuko Tsurumi et al., "Asahigaoka Chūgakkō no Fukei no Kōdō to
Ishiki" ("The Conduct and Consciousness of the Parents of Asahigaoka

This episode occurred when Kitakōji was in his second year of high school. Although his father's involvement in the incident must have provided the initial emotional impetus for his interest in the event, the son denies that his interest was altogether personal: "This incident revealed to me that people cannot defend their own constitutional rights unless they are organized to fight against the government's suppression of their movements for self-expression."[2]

After this experience he began to read the *Communist Manifesto* and *Socialism: Utopian and Scientific.* In the following year he joined the Communist Party. Here again he flatly denies that his father influenced his decision to become a communist. Instead, he mentions his friends and teachers at the senior high school as the persons who contributed most to turning him to communism.

Takeo Shimizu, a student at Tokyo University, was born in 1937, the son of a tenant farmer who became an owner-cultivator of 1.2 chō of land after the land reform of 1946. His parents, wishing him to grow strong enough to become a soldier, named him "Takeo," meaning "strong boy." He was in the second grade at a primary school when the war ended. Hearing the news of Japan's defeat, he cried aloud, shut himself up all day, and refused to go out to play with his friends. He, too, asserts that he was "a boy fascist." His interest in politics has persisted since his boyhood, but it has developed in a direction different from that in which his previous political sympathies had impelled him.

His two elder brothers were engine drivers with the National Railway Corporation. When he was in the sixth grade, the National Railway workers went on strike, and under the influence of his elder brothers he became sympathetic to their cause. At school he was taught the equality of all men in a democracy, but at home his brothers talked about the inequalities between the wealthy and the poor. Thus he became aware of the gap between the democratic values set forth in the Constitution and the hard realities of everyday existence.

When Shimizu was in his second year of high school, he attempted to persuade his classmates to refrain from observing a silent prayer, ordered by the school authorities on the death of the Empress Dowager. He told his classmates: "after all, this

High School"), *Tokyo Daigaku Kyōikugakubu Kiyō* (*Bulletin of the Department of Education, Tokyo University*), 1957, ii, 72-114.

[2] From the author's interview with Kitakōji on August 28, 1962.

is nothing but the death of an old woman, and we do not need to perform any special ritual of deference for the occasion." If any school child had acted in this way before the defeat, he would have been severely punished. But nothing happened to Shimizu when he thus agitated against the Imperial Household. At about the same time he began to read the *Communist Manifesto*, and his spontaneous reaction was: "Marxism is right. We've got to prepare for the coming revolution." Again he gathered his friends and told them what he thought about Marxism and revolution.

He joined the Communist Party in 1957 after entering Tokyo University. In deciding to join, he made up his mind that he would have to accept two conditions. First, he knew that as a communist he would not be able to get an ordinary job; thus he was determined to become a lifetime professional revolutionary. Second, since a communist revolution resorts to violence, he had to be prepared to take part in armed insurrection. He observes that, "out of the 350,000 Zengakuren members, only three or four individuals per year make up their minds as firmly as I did to become a lifetime professional revolutionary."[3]

The Structural Reformists

G, a student at Tokyo University, was born in 1940 in Tokyo, the eldest son of a civil servant. His teachers in the elementary school he attended recommended that the children read *Echoes from a Mountain* and *The Yam*, a collection of poems written by a peasant boy during his primary school days.[4] The publication of these children's compositions and poems heralded the postwar revival of the life-composition movement in education at the primary and high school levels. (For an account of the life-composition movement, see Chapter Six, Section 1.) G and his classmates were encouraged to write compositions and poems about whatever subjects interested them, to think on their own, and to express their ideas in their own words rather than in stereotyped formal language.

At G's high school there were many young teachers who pro-

---

[3] Both Kitakōji and Shimizu are the leaders now (1968) of the Revolutionary Communist League and are living up to their own goal of becoming "professional revolutionaries."

[4] Seikyō Muchaku, ed., *Yamabiko Gakkō* (*Echoes from a Mountain School*), Tokyo, Seidōsha, 1951. Michio Sagawa, *Ōzeki Matsusaburō Shishū Yamaimo* (*The Yam, A Collection of Poems by Matsusaburō Ōzeki*), Tokyo, Yuri Shuppan, 1951.

moted the formation of study circles and the involvement of their students in other voluntary research and recreational activities, such as "pupils' cultural festivals." In their social studies classes, some teachers asked their pupils to listen to radio programs, to read different newspapers, and to write up reports on national and international affairs, instead of listening only to the teachers' own interpretations of events. G relates:

> I read newspapers and listened to radio programs carefully, so that I might crosscheck information I got from one source with what I acquired from another. Thus I became aware of discrepancies in the reporting of facts from different sources. Through our education at the primary and high school levels, we were trained to detect the distortions of facts that often appear in mass communication media. It became a habit with us to try to build up our own generalizations step by step from the data we collected ourselves. That was why I did not become a member of the communist cell at the senior high school. The dogmatism that then prevailed in that communist cell was repulsive to my previous training.[5]

It was the demonstration against the attempted revision of the Police Duty Bill that led G to think seriously of the importance of organized political activities. He was an off-school student when this happened. Subsequently he entered the university and there joined the Communist Party; he left the party after the anti-*anpo* campaign. He emphasizes that the kind of education he and other students of his generation received both in elementary and in high school was "the essential factor contributing to the formation of the New Left."

Junichi Kuroha, a student at Kyōiku University (the National University of Education), was born in the same year as Kitakōji. His father was a clerk at the stock exchange. He says the influence of his father, from whom he learned to think rationally, was so deep-rooted that he could not accept wholeheartedly all that he was taught at the primary school he entered during the war. For instance, he recalls feeling repelled by such a widely circulated expression as "the Americans and the British are devilish beasts." On the other hand, he was excited over the news of Japan's victories in the earlier stages of the war since, he says, he "romanticized the policy of the Great Asiatic Co-

---

[5] From the author's interview with G on May 29, 1962.

prosperity Sphere." Thus his wartime education created an ambivalent attitude in him.

His father died when Kuroha was in third grade. Upon reaching fifth grade he began to work as a newsboy to help his mother, who had remarried and was poor.

The experiences of poverty and the early necessity of working for a living underlay his interest in the leftist movement, although they were not the conscious and immediate motives in his conversion to communism. A conscious interest in communist movements was aroused during his first year in high school when a teacher whom he respected was discharged from his school in accordance with the government's Red purge policy. In his farewell speech the teacher told his pupils: "You may not understand now why I have to say good-bye to you, but you will eventually understand." These words made Kuroha curious to know what lay behind the discharge of his teacher.

His curiosity drove him to read many books during his high school days, among which were the *Communist Manifesto* and other works by Marx and Engels, recommended as reference books for social study in his class on the history of the Western world. In his first year at senior high school he encountered another shocking experience when some upperclassmen and teachers were arrested by the police for their part in the Bloody May Day incident. At this time he understood in his own way the meaning of their arrest, and he decided to become a member of the Democratic Youth League.

The Socialist Student League—the Secretariat Faction

N, a student at Tokyo University, had been a leader of the Bund and was a leader of the Socialist Student League at the time of the survey. He was born in 1933 at Tailin in Manchuria. His father at that time was an engineer; he later became a manager of his company and after the war went into the Christian ministry. The son was brought up as a devout Christian and refused to accept the doctrine of militarism taught at the Japanese school in Tailin. He often cut his classes and went to the park to play with doves, as a way of protesting against certain teachers whom he detested.

After the war he returned with his parents to Japan and entered a high school. He joined the Youth for Christ and began preaching in the street. During these days he read Kropotkin's *Appeal to Youth* and the *Communist Manifesto*. In his second year in junior high school he became a member of the Democratic Youth League and tried to make communism and Christianity compatible. His second year at senior high school saw him leave his church to devote himself single-heartedly to communism. His primary motives in joining the communist party were humanism and "the spirit of public service." He was purged from the party just half a year after he had entered it. In his university days he came under the spell of the existentialism of Jean-Paul Sartre.

Shigerō Shima, a graduate student at Tokyo University, was a top leader of the Bund until its dissolution, after which he became sympathetic to the Socialist Student League. He was born in 1931 in Tokyo, the third son of a government-employed engineer. His two elder brothers were in the navy. But, since he suffered from asthma from his childhood, he was determined not to have a military career. Instead, he wished to be a scientist. In his early days at high school during the war, one of his teachers returned from China as a veteran. The teacher insisted that, even if the war should end with Japan's temporary defeat, the true war would be launched again and youth should be trained for that next war. He opened up a farm in the suburbs of Tokyo where military training was combined with regular classroom teaching. At this farm-school Shima became disrespectful of his teachers, since he observed that they secretly exchanged their farm products for food and other items on the black market and then kept these goods for themselves. After Japan's defeat it was these same militaristic teachers who changed their views the fastest and claimed to be democrats, an about-face which made Shima even more contemptuous of them.

When he was in senior high school, the Korean War broke out, and soon afterward a purge of communists among civil servants was decided upon by the Japanese cabinet. Shima was opposed to the Red purge mainly on two grounds. First, it was a part of his revolt against his father, who was a member of the executive group in the civil service which was promoting the purge. Second, the Red purge policy evoked among the public the image of government oppression of free speech and the sense of crisis which were directly associated with the gloomy experiences of the 1930's, when thought control was exercised by a government which had eventually led the country into war. It was the Red purge and the sentiments it aroused in him against the symbols of oppression—his own father, on the one hand, and the conservative government, on the other—that initially induced Shima to enter the Communist Party. When he fought with the party against the purge, he says, his primary motivation was the spirit of resistance to suppression. And, in that sense, his attitude was continuous with the basic affective posture of the prewar communists, who fought against suppression by the state power.

On the other hand, Shima asserts, a quite different motive was present among students who had been purged from the Communist Party, including himself, when independently of the party they launched their campaign against the Security Treaty.

At the time of the anti-*anpo* campaign, the situation in Japan on the whole was not dark and oppressive as it was at the time of the Red purge. The general atmosphere surrounding us was full of light, and we also felt full of light within ourselves. Our primary motivation was to revive our own humanity. We had been reading Marx's earlier writings and came to realize that our basic problem was self-renewal, for we had been alienated to such an extent under the capitalist system as to become part of the machine, completely losing our humanity.

We feel there is a clear line of demarcation between ourselves and the communists of the prewar days. Their primary motivation was the spirit of martyrdom. They said they were sacrificing themselves for the sake of the proletariat. In contrast, emancipation of ourselves as human beings has become our primary concern since the time of the anti-*anpo* campaign.[6]

Shima, Kitakōji, Shimizu, Kuroha, and N were first subjected to the system of education based on the Emperor cult and then later exposed to the postwar educational pattern based on the Constitution of 1947. G is the only one of the six leaders who received his education entirely in the postwar era. We have characterized education before the defeat as predominantly a negative affect type of socialization in which fear, terror, humiliation, and contempt are emphasized. Postwar education based on the new Constitution, in contrast, is predominantly a positive affect type of socialization in which joy, excitement, and interest in new things are encouraged. Thus the first five leaders have been exposed to two different types of socialization at school, whereas the last one knows only one type.

[6] From the author's interview with Shima on July 29, 1962.

The five who have been exposed to contrasting kinds of socialization have reacted differently to the earlier kind. Kitakōji and Shimizu accepted wholeheartedly, at least until the end of the war, the previous type of socialization, whereas Kuroha was ambivalent in his attitude toward it, and N and Shima rejected it. All six leaders accepted the positive affect type of socialization once they were exposed to it. The predominance of positive affective postures developed through preuniversity education was a prominent feature of the leaders of the student movement in early 1960, in marked contrast to the prewar communist leaders, whose affective postures were predominantly negative.

2. PROLIFERATION OF INDEPENDENT MARXIST GROUPS: IDEOLOGICAL POSTURES

The National Committee of the Revolutionary Communist League

Kitakōji explains the basic program of his organization:

We are opposed to the imperialism of both West and East. In other words, we are against the imperialism of any country, including the United States, Japan, and Soviet Russia, and at the same time we stand against the Stalinist type of dictatorship within the Communist Party of any country.

We have criticisms of the present system in Soviet Russia. According to our observations, the Russians are strengthening the capitalist structure of wages, prices, and the money economy, instead of abolishing it as they should if they seriously aim at the realization of a socialist, and eventually a communist, society. At the moment Soviet Russia is not a socialist country, but rather a distorted form of a transitional society, where the workers' initiatives are dulled within a mass society. The Soviets are not able at present to provide the revolutionary ethos to the workers of other countries.

We are opposed to nuclear tests by any country, including those by both the United States and the Soviet Union. It is our aim to spread our movement among our own Japanese people against nuclear tests by all countries and also to work for cooperation with people in similar movements in every country. The organization of an international antiwar league is one of our major goals.[7]

[7] From the author's interview with Kitakōji.

Takeo Shimizu distinguishes his group from the Communist Party of Japan:

> We feel strongly that materialism without a proper emphasis on humanity cannot claim to be Marxism. For that reason the Communist Party of Japan does not represent Marxism in Japan. It represents only the distorted version of Marxism held by Stalin and his followers. Curiously enough, it is outside of the Communist Party that theoretical works designed to recover the original meaning of Marxism are being produced. Katsumi Umemoto [1912-], Akihide Kakehashi [1902-], and Hirokazu Kuroda [1927-][8] are philosophers who are not affiliated with the Communist Party but have been working vigorously to give a humanist orientation to Marxism.
>
> It is the basic aim of our organization to reconsider and reconstruct Marxism by studying Marx's own writings from the very beginning of the formulation of his ideas. Trotsky's writings are very helpful in this search for a reconstructed Marxism. However, we feel that Trotsky failed because he did not form his own organization among the workers. Without organizing the workers, we cannot possibly achieve our political goal, even if we base our political goal on the *right* philosophical foundations. That is why we are attempting to form a new party.
>
> Among the student movements there are many factions, because we differ on theoretical points. The more theoretical controversies we have, the better I think. Since students do not constitute a class, it is natural that we should hold different theories and opinions and thus form different factions. However, we do try our best to acquire as large a following as possible.[9]

[8] Hirokazu Kuroda, usually called by students Kanichi Kuroda, is a blind philosopher who was then the most influential theoretical leader of the Revolutionary Communist League. On account of his illness he left Tokyo Senior High School in 1949 and has since devoted himself to writing. He has published militant critiques of Stalinism in its philosophical aspect and of its strategy of revolution. The following is an abbreviated list of his works: *Hēgeru to Marukusu* (*Hegel and Marx*), Tokyo, Rironsha, 1952; *Keizaigaku to Benshōhō* (*Economics and Dialectics*), Tokyo, Jinseisha, 1956; *Sutārinshugi no Hihan* (*A Critique of Stalinism*), Tokyo, Jinseisha, 1956; *Puroretariateki Ningen no Ronri* (*The Logic of the Proletarian Person*), Saitama, Kobushisha, 1960; *Hyūmanizumu to Marukusushugi* (*Humanism and Marxism*), Saitama, Kobushisha, 1963; *Shihonron igo Hyakunen* (*One Hundred Years After Capital*), Saitama, Kobushisha, 1967; *Gendai Yuibutsuron no Tankyū* (*An Inquiry into Contemporary Materialism*), Saitama, Kobushisha, 1968.

[9] From the author's interview with Shimizu on Sept. 4, 1962.

It is interesting to find the leader of the Revolutionary Communist League, which is considered the most belligerent group of all the factions, encouraging diversity in theoretical approaches to Marxism. Shimizu also asserts, of course, that his group should exert its influence to gain the largest possible following. How does his group attempt to expand its sphere of influence among students? When its members differ on theoretical issues with other factions in the student movement, do they stick to the method of persuasion or do they resort to the use of violence? Kitakōji tries to defend his group's position on the use of interfactional violence:

> We are not basically against the use of violence. Since the existing society is based on violence, we cannot overthrow it without organized violence of the masses. We do make a distinction, however, between the use of violence against the establishment and violence among ourselves. It is better not to have any trouble among ourselves. Nevertheless, when some groups among our movements stick to *mistaken* views, we should exert our utmost influence to win the masses to the *right* side, which is ours. In doing so, occasions may arise when the use of violence cannot be avoided.[10]

Both Kitakōji and Shimizu maintain that they welcome divergent opinions and theories within the student movement. This attitude is logically consistent with their rejection of authoritarian thought control in the Communist Party, against which they fought until they were finally thrown out of the party. To this extent their ideological posture is rational. At the same time, they often use the expressions the "right" and the "mistaken" views. When controversies arise among the Marxists, who decides who is on the "right" side? They try to justify resorting to violence to decide controversial issues, although "right" and "wrong" in the matter may not be verified immediately. In this respect their ideological postures are nonrational. Thus rational and nonrational attitudes coexist within the personalities of Kitakōji and Shimizu without their being aware of any discrepancies. The persistence of nonrational postures within dominantly rational persons, such as these leaders are, may be linked to the intrusion of negative affective postures, the residues of a negative affect type of pre-defeat school education within personalities in which positive affects predominate.

[10] From the author's interview with Kitakōji.

The leaders of this faction are consistently universalistic; they apply the same principle of judgment to every society regardless of its dominant political institution and ideological stand. Both Kitakōji and Shimizu are against nuclear tests by *any* country, including the United States and the Soviet Union, since they maintain that "nuclear tests precipitate trends toward war." They support neither the action of the Soviets in the Hungarian revolt in 1956 nor the United States' involvement in the invasion of Cuba in 1961, because they are against military intervention by any state to suppress revolutionary movements in other countries. They make a clear distinction between people and governments, and, even when they are opposed to the policy of the government of a particular country, they manifest no ill-will toward its people.

This attitude was exemplified at the height of the anti-*anpo* demonstrations, one of whose aims was to stop President Eisenhower's visit to Japan at that particular time, in the freedom allowed American correspondents and individual citizens to walk around and talk with the student demonstrators with complete impunity.[11] During the demonstrations the author had occasion to arrange for an American newspaperman to meet leaders and rank-and-file students at the Komaba branch of Tokyo University. The classroom where we met was packed with students, who talked with the American openly and most enthusiastically. The absence of xenophobia is a distinguishing mark of those postwar student activists who are not affiliated with the Communist Party.

The Structural Reformists

G claims that his group is the most "modernized" of all the factions, because it emphasizes the defense of constitutional rights as the effective means of changing the existing system. Kuroha gives a fuller account of his group's ideological stance:

Since I entered the National University of Education, I have been reading Marxist literature as widely as possible, from Trotsky on the extreme left to Bernstein on the extreme right; in doing so, I came across Togliatti's works, which I read in both Japanese and in the original Italian texts. Through

---

[11] Shunsuke Tsurumi, "Nemoto kara no Minshushugi" ("Democracy from the Grass-roots"), *Secchushugi no Tachiba* (*In Defense of Eclecticism*), Tokyo, Chikuma Shobō, 1961, pp. 133-134.

reading Togliatti, my old concept of the relationship between democracy and socialism changed. When I was a member of the Democratic Youth League, we used to be faced with a dilemma concerning our attitude toward the new Constitution. According to the traditional communist approach, we were told to criticize the Constitution for its limitations and biases as a product of the bourgeois class. But we belonged to the generation that had been brought up with this Constitution. For us to deny the values embodied in the Constitution was tantamount to denying our own existence. If we insisted on the traditional communist approach to the Constitution, we had to deprive our own generation not only of its constitutional rights but of the future possibilities guaranteed by those rights. It was Togliatti who helped us out of this dilemma. With his help we can now assert that defense of our constitutional rights is compatible with the structural transformation of the existing society into socialism. This is the first point of departure from the traditional communist party line.

The second point of difference lies in the fact that the Communist Party accepts Marxism as a total, theoretical system. We, on the other hand, try to test Marxian theories with reference to our own experiences in participating in various campaigns, such as the fight against the expansion of the military base in Sunagawa and the anti-*anpo* struggle. We take Marxian theories as propositions whose effectiveness should be tested in the actually changing situations in which we live.

The third point of distinction between us and the Communist Party concerns the concept of the dictatorship of the proletariat. According to the Communist Party, it means one-party rule. We do not insist on one-party rule, however. We feel that, by insisting on the hegemony of the one and only party, some strata of the workers might be alienated from participation in government. It is up to them to decide whether they should have one-party rule or should form multiple parties.

The fourth point of distinction pertains to the problem of violence. We have learned from Gramsci that there are two different means to establish control. The one is coercion and the other is persuasion. In order to persuade, one has to use education and propaganda. At the time of Lenin, since the czarist power was based upon coercive force, one had no other choice but to use violence in order to overthrow that coercive mechanism of control. In a society where capitalism is highly developed, however, the proletariat are controlled through the government's manipulation of their consensus. Is violence an effective means of shifting their consensus to our side? Suppose we wish to work on the workers in an ammunition factory. We cannot depend on violence, but we should attempt to win them over to our side.

Fifth, although we have learned from both Togliatti and Gramsci, we do not worship their teachings as immutable dogmas.[12]

Of the leaders of the three factions, the Structural Reformists are the most consistently rational in their ideological postures. They maintain that theories should be tested with reference to the everyday experience of the people, and they consistently reject resort to violence as a means of resolving differences of opinion and judgment, stressing instead the importance of persuasion and the exercise of constitutional rights.

The leaders of this group are critical of the policy of the Central Committee of the Communist Party of Japan and are striving to become independent of the party. Yet they are dependent on the exogenous version of Marxism developed by the Italian communist leaders, such as Togliatti and Gramsci. Thus their ideological postures are partly independent and partly dependent.

The Socialist Student League—the Secretariat Faction

N tries to define the essential ideological postures of the Bund and to show how those postures have been partially transmitted to the Socialist Student League. He uses three key words: "alienation," "existence," and "experiment."

> When we formed the Bund, we were interested essentially in making an *experiment* in *a Japanese style* of communism. Owing to the advent of the political crisis [over the ratification of the revised Japanese-American Security Treaty], we could not afford the time for experiment. Thus the original members of the Bund, like myself, who were primarily interested in social experiment had to step aside from the main current of the movement. Finally, we were forced by the

12 From the author's interview with Kuroha on July 25, 1962.

exigencies of circumstances to take an active part in the demonstrations.[13]

Exactly what was the experiment on which they embarked? Instead of explaining it directly, N gives a brief account of the history of the concepts "existence" and "alienation." The word "existence" was imported to Japan around 1948 with the introduction of French existentialism. But the word did not catch fire among students until the Sixth National Party Conference, where the announcement of a sudden change in Communist Party policy shocked the student members of the party. This unexpected move was followed by a series of purges of students from the party ranks. Being thus torn away from the party organizations that had enveloped them, the expelled students felt themselves naked, so to speak, vis-à-vis their own *existence*. In this way the exogenous concept acquired experiential significance for them. In 1956 they sympathized with the Hungarian workers, whose revolt against the authoritarian rule of the party was put down by the Soviet army. At this stage the students were very enthusiastic about Sartre's existentialism.

When the Bund was formed, they began to talk about the concept of "alienation" and were attracted to Marx's earlier writings on this subject. The concept of alienation was especially congenial to the student activists who had been purged from the party, since they could interpret their experience as a specific form of "alienation" and thus tie it to the more general meaning of the concept—man's loss of his humanity in a class society.

Thus, according to N, the students' interests in these two words, "existence" and "alienation," have a common source in their experiences of being estranged from what they had previously cherished. An "alienated" person is able to look face-to-face at his own "existence." N maintains that the aim of the Socialist Student League is to probe into the question: "What does existence mean for students?" How is this inquiry connected with "an experiment in a Japanese-style communism," which was the initial target of the Bund?

Shima's comment throws light on this point:

> The Bund was a revolutionary movement that was launched by people who had a sense of alienation and whose goal was to overcome that feeling.

[13] From the author's interview with N on July 10, 1962.

Its prewar counterpart may be found in the orthodox right-ist movement led by Ikki Kita.[14] It is probably important for us to study how Kita formed his theory of Japan's reform. The contrast between the prewar rightist reformist movement and the Bund is that the latter was a movement launched within a social milieu full of a vital and exuberant spirit, whereas the former grew out of the most critical and the darkest period in our recent history.

There is always something of the Bund in our movement that cannot be precisely defined by stereotyped words. Expressions like "antiimperialist struggle" or "fight against monopoly capitalism" characterize our movement only partially.[15]

How are the early spirit and aims of the Bund appropriated by the Socialist Student League? We shall quote from a leaflet issued by the Secretariat office on Christmas Eve of 1961. It appeals to students to join a study group on the Constitution and explains the Secretariat's basic purposes in organizing the group.

We believe that people, through studying the Constitution, will eventually formulate their own theory of revolution in a "Japanese style." In the process of formulating our own theory, we can learn from Ikki Kita, the only true revolutionary in Japan and a Japanese-style fascist, who was executed on account of his involvement in the February 26th incident. It was through the rigorous examination of the essence of the Meiji Constitution [of 1889] that he managed to build up his original theory of revolution. A formulation of our own theory of revolution through studying the Constitution of 1947, as Kita formulated his theory by examining the Con-

[14] Ikki Kita (1883-1937) was the most important ideological leader of the young officers' uprising on February 26, 1936. His work *Nihon Kaizō Hōan Taikō* (*An Outline Plan for the Reorganization of Japan*) became a bible for the rebels. He participated in the Chinese revolution of 1911 and learned from that experience how deeply rooted indigenous nationalism was in the minds of the people. He came to the conviction that, without full use of this indigenous nationalist feeling, it is impossible to achieve a revolution in the society. See "Kita Ikki and the Reform Wing of Ultranationalism," in *Sources of Japanese Tradition*, ed. William T. DeBary et al., New York, Columbia University Press, 1958, II, 266-277. See also Osamu Kuno and Shunsuke Tsurumi, *Gendai Nihon no Shisō* (*Contemporary Japanese Thought*), Tokyo, Iwanami, 1956, pp. 118-182; Sōgorō Tanaka, *Kita Ikki*, Tokyo, Miraisha, 1959.

[15] From the author's interview with Shima.

stitution of 1889, will provide the only theory of revolution that can serve as an effective and practical guide to our political movements. "The Theory of a Democratic-Independent Revolution" [advocated by the Communist Party], "the Theory of a Socialist Revolution through Democratic Structural Reforms" [proposed by the Structural Reformists], and "the Theory of an Anti-Imperialist Anti-Stalinist Proletarian Revolution" [as upheld by the Revolutionary Communist League —the National Committee] cannot claim to be as effective and practical as our theory would be.

. . . To this study group on the Constitution we welcome everybody, including rightists and supporters of the Liberal-Democratic Party, with the hope of developing it into a most pleasant bull session. . . .

Finally, we wish to clarify our attitude toward nuclear tests by the United States and Soviet Russia. . . .

. . . It is a matter of course that we are against nuclear tests by any imperialist nation. But we should emphasize that we are opposed unconditionally to the nuclear tests by a Soviet government which audaciously claims to rule "a socialist nation."

To see the rationale for protest against nuclear tests, we need not begin with any broad analysis of the present world situation. Instead, it is the sense of the threat of death that all of us feel in our everyday lives that provides the starting point for our protest movement. And this protest movement against nuclear tests by any country will develop into a fight against the imperialist government of our own country and into a still larger movement for the eventual abolition of national sovereignties throughout the world.[16]

The leaders of the Secretariat faction of the Socialist Student League are predominantly rational, for they do not hold Marxism as totally and absolutely true but encourage an eclectic approach to theory. Moreover, they are predominantly open in that they welcome communication with people of different ideologies, including rightists and conservatives. As a group, however, the Secretariat faction of the Socialist Student League is not as consistently rational as the Structural Reformist faction, because nonrational elements are also allowed to exist within the

[16] This four-page leaflet is signed by Hiroshi Tonami of the Secretariat faction of the Socialist Student League.

group. The coexistence of heterogeneous ideologies and affects is the essential characteristic of this group.

Both the leaders and the rank-and-file members of this group are predominantly independent in two senses. First, they stress the importance of the individual as the locus of feeling and judgment, as shown in their attitude toward the antinuclear test campaign. Second, they do not take any existing interpretation of Marxism as the authoritative version, as the Revolutionary Communist League does with Kuroda's interpretation of Marxism and as the Structural Reformists do with Togliatti's version of Marxism. The Secretariat faction of the Student Social League is probably the most independent, not only from the official Communist Party interpretation of Marxism but from any other existing versions of Marxism.

The leaders of this group are unique among the leaders of the different factions of the student movement in recognizing the importance of learning from the past experiences of revolutionary movements in Japan. In Section 5 of Chapter I, where we examined ideological conversion among communist intellectuals of the 1930's, we pointed out that their vital failure to make their revolutionary ideology effective in the Japanese situation was due partly to their rashness in applying the exogenous ideology which they held to be absolute, without sufficient attention to the indigenous patterns of ideas and feelings of the people. Thus they were alienated from the people for whom they had allegedly been working. This attitude we have called "above-the-people universalism." It is to the avoidance of this shortcoming of the prewar communist intellectuals that the leaders of the Student Socialist League have addressed themselves most vigorously, in comparison to the leaders of the other factions. The leaders of the Student Socialist League, as we have quoted them, suggest that they study the case of Ikki Kita, who attempted to combine the theory of revolution with the cult of the Emperor. Some leaders, like N, also propose to reconsider the works of Kunio Yanagida, the pioneering scholar who established the science of folklore in Japan. It is characteristic of the leaders of this group to stress the importance of learning from the works of non-Marxist and indigenous Japanese thinkers, rather than limiting themselves to learning from Marxist thinkers in Japan or from Marxist and non-Marxist thinkers abroad. By so doing, they strive to match universalism with the peoples' indigenous ways of feeling and thinking. This attitude we may call "to-the-people universalism," in contrast to above-the-people universalism.

We may conclude that the leaders of the Socialist Student League are just as rational as the leaders of the Structural Reformists and just as universalistic as the leaders of the Revolutionary Communist League. They are distinguished from the leaders of other factions by their emphasis on open communication within and without their own group and by their endeavor to maintain independence of thinking from any established ideologies, Marxist and non-Marxist alike.

The coexistence of heterogeneous and often conflicting ideas and ideologies within this group has both functional and dysfunctional aspects from the point of view of the leaders. It is functional in the sense that they might be able to achieve some new patterns of theoretical integration of now conflicting ideologies, both indigenous and exogenous. But that process of integration would require a considerable length of time. On the other hand, it is dysfunctional insofar as the very existence of the multiplicity of ideas and ideologies within the group tends to make the group antagonistic rather than solidary. Such a group is not likely to persist long enough for both its leaders and its members to achieve the attempted theoretical integration.

3. GENERALIZATIONS AND HYPOTHESES

How far do the postwar student leaders diverge in their ideological postures from the prewar communists in Japan? The samples chosen for the intensive analysis made above are too small to serve as a basis for a definitive conclusion. Nevertheless, we may still make a tentative comparison between the prewar communists and the postwar Marxist student leaders with respect to their ideological postures.

To begin with, both the prewar communists and the postwar student leaders claim to be Marxists, although their ideological postures differ even among themselves. Thus we can assert that the same ideology—in this case, Marxism—is being held by different persons with different ideological postures. For instance, there are both rational and nonrational, universalistic and particularistic, open and secret, and independent and dependent approaches to Marxism. This observation leads us to suspect that a specific ideological posture is not intrinsic to any particular ideology.

Furthermore, the sources of variation of ideological postures associated with a specific ideology may be manifold. As far as our study goes, we can point out three major sources of variation. The first probable source is the type of affect development which individuals evolve during their socialization throughout their life cycles. The second probable source of variation lies in the divergent structures of relationships within the groups that support similar ideologies. The third possible source of variation in ideological postures, especially of the leaders of a movement, is to be found in the levels of participation by the grass-roots members of the group in the activities advocated by the leaders.

However much they differ among themselves, the postwar student leaders on the whole are more rational, to-the-people universalistic, open, and independent than the prewar communists. There is no doubt that the level of participation in protest movements on the part of ordinary citizens is much higher in the postwar period than in the 1930's, when practically all the mass protest movements were under severe suppression. The predominantly nonrational, above-the-people universalistic, secret, and dependent ideological postures of the postwar communist leaders can be partially related to the very low level of participation on the part of working-class people in the protest movements sponsored by communist leaders.

On the basis of these observations about the sources of variation in the ideological postures of the student leaders, we can make some predictions about the future types of leadership in the student movements in Japan.

In the first place, to the extent that national educational policy from the primary school to the university level reverts to emphasis on a negative affect type of socialization, as in prewar Japan, it is likely that negative affects will predominate in the personalities of the emergent leaders of the student movements and that their ideological postures will become more nonrational, above-the-people universalistic, secret, and dependent. Conversely, to the extent that positive affect types of socialization at any level of schooling are promoted, positive affects will predominate in the personalities of the emergent leaders, and rational, to-the-people universalistic, open, and independent ideological postures will be developed among them.

The cumulation of positive or negative affects within a personality is also likely to be influenced by the types of experience a person encounters. If, for instance, police suppression of protest movements is intensified and terror used, as in the 1930's, one may expect that negative affects will predominate in the personalities of the student leaders, whose ideological postures will then become predominantly nonrational, above-the-people universalistic, secret, and dependent. Should that come about, the use of violence would almost certainly be promoted.

In the second place, if the student leaders succeed in engaging students in general in the activities of the student governments at every university, as well as on the national level, they are likely to maintain and develop rational, to-the-people universalistic, open, and independent ideological postures. If, however, they fail to solicit wide support from their fellow students in their activities, they will probably seek to fortify themselves with nonrational, above-the-people universalistic, secret, and dependent ideological postures. The more alienated the leaders are from the ordinary members of their groups, the more nonrational they are likely to be.

Success or failure in cultivating more rational, universalistic, open, and independent approaches to Marxism seems to hinge partly on the type of preuniversity and university education that is available. It also depends on the ability of the student leaders themselves to renovate the structure of relationships within their groups and also to overcome the apathy now prevalent among the student masses.

Personality and Society: A Critical Review of Current and Classical Views

1. PREOCCUPATION WITH CHILDHOOD SOCIALIZATION IN CURRENT THEORY

Talcott Parsons analyzes the learning process of a neonate in "the first few weeks," in which supposedly "the infant . . . comes to be integrated into a social system,"[1] and proceeds to make this process the model of the interaction patterns of adult persons.

> An established state of a social system is a process of complementary interaction of two or more individual actors in which each conforms with the expectations of the other(s) in such a way that alter's reaction to ego's action are positive sanctions which serve to reinforce his given need-dispositions and thus to fulfill his given expectations. This stabilized or equilibrated interaction process is the fundamental point of reference for all dynamic motivational analysis of social process.[2]

[1] Talcott Parsons, "Social Structure and the Development of Personality: Freud's Contribution to the Integration of Psychology and Sociology," in *Personality and Social Systems*, eds. Neil J. Smelser and William T. Smelser, New York, John Wiley and Sons, 1963, p. 38.

[2] Talcott Parsons, *The Social System*, Glencoe, Ill., The Free Press, 1951, p. 204. There is a terminological difficulty. As pointed out by Levy in his seminar on "Social Systems" given in the fall of 1963 at Princeton University, the term "complementarity" is borrowed from the quantum theory of physics. According to quantum physics, the structure of matter has been discovered to have two distinctly different aspects, namely, the aspect of being particles and that of being waves. In order to observe either of the aspects, the observer's intervention with some measuring apparatus is necessary. But the wave aspect and the particle aspect cannot be observed at the same time with precision. The incompatibility of simultaneous measurement with precision applies also to the position and velocity of an electron at a given time. The concept of complementarity in quantum physics designates the two aspects of the same element which cannot be observed simultaneously with precision. Parsons borrows this term from physics to indicate a set of two actors whose roles are not identical but who nevertheless interact in such a way as to conform mutually to each other's expectations and thus to gratify mutually each other's need-dispositions. Alvin Gouldner points out that Parsons uses the term "complementarity" as though it were synonymous with "reciprocity," which means "a mutually contingent exchange of equal benefits"; this usage he thinks misleading, since "complementarity" means "exchange of unequal benefits." In the original meaning

Parsons's attempt to generalize from the basic pattern of inter-action between an infant and its mother leads to some limita-tions in his theory as a tool of analysis for both personality and society.

According to Parsons, the process of the ego and alter con-forming mutually to the expectations of each other for the mutual gratification of need-dispositions is the basic model of all the human interaction within a social system. This is called by his critics an "equilibrium model" or a "consensus model." Is this model adequate for the analysis of socialization in adulthood?

Parsons demonstrates his keen awareness of the role of affects in socialization.[3] His model, however, emphasizes the function of positive affects only and does not take into account the role which negative affects such as shame, fear, hatred, and anger play in socialization. Negative affects are implanted just as often as positive affects in the course of both adult and childhood socialization.

The critics of the "consensus model" argue that a "dissensus model" or a "conflict model" is more fundamental and that the latter should replace the former.[4] There are also critics like Ralf Dahrendorf who, while maintaining the primacy of a conflict model, propose to use both models for more adequate explana-tions.[5]

How do the two models, consensus and conflict, contribute to the study of socialization? Even in childhood, as soon as an individual is exposed to extra-familial influences such as peer groups, schools, television, and radio, he cannot always expect others to conform to his expectations. The greater part of his relationships at home may continue to be gratifying, but, still,

---

of "complementarity" in quantum physics, the focus is not upon the inter-action between the two aspects of a unit but upon the incompatibility of observation of the two aspects, which, in spite of their incompatibility, belong to the same unit. For discussions of the concept of complementarity in quantum physics, see Albert Einstein and Leopold Infeld, *The Evolution of Physics*, New York, Simon and Schuster, 1961, p. 279; Ernest Nagel, *The Structure of Science*, New York, Harcourt, Brace and World, 1961, pp. 294-295. For a sociologist's discussion of the concepts of complementarity and reciprocity, see Alvin W. Gouldner, "The Norm of Reciprocity: A Pre-liminary Statement," *American Sociological Review*, xxv, April 1960, 164.

[3] Talcott Parsons and Robert F. Bales, *Family, Socialization and Inter-action Process*, Glencoe, Ill., The Free Press, 1955, p. 304.

[4] Lewis A. Coser, "Social Conflict and the Theory of Social Change," *British Journal of Sociology*, viii, Sept. 1956, 198-203.

[5] Ralf Dahrendorf, "Out of Utopia: Toward a Reorientation of Socio-logical Analysis," *American Journal of Sociology*, lxiv, Sept. 1958, 127.

his interactions outside of the family may give rise to conflicts which may eventually react upon his way of relating to others at home. In adulthood the husband-wife and the parent-child relationships may be gratifying; nevertheless, strains may occur in the husband's relations with his boss at his place of work, and this friction may have an effect upon his family relationships, and vice versa. In childhood, and even more in adulthood, individuals are faced with both consensus-generating and conflict-evoking relationships with others. And it can be assumed that a conflict-evoking relationship is just as effective as a consensus-generating relationship in influencing the individual's attitudes and values. The use of more than one model of the basic pattern of interaction has proved to be more heuristic than the application of only one. A good example is E. R. Leach's *The Political System of Highland Burma*. This study describes "the structure of a system that is not in equilibrium," and his "method of demonstration has involved trying to display two or three different ideal systems at one and the same time." These are the Gumsa system based upon hereditary aristocracy and the Gumlao system which repudiates "all notions of hereditary class difference."[6] The persuasiveness of work such as Leach's demonstrates the soundness of using more than one model of interaction for empirical research.

Theoretical limitations due to the preoccupation with childhood socialization also hamper analysis of the relationship between social systems and personality development. According to Parsons, "throughout the course of personality development, identification, object-choice, and internalization are processes of relating the individual to and integrating him in the social system, and, through it, the culture."[7] He further maintains:

> . . . though personalities differ greatly in their degrees of rigidity, certain broad fundamental patterns of "character" are laid down in childhood . . . and are not radically changed by adult experience. . . . it is the internalization of the value-orientation patterns embodied in the role-expectations for ego of the significant socializing agents, which *constitutes the strategic element of this basic personality structure.* And it is because these patterns can only be acquired through the

[6] E. R. Leach, *Political Systems of Highland Burma*, Cambridge, Harvard University Press, 1954, pp. 198, 283.
[7] Parsons, "Social Structure and the Development of Personality," p. 52.

mechanism of identification, and because the basic identification patterns are developed in childhood, that the childhood structure of personality in this respect is so stable and unchangeable.[8]

The major assumptions involved are, first, that the child, through the processes of identification and internalization, takes into himself the basic norms and value orientations of the society into which he is born and, second, that the results of childhood socialization are so potent that they can hardly be changed by his later experiences, especially in the realm of value orientation. These assumptions are shared by the "basic personality" school of social psychologists and anthropologists like Abram Kardiner, Ralph Linton, Geoffrey Gore, Margaret Mead, and Ruth Benedict.

The idea of "basic personality" was first conceptualized by Linton and Kardiner.[9] According to this view, if one investigates the child-rearing habits of a society, one can tell the personality structure of the majority of the population not only for a generation but from generation to generation, assuming that similar child care persists.[10] The theorists of "basic personality" are also identified as the "personality and culture" school. Parsons cannot be classified as one of them, since he distinguishes himself from them on a point crucial to his general theory: "To a point the position taken by the personality and culture school is . . . correct. But it is not the 'culture' in the most general sense, but the circumstantially detailed role structure of the social system which is the focus of personality structure and its development."[11] In spite of this difference, Parsons shares with these theorists their major postulates about the effect of childhood socialization.

The critics of the "basic personality" school attack it on two major points. The first concerns the unchangeability of the results of childhood socialization. Lindesmith and Strauss comment that "the effects of infant experience are undemonstrated." They further state:

> The idea that basic personality patterns are established in the first couple of years of life or in pre-adolescent childhood

[8] Parsons, *The Social System*, pp. 227-228. Italics in the original.

[9] Abram Kardiner, *The Psychological Frontier of Society*, New York, Columbia University Press, 1945, pp. viii-ix.

[10] Geoffrey Gore, "The Concept of National Character," in *Science News*, ed. J. L. Crammer, 1950, pp. 105-122.

[11] Talcott Parsons, "Malinowski and the Theory of Social Systems," *Man and Culture: Bronislaw Malinowski*, ed. R. Firth, New York, Harper and Row, 1957, p. 68.

involves the assumption that personality does not change, or changes only in minor ways, in response to later experiences and cultural influences. . . . It may be pointed out that if personality is conceived as a system of responses arising in a cultural matrix, the individual lives his entire life within such a matrix and is never independent of it. Why, then, unless one assumes that learning and the organization of responses takes place only in childhood, should later experiences be largely ruled out?[12]

Gordon Allport warns that "basic personality is a misleading conception unless we keep in mind the variability always present in real culture and in child-training."[13] Tamotsu Shibutani bases his criticism upon empirical data and supports the view that personality *does* change after childhood and may change drastically depending upon the circumstances.[14] He specifically points out the effects of "dramatic experience, especially if it is traumatic," and shows how different social settings release "previously suppressed impulses" to permit possible drastic changes in personality.[15]

The second point of objection concerns the relationship between personality and social systems. Anthony Wallace criticizes the "basic personality" approach as the conception of "the replication of uniformity." Instead of looking at personality as a little replica of society, he proposes to conceive of society as "the organization of diversity." He maintains that "a diversity of habits, of motives, of personalities, of customs" coexists within the boundaries of any organized society.[16] Alfred Baldwin, after a careful examination of Parsons's theory of personality, concludes that "a basic difficulty" stems from "a rigid insistence upon *isomorphism between one personality system and the social system.*"[17]

[12] Alfred R. L. Lindesmith and Anselm L. Strauss, "A Critique of Culture-Personality Writings," *American Sociological Review*, xv, Oct. 1950, 596-598.

[13] Gordon W. Allport, *Pattern and Growth in Personality*, New York, Holt, Rinehart and Winston, 1961, pp. 172, 295.

[14] Tamotsu Shibutani, *Society and Personality*, Englewood Cliffs, N.J., Prentice-Hall, 1961, p. 543.

[15] *Ibid.*, pp. 523-524.

[16] Anthony F. C. Wallace, *Culture and Personality*, New York, Random House, 1963, p. 26.

[17] Alfred L. Baldwin, "The Parsonian Theory of Personality," in *The Social Theories of Talcott Parsons*, ed. Max Black, Englewood Cliffs, N.J., Prentice-Hall, The Free Press, 1955, p. 190. Italics in the original.

The Parsonian theory of personality and society distinguishes two sources of possible change. On the personality side there is "deviant behavior" (defined as unsocialized or undersocialized) and, on the social system side, alterations in its role structure. According to this view, if the role structure of a society changes, changes in personality structure will follow. This is an empirically fruitful hypothesis, and it is to Parsons and his associates that we owe the role theory of personality.[18] On the other hand, given the Parsonian concept of personality, it is difficult to classify the individuals with nonconformist "creative intelligence," upon which John Dewey places much importance, except for categorizing them as deviants. Deviance implies "a right way or a standard" with which it is contrasted. Hence, it has a moral overtone. It is one of the major difficulties of the Parsonian concept of personality that it makes creativity appear almost criminal.

Dennis Wrong makes a potent criticism by questioning the basic postulate of the conformist theory of human nature:

> The same may be said of the assumption that people seek to maximize favorable evaluations by others; indeed this assumption has already fathered such additional concepts as "reference group" and "circle of significant others." Yet the question must be raised as to whether we really wish to, in effect, define sociology by such partial perspectives. The assumption of the maximization of approval from others is the psychological complement to the sociological assumption of a general value consensus. And the former is as selective and one-sided a way of looking at motivation as Dahrendorf and others have argued the latter to be when it determines our way of looking at social structure. The oversocialized view of man of the one is a counterpart to the overintegrated view of society of the other.[19]

[18] "A role-learning approach to personality development . . . would view personality as composed of learned roles, and role components, rather than of general traits descriptive of behavior across situations. . . . the learned repertoire of roles is the personality." Orville G. Brim, Jr., "Personality Development as Role-Learning," in *Personality Development in Children,* ed. Ira Iscoe and Harold W. Stevenson, Austin, University of Texas Press, 1960, pp. 133, 141.

[19] Dennis H. Wrong, "The Oversocialized Conception of Man in Modern Sociology," in *Personality and Social Systems,* p. 76.

2. Some Current Hypotheses on Adult Socialization

Recently there has emerged some interest in adult socialization, and efforts have been made to formulate general theories which encompass both childhood and adult socialization. Irving Rosow defines adult socialization as

> ... the process of inculcating new values and behavior appropriate to adult positions and group memberships. These changes are internalized, usually in the course of induction and indoctrination procedures. They are attended by the development of new self-images and new orientations, expectations, skills and norms, both as the person views himself and others view him. Thus, there are both external and internal changes of behavior, cognition, affect and even personality elements (as in self-conception). The prototype of adult socialization appears in status successions and new group memberships. Thereby, new standards and conformity to them are presumably built into the person so that he is significantly altered as a social being.[20]

The learning of specific roles, as Parsons defines socialization, involves both values and behavior. And Rosow's definition is similar to Parsons's. Orville Brim assesses the relative weight of "value and behavior":

> With respect to changes during the life cycle, the emphasis in socialization moves from motivation to ability and knowledge, and from a concern with values to a concern with behavior. ...
>
> In general, the socialization after childhood deals primarily with the overt behavior of the role and makes little attempt to influence motivation of a fundamental kind, or to influence basic values.[21]

Rosow makes the same point. According to him, there are four referents of socialization in general: "(1) culture and personality, (2) basic social values, (3) group membership, (4) social roles." The first two referents are more pertinent to childhood

[20] Irving Rosow, "Forms and Functions of Adult Socialization" (ms), Russell Sage Foundation, Socialization Conference, May 17-19, 1963, p. 1.
[21] Orville G. Brim, Jr., "Socialization through the Life Cycle," in Orville G. Brim, Jr., and Stanton Wheeler, *Socialization after Childhood: Two Essays*, New York, John Wiley and Sons, 1966, pp. 26-27.

socialization, while the latter two are more pertinent to adult socialization.

Normally by the time of adolescence, his basic cultural personality is established and he has a pretty clear idea of social reality, of what is worthwhile and worthless, of what scarcities have social utility, of the principles which govern the distribution of property, power and prestige, of what constitutes the good life. . . . It is most unusual for discontinuities in adulthood to reverse drastically the cultural personality and basic values established earlier. . . . Of the four referents, modal personality is the least relevant to adult socialization while basic values are slightly more so.[22]

If we follow these arguments, it seems to be very difficult to see adult socialization as an instrument in effectuating changes in a person's basic values. For example, it is one thing to acquire the values and behavior proper to old age, in which one has to live alone separated from one's married children, when that kind of old-age role was fully anticipated from early life. And it is another thing entirely to have to adjust to such circumstances in middle age if one has been living solely for the sake of one's children, taking it for granted that rearing children is a good investment as an old-age pension. In the latter case the individual is affected by a change in the basic value-orientation pattern of society, whereas in the former case he is not; in both instances the individual faces the need to change roles as he grows old. Any theory of socialization that fails to account for the latter type of change and focuses only on the former type cannot assist the analysis of societies undergoing basic changes in value orientation.

In spite of such shortcomings as these, the role theory of personality developed by Parsons, Orville Brim, William Goode, and others has produced some hypotheses applicable to adult socialization. Brim states that "the learned repertoire of roles is the personality" and that the self consists of many selves, each one of which conforms to the role expectations of an individual's various reference groups.[23] Goode develops the role concept of personality into "a theory of role strain." An adult individual occupies specific positions in a variety of reference groups, such

[22] Rosow, "Forms and Functions of Adult Socialization, pp. 2-3.
[23] Brim, "Personality Development as Role-Learning," p. 141.

as his place of work, his family, club, neighborhood, and political party. Each position prescribes for him a different role. The roles multiply as the individual's affiliation with reference groups expands. They often demand conflicting obligations and place the individual under great strains. He tries to reduce these strains with various mechanisms, such as "compartmentalization" (defined by Goode as "the ability to ignore the problem of consistency"), "delegation" of some roles to others, the "elimination" of some roles, and "extension." The individual may even expand his role relations in order to make that an excuse for not fulfilling certain other obligations. The ways in which individuals manage their role strains result in some rearrangement of society's role structures; this management in turn changes some segments of the society.[24]

Goode further develops the idea of the personality as the agent of "role-bargaining" to solve role strains. He uses this concept to account specifically for the changes in family patterns in various countries under the impact of industrialization and urbanization.[25] He considers the family to be "the role budget center for adult or child," since "family members are often the only persons who are likely to know how an individual is allocating his *total* role energies, managing his whole role system." This description does not necessarily apply to Japanese experience, however, for in Japan frequently husbands are not expected to account to their wives "for what they spend in time, energy and money outside of the family."[26] Some agrarian women even lose track of their husbands who temporarily or permanently leave their villages to work in cities and towns as migrants. Yet even though this view of personality as the agent of role bargaining assumes an intimacy not always present in Japan, it is still a fruitful hypothesis for the analysis of the process of Japanese adult socialization.

Goode begins with a role theory of personality similar to Parsons's but arrives at a more positive concept: he finds personality to be the agent of reorganization of the social structure. It is interesting to note that Goode's concept of "bargaining" originates in Parsons's interpretation of Marx: "starting as Marx

[24] William J. Goode, "A Theory of Role Strain," *American Sociological Review*, xxv, No. 4 (Aug. 1960), 483-496.

[25] William J. Goode, *World Revolution and Family Patterns*, Glencoe, Ill., The Free Press, 1963.

[26] Goode, "A Theory of Role Strain," p. 493.

did from the element of class conflict, the center of his attention was on bargaining power. Thus in a particular case he reintroduced the factor of differences of power into social thinking, which had been so important in Hobbes' philosophy and so neglected since."[27]

The second set of hypotheses in current theories of adult socialization is concerned with the continuity and discontinuity between childhood and adult personality.

Everett Hagen identifies two types of personality: the authoritarian type, who "perceives the world as an arbitrary place rather than an orderly one amenable to analysis and responsive to his initiative," and the innovative type, who organizes "reality into relationships embodying new mental or aesthetic concepts, the new relationships serving the purpose of the innovator," a process which involves two steps: arriving at a new mental conception, and converting it into action or into material form."[28] Hagen assumes that it is the character of childhood socialization and experience that determines these two different personality types:

> . . . no individual becomes a reformer of his community or society who does not feel both that the institutions of his community or society threaten him deeply and that they can be changed by his efforts: and no individual feels this who did not in childhood feel that institutions which governed him in childhood threatened him, and also that he could and must escape from the childhood threat by changing those institutions through his own efforts.[29]

The assumption of basic personality types suggests that the concept and the fact of changes are built into the personality by specific childhood experiences. According to Erik Erikson and Hagen, it is the authoritarian father or father-surrogate who creates a reformer. Yet, according to Rosow, D'Andrade, Strodtbeck, and Abegglen, the existence of paternal dominance produces low need for achievement, while success in the business world in the United States shows a high correlation with the

[27] Talcott Parsons, *The Structure of Social Action*, Glencoe, Ill., The Free Press, 1937, pp. 109-110.

[28] Everett F. Hagen, *On the Theory of Social Changes: How Economic Growth Begins*, Homewood, Ill., Dorsey, 1962, pp. 86-98.

[29] *Ibid.*, p. 156.

absence of paternal dominance.[30] These two seemingly contra-
dictory hypotheses may be interpreted in such a way as to suggest that domineering fathers tend to make their children non-
conformist and highly motivated to change the existing institutions, whereas the absence of such domineering fathers tends to
make their children conformist and highly motivated to get
ahead on the social ladder. Both hypotheses emphasize the persistence of childhood socialization and experience.

Erikson has made adolescence the important link between
childhood and adulthood in personality development. His analysis of adolescence centers upon the concept of identity. Identity
consists of two basic desires: the desire to retain self-identity,
and the desire to share values with others. Erikson gives four
"varieties of angles" to the concept of identity: (1) "a conscious
sense of individual identity"; (2) "an unconscious striving for
a *continuity of individual identity*"; (3) "a criterion for the silent
doings of *ego synthesis*"; and (4) "a maintenance of an inner
solidarity with a group's ideals and identity."[31] He observes the
development of personality in terms of eight stages, each stage
involving a crisis in the sense that the value attained in the previous stage is tested in confrontation with new experiences and
role obligations appropriate to each succeeding age of man. And
he considers adolescence to be the most crucial period in personality formation because that is the period when the individual
examines what he has been and what he wishes to be.[32] This
view of adolescence as the period of identity crisis is an interesting hypothesis, and Erikson uses it in a most effective manner in
his substantive study *Young Man Luther*.[33] The variety of meanings included in his concepts limits their use in actual analysis
to expert craftsmen.

Robert Lifton puts some of Erikson's concepts and hypotheses
to use in his analysis of Chinese ideological transformations under the Communist regime. His is perhaps the first scholarly
study in English to deal with the transformation of basic social

[30] David C. McClelland, *The Achieving Society*, Princeton, D. Van
Nostrand, 1961, p. 404.
[31] Erik H. Erikson, "The Problem of Ego Identity," *Identity and Anxiety*,
ed. Maurice Stein, Arthur J. Vididi, and David M. White, Glencoe, Ill., The
Free Press, 1960, p. 38.
[32] Erik H. Erikson, *Childhood and Society*, New York, W. W. Norton,
1963, pp. 262-263.
[33] Erik H. Erikson, *Young Man Luther*, New York, W. W. Norton, 1958.

values in adults.[34] Lifton describes the process of change in adult personality in three stages: "confrontation," "reordering," and "renewal." In the final stage of renewal "the new sense of fit—between personal emotions and personally held ideas about the world"—or "a new interplay between identity and ideology" is successfully worked out. In analyzing the process of personality transformation, Lifton tries to show that the success of ideological transformation in China hinges upon the "ideological fit" between Marxism and Confucianism.[35] It should also be added that, if a permanent personality transformation is to occur, the fit must exist not only on the level of ideology but also between affect and ideology. The theory that childhood socialization is definitive and that an individual cannot change his value orientations as an adult does not stand up to empirical test. It can apply only to those societies which have not seen their values undergo basic change.

The third hypothesis that has a relevance to adult socialization and social change is suggested by Alex Inkeles. He stresses the parental role in mediating generational changes: "parents who have experienced extreme social change seek to raise their children differently from the way in which they were brought up, purposefully adapting their child rearing practices to train children better suited to meet life in the changed world as the parent now sees it."[36] This hypothesis is especially pertinent to the analysis of the changing role of mothers in postwar Japan, which is dealt with in detail in Chapter VII.

3. SOME CLASSICAL VIEWS OF PERSONALITY AND SOCIETY CURRENTLY NEGLECTED

Parsons pays tribute to Freud, Durkheim, Cooley, and Mead in formulating his theory of personality and society.[37] But, as Wrong points out, Parsons puts so much emphasis upon superego controls that he leaves out the id in his picture of personality.[38] In a like manner some present-day theorists have been one-

[34] Robert J. Lifton, *Thought Reform and the Psychology of Totalism: A Study of "Brainwashing" in China*, New York, W. W. Norton, 1961, p. 463.

[35] *Ibid.*, p. 391.

[36] Alex Inkeles, "Social Change and Social Character: The Role of Parental Mediation," in *Personality and Social Systems*, p. 359.

[37] Parsons, "Social Structure and the Development of Personality," p. 34.

[38] Wrong, "The Oversocialized Conception of Man in Modern Sociology," p. 72.

sided in their adoption of the views of Durkheim, Mead, and W. I. Thomas.

Durkheim describes childhood socialization as the process of conforming to the existing norms. (See Introduction, n. 1.) In his differentiation between mechanical and organic types of society, Durkheim distinguishes two different relationships between personality and society. ("These two societies really make up only one. They are two *aspects* of one and the same reality, but nonetheless they must be distinguished.")[39] In the first type, personality replicates social values and norms; in the second type, there are varieties of personalities existing within a society, and each personality retains something unique and distinguishable from "the collective consciousness." Durkheim uses both of these conceptions of personality and society and conceives of personality as capable of dynamic change in adulthood. Had he believed in the unalterable character of childhood socialization, he could not have been so zealous an interpreter of Saint-Simon, who was born nearly four decades before the French Revolution and was no doubt socialized under the *ancien régime* to the point of being "weighed down with teachers without having time to reflect on what they were teaching"[40] him, and yet was able in his later years to behold new visions of a highly industrialized society. *Socialism* is a testimony to Durkheim's recognition of the function of conflict in the process of adult socialization. It is to Saint-Simon that Durkheim owes a profound insight into the concept of social change.[41] In the womb of the *ancien régime* and under the authority of the clergy and the nobility were germinated the new forces of "the free commune and exact science." And it was to the clash of those opposing values that Saint-Simon was exposed as a young man—an experience which proved even more potent than the training he received from his parents in conformity to established authority. Current theorists have adopted Durkheim's theory of childhood socialization and have neglected his insights into adult socialization.

Current sociologists have also made extensive use of Mead's concept of "the generalized other." "The generalized other" represents the established values and norms of the society of

[39] Emile Durkheim, *The Division of Labor in Society*, tr. George Simpson, Glencoe, Ill., The Free Press, 1960, pp. 129-130.

[40] Emile Durkheim, *Socialism*, ed. Alvin W. Gouldner, New York, Collier Books, 1962, p. 119.

[41] *Ibid.*, p. 147.

which the individual is a member. It is important to note, however, that what is "internalized," according to Mead, is not exactly the values and norms of the society but "a universe of discourse" or an "internalized conversation." By communicating with others and by coming to understand the connection between a sign and its meanings, as established by convention within a society, the individual comes to converse within himself as though he were conversing with others. In this way Mead formulates his theory of the thinking process. To make a conversation, though, one must address another. Out of this concept of thinking as the process of internalized conversation emerged the concepts of "I" and "me" in the self. "The 'I' is the response of the organism to the attitudes of others which one assumes oneself."[42] In the Parsonian concept of personality there exists a "me," but the "I" is conspicuously absent. Parsons's assertion that "a role-expectation itself may legitimately be called a need-disposition within the personality"[43] identifies the unit of personality with the unit of the social system—that is, a role or a role-expectation —and thus he has virtually denied the possibility of the existence of "I." By denying the existence of "I," the conversant, the meaning of personality as a continuing internalized discourse, which is so crucial in Mead's formulation of the theory of the self, is lost. The implication of this point has some significance since, in Mead's theory, it is exactly this dynamic process of conversation between the "I" and the "me" within one's personality that brings forth novelty.[44]

This process of arriving at the novel is for Mead a capacity with which every individual is endowed. There are differences, of course, in the degrees of achieving the novel. A person who achieves a high degree of the novel Mead calls a leader.[45] Stated in a general propositional way, leaders are characterized as follows: in any society those persons who are most able to absorb the attitudes of others and to give a novel organization to those attitudes become leaders. Mead makes no sharp distinction between the leaders and the led, placing them in the same continuum. It is a matter of the degrees of range and magnitude of influence. Even an unimportant person contributes to changes in

[42] George H. Mead, *Mind, Self and Society*, Chicago, University of Chicago Press, 1940, pp. 154-156.
[43] Talcott Parsons and Edward A. Shils, eds., *Toward a General Theory of Action*, New York, Harper and Row, 1962, p. 115.
[44] Mead, *Mind, Self and Society*, p. 175.
[45] *Ibid.*, p. 216.

the social milieu in his own way. Thus the relationship between the self and society is one of mutual interaction: the person is molded by his social institutions, which he in turn remolds and, in so doing, undergoes further change himself. This idea of a two-way exchange of influence between the individual and society is also present in Cooley's work.[46]

Among the American classical sociologists in the tradition of Mead and Cooley, W. I. Thomas develops the most dynamic theory of the interrelationship between personality and society. The views of Cooley, Mead, Thomas, and Parsons all fall into the general framework of a theory of action which is characterized by Roscoe Hinkle as "voluntaristic nominalism."[47] This designation is intended to direct attention to the individual actor as the locus of action and to the selectivity of the actor in determining means and ends in his course of action. There is, however, a marked difference between Parsons, on the one hand, and Thomas in particular, on the other. In the Parsonian scheme the actor is an analytical point of reference which does not designate any specific individual in the empirical sense,[48] whereas in the sociological theory of Thomas and Znaniecki, just as in the philosophical system of the former's colleague John Dewey, the concept of the individual actor is derived as an empirical generalization from a study of actually living and changing men.[49] Within the general framework of action theory, perhaps Thomas stands in the most marked contrast to Parsons.

The contribution of Thomas to sociological theories centers upon the idea of "four wishes," the concept of "definition of the situation," the "dynamic personality typology" in the process of social change, and the use of human documents in sociological studies. Although the idea of "four wishes" is arbitrary in the sense that it is not verifiable, and is left out by Thomas himself

[46] Charles H. Cooley, *Social Organization*, New York, Schocken Books, 1962, p. 314.

[47] Roscoe C. Hinkle, Jr., and Gisela J. Hinkle, *The Development of Modern Sociology*, New York, Random House, 1954, p. 5.

[48] Edward C. Devereux, Jr., "Parsons' Sociological Theory," in *The Social Theories of Talcott Parsons*, p. 21.

[49] Dewey was chairman of the Department of Philosophy at Chicago University from 1894 to 1905. Thomas taught sociology at the same university from 1894 to 1918. The difference between Parsons's concept of action and Dewey's is pointed out by Lewis Feuer in his review of *The Social Theories of Talcott Parsons*: "Although Parsons describes his general theory as 'pragmatic' in intent . . . and its basic term as 'action,' his theory is clearly devoid of the pragmatic stimulus to social science as Dewey, for instance, described it." *The Journal of Philosophy*, LIX, No. 7 (March 29, 1962), 185.

in his later writings, nevertheless it points to an important issue in the formation of theory about the relationship between personality and society. "The human wishes have a great variety of concrete forms but are capable of the following general classification: desire for new experience, for security, for response, for recognition."[50] Any social theory makes some basic assumptions about what man is or includes some basic presuppositions about "human nature," even if they are not stated in an obvious fashion. Erich Fromm argues for the importance of postulating some fundamental and universal qualities of men, lest comparative studies of societies and personalities dissolve into complete relativism.[51] At this stage in the development of the social sciences, postulates about an essential human nature are not testable. In Parsons's system the basic tendency of man is to conform. This corresponds to the desires for response and for recognition in Thomas's formulation. Desire for new experience, however, is conspicuously absent from Parsons's theory. Levy, on the other hand, in his general theory of comparative social structures, makes the following assumption about universal human nature:

> To some extent individuals can have their preoccupation with other problems alleviated by increased acquisitions of goods and services in general and of new and different goods and services in particular. The appeal of both sorts follows from two exceedingly general aspects of the behavior of human beings wherever they are found. *One is the irreducible interest always found in material goods and services and in being relatively better off in terms of them. The other is the fascination with novelty.* The extent to which the novel is likely to be regarded with fear and suspicion varies widely from the members of one society to the members of another, *but there has never been a society whose members were indifferent to novelty or found it totally lacking in a favorable fascination for them.*[52]

Levy's postulate of a desire to be better off corresponds to Thomas's assumption of a desire for security. And his "fascination with novelty" parallels Thomas's "desire for new experience."

[50] W. I. Thomas, *The Unadjusted Girl*, Boston, Little, Brown, 1923, p. 4.
[51] Erich Fromm, *Escape from Freedom*, New York, Holt, Rinehart and Winston, 1961, pp. 287-289.
[52] Marion J. Levy, Jr., *Modernization and the Structure of Societies*, Princeton, Princeton University Press, 1966, ii, 783.

Thomas has, in addition, introduced an original concept, "definition of the situation," to sociological thinking.

The situation involves three kinds of data: (1) The objective conditions under which the individual or society has to act, that is, the totality of values—economic, social, religious, intellectual, etc.—which at the given moment affect directly or indirectly the conscious state of the individual or the group. (2) The pre-existing attitudes of the individual or the group which at the given moment have an actual influence upon his behavior. (3) The definition of the situation, that is, the more or less clear conception of the conditions and consciousness of the attitudes. And the definition of the situation is a necessary preliminary to any act of the will, for in given conditions and with a given set of attitudes an indefinite plurality of actions is possible, and one definite action can appear only if these conditions are selected, interpreted, and combined in a determined way and if a certain systematization of these attitudes is reached, so that one of them becomes predominant and subordinates the others.[53]

The concept of definition of the situation is employed, together with the concept of the primary group borrowed from Cooley, to explain the process of socialization.

This defining of the situation is begun by the parents in the form of ordering and forbidding and information, is continued in the community by means of gossip, with its praise and blame, and is formally represented by the school, the law, the church.

As process, they [definitions of situations] occur in socialization; individuals learn how to behave properly by having situations defined for them. As product, definitions are embodied in social codes, the norms of behavior.[54]

Thomas observes that the common definition of the situation, upon which stable social organization hinges, is lacking in modern society, which is characterized by the rise of "conflicting definitions of situations" symptomatic of social disorganization.

[53] W. I. Thomas and Florian Znaniecki, *The Polish Peasant in Europe and America*, New York, Dover, 1921, i, 68.
[54] Edmund H. Volkart, ed., *Social Behavior and Personality: Contribution of W. I. Thomas to Theory and Social Research*, New York, Social Science Research Council, 1951, pp. 8, 226.

And it is at this stage that these individuals who have worked
out the most adequate redefinition of the situation promote social
reorganization.

> The conflict arises from the fact that the individual intro-
> duces other definitions of the situation and assumes other atti-
> tudes toward values than the conventionalized ones and con-
> sequently tends to change plans of action and introduce dis-
> order, to change the existing norms. . . . Society desires stabil-
> ity, and the individual desires new experience and introduces
> change. But eventually all new values, all the new cultural
> elements of a society are the result of the changes introduced
> by the individual.[55]

Unlike Parsons, who bases his theory on the model of consensus
and conformity, Thomas sees the relationship between the individual and society in terms of both conformity and conflict. His
expression "society desires stability" sounds like the organismic
fallacy. If "dominant social group" is substituted for "society,"
however, it comes close to a modern conflict model.

The individual variation of response to the social situation is
classified by Thomas and Znaniecki into three types: the "philistines" or the conformists, who are inclined to accept the established definition of the situation; the "bohemians," who subject
themselves to conflicting definitions of the situations and whose
essential trait is inconsistency; and the "creative," who bring
forth the redefinition of the situation. The third type has a
character "settled and organized" and "values the possibility
and even the necessity of evolution."[56] These are the "ideal limits
of personal evolution," and real characters are more or less
mixed types. In the philistines desire for security is dominant,
in the bohemians desire for new experience, while in the creative the two polar desires are in harmony. These three types of
personality correspond to the three stages of social change. In
the period of relatively stable organization the philistine type
prevails. At the time of crisis or revolutionary upheaval the
bohemian type prevails. And during the period of reconstruction
the creative type predominates. The philistine type most nearly
approximates the Parsonian model of the normal actor, but both
the bohemian and the creative would have to be classified as

[55] Thomas, *The Unadjusted Girl*, p. 234.
[56] Thomas and Znaniecki, *The Polish Peasant in Europe and America*, ii,
1861-1962.

deviants in the Parsonian system. Thomas's three personality types perhaps have their closest counterparts in current theory in David Riesman's three types of adjustment patterns, namely, *the adjusted, the anomic,* and *the autonomous.*[57] Thomas himself places the greatest weight on the creative type and values most highly the type of society that encourages the development of that kind of personality.[58]

In the preceding discussion of current and classical theories of socialization, one point stands out clearly. According to current usage, the concept of socialization designates specifically childhood socialization, and the aspect of conformity to the norms and values of the dominant social group is therefore emphasized. But, as soon as the concept of socialization is applied to the process of learning all through an individual's life, the aspect of conflict with established norms and values also comes into the picture. An examination of some of the classical theories shows that the concepts of novelty and creativity have been stressed in the study of personality development. Unfortunately, in current work, these concepts are frequently neglected where they might provide important insight. If given their proper due, they should contribute to a more comprehensive general theory of adult socialization and social change.

[57] David Riesman, Nathan Glazer, and Ruel Denning, *The Lonely Crowd,* New York, Doubleday, 1953, Ch. XV.
[58] Thomas and Znaniecki, *The Polish Peasant in Europe and America,* II, 1906-1907.

Bibliography

1. Works in English

Allport, Gordon W., *Pattern and Growth in Personality*, New York, Holt, Rinehart and Winston, 1961.

Basabe, Fernando M., et al., *Japanese Youth Confronts Religion*, Tokyo, Sophia University, 1967.

Bellah, Robert N., *Tokugawa Religion*, Glencoe, Ill., The Free Press, 1957.

Bendix, Reinhard, and Seymour M. Lipset, eds., *Class, Status and Power*, Glencoe, Ill., The Free Press, 1953.

Benedict, Ruth, *The Chrysanthemum and the Sword*, New York, Houghton Mifflin, 1946.

Black, Max, ed., *The Social Theories of Talcott Parsons*, Englewood Cliffs, N.J., Prentice-Hall, The Free Press, 1955.

Bloch, Marc, *Feudal Society*, tr. L. A. Manyon, London, Routledge and Kegan Paul, 1961.

Braibanti, Ralph, and Joseph J. Spengler, eds., *Tradition, Values, and Socio-Economic Development*, Durham, N.C., Duke University Press, 1961.

Brim, Orville G., Jr., and Stanton Wheeler, *Socialization after Childhood: Two Essays*, New York, John Wiley and Sons, 1966.

Clark, Colin, *Conditions of Economic Progress*, London, Macmillan, 1957.

Coale, Ansley J., Lloyd A. Fallers, Marion J. Levy, Jr., David M. Schneider, and Silvan S. Tomkins, *Aspects of the Analysis of Family Structure*, Princeton, Princeton University Press, 1965.

Cooley, Charles H., *Social Organization*, New York, Schocken Books, 1962.

Coser, Lewis A., "Social Conflict and the Theory of Social Change," *British Journal of Sociology*, Vol. viii, Sept. 1956.

Cumming, Elaine, and William E. Henry, *Growing Old: The Process of Disengagement*, New York, Basic Books, 1961.

Dahrendorf, Ralf, *Class and Class Conflict in Industrial Society*, Stanford, Stanford University Press, 1957.

———, "Out of Utopia: Toward a Reorientation of Sociological Analysis," *American Journal of Sociology*, Vol. lxiv, Sept. 1958.

Davis, Kingsley, *Human Society*, New York, Macmillan, 1961.

Dazai, Osamu, *No Longer Human*, tr. Donald Keene, Norfolk, Conn., New Directions, 1958.

De Bary, William T., et al., eds., *Sources of Japanese Tradition*, New York, Columbia University Press, 1958.

DeVos, George, "The Relation of Guilt toward Parents to Achievement and Arranged Marriage among the Japanese," *Psychiatry: Journal for the Study of Interpersonal Processes,* Vol. xxiii, No. 3 (Aug. 1960).

Dewey, John, *Characters and Events,* New York, Henry Holt, 1929.

Dore, R. P., ed., *Aspects of Social Change in Modern Japan,* Princeton, Princeton University Press, 1967.

———, *City Life in Japan,* London, Routledge and Kegan Paul, 1958.

———, *Education in Tokugawa Japan,* Berkeley, University of California Press, 1965.

———, *Land Reform in Japan,* London, Oxford University Press, 1959.

Dornbusch, Sanford M., "The Military Academy as an Assimilating Institution," *Social Forces,* Vol. xxxiii, May 1955.

Durkheim, Emile, *The Division of Labor in Society,* tr. George Simpson, Glencoe, Ill., The Free Press, 1960.

———, *The Rules of Sociological Method,* tr. Sarah A. Solovay and John H. Mueller, Glencoe, Ill., The Free Press, 1938.

———, *Socialism,* ed. Alvin W. Gouldner, New York, Collier Books, 1962.

Effrat, Andrew, "Another Analytic Aspect of Relationship Structures" (ms).

Einstein, Albert, and Leopold Infeld, *The Evolution of Physics,* New York, Simon and Schuster, 1961.

Erikson, Erik H., *Childhood and Society,* New York, W. W. Norton, 1963.

———, ed., *The Challenge of Youth,* New York, Doubleday, 1963.

———, *Young Man Luther,* New York, W. W. Norton, 1958.

Feldman, Arnold S., and Wilbert E. Moore, "Industrialization and Industrialism: Convergence and Differentiation," *Transactions of the Fifth World Congress of Sociology,* Vol. ii, The International Sociological Association, Sept. 1962.

Feuer, Lewis S., ed., *Marx and Engels: Basic Writings on Politics and Philosophy,* New York, Doubleday, 1959.

———, *Psychoanalysis and Ethics,* Springfield, Ill., Charles C. Thomas, 1955.

———, *The Scientific Intellectual,* New York, Basic Books, 1963.

———, "A Talk with the Zengakuren," *The New Leader,* May 1, 1961.

Firth, R., ed., *Man and Culture: Bronislaw Malinowski,* New York, Harper and Row, 1957.

Fromm, Erich, *Escape from Freedom,* New York, Holt, Rinehart and Winston, 1961.

Fukutake, Tadashi, *Man and Society in Japan,* Tokyo, University of Tokyo Press, 1962.

Goode, William J., "A Theory of Role Strain," *American Sociological Review,* Vol. xxv, No. 4 (Aug. 1960).

———, *World Revolution and Family Patterns*, Glencoe, Ill., The Free Press, 1963.

Goodman, Paul, *Growing up Absurd*, New York, Random House, 1960.

———, *Utopian Essays and Practical Proposals*, New York, Random House, 1964.

Gorer, Geoffrey, "The Concept of National Character," *Science News*, ed. J. L. Crammer, 1950.

Gould, Julius, and William L. Kalb, eds., *A Dictionary of the Social Sciences*, Glencoe, Ill., The Free Press, 1964.

Gouldner, Alvin W., "The Norm of Reciprocity: A Preliminary Statement," *American Sociological Review*, Vol. xxv, April 1960.

Hagen, Everett F., *On the Theory of Social Changes: How Economic Growth Begins*, Homewood, Ill., Dorsey, 1962.

Hall, Calvin S., and Gardner Lindzey, *Theories of Personality*, New York, John Wiley and Sons, 1957.

Henderson, Lawrence J., *Pareto's General Sociology: A Physiological Interpretation*, Cambridge, Harvard University Press, 1937.

Hinkle, Roscoe C., Jr., and Gisela J. Hinkle, *The Development of Modern Sociology*, New York, Random House, 1954.

Howes, John F., "Japan's Enigma: The Young Uchimura Kanzō," Ph.D. diss., Columbia University, 1965.

International Military Tribunal for the Far East, *Judgment*, Nov. 1948.

Iscoe, Ira, and Harold W. Stevenson, eds., *Personality Development in Children*, Austin, University of Texas Press, 1960.

Jansen, Marius B., ed., *Changing Japanese Attitudes toward Modernization*, Princeton, Princeton University Press, 1965.

———, *Sakamoto Ryōma and the Meiji Restoration*, Princeton, Princeton University Press, 1961.

Jaspers, Karl, *The Question of German Guilt*, tr. E. B. Ashton, New York, The Dial Press, 1947.

Kardiner, Abram, *The Psychological Frontier of Society*, New York, Columbia University Press, 1945.

Kennedy, John F., *Profiles in Courage*, New York, Harper and Brothers, 1956.

Kerr, Clark, et al., *Industrialism and Industrial Man*, New York, Oxford University Press, 1960.

Kinoshita, Junji, *Twilight of a Crane*, tr. Kuraishi Kenji, Tokyo, Miraisha, 1952.

Kornhauser, William, *The Politics of Mass Society*, Glencoe, Ill., The Free Press, 1959.

Koyama, Takashi, *The Changing Social Position of Women in Japan*, UNESCO, 1961.

Kuznets, Simon, *Economic Growth and Structure*, New York, W. W. Norton, 1965.

Lazarsfeld, Paul, "The American Soldier—An Expository Review," *Public Opinion Quarterly*, Vol. xiii, Fall 1949.

Leach, E. R., *Political Systems of Highland Burma*, Cambridge, Harvard University Press, 1954.

Levenson, Joseph R., *Confucian China and Its Modern Fate*, Berkeley, University of California Press, 1965.

Levy, Marion J., Jr., "Contrasting Factors in the Modernization of China and Japan," *Economic Development and Cultural Change*, Vol. ii, Oct. 1953.

———, *The Family Revolution in Modern China*, Cambridge, Harvard University Press, 1949.

———, *Levy's Six Laws*, MPH, Princeton, 1966.

———, *Modernization and the Structure of Societies*, Princeton, Princeton University Press, 1966.

———, *The Structure of Society*, Princeton, Princeton University Press, 1952.

Lifton, Robert J., *Thought Reform and the Psychology of Totalism: A Study of "Brainwashing" in China*, New York, W. W. Norton, 1961.

Lindesmith, Alfred R.L., and Anselm L. Strauss, "A Critique of Culture-Personality Writings," *American Sociological Review*, Vol. xv, Oct. 1950.

Linton, Ralph, *The Study of Man*, New York, Appleton-Century, 1936.

McClelland, David C., *The Achieving Society*, Princeton, Van Nostrand, 1961.

Malinowski, Bronislaw, "Culture," *Encyclopaedia of the Social Sciences*, Vol. iv, Macmillan, 1937.

Maruyama, Masao, *Thought and Behavior in Modern Japanese Politics*, ed., Ivan Morris, London, Oxford University Press, 1963.

Mead, George H., *Mind, Self, and Society*, Chicago, University of Chicago Press, 1940.

Merton, Robert, *Social Theory and Social Structure*, Glencoe, Ill., The Free Press, 1951.

Moore, Wilbert E., *Order and Change: Essays in Comparative Sociology*, New York, John Wiley and Sons, 1967.

———, "A Reconsideration of Theories of Social Change," *American Sociological Review*, Vol. xxv, Dec. 1960.

———, *Social Change*, Englewood Cliffs, N.J., Prentice-Hall, 1963.

———, and Arnold S. Feldman, eds., *Labor Commitment and Social Change in Developing Areas*, New York, Social Science Research Council, 1960.

Muchaku, Seikyō, ed., *Echoes from a Mountain School*, tr. Michiko Kimura, Tokyo, Kenkyūsha, 1954.

Nagel, Ernest, *The Structure of Science*, New York, Harcourt, Brace and World, 1961.

Nakamura, Hajime, *Ways of Thinking of Eastern Peoples*, Honolulu, Hawaii, East-West Center, 1964.

Nakano, Takeshi, "Recent Studies of Change in the Japanese Family,"

International Social Science Journal, Vol. xiv, No. 3, UNESCO, 1962.

Noma, Hiroshi, *Zone of Emptiness,* tr. Bernard Frechtman, Cleveland, World, 1956.

Norman, E. Herbert, *Soldier and Peasant in Japan: The Origins of Conscription,* New York, Institute of Pacific Relations, 1943.

Parsons, Talcott, *Essays in Sociological Theory,* Glencoe, Ill., The Free Press, 1958.

———, *The Social System,* Glencoe, Ill., The Free Press, 1951.

———, *The Structure of Social Action,* Glencoe, Ill., The Free Press, 1949.

———, et al., eds., *Theories of Society,* Glencoe, Ill., The Free Press, 1961.

———, and Robert F. Bales, *Family, Socialization and Interaction Process,* Glencoe, Ill., The Free Press, 1955.

———, and Edward A. Shils, eds., *Toward a General Theory of Action,* New York, Harper and Row, 1962.

Peirce, Charles, *Philosophical Writings of Peirce,* ed. Justus Buchler, New York, Dover, 1955.

Popper, Karl, *Conjectures and Refutations,* London, Routledge and Kegan Paul, 1963.

———, *The Open Society and Its Enemy,* Princeton, Princeton University Press, 1950.

Riesman, David, Nathan Glazer, and Ruel Denning, *The Lonely Crowd,* New York, Doubleday, 1953.

Rosow, Irving, "Forms and Functions of Adult Socialization" (ms), Russell Sage Foundation, Socialization Conference, May 17-19, 1963.

Scalapino, Robert A., *The Japanese Communist Movement 1920-1966,* Berkeley, University of California Press, 1966.

———, et al., *Parties and Politics in Contemporary Japan,* Berkeley, University of California Press, 1962.

Scheler, Max, *Ressentiment,* Glencoe, Ill., The Free Press, 1961.

Shibutani, Tamotsu, *Society and Personality,* Englewood Cliffs, N.J., Prentice-Hall, 1961.

Simmel, Georg, *The Sociology of Georg Simmel,* ed. and tr. Kurt H. Wolff, Glencoe, Ill., The Free Press, 1950.

Smelser, Neil J., and William T. Smelser, eds., *Personality and Social Systems,* New York, John Wiley and Sons, 1963.

Sorokin, Pitirim A., *Society, Culture, and Personality: Their Structure and Dynamics,* New York, Cooper Square Publishers, 1962.

Spencer, Herbert, *The Principles of Sociology,* New York, D. Appleton, 1896.

Stein, Maurice, et al., eds., *Identity and Anxiety,* Glencoe, Ill., The Free Press, 1960.

Stouffer, Samuel A., et al., *The American Soldier: Adjustment during Army Life*, Princeton, Princeton University Press, 1949.

Thomas, W. I., *The Unadjusted Girl*, Boston, Little, Brown, 1923.

——, and Florian Znaniecki, *The Polish Peasant in Europe and America*, New York, Dover, 1958.

Tiedemann, Arthur E., *Modern Japan*, Princeton, Van Nostrand, 1955, 1962.

Toennies, Ferdinand, *Fundamental Concepts of Sociology*, tr. C. P. Loomis, New York, American Book, 1940.

Tomkins, Silvan S., *Affect, Imagery, Consciousness*, New York, Springer, 1962.

——, "Ch. 7. Ideology and Affect in the Volume Ideology and Affect" (MS).

——, and Carroll E. Izard, eds., *Affect, Cognition, and Personality*, New York, Springer, 1965.

Tumin, Melvin, "Final Seminar in Social Stratification" (MS), Feb. 1963.

Vogel, Ezra F., *Japan's New Middle Class*, Berkeley, University of California Press, 1963.

Volkart, Edmund H., ed., *Social Behavior and Personality: Contribution of W. I. Thomas to Theory and Social Research*, New York, Social Science Research Council, 1951.

Wallace, Anthony F.C., *Culture and Personality*, New York, Random House, 1963.

Ward, Robert E., ed., *Political Development in Modern Japan*, Princeton, Princeton University Press, 1967.

Weber, Max, *The Theory of Social and Economic Organization*, tr. A. M. Henderson and Talcott Parsons, Glencoe, Ill., The Free Press, 1947.

White, Robert W., ed., *The Study of Lives*, New York, Atherton Press, 1963.

Zollachan, George K., and Walter Hirsch, eds., *Exploration in Social Change*, Boston, Houghton Mifflin, 1964.

2. WORKS IN JAPANESE

Abe, Hirosumi, "Gendai Tennō-sei no Mondaisei" ("The Problems of the Contemporary Emperor System"), *Rekishi to Gendai*, Dec. 1964.

Arai, Naoyuki, ed., "Sengo Jānarizumushi Nenpyō" ("A Chronological Table of the Postwar History of Journalism"), *Shisō no Kagaku*, Feb. 1965.

Aruga, Kizaemon, *Nihon Kazokuseido to Kosakuseido (The Japanese Family System and Tenancy)*, Tokyo, Kawade, 1943.

——, "Nihon no Ie" ("The Japanese Family"), in *Nihon Minzoku (The Japanese Race)*, ed. Nihon Jinrui Gakkai (The Japanese Anthropological Association), Tokyo, Iwanami, 1959.

Asahi Nenkan (*Asahi Year Book*), Tokyo, Asahi Newspaper Publishing Co., 1965.

Asahi Shinbun Hōtei Kishadan, *Tokyo Saiban* (*The Tokyo War Tribunal*), Tokyo, Tokyo Saiban Kankōkai, 1962.

Ashi Ato (*Footsteps*), Tokyo, Dōin Gakuto Engo Kai (Society to Aid the Mobilized Students), 1960.

Ashida, Keinosuke, *Keiu Jiden* (*Autobiography*), Tokyo, Kaigensha, 1950.

Ashizu, Uzuhiko, *Nihon no Kunshusei* (*The Japanese Monarchy*), Tokyo, Shinseiryokusha, 1966.

Awata, Yasuko, "Shufu no Mezame to 'Chiisana Kōfuku'" ("The Awakening of Housewives and Their 'Small Happiness'"), *Shisō*, No. 424 (Oct. 1959).

Chihō (*Our Local World*), circle pamphlets, ed. Tomoe Yamashiro, Miharashi, Nos. 1 (Dec. 10, 1962), 2 (June 10, 1963), and 3 (Dec. 15, 1963).

Chūgoku, Shinbunsha, ed., *Hiroshima no Kiroku* (*The Record of Hiroshima*), Tokyo, Miraisha, 1966.

Dai Jukkai Zenkoku Ie no Hikari Taikai Keiken Happyō Kai Shiryō (*Proceedings of the Tenth Annual National Convention of the Readers of the* Ie no Hikari), Tokyo, Ie no Hikari Kyōkai, Feb. 6, 1968.

Dazai, Osamu, *Dazai Osamu Shū* (*Selected Works of Osamu Dazai*) *Gendai Nihon Bungaku Zenshū*, Vol. XLIX, Tokyo, Chikuma Shobō, 1954.

Endō, Shōkichi, ed., *Nihon no Keizai* (*Japan's Economy*), Vol. II of *Gendai Nihon no Bunseki* (*Analysis of Contemporary Japanese Economy Series*), Tokyo, Yūhikaku, 1961.

———, *Sengo Nihon no Keizai to Shakai* (*The Economy and Society of Postwar Japan*), Chikuma Shobō, 1966.

Fuji, Masaharu, *Teikoku Guntai niokeru Gakushū Jo* (*A Preface to Learning in the Imperial Army*), Tokyo, Miraisha, 1964.

Fujita, Shōzō, *Tennō-sei Kokka no Shihaigenri* (*The Principle of Control of the Emperor-governed State*), Tokyo, Miraisha, 1966.

Fujiwara, Akira, *Gunjishi* (*Military History*), *Nihon Gendaishi Taikei* (*Contemporary Japanese History Series*), Tokyo, Tōyōkeizai, 1961.

Fukazawa, Shichirō, "Fūryū Mutan" ("A Dream Story of the Floating World"), *Chūōkōron*, Dec. 1960.

Fukutake, Tadashi, *Nihon Sonraku no Shakai Kōzō* (*The Social Structure of the Japanese Village*), Tokyo, Tokyo Daigaku Shuppankai, 1959.

Gakusei Undō Kenkyūkai (Study Group of Student Movements), *Gendai no Gakusei Undō* (*Contemporary Student Movements*), Tokyo, Shinkō Shuppan, 1962.

Gamō, Masao, *Nihonjin no Seikatsu Kōzō Josetsu* (*An Introduction to the Life Structure of the Japanese*), Tokyo, Seishin Shobō, 1960.

Gekkōhara Shōgakkō, ed., *Gakudō Sokai no Kiroku* (*The Records of School Children on Evacuation*), Tokyo, Miraisha, 1960.

Hashikawa, Bunzō, *Nihon Rōmanha Hihan Josetsu* (*An Introduction to the Critique of the Japan Romantic School*), Tokyo, Miraisha, 1965.

Hashiura, Yasuo, *Minkan Denshō to Kazokuhō* (*Folklore and Family Law*), Tokyo, Nihon Hyōronsha, 1942.

Hidaka, Rokurō, "Seikatsu Kiroku Undō" ("Life-Record Movement"), *Kōza Seikatsu Tsuzurikata* (*Lectures on Life-Composition*), Vol. v, Tokyo, Yuri Shuppan, 1963.

Higuchi, Shigeko, *Hijō no Niwa* (*The Garden of Disillusionment*), Tokyo, Sanichi Shobō, 1957.

Hirano, Yoshitarō, *Nihon Shihonshugi Shakai no Kikō* (*The Structure of the Capitalist Society of Japan*), Tokyo, Iwanami, 1934; rev. edn., 1959.

Honda, Shūgo, *Tenkō Bungaku Ron* (*Essays on Conversion Literature*), Tokyo, Miraisha, 1964.

Hosoi, Wakizō, *Jokō Aishi* (*A Tragic History of Female Workers*), Tokyo, Kaizōsha, 1929.

Ichikawa, Shōichi, *Nihon Kyōsantō Tōsōshōshi* (*A Short History of the Japanese Communist Party*), Tokyo, Shōkōshoin, 1946.

Ienaga, Saburō, *Nihonjin no Shisō no Ayumi* (*The Development of the Thought of the Japanese*), Tokyo, Rironsha, 1956.

——, et al., eds. *Jiyūminken Shisō* (*The Idea of Freedom and People's Rights*), Tokyo, Aoki Shoten, 1957.

Iizuka, Kōji, *Nihon no Guntai* (*The Japanese Army*), Tokyo, Tōdai Kyōdō-kumiai Shuppanbu, 1950.

Imai, Takajirō, and Mitsushige Mineji, *Sakubun Kyōiku* (*Composition Education*), Tokyo, Tōyōkan, 1957.

Inoue, Kiyoshi, *Tennō-sei* (*The Emperor System*), Tokyo, Tokyo Daigaku Shuppankai, 1953.

Ishida, Takeshi, *Kindai Nihon Seiji Kōzō no Kenkyū* (*Studies of the Modern Political Structure of Japan*), Tokyo, Miraisha, 1956.

——, *Meiji Seiji Shisōshi* (*History of Political Thought in the Meiji Period*), Tokyo, Miraisha, 1954.

Ishimoda, Tadashi, *Rekishi to Minzoku no Hakken* (*The Discovery of History and Nation*), Tokyo, Tokyo Daigaku Shuppankai, 1952.

Isono, Seiichi, Junji Kinoshita, Kazuko Tsurumi, Rokurō Hidaka, and Hideko Maruoka, eds., *Nakama no naka no Renai* (*Love in the Group*), Tokyo, Kawade Shobō, 1956.

Iwateken Nōson Bunka Kondan-kai (A Conference on Culture in Agrarian Villages of Iwate Prefecture), ed., *Senbotsu Nōmin Heishi no Tegami* (*Letters of the Peasant-Soldiers Who Died in the War*), Tokyo, Iwanami, 1961.

Izumi no Kai, ed., *Shufu no Sensō Taikenki* (*The Records of the Housewives' Experience of the War*), Nagoya, Fūbaisha, 1965.

Jiyū Minken Hen, Meiji Bunka Zenshū (*The Collected Works of Meiji Culture*), Tokyo, Nihon Hyōronsha, 1927.

Jūnen no Kiroku (*A Record of Ten Years*), Tokyo, Kusanomi Kai, 1964.

Junpō Gakusei Seinen Undō (*Trimonthly Review of Student and Youth Movements*), Tokyo, Nihon Kyōiku Kyōkai, Sept. 1, 1962.

Kajinishi, Mitsuhaya, et al., *Seishi Rōdōsha no Rekishi* (*A History of Silk Mill Workers*), Tokyo, Iwanami, 1955.

Kamishima, Jirō, *Kindai Nihon no Seishin Kōzō* (*The Mental Structure of Modern Japan*), Tokyo, Iwanami, 1961.

————, "Tennō-sei to Sengo Shisō" ("The Emperor System and Postwar Thought"), *Shisō no Kagaku*, Jan. 1963.

Kamiyama, Makoto, *Tennō no Taii o Semaru Otoko* (*The Man Who Tried to Force the Emperor to Resign*), Tokyo, Daini Shobō, 1957.

Kanba, Toshio and Mitsuko, *Shi to Kanashimi o Koete* (*Beyond Death and Sorrow*), Kyoto, Yūkonsha, 1967.

Karasawa, Tomitarō, *Gakusei no Rekishi* (*History of Students*), Tokyo, Sōbunsha, 1955.

————, *Kyōkasho no Rekishi* (*History of Textbooks*), Tokyo, Sōbunsha, 1956.

————, *Nihonjin no Rirekisho* (*The Curriculum Vitae of the Japanese People*), Tokyo, Yomiuri Shinbunsha, 1957.

Kasahara, Yoshimitsu, "Sengo Tennō-sei no Henbō" ("The Metamorphosis of the Emperor System After the War"), *Shisō no Kagaku*, Jan. 1966.

Kashō, Fumiko, "Katei de" ("In the Family"), *Bungaku no Sōzō to Kanshō* (*The Appreciation and Creation of Literature*), Vol. III, Tokyo, Iwanami, 1955.

Katō, Shūichi, *Sandai Banashi* (*A Trilogy*), Tokyo, Chikuma Shobō, 1965.

Katsuta, Moriichi, and Toshio Nakauchi, *Nihon no Gakkō* (*Schools in Japan*), Tokyo, Iwanami, 1964.

Kawaguchi, Hiroshi, et al., *Nihon Keizai no Kiso Kōzō* (*The Basic Structure of Japan's Economy*), Tokyo, Shunjūsha, 1962.

Kawakami, Hajime, *Jijoden* (*Autobiography*), Tokyo, Sekai Hyōronsha, 1947.

Kawashima, Takeyoshi, *Ideorogii toshiteno Kazokuseido* (*The Family System as an Ideology*), Tokyo, Iwanami, 1959.

Kikuchi, Keiichi, and Ryō Ōmura, eds., *Anohito wa Kaette Konakatta* (*He Never Returned*), Tokyo, Iwanami, 1964.

Kikuchi, Kunisaku, "Tennōseika no Guntai ni okeru Itan" ("The Heresy in the Army under the Emperor System"), *Misuzu*, Nov. 1964.

Kinoshita, Junji, and Kazuko Tsurumi, eds., *Haha no Rekishi* (*History of Mothers*), Tokyo, Kawade Shobō, 1954.

Kinoshita, Naoe, ed., *Tanaka Shōzō no Shōgai* (*The Life of Shōzō Tanaka*), Tokyo, Kokumin Tosho, 1928.

Kitakōji, Satoshi, et al., "Gakusei Undō no Genjō to Tenbō" ("The Present Situation and the Future Prospect of Student Movements") *Shisō no Kagaku*, No. 62 (May 1967).

Kobayashi, Bunjō, *Rōjin wa Kawaru* (*Old Folks Change*), Tokyo, Kokudosha, 1961.

Kobayashi, Takiji, *Kobayashi Takiji Shū* (*Selected Works of Takiji Kobayashi*), *Gendai Nihon Bungaku Zenshū*, Vol. xxxviii, Tokyo, Chikuma Shobō, 1954.

Kodama, Kōta, *Kinsei Nōmin Seikatsu Shi* (*History of the Life of Farmers in the Near-Modern Period*), Tokyo, Yoshikawa Kōbunkan, 1960.

Kokubun, Ichitarō, ed., *Ishi o mote Owaruru Gotoku* (*To Be Driven Away as Though with Stones*), Tokyo, Eihōsha, 1956.

Kokugo Kyōiku: Ashida Keinosuke Tokushū (*Japanese-Language Education: A Special Edition on Keinosuke Ashida*), No. 31 (July 1961).

Kome to Nōson Fujin (*Rice and Village Women*), Tokyo, Zenkoku Nōgyō Fujin Soshiki Kyōgikai (National Council of Agricultural Women's Organizations), 1959.

Koyama, Kōken, *Sengo Nihon Kyōsantō Shi* (*A History of the Communist Party in Postwar Japan*), Tokyo, Haga Shoten, 1966.

Kumagaya, Motoichi, *Mura no Fujin Seikatsu* (*The Life of Women in a Village*), Tokyo, Shinhyōronsha, 1954.

Kuno, Osamu, and Shunsuke Tsurumi, *Gendai Nihon no Shisō* (*Contemporary Japanese Thought*), Tokyo, Iwanami, 1956.

——, et al., *Sengo Nihon no Shisō* (*Postwar Japanese Thought*), Tokyo, Chūōkōronsha, 1959.

Kuroda, Hirokazu, *Gendai Yuibutsuron no Tankyū* (*An Inquiry into Contemporary Materialism*), Saitama, Kobushisha, 1968.

——, *Hēgeru to Marukusu* (*Hegel and Marx*), Tokyo, Rironsha, 1952.

——, *Hyūmanizumu to Marukusushugi* (*Humanism and Marxism*), Saitama, Kobushisha, 1963.

——, *Keizaigaku to Benshōhō* (*Economics and Dialectics*), Tokyo, Jinseisha, 1956.

——, *Puroretariateki Ningen no Ronri* (*The Logic of the Proletarian Person*), Saitama, Kobushisha, 1960.

——, *Shihonron igo Hyakunen* (*One Hundred Years After Capital*), Saitama, Kobushisha, 1967.

——, *Sutārinshugi no Hihan* (*A Critique of Stalinism*), Tokyo, Jinseisha, 1956.

Kusanomi Kai Daishichi Gurūpu, ed., *Sensō to Watakushi* (*The War and I*), Tokyo, Chūōkōron Jigyō Shuppan, 1963.

Maruoka, Hideko, *Nihon Nōson Fujin Mondai* (*The Problems of the Japanese Agrarian Women*), Tokyo, Yakumo Shoten, 1948.

Maruyama, Kenji, and Kensuke Ikeda, eds., *Inadani ni Tsuzuru* (*Voices from the Ina Valley*), Tokyo, Ie no Hikari Kyōkai, 1965.

Matsushita, Keiichi, "Taishū Tennō-sei Ron" ("Mass Emperor System"), *Chūōkōron*, April 1959.

Matsuura, Tatsuhisa, "Sākuru-shi no Seiri Chūkan Hōkoku" ("An Interim Report on Circle Pamphlets"), *Shisō no Kagaku*, June 1965.

Mita, Sōsuke, *Gendai Nihon no Seishin Kōzō* (*The Mental Structure of Contemporary Japan*), Tokyo, Kōbundō, 1965.

Miyazawa, Toshiyoshi, *Kokumin Shuken to Tennō-sei* (*Popular Sovereignty and the Emperor System*), Tokyo, Keisō Shobō, 1957.

Monbushō, *Kokutai no Hongi* (*The Fundamentals of Our National Polity*), Tokyo, 1939.

――――, *Shingaku to Ikuei Shōgaku* (*University Education and Scholarships*), Tokyo, 1961.

――――, *Waga Kuni no Kōtō Kyōiku* (*Higher Education of Japan*), Tokyo, 1964.

Monbushō Chōsa-kyoku (Research Bureau of the Ministry of Education), *Nihon no Seichō to Kyōiku* (*Japan's Growth and Education*), Tokyo, 1963.

Mori, Shigeru, "Sogairon no Tankyū" ("In Quest of the Theory of Alienation"), *Kyōsanshugi*, April 1, 1959.

Muchaku, Seikyō, ed., *Yamabiko Gakkō* (*Echoes from a Mountain School*), Tokyo, Seidōsha, 1951; Tokyo, Yuri Shuppan, 1957.

Murayama, Tomoyoshi, *Murayama Tomoyoshi Shū* (*Selected Works of Tomoyoshi Murayama*), Gendai Nihon Bungaku Zenshū, Vol. LXXVII, Tokyo, Chikuma Shobō, 1957.

Mutō, Ichiyō, "Marukusushugi to Atarashii Kakumei Shutai" ("Marxism and the New Selfhood of Revolution"), *Shisō no Kagaku*, Oct. 1967.

Nabeyama, Sadachika, *Watashi wa Kyōsantō o Suteta* (*I Have Left the Communist Party*), Tokyo, Daitō Shuppan, 1949.

Nagai, Michio, "Chishikijin no Seisan Rūto" ("The Route for the Production of Intellectuals"), *Kindai Nihon Shisōshi Kōza* (*Lectures on the Intellectual History of Japan*), Vol. IV, Tokyo, Chikuma Shobō, 1959.

――――, "Habatsu to Yūmono" ("What We Call Cliques"), *Mainichi Shinbun*, July 26, 1962.

――――, *Nihon no Daigaku* (*The Japanese University*), Tokyo, Chūōkōronsha, 1965.

Nagano-ken Shimo Ina-gun Seinendan Shi Hensan Iinkai, ed., *Shimo*

Ina Seinen Undō Shi (*A History of the Movement of the Youth Organization in Shimo Ina*), Tokyo, Kokudosha, 1960.

Nakamura, Mitsuo, "Meiji," *Gendai Nihon Bungaku Zenshū* (*The Collected Works of Contemporary Japanese Authors*), Bekkan Vol. I, Tokyo, Chikuma Shobō, 1959.

Nakano, Shigeharu, *Nakano Shigeharu Shū* (*Selected Works of Shigeharu Nakano*), *Gendai Nihon Bungaku Zenshū*, Vol. XXXVIII, Tokyo, Chikuma Shobō, 1954.

Nakayama, Tarō, *Nihon Wakamono Shi* (*A History of the Youths in Japan*), Tokyo, Nichibunsha, 1958.

Natsume, Sōseki, "Gendai Nihon no Kaika" ("The Evolution of Contemporary Japan"), *Sōseki Zenshū* (*The Collected Works of Sōseki Natsume*), Vol. XIV, Tokyo, Iwanami, 1929.

Nihon Hyōron, May 1939.

Nihon Jidō Bungakukai (The Japanese Association of Children's Literature), ed., *Akaitori Kenkyū* (*A Study of The Red Bird*), Tokyo, Komine Shoten, 1960.

Nihon Senbotsu Gakusei Shuki Henshū Iinkai (Committee for the Compilation of the Letters of the Student-Soldiers Who Died in the War), ed., *Kike Wadatsumi no Koe* (*Listen, the Voice of the Sea*), Tokyo, Tokyo Daigaku Shuppankai, 1952.

Niida, Noboru, *Chūgoku no Nōson Kazoku* (*The Agrarian Family in China*), Tokyo, Tokyo Daigaku Tōyōbunka Kenkyūjo, 1952.

Nikkyōso Jūnenshi (*Ten Years of the Japanese Teachers' Union*), Tokyo, Kyōshokuin Kumiai, 1958.

Noma, Hiroshi, *Shinkū Chitai* (*Zone of Emptiness*), Tokyo, Kawade Shobō, 1952.

Nōrinshō (Ministry of Agriculture and Forestry), *Nōgyō no Dōkō ni kansuru Nenji Hōkoku* (*Annual Report on the Trends of Agriculture*), 1967.

Nōrinshō Tōkei Chōsabu (Statistical Survey Section of the Ministry of Agriculture and Forestry), *Nōgyō Chōsa Kekka Gaiyō* (*Outline Report on the Results of the Agricultural Survey*), July 1967.

Obara, Tokushi, ed., *Ishikoro ni Kataru Hahatachi* (*The Mothers Who Talked to Pebbles*), Tokyo, Miraisha, 1964.

Odaka, Tomoo, *Kokumin Shuken to Tennō-sei* (*Popular Sovereignty and the Emperor System*), Tokyo, Seirin Shoin, 1954.

Ogawa, Tarō, and Ichitarō Kokubun, eds., *Seikatsu Tsuzurikatateki Kyōiku Hōhō* (*The Life-Composition Method of Education*), Tokyo, Meiji Tosho, 1955.

Oikawa, Wakō, ed., *Yome to Shūtome* (*Daughters-in-Law and Mothers-in-Law*), Tokyo, Miraisha, 1963.

Ōkōchi, Kazuo, *Nihon no Chūsan Kaikyū* (*The Middle Class in Japan*), Tokyo, Bungeishunjū Shinsha, 1961.

————, ed., *Nihon Rōdō Kumiai Ron* (*Essays on Labor Unions in Japan*), Tokyo, Yūhikaku, 1954.

Ōkubo, Riken, et al., eds., *Shiryō niyoru Nihon no Ayumi: Kindaihen* (*A Documentary History of Japan: The Near-Modern Period*), Tokyo, Yoshikawa Kōbunkan, 1951.

Ōkuma, Nobuyuki, *Kokka Aku—Sensō Sekinin wa Dare no Monoka* (*The Evils of the State—To Whom Does Responsibility for the War Belong?*), Tokyo, Chūōkōronsha, 1957.

Ōno, Akio, *Zengakuren Keppūroku* (*The Blood and Wind Record of the Zengakuren*), Tokyo, Nijusseikisha, 1967.

Ōtani, Shōzō, "Nihon Nōgyō no Kadai (1)" ("The Issues of Agriculture in Japan"), *Ekonomisuto*, Jan. 1965.

Ōuchi, Hyōe, et al., *Nihon Keizai Zusetsu* (*Japan's Economic Statistics in Graphs*), Tokyo, Iwanami, 1965, 1967.

Rekishigaku Kenkyūkai (Association for the Study of History), ed., *Sengo Nihonshi* (*A History of Postwar Japan*), Tokyo, Aoki Shoten, 1965.

Rōdō Daijin Kanbō Rōdō Tōkei Chōsabu (Statistical Survey Section of the Labor Minister's Secretariat), *Chingin Kōzō Kihon Tōkei Chōsa Kekka Sokuhō* (*Quick Report on the Results of the Statistical Survey of the Structure of Wages*), March 1968.

Rōdōshō Fujin Shōnen Kyoku (Women and Minors' Bureau of the Labor Ministry), *Fujin Rōdō no Jitsujō* (*The Conditions of Women Labor*), Tokyo, 1966.

————, *Fujin to Shokugyō* (*Women and Occupations*), Tokyo, 1948.

————, *Kinrōsha Katei no Shōhi Seikatsu Suijun ni Kansuru Ishiki Chōsa* (*An Opinion Survey on the Consumption Level of Working Men's Families*), Tokyo, Finance Ministry Printing Office, 1964.

————, *Nōka Fujinseikatsu ni Kansuru Ishiki Chōsa* (*An Opinion Survey on the Life of Agrarian Women*), Tokyo, Finance Ministry Printing Office, 1962.

————, *Rōdōsha Kazoku no Genjō* (*The Present Condition of the Working Man's Family*), Tokyo, Finance Ministry Printing Office, 1965.

————, ed., *Seikatsu Jikan Hakusho* (*White Paper on the Time Allocation*), Tokyo, Finance Ministry Printing Office, 1961.

Saegusa, Yasutaka, *Dazai Osamu to Sono Shōgai* (*Osamu Dazai and His Life*), Tokyo, Shinbisha, 1965.

Sagawa, Michio, *Ōzeki Matsusaburō Shishū Yamaimo* (*The Yam, A Collection of Poems by Matsusaburō Ōzeki*), Tokyo, Yuri Shuppan, 1951.

Sakata, Yoshio, ed., *Meiji Zenhanki no Nashonarizumu* (*Nationalism of the Early Part of the Meiji Period*), Tokyo, Miraisha, 1958.

Sakuda, Keiichi, ed., *Ningen Keisei no Shakaigaku* (*Sociology of the*

Character Formation of Man), *Gendai Shakaigaku Kōza* (*Lectures on Contemporary Sociology*), Vol. v, Tokyo, Yuhikaku, 1964.

———, "Shi to no Wakai—Senpan Keibotsusha no Ibun ni Arawareta Nihonjin no Sekinin no Ronri" ("Rapprochement with Death—The Logic of Responsibility of the Japanese as Appeared in the Messages of the War Criminals Convicted to Death"), *Tenbō*, No. 72 (Dec. 1964).

Sakuma, Gen, "Jinmin Minshushugi to Heiwa Undō" ("People's Democracy and Peace Movements"), *Kyōsanshugi*, Oct. 1, 1959.

Sasaki, Sōichi, *Tennō no Kokkateki Shōchōsei* (*The Emperor as the National Symbol*), Tokyo, Kōbunsha, 1949.

Seiji Keizai Kenkūjo (Political and Economic Research Institute), *Fujin Rōdō no Kihon Mondai—Sengo Bōshoku Kōjō no Jittai Chōsa* (*The Basic Problems of Female Labor—A Survey of the Postwar Spinning and Weaving Factories*), Tokyo, Chūō Rōdō Gakuen, 1948.

Seikatsu o Tsuzuru Kai, ed., *Okāsan to Seikatsu Tsuzurikata* (*Mothers and Life-Composition*), Tokyo, Yuri Shobō, 1957.

Sekai Dai Hyakka Jiten (*The Great World Encyclopaedia*), Tokyo, Heibonsha, 1959.

Sekiyama, Naotarō, *Kinsei Nihon no Jinkō Kōzō* (*The Population Structure of Near-Modern Japan*), Tokyo, Nishikawa Kōbunkan, 1958.

Shibata, Michiko, "Bundo no Seiritsu" ("The Emergence of the Bund"), *Shisō no Kagaku*, May 1964.

Shimazu, Chitose, *Joshi Rōdōsha—Sengo no Menbō Kōjō* (*Woman Workers—Cotton Spinning Mills in the Postwar Period*), Tokyo, Iwanami, 1953.

Shioda, Shōbei, *Kōtoku Shūsui no Nikki to Shokan* (*The Diary and Letters of Shūsui Kōtoku*), Tokyo, Miraisha, 1954.

Shiratori, Kunio, *Mumei no Nihonjin* (*The Anonymous Japanese*), Tokyo, Miraisha, 1961.

Shisō no Kagaku, April 1962 (a special issue on the Emperor system).

Shisō no Kagaku Kenkyūkai, ed., *Tenkō* (*Ideological Conversion*), Tokyo, Heibonsha, 1959-1962.

Suekawa, Hiroshi, ed., *Kihon Roppō* (*The Six Basic Laws*), Tokyo, Iwanami, 1962.

Sugamo Isho Hensankai, ed., *Seiki no Isho* (*The Last Testament of the Century*), Tokyo, Shiragikukai, 1954.

Sugiura, Minpei, "Kawakami Hajime Ron" ("On Hajime Kawakami"), *Shisō no Kagaku*, No. 44 (1965).

Sumiya, Etsuji, *Kawakami Hajime*, Tokyo, Yoshikawa Kōbunkan, 1962.

Takahashi, Ryōzō, *Otō o Kaese* (*Give Me Back My Daddy*), Tokyo, Ie no Hikari Kyōkai, 1965.

Takeda, Kiyoko, *Tennō-sei Shisō to Kyōiku* (*The Idea of the Emperor System and Education*), Tokyo, Meiji Tosho, 1964.

Takeuchi, Yoshimi, *Fufukujū no Isan* (*The Heritage of Disobedience*), Tokyo, Chikuma Shobō, 1961.

——, "Kindai no Chōkoku" ("Overcoming the Modern"), *Kindai Nihon Shisōshi Kōza* (*Lectures on the Intellectual History of Modern Japan*), Vol. VII, Tokyo, Chikuma Shobō, 1959.

——, *Kokumin Bungaku Ron* (*Theory of National Literature*), Tokyo, Tokyo Daigaku Shuppankai, 1954.

——, *Takeuchi Yoshima Hyōronshū: Nihon to Ajia* (*Selected Essays of Yoshimi Takeuchi: Japan and Asia*), Vol. III, Tokyo, Chikuma Shobō, 1966.

Takikawa, Masajirō, *Tokyo Saiban o Sabaku* (*My Judgment of the Tokyo Tribunal*), Tokyo, Tōwasha, 1952.

Tamaki, Motoi, *Nihon Gakusei Shi* (*A History of the Japanese Students*), Tokyo, Sanichi Shobō, 1961.

Tanaka, Sōgorō, *Kita Ikki*, Tokyo, Miraisha, 1959.

Tezuka, Tomio, "Daigakusei no Seishin Shōgai" ("Mental Disturbance among University Students"), *Mainichi Shinbun,* May 27, 1962.

Tokyo Daigaku Gakuseibu (Student Section of the Administration of Tokyo University), *Sengo ni okeru Tōdaisei no Keizai Seikatsu* (*The Economic Life of Tokyo University Students After the War*), Tokyo, Tokyo University, 1960.

Tomin Kyō Dayori (*A Newspaper Put Out by the Citizens' Council on the Problems of Entrance into Senior High Schools*), Sept. 1, 1962.

Tōyama, Shigeki, et al., *Kindai Nihon Seijishi Hikkei* (*A Compendium to the Political History of Modern Japan*), Tokyo, Iwanami, 1961.

——, et al., *Shōwashi* (*A History of the Shōwa Period*), Tokyo, Iwanami, 1959.

Tsurumi, Kazuko, *Chichi to Haha no Rekishi* (*The History of Our Fathers and Mothers*), Tokyo, Chikuma Shobō, 1962.

——, ed., *Dewey Kenkyū* (*Studies of John Dewey*), Tokyo, Shunjūsha, 1952.

——, *Dewey Koraidosukōpu* (*Dewey Kaleidoscope*), Tokyo, Miraisha, 1963.

——, ed., *Enpitsu o Nigiru Shufu* (*The Housewives with Pencils in Their Hands*), Tokyo, Mainichi Shinbunsha, 1954.

——, "Kazoku ni okeru Fujin no Yakuwari Henka" ("Women's Role Change in the Family"), *Shisō*, March and May 1968.

——, *Seikatsu Kiroku Undō no Naka de* (*An Essay on the Life-Record Movement*), Tokyo, Miraisha, 1963.

——, et al., "Asahigaoka Chūgakkō no Fukei no Kōdō to Ishiki" ("The Conduct and Consciousness of the Parents of Asahigaoka High School"), *Tokyo Daigaku Kyōikugakubu Kiyō* (*Bulletin of the Department of Education, Tokyo University*), Vol. II, 1957.

——, and Kikue Makise, eds., *Hikisakarete: Haha no Sensō Taiken*

(*To Be Torn Apart: Mothers' War Experiences*), Tokyo, Chikuma Shobō, 1959.

Tsurumi, Shunsuke, "Chishikijin no Sensō Sekinin" *Chūōkōron*, Jan. 1956.

———, *Secchūshugi no Tachiba* (*In Defense of Eclecticism*), Tokyo, Chikuma Shobō, 1961.

———, et al., eds., *Nihon no Hyakunen* (*A Hundred Years of Japan*), Vol. IX, Tokyo, Chikuma Shobō, 1953.

———, Akira Yamamoto, and Hideo Kitamura, *Rokudai Toshi to Shimin: Bunkado Chōsa Hōkōkusho* (*The Six Major Cities and Their Citizens: A Survey on Their Cultural Levels*), published under the auspices of Shitei Toshi Kikaku Chōsa Jimu Shukansha Kaigi (Council of the Planning and Research Directors of the Major Cities), Kyoto, 1966.

Uchiyama, Shōzō, *Kensetsu Rōdōron* (*Theory of Construction Labor*), Tokyo, Hōsei Daigaku Shuppan Kyoku, 1963.

Ueyama, Shunpei, *Dai Tōa Sensō no Imi* (The Meaning of the Great Asiatic War), Tokyo, Chūōkōronsha, 1964.

Umetani, Noboro, *Meiji Zenki Seijishi no Kenkyū* (*A Study of the Political History of the Early Meiji Period*), Tokyo, Miraisha, 1963.

Wadatsumi-kai, ed., *Senbotsu Gakusei no Isho ni Miru Jūgonensensō* (*The Fifteen Years' War Seen Through the Messages of the Students Who Died in the War*), Tokyo, Kōbunsha, 1963.

Wakamori, Tarō, ed., *Nihon Rekishi Jiten* (*Encyclopaedia of Japanese History*), Tokyo, Jitsugyō no Nihonsha, 1952.

Wataya, Takeo, "Nōminsō no Ryōkyoku Bunkai to Sono Igi" ("The Polarization of the Farmers and Its Implications"), *Keizai Hyōron*, Feb. 1962.

Watsuji, Tetsurō, *Kokumin Tōgō no Shōchō* (*The Symbol of National Unity*), Tokyo, Keisō Shobō, 1948.

Yamabe, Kentarō, et al., eds., *Kominterun Nihon ni kansuru Tēze Shū,* (*Collection of the Comintern Theses on Japan*), Tokyo, Aoki Shoten, 1961.

Yamada, Sōboku, "Jānarizumu towa Nani ka" ("What is Journalism?"), *Shisō no Kagaku*, Feb. 1965.

Yamamoto, Tsunetomo, *Hagakure*, ed., Tetsurō Watsuji et al., Tokyo, Iwanami, 1965.

Yamanaka, Akira, *Sengo Gakusei Undō Shi* (*A History of the Postwar Japanese Movements*), Tokyo, Aoki Shoten, 1961.

Yanagida, Kunio, *Kokyō Shichijūnen* (*Seventy Years of My Native Village*), Kobe, Nojigiku Bunko, 1959.

———, *Yanagida Kunio Shū* (*Selected Works of Kunio Yanagida*), Tokyo, Chikuma Shobō, 1962-1964.

Yano Tsunetarō Kinenkai, ed., *Nihon Kokusei Zue* (*Japanese Census in Graphs*), Tokyo, Kokuseisha, 1961.

Yasuda, Takeshi, *Sensō Taiken: Issen Kyūhyaku Shichijūnen e no Isho* (*My War Experience: A Will for 1970*), Tokyo, Miraisha, 1963.

Yoshimoto, Ryūmei, *Geijutsuteki Teikō to Zasetsu* (*Artists' Resistance and Their Failure*), Tokyo, Miraisha, 1959.

————, *Gisei no Shūen* (*The End of Pseudo-Systems*), Tokyo, Gendai Shichōsha, 1962.

————, *Takamura Kōtarō*, Tokyo, Iizuka Shoten, 1957.

————, "Tenkōron" ("An Essay on Ideological Conversion"), *Gendai Hihyō*, Jan. 1959.

————, et al., *Minshushugi no Shinwa: Anpo Tōsō no Shisōteki Sōkatsu* (*The Myth of Democracy: The Intellectual Generalizations of the Anti-Security Treaty Campaign*), Tokyo, Gendai Shichōsha, 1960.

INDEX